The
Department
of State in the
Middle East
1919-1945

Phillip J. Baram

The
Department
of State in the
Middle East

1919–1945

University of Pennsylvania Press
1978

Library of Congress Cataloging in Publication Data

Baram, Phillip J
    The Department of State and the Middle East,
1919-1945.

    Includes bibliographical references and index.
    1. Near East—Foreign relations—United States.
2. United States—Foreign relations—Near East.
3. United States. Dept. of State. 4. United
States—Foreign relations—1933-1945. I. Title.
DS63.2.U5B35   327.73′056   77-20302
ISBN 0-8122-7743-0

For my mother and father

Contents

Preface

The purpose of this work is to examine Department of State policies in the
Middle East (understood as the current states of Iraq, Egypt, Syria,
Lebanon, Saudi Arabia, Israel, and Jordan) in the period 1919–45, with
emphasis on 1939–45. The examination seeks to answer in detail and with
nuance such questions as: What were these policies? Why were they the
Department's policies, and who made them? Were they "realistically"
grounded and wisely conceived? Were they implemented as official
American policies, and if so, what happened to them? Were they important? Did they "make a difference"? To a large degree, the examination
is based on the vantage point that an empathetic, but not necessarily
sympathetic, contemporary observer might have had if he had stood
within the Department in Washington, "looking out" across the miles
toward the Middle East, as well as across the street towards Congress,
the White House, and other Cabinet departments.

There are several other perspectives used in this work. One could be
called the microscopic view of Department decision making. I have concentrated on the swirling yet orderly beehive activities of individual
decision makers—the shuttle of ideas and intelligence between divisional
deskmen, the flow of clarifications to and from Foreign Service Officers,
the inter-echelon screening procedure and chain of command, and the
interactions of personal anxieties, styles, tacit assumptions, and first
principles. This approach means that the focus has been more on the
"soft" and developmental terms of the Department's decision making process, terms like premise, preference, principle, viewpoint, tendency, than
on "hard" and final terms like power, authority, execution, implementation.

xi

Another perspective used is the concentric-circles view. I have tried to see to what degree the general and global foreign policy positions (visualized as "circles") of the pre-World War II Department, the wartime Department, and the postwar Department coincided with the corresponding "circles" covering the Department's more specific positions in the Middle Eastern countries surveyed. Similarly, I have tried to see if and how these Departmental policy circles coincided, or collided, with the policy circles represented by other departments, notably the Department of War; by Congress, the President, and public opinion; by the other great powers; by the Arabs and the Jews; and by other relevant parties, like the oil companies and the Vatican. The purpose, in short, has been to treat Departmental Middle Eastern policy within the context of the Department's general foreign policy and in the broader context of other American and non-American foreign policy positions.

A third perspective deals directly with the Palestine issue and is what can be called a History-in-the-Round viewpoint. Many studies of the region tend either to treat "Palestine" as one more Middle Eastern area, with little detail on its continuous historical atypicalities, or to concentrate on Palestine to the near exclusion of adjacent countries. The result of either tendency is incomplete in both information and a sense of the whole. That this is so is probably less due to ideological dispositions over whether Palestine is, or is not, primarily, a part of the "Arab world," than it is to the research problem that Palestine always presents. The enormous bulk of material, largely non-Arab in character, makes it difficult for an author to research both the Arab states and Palestine and to synthesize the information. Such a synthesis has nonetheless been my intent. I leave to the reader to judge whether I have succeeded.

A fourth perspective is the long overview, from which height one discerns a remarkable pattern of continuity over the decades in the State Department's personnel, philosophy, and policies. In so many respects, the more things changed, the more they remained the same. This continuity is most clearly evidenced when one examines the sequence of external events and of intra-Departmental relations from World War I through World War II and then notes within subperiods of this time span how and why the Department's reactions to external events invariably led it to reconfirm its traditional goals.

To show this continuity a detailed narrative form has been adopted in this work; and while much of Part I and some of Part II are topical and thematic, most of the material on Departmental policy making is treated on a country-by-country and period-by-period, sometimes year-by-year, basis. Perhaps an "issue-oriented" approach, with grand conceptions, Prime Mover theories, and the inevitably selected, truncated evidence, is more exciting and more in vogue in American academia today, but I do not think history is well served thereby. As Herbert Feis wrote not many years ago of his own approach to explaining World War II:

I have favored consecutiveness over concentration on a few main dramatic occasions or acts. Since the fullness of reality—or truth, if you will—resides in the continuity of influence and behavior, it is to be perceived only by slow travel along the whole stream of eventful detail.[1]

There are several problems in this work. First, it is large, yet there is a considerable amount of compression and generalization, notably in the first three chapters. There, political scientists and Middle East area experts might wish that I had offered more clarification regarding, as random examples, the Department's prewar global policy or the British mandate in Iraq.

Second, there are a few problems relative to the research material. My primary sources are mainly the voluminous official Departmental files, and to a slightly lesser degree the private papers, memoirs, and publications of key Departmental and other participants in the period under review. Also, interviews and correspondence were conducted with, among others, some fifteen officers of the wartime Department who were closely associated with the Middle East.

Anyone working with official papers and memoirs several decades after the event knows the questions inevitably posed: to what extent does a given document omit or distort relevant information because its author misunderstood realities, or, having been concerned with his career or the judgment of posterity, concealed his feelings and motives and instead wrote a bland, deodorized memorandum "for the record"? To what extent is a given document incomplete because the really important decision was made orally, not in writing? And to what extent is the researcher himself, using his documentary "bone fragments" (like a paleontologist trying to picture the body shape of a prehistoric behemoth on the basis of fossil fragments), reduced to educated guessing in his attempt to picture "in the flesh" the vast wartime policy making process?

Two unintended caveats straight from the horses' mouths, as it were (Assistant Secretary Breckinridge Long and Presidential Adviser Harry Hopkins), illustrate the researcher's problems in reconstructing the past *and* in finding, despite the abundance of words, statements of candor, quotable quotations, and admissible evidence:

One who has not been through one of those searching, prolonged [Departmental speech drafting] sessions cannot realize what microscopic examination is given to every phrase in the lights of grammar, inflexes, syntax, history, politics, psychology and structural position—all the nuances of meaning and all the implications of use—alone or in relation to its context. Such a session is truly an ordeal—but an interesting experience. The result is a short, compact, logical, correct statement of a political situation—and hard to deny or refute.

I don't know [about appraising the Potsdam Conference]. It looks as if President Truman and Jimmy Byrnes did a good job—but you can't tell what the real problems are unless you're *there* and intimately involved in them and understand all the background circumstances and the implications of what is said and what isn't said. The way the situation changes from day to day—or minute to minute—if you lose touch with it for as long as I have [one month] you're just about as ignorant of it as anybody else.[2]

To be sure, I have tried to "flesh out" the documentary bones used, by extensive readings in most of the secondary sources in English, and to a minor extent in Hebrew and French, on most facets of American economic, political and diplomatic history, the interwar period and World War II, the foreign policies of the British, French, Soviets and Axis, and Jewish and Middle Eastern political history. (I might comment at this point that a number of secondary sources were used that are not, however, cited in the notes; and, of course, there were other secondary sources, hopefully few, which for various reasons I was unable to use.) Given, then, the problems inhering in official papers and the fact that I have not been able to research with comparable depth the official papers on the non-American side, whatever picture emerges from this work is still short of being full sculpture-in-the-round.

Despite these problems, there are several advantages in having access to the Department's records. One is that while the sense of contemporary atmosphere is often absent in a formal memorandum, the totality of formal memoranda offers an evolutionary sense of the whole. Official records can also provide "backroom" news, as well as a broader picture than the participants themselves, so close to the trees, often had.

The specific advantage in this work, apart from its efforts to integrate several perspectives and bodies of specialized information, is that I have exhaustively used several sets of documents relative to the Middle East that were hitherto closed. I am the first researcher to have studied the William Yale Papers at Harvard (mainly on wartime planning for postwar Palestine); and, as far as I know, this work incorporates for the first time the Departmental planning discussions, minutes, and positions on Middle Eastern countries, as found in the Harley Notter Papers and Edward Stettinius Papers. Other collections of value are referred to in the notes, where appropriate.

I wish to acknowledge with gratitude the encouragement of Professor Sidney Burrell, chairman, Department of History, Boston University; and the helpfulness of several critiques, chiefly those of Professor Uri Ra'anan of the Fletcher School of Law and Diplomacy and Professor Ben Halpern of Brandeis University. They are of course not responsible for whatever errors exist in this work. Finally, I want to express my appreciation for their patience and affection to my wife Eleanor, my sons Yoav and Yaakov, and my parents, Max and Eva Baram.

NOTES

1. Herbert Feis, *Churchill, Roosevelt, Stalin: The War They Waged and the Peace They Sought* (Princeton, N.J.: Princeton Univ. Press, 1957), p. v of Foreword.

2. The first quotation, from Long, is in Fred Israel, ed., *The War Diary of Breckinridge Long, Selections from the Years 1939–1944* (Lincoln, Nebraska: Univ. of Nebraska Press, 1966), p. 334. The second, from Hopkins, is from Robert Sherwood, *Roosevelt and Hopkins, An Intimate History* (New York: Harper, 1948), pp. 925–26.

Document and Manuscript Sources

The External Political Files of the Department of State's diplomatic correspondence. The National Archives, Washington, D.C. (For particulars, see note 1 of chapter three.)

The Harley Notter Papers (committee and research material of the Department of State's postwar planning apparatus, 1942–1945). The National Archives, Washington, D.C.

The Research & Analysis political reports of the Office of Strategic Services, regarding Palestine, 1942–1945. The National Archives, Washington, D.C.

The Edward R. Stettinius, Jr., Papers. University of Virginia, Charlottesville, Va.

The James F. Byrnes Papers. Clemson University, Clemson, South Carolina.

The Franklin D. Roosevelt Papers. Franklin D. Roosevelt Library, Hyde Park, N.Y.

The Harry Hopkins Papers. Franklin D. Roosevelt Library, Hyde Park, N.Y.

The Joseph Grew Papers. Houghton Library, Harvard University, Cambridge, Mass.

The William Yale Papers. Houghton Library, Harvard University, Cambridge, Mass.

The William Yale Papers. Mugar Library, Boston University, Boston, Mass.

The public papers of, in order of importance for this work, Breckinridge Long, Cordell Hull, James Landis, Archibald MacLeish, Leo Pasvolsky, Herbert Feis, Lawrence Steinhardt, Felix Frankfurter. Library of Congress, Washington, D.C.

Recollections of Walter K. Lowdermilk, William Clayton, and William Phillips. Oral History Library, Columbia University, New York, N.Y.

The James G. McDonald Papers. Herbert Lehman Papers, School of International Affairs, Columbia University, New York, N.Y.

The Abba Hillel Silver Papers. The Temple, Cleveland, Ohio.

Interviews and correspondence (mainly during the summer of 1972) were also conducted with former Department of State officers and with public figures, all of whom were intimate with Departmental Middle East policy during World War II: Loy Henderson, Harry Howard, Ray Hare, Gordon Merriam, Gordon Mattison, Philip Ireland, William Yale, George Warren, Evan Wilson, Benjamin V. Cohen, Harold B. Hoskins, Joseph Satterthwaite, H. Schuyler Foster, H. Freeman Matthews, J. C. Hurewitz, Emmanuel Neumann, John J. McCloy, Abe Fortas, Oscar Gass, Leroy Stinebower, Morris Lazaron.

Chronology of Relevant Events During World War II

THE COURSE OF WAR OUTSIDE THE MIDDLE EAST

September 1938	Munich Conference
May 1939	German-Italian military alliance
August 1939	Russo-German nonaggression pact
September 1939	World War II begins
June 1940	Paris falls
July 1940	Battle of Britain
June 1941	Germany invades Russia
December 1941	Japan attacks Pearl Harbor
November 1942	Germany occupies Vichy France
November 1942	Soviet counteroffensive at Stalingrad
May 1944	Rome captured by Allies
June 1944	Allied invasion of Normandy
August 1944	Soviet offensive in Eastern Europe
August 1944	Paris liberated
May 1945	Germany surrenders
August 1945	Atomic bomb used
August 1945	Japan surrenders

GREAT-POWER INTERRELATIONS

May 1939	Churchill succeeds Chamberlain
September 1939	Anglo-American destroyer-base exchange

August 1941	Roosevelt and Churchill announce Atlantic Charter
December 1941–January 1942	First Washington Conference; United Nations Declaration signed
June 1942	Second Washington Conference; North African campaign planned
November–December 1943	Teheran Conference; Russian and British withdrawals from Iran projected
April 1944	London (Stettinius) Mission; Anglo-American ministerial exchange of views on Middle East
August–September 1944	U.N. organizational conference (Dumbarton Oaks)
October 1944	Free French under De Gaulle recognized as government of France by U.S., U.S.S.R., Britain
February 1945	Yalta Conference
April 1945	Reports from Moscow (Harriman) of deteriorating U.S.–U.S.S.R. relations
April–June 1945	Founding conference of U.N. (San Francisco)
July 1945	Atlee succeeds Churchill
July–August 1945	Potsdam Conference
Fall 1945	British postwar economic problems acute; wartime dependence on American aid continues

REGARDING THE JEWS, IN PALESTINE, EUROPE, AND THE UNITED STATES

May 1939	MacDonald White Paper rejects Balfour Declaration
Summer 1939	Beginnings of Palestinian Zionist defensive and Jewish rescue operations
May 1941	The Haganah forms the Palmach (strike forces)
January 1942	Nazi Wannsee Conference decides on "final solution" of Jewish Problem
May 1942	Biltmore Program; American Zionists agree to work for Jewish state of Palestine
Summer 1942	Zionists lobby in U.S. for Jewish army
Fall 1942	First leaks in West of the Final Solution

November 1942   Formation of anti-Zionist American
                 Council for Judaism
April–May 1943   Warsaw Ghetto uprising and destruction
April 1943   Abortive Anglo-American Refugee
                 Conference (Bermuda)
August–September 1943   American Jewish Conference; most
                 American Jewish organizations, Zionist
                 and non-Zionist, endorse Biltmore
                 Program
August 1943   American Zionist Emergency Council is
                 led by Abba Hillel Silver
March 1944   Britain maintains 1939 White Paper past
                 its five-year expiration
August 1944   Jewish Brigade formed
November 1944   Stern Gang kills Lord Moyne
September 1945   Earl Harrison Report on Jewish Dis-
                 placed Persons
Fall 1945   Truman-Bevin argument over D.P.
                 immigration to Palestine
Fall 1945   Escalation in Palestine of Jewish resis-
                 tance, terrorism, and rescue operations
November 1945   Anglo-American Inquiry Commission
                 appointed

IN THE MIDDLE EAST

July 1940   Britain destroys Vichy French fleet off
                 coast of Algeria
Fall 1940   Britain makes Transjordan's Arab Legion
                 most effective of all Arab armies
March 1941   German counteroffensive in North Africa
April 1941   Britain establishes Middle East Supply
                 Council (MESC), with headquarters
                 in Cairo
May 1941   Germany invades Crete
May 1941   Britain suppresses pro-Axis coup in Iraq
May 1941   Eden's Mansion House speech favoring
                 Arab unity
June 1941   Britain and Free French invade Vichy
                 Syria
June 1941   German-Turkish nonaggression treaty
August 1941   British and Russian troops enter Iran

November 1941	British offensive in Libya
January 1942	German counteroffensive in North Africa
May 1942	German counteroffensive in North Africa
June 1942	Germany takes Tobruk
June 1942	U.S. joins MESC
October 1942	British counteroffensive at El Alamein
November 1942	American and British troops launch Operation TORCH
January 1943	Iraq declares war on Axis
May 1943	Axis resistance ends in North Africa
August 1943	Hoskins's mission to Riyadh fails; Ibn Saud refuses to meet with Zionists
Fall 1943	Nuri Said promoting Fertile Crescent plan and Iraqi pan-Arab leadership
July 1944	U.S.S.R. recognizes independence of Syria and Lebanon
September 1944	U.S. recognizes independence of Syria and Lebanon
January 1945	Turkish straits opened to shipping to Russia
January 1945	Lend-Lease extended to Saudi Arabia, Egypt and Iraq by this date
February 1945	Ibn Saud and Roosevelt meet
February–March 1945	Turkey and Arab states declare war on Axis
March 1945	Arab League founded in Cairo
May 1945	Anti-French riots in Syria and Lebanon
July 1945	U.S.S.R. expresses interest in Middle Eastern-North African trusteeships
November 1945	U.S. terminates funding and participation in MESC
December 1945	Soviet expansionism in northern Iran

IN THE UNITED STATES

March 1940	Lend-Lease bill enacted
December 1942	Consensus crystallizes in administration that Saudi oil is vital national interest
July 1943	Interior Secretary Ickes heads federal Petroleum Reserves Corporation
February 1944	Pro-Zionist Congressional resolutions tabled

March 1944	Roosevelt makes pro-Zionist statement; Department of State assures Arabs otherwise
November 1944	Roosevelt reelected
December 1944	Pro-Zionist Congressional resolutions tabled
March 1945	Roosevelt makes pro-Zionist statement; Department of State assures Arabs otherwise
April 1945	Roosevelt dies; Truman is successor
May 1945	Truman meets Iraqi regent
July 1945	Truman endorses building of Dhahran airbase
July 1945	ARAMCO forms Tapline
August 1945	Lend-Lease terminated; Saudi Arabia excepted
August 1945	Wage-price controls relaxed as preventative against feared postwar depression
November 1945	Congress approves large tax reductions
November 1945	Congress passes pro-Zionist resolutions
November 1945	State-War-Navy Coordinating Committee formed
December 1945	American wartime military forces reduced 50%, from approximately 8 million (August 1945) to approximately 4 million

DEPARTMENT OF STATE

February 1941	A. Kirk appointed minister to Egypt and Saudi Arabia
March 1942	Departmental postwar planning apparatus in full operation
December 1942	W. Yale heads Palestine desk for postwar planning
January 1943	Departmental reorganization and expansion
August 1943	Most postwar plans on Palestine, and on all other Middle Eastern countries and topics, finalized
September 1943	S. Welles resigns as undersecretary
December 1943	P. Ireland presides over Departmental Interdivisional Country Committee on the Arab Countries

December 1943	New consulates established during the year include Basra and Suez
January 1944	Departmental reorganization and expansion
March 1944	Petroleum Division established; other new economic divisions are subsequently created and expanded
April 1944	Department frames final U.S. postwar global oil strategy
May 1944	Lt. H. Hoskins heads American representation in MESC
August 1944	Consulate established at Dhahran
September 1944	Col. W. Eddy appointed minister to Saudi Arabia
September 1944	G. Wadsworth elevated to rank of minister to Syria and Lebanon
November 1944	Summations of postwar plans made; postwar planning apparatus partially discontinued, partially absorbed into Department's regular divisions
November 1944	Department reaffirms anti-imperialist Atlantic Charter principles
November 1944	Concern over Soviet-Arab mutual interests
November–December 1944	Secretary Hull and assistant secretaries B. Long and A. Berle resign; E. Stettinius, Jr., J. Grew, and D. Acheson are successors
December 1944	Culbertson Mission to Mediterranean countries; finalization of open-door economic policy
April 1945	L. Henderson and G. P. Merriam are successors to W. Murray and P. Alling in Office of Eastern and African Affairs
July 1945	James Byrnes becomes Secretary of State
September 1945	Office of Strategic Services partially discontinued, partially integrated into Department
Fall 1945	Department campaigns for elevation of its diplomatic rank in Middle East and for increased Arab-American bilateralism

I
Departmental Structure and Middle East Background

1

Departmental Global Outlook and Postwar Plans

To 1939

Long before September 1939, external phenomena toward which the Department of State customarily took a negative view included political and social revolution, militant ideology, radical nationalism, armed aggression, entangling alliances, Old World power politics, despotism, commercial discrimination, and imperialistic spheres of influence. Mainly from the pragmatic viewpoint of the American "national interest," though also from the moral viewpoint, these phenomena and the images associated with them often fell into one of two sets of extremes along the political spectrum. They signified to the Department either great change, due to the dissolution of peace and stability; or the blockage of change, due to the consolidation of a status quo to the advantage of rival powers.

To be sure, the undesirability of all such phenomena and trends abroad did not necessarily mean that the Department was willing to forswear ideological and militant efforts of its own as instruments to promote policy: Witness the Caribbean. Nor did its dislikes mean that it was willing to act with other nations for preventive purposes. Nonaction was particularly evident in the fact that throughout the 1920s and 1930s the Department had no wish to promote Woodrow Wilson's mission of American participation in the League of Nations.

Still, even if it was not physically responsive, the post-1919 Department was highly sensitive to echoes of overseas disruption or competition. In part, this was due to American diplomacy's hypercritical, and often hypo-

3

critical, moralistic-legalistic traditions, revived during the Progressive period of American politics after the turn of the century. In greater part, Departmental sensitivity derived from a combination of old and new emotions, such as an increasing anxiety over America's prestige, potency, and acceptability as an emerging and "mature" world power; a residual middle-class fear of violence and instability; and an ingrained patriotic phobia toward presumed European machinations. (One should note, however, that right up through and beyond September 1939, fear of another lengthy "World War" was *not* a typical emotion or reason for the Department's increased sensitivity to undesirable phenomena abroad.)

Conversely, the Department viewed as desirable—for both the people and government of the United States, and for the people, but not necessarily the governments, of the world—the economic principles of the open door and nondiscrimination; the political principles of native majority rule and national self-determination; and the combined moral-political-economic principle of the good neighbor and its corollary, anti-imperialism. Operative here was the wish, at once opportunistic and benevolent, capitalistic and Progressive, for good, stable relations with all countries that did not represent a threat to the United States. The traditional American beliefs in the salutary effects of competition and free enterprise, and in the exportability of the American Constitution's wisdom, were equally motivating. Finally, the Department believed deeply in America's unique moral mission and its example, in domestic and hemispheric relations, of evolutionary, not revolutionary, reformism.[1]

On the historical level, all these negative and positive viewpoints and emotions, taken together as a creed, gave sustenance to the Department's fundamental impulse to conceive of American foreign policy in terms of (1) political-military isolationism, and *simultaneously* (2) expansive economic internationalism. This was an impulse which went back beyond Wilson to the early nineteenth century, when Federalist and Jeffersonian theories had intermixed and produced precisely this kind of syncretic tradition of simultaneous isolationism and internationalism.

On the psychological level, all these viewpoints and emotions, taken together as a personal value system, were eminently appropriate for the Department's officers, given their role and personal backgrounds. First, Department officers were by definition the established watchmen of the national interest, the loyal shepherds at home and abroad of the American creed.

But role-playing was unnecessary. Upholding the value system was instinctive, as most members of the Department came from a stratum which particularly nourished that system. This was the stratum of urban upper- and middle-class white Anglo-Saxon Protestants of the late nineteenth century, a stratum which gave its sons education at private boarding schools and the better colleges and instilled in them a personal drive for success and respectability. Like their counterparts in the British Foreign Office, Department officers were often bred with an at least half-conscious sense of belonging to a patrician class, clubby yet with a strong sense of civic duty. Moreover, although it is a simplification to say so, basic qualities of their stratum were a staunch conformist patriotism, leaning toward chauvinism; a predisposition toward legalism and self-righteousness (not necessarily the same as moralism or idealism); and an ambivalent condescension toward hyphenated Americans and most foreigners, with a tendency to interact with them either naively or exploitatively, defensively or aggressively. Finally, this was a stratum that had a somewhat Pavlovian reaction to private property, contracts, free trade, and the open door as automatically good words, and to cartels, privilege, European power politics, and spheres of influence as automatically bad words.[2]

In retrospect, it might appear that the "best word" of all to this stratum, and hence the most important principle of Department officers, was the economic open door. This conclusion would seem to be warranted on the basis of the fact that the great bulk of the diplomatic record for the interwar period deals with the Department's direct efforts to guard or gain "rights" overseas for private American economic interests. For all the visibility and genuine significance of the Department's economic push, however, it is a thesis of this work that to slight noneconomic desiderata as mere wind is an error. *All* Departmental "pushes" and desiderata, as shall be seen, had as their object not only the enhancement of private American capitalism, but also the enhancement of the American government's *status* as a great power. Moreover, greater American prestige abroad would, by clear implication, increase the domestic prestige of the officers and the "institution" of the Department of State in the eyes of other executive departments and the public at large.

1939 to 1941

When Germany invaded Poland in September 1939, this was *not* a signal to the Department that both the world's and America's foreign policies were about to experience considerable change. True, watchful waiting over the increasingly disturbed international relations of the late 1930s had been mounting in the Department, as elsewhere. It was true, too, that the idea was gaining currency that at the end of the new "conflict" the controversies and alleged inadequacies of the peace settlements following World War I ought not be repeated. The corollary was that America's stance after the conflict ought somehow to be more active than, or at least different from, its conventional isolationist stance.

Despite these signs of tossing and turning, there was no major Departmental change in the wake of the 1939 hostilities, whether from the point of view of organization, procedures, personnel, or ideas. For the duration of 1939 and the early part of 1940, the prewar dual axioms of political-military isolationism and economic internationalism continued to be applied by the Department as relevant to all regions of the globe, along with all the other prewar desiderata like anti-imperialism and the good neighbor.[3]

Only by 1941 did a nonisolationist approach emerge in the Department. The shift was due to external currents such as Congress's progress in repealing neutrality legislation, Axis ideological and territorial expansion, and the growing, if still uncommitted, anti-Axis mood of the American public. The import of these was intensified by the pro-British, pro-internationalist, and increasingly pro-interventionist position of many private groups. Similarly catalytic was Franklin Roosevelt's personal magnetism and the prospect of his leadership of the entire "democratic" world in a war to the finish with the Axis. Moreover, the second half of 1940 had witnessed several actions which, while dealing primarily with hemispheric defense, assisted in eroding isolationism and neutralism by the end of that year: for example, the Act of Havana in July and the Destroyer-Bases Exchange in September.

Roosevelt's Four Freedoms Speech in January 1941, with its allusion to America as arsenal of democracy, the Lend-Lease Act in March, the Proclamation of Unlimited Emergency in May, and the Atlantic Charter in August were additional steps in the process of erosion and conversion. In this period the Department of State also helped, by means of counsel to the President and by many public speeches and releases, to turn the country away from smug isolationism. Then and later, it stressed the global applicability of the open door and good neighbor principles, and of the Monroe Doctrine; and it emphasized preparedness, pride, and loyalty to the American heritage, the virtues of international law and comity, and the final need for a just and lasting postwar peace, banning aggression and imperialism.[4]

On balance, however, the Department was more the recipient of, than the donor to, the new zeitgeist. In any case, the zeitgeist made personally incompatible officers, like Secretary Cordell Hull and Undersecretary Sumner Welles, more willing to act together than they might have. It clearly helped to resurrect Wilson's missionism, dead since 1920, on behalf of political internationalism and military interventionism.

Thus did 1941—before Pearl Harbor—represent an activating stage of nonisolationism between earlier passive isolationism and later fully active anti-isolationism. It is essential to note, however, that there was no such change with regard to any of the other traditional desiderata and principles of the Department.

Indeed, economic nondiscrimination and the open door, self-determination and native majority rule, the good neighbor policy, and antipathy to spheres of influence were all reaffirmed in 1941 and in the subsequent war years, in general and in the French and British sectors of the Middle and Far East in particular, as benign, democratic, *and more appropriate than ever.* The activism aborning in 1941 thus foretold an intensification rather than a revision of prewar shibboleths. A policy of expansive economic internationalism, now wedded to a policy of political-military internationalism, clearly promised to be more potent than that same economic policy wedded to political-military isolationism.

Still, the Department recognized that it had to keep a steady head and that the first imperative in 1941 was to cope with the moral, political, economic, and military sense of threat and radical change represented by an increasingly Axis-dominated Europe. Translated, this meant helping Britain defend itself and trying to keep Vichy France from open collaboration with the Nazis. Under the immediate circumstances, therefore, too much chipping away at French and British overseas spheres of influence was counterproductive. Indeed, in the case of the Middle East, an active American policy of anti-French and anti-British colonialism would play into the hands of German-Italian power which in 1941 and most of 1942 was already threatening to replace British-French power.

Yet even the slightest diminution of its anti-colonialist creed in the face of wartime imperatives had to be, like every other Departmental policy, delicately calibrated and weighed with other considerations in mind. As shall be demonstrated, neither in the 1939–1941 period nor after that time did the Department *ever* lose sight of its traditional value system and its hopes for success in the Middle East. Nor did it ever ignore the salient fact that the Arab–Moslem majority, whose friendship America had long cultivated, was opposed to the British-French hegemony in the region.

THE DEPARTMENT'S WARTIME ROLE

Despite similar background and outlook which approached country-club homogeneity, Department officers who served during the war years have divided, in their postwar reflections, over the question of whether the Department responded well to the war's challenges. Dean Acheson, then an assistant secretary, has disparaged the wartime Department as "without direction, composed of a lot of busy people working hard and usefully but as a whole not functioning as a foreign office. It did not chart a course to be furthered by the success of our arms, or to guide our arms."[5]

In contrast, Harley Notter, a planning chief and an official historian of the Department, has contended that the Department was an efficient policy-making machine to begin with and was galvanized by Pearl Harbor into resolute and wise action. It marched right behind Roosevelt, embodying the President's fighting words in his address of 9 December 1941: "We are going to win the war and we are going to win the peace that follows."[6]

Acheson's foggy-bottom thesis of the Department as a busy but captainless ship, drifting nowhere, is an exaggeration. But so is Notter's emphasis on the Department's purposeful activism.

It is true of course that the Department's personnel and structure did expand considerably over the war years. One index is the fact that upper-echelon officials rose from approximately 42 in 1939 to 57 in 1942, to 96 in 1944, to 104 in early 1945. (Upper-echelon officials can be defined as the Secretary's staff of undersecretaries, assistant secretaries, special assistants, advisors on political relations; also, although on the fringes of the middle echelons as well, office directors and divisional chiefs.) Especially augmented was the number of advisers on political relations and special assistants to the Secretary. Additions were also made to the number and variety of offices and specialized divisions dealing with wartime economic affairs, public and cultural affairs, international trade policy, and postwar studies and planning—notably planning on international organization, international security, and the future of dependent areas. As of January 1944, the regular geographic divisions were also expanded and reshaped. The same applied to foreign service posts and their personnel.[7]

On the other hand, compared with the expansion of the personnel and foreign policy role of the Departments of War, Navy, Interior, and Treasury, and of new federal agencies like the Board of Economic Warfare and the Lend-Lease Administration, the Department of State's internal expansion was not extraordinary. Indeed, despite that internal expansion, most of those in the State Department's upper and middle echelons were the same men who had begun career service long before the war. Names of offices and titles of officers changed, but the faces did not. Even after Edward Stettinius, Jr., and his "new look" and clean-broom approach replaced the tired Hull and several of Hull's associates, like Breckinridge Long and Adolph Berle, Jr., in December 1944, most of those in the new regime were already old hands. The result of such longevity and continuity was that the substructure of values, class, and emotions and the superstructure of Departmental policy remained largely the same.[8]

In general, despite its traditional cabinet seniority, the State Department had less unchallenged authority in handling foreign affairs in 1945 than in 1939. Though this was due principally to the faster rate of growth of rival departments, there were other reasons, too, such as Roosevelt's secretive style, his personal interest in foreign affairs, and his summit diplomacy. Another factor was the manifest importance of the military point of view in shaping wartime foreign policy. An additional factor, the origin of which was much older than the war, was the steady erosion of esteem suffered by the Department as a whole in the eyes of the public and liberal press. The most common charges were that it was inept, elitist, timid to the point of being appeasing, pro-fascist and somehow "unAmerican."[9]

And yet, notwithstanding the poor impressions it made or the sense of frustration it often felt, the Department succeeded in the great majority of instances in ultimately making its positions official national policy. But the process was far less tidy and straightforward than Notter suggests. Its ability to manipulate and its sheer pertinacity were among the Department's most vital talents. Defensively, it blocked or greatly diluted positions contrary to its own. Offensively, it took initiatives, followed them through, and saw to it that they were "sold" and adopted, with usually but minimal modification, as official executive policy. Certainly a record of success, as will be demonstrated, applied to almost all final official policies bearing on the Middle East during World War II.

Particularly helpful in enabling the Department to outdo other departments in long-run policy formulation was a third talent, that of intelligence gathering, impressively expressed in the State Department's early establishment and expansion of offices dealing exclusively with research and long-run planning. The Department's postwar planning apparatus, therefore, merits special examination.

ORIGINS OF THE POSTWAR PLANNING
   APPARATUS

In the second half of 1941, the predominant mood of both the executive and legislative branches passed quickly from traditional isolationism through an intermediate phase of nonisolationism and into a third phase of armed interventionism and anti-isolationism. After 7 December, the officially proclaimed goal in the short run was all-out war against the Axis with a view towards total victory—later understood (as expressed by Roosevelt at the Casablanca Conference of January 1943) as a policy of unconditional surrender. In the long run, the administration's goal was to create, then conserve, a new and peaceful global status quo.

To the Department of State, the Ten Commandments of this new world order was the Atlantic Charter, with particular emphasis on its clauses espousing the traditional American dogmas of majority rule, native self-determination, and economic nondiscrimination. In this vein, Department officers undertook to serve as the Charter's special evangelists, bringing its gospel to the ignorant, the scoffers, and the doubters alike. Concomitantly, the Department began to devote much of its energy and staff to planning the world's future in the postwar period—and indirectly, the Department's own institutional future. It apparently hoped that by concentrating on such planning, which other departments and agencies were less preoccupied with, to prove its indispensability in the President's Cabinet. Given the fact that it felt excluded from the immediate management of wartime diplomacy, long-run planning seemed the best way to retrieve status and control over foreign policy.[10]

Actually, the idea of postwar planning preceded both Pearl Harbor and the Atlantic Charter. It was in the intermediate phase of nonisolationism after September 1939 that the Department had begun to plan its postwar planning apparatus, despite the uncertainties and the residual weight of isolationism at that time. The invasions instigated by Hitler and the reverberations and dislocations they caused in international relations were the primary stimuli. A second reason was the Department's fear of competition and encroachment in policy making by the military, the established departments, and new federal agencies. On the level of personal influence at the White House, Secretary Hull's many prewar rivals, like Vice President Henry Wallace, Treasury Secretary Henry Morgenthau, Jr., Interior Secretary Harold Ickes, Commerce Secretary Jesse Jones, and Presidential Adviser Harry Hopkins, seemed after 1939 to loom larger, overshadowing Hull.[11]

The Department also gave attention to the need for planning because of an anxiety that the country might fall into the allegedly mistaken ways of postwar planning attendant to World War I. At that time, most of the peace-making studies had emanated, at President Wilson's suggestion, not from the State Department but from the Commission of Inquiry set up by Colonel Edward House in 1917. In anticipation of a similar bypassing of the Department and, as a result, a similar "losing of the postwar peace," Hull wanted to begin early to construct an elaborate body of postwar planning studies, better and more elaborate than House's.[12]

For a somewhat different reason, Undersecretary Welles also came to the conclusion that large-scale planning ought to be begun quickly. It was Welles's organic view of policy making that military considerations should never be separated from nonmilitary considerations, and by the same token, that short-run policy should never be separated from long-run policy. On these premises he maintained that postwar planning on the political and economic level should not be postponed as if it were irrelevant to the immediate military imperatives.[13]

For all these reasons, the Department had already laid the groundwork for comprehensive postwar planning before Pearl Harbor. The person, then and later, most directly responsible for "planning for postwar planning" was Leo Pasvolsky, Hull's longtime special assistant and also chief of the Division of Special Research. As this division, before 1939, had coordinated research and analysis (albeit on a limited scale), it was the Department's closest prototype to a planning division, and its head was a natural choice as coordinator of a new planning apparatus.[14]

A Russian-Jewish naturalized citizen, Pasvolsky had a doctoral degree, was an author in Russian and English on international monetary policy, and was prominently associated with the Brookings Institution. An owlish, taciturn person, he was long an exponent of reduced tariffs and multi-lateralism, and to a degree he served as Hull's theorist. It may be noted, however, that Pasvolsky's own open door perspective was different from that of the majority of the Department. In essence, Pasvolsky assumed that because the open door and free trade were good for the world, they were good for America. Most of his colleagues assumed, conversely, that because the open door and free trade were good for America, they were good for the world. (It may also be noted that Pasvolsky never demonstrated any interest in Russian, Middle Eastern, and Jewish issues, even though he took part in numerous planning meetings bearing on such issues. True, in terms of bureaucratic function, he was a coordinator, not a decision maker or regional expert. Still, he was in a natural position to exert at least minimal influence on these issues; that he chose not to suggests personal, in addition to bureaucratic, reasons for abstention.)[15]

In any event, prior to Pearl Harbor, Pasvolsky, with of course many others in the Department's upper echelons, was already active in making public addresses calling for more postwar planning. In the language of some of the speech titles, the purpose of planning was to build and "pioneer" the peace. Moreover, Hull and his planning coordinator wanted a special Advisory Committee set up by the Department to be authorized by the President, so as to coordinate all phases of present and future deliberations on the postwar period emanating increasingly from *all* federal departments and agencies. The purpose was not only to make the totality of planning more efficient on the interdepartmental level; it was also to preclude the possibility that the Department of State might lose control over planning to others.

The Advisory Committee was set up in February 1942. Its members came from Congress, the Department itself, and from private life. Representation from the Council on Foreign Relations, the most prestigious and influential of all wartime private interest groups, was especially strong, then and later. Men like Dr. Isaiah Bowman, president of Johns Hopkins University, were interchanged directly between the Department's planning apparatus and the Council, whose own postwar planning apparatus predated the Department's. Council executives like Bowman had also already served the Department in the 1917–19 planning period. (Bowman, then of the American Geographic Society, had been chief territorial specialist of House's Commission of Inquiry.)[16]

When the Advisory Committee met initially, it was stimulated by the administration's determination to win a total victory of arms. Though this objective did not yet expressly include the corollary of unconditional surrender, that corollary was inherent in the fact that all discussions and plans of the Committee, and of subsequent planning committees, were based squarely on the assumption of total Allied victory. Neither then nor later would any Departmental plans, even of a contingency or specu- lative nature, be based on the assumptions of ultimate stalemate, nego- tiated peace, or American defeat. However, this confidence and resolve were countered by a mounting sense of urgency in 1942, born of the awareness that the planning tasks were larger than expected, and that postwar policy in a number of geographic areas had possibly to be ready for implementation before final and total military victory was achieved.[17]

Under the aegis of the Advisory Committee, a roster of subcommittees was formed, often with common or rotating members, most of whom were careermen in the Foreign Service, recent lateral entrants, and academic experts hired or on loan. By March 1942 these subcommittees—of eco- nomic reconstruction, economic policy, security problems, political prob- lems, and territorial problems—began their business. All were formed outside public scrutiny and most of their activities would remain secret during the war. All were coordinated with the traditional operational activities of the Department's regular geographic and economic divisions, like the Divisions of European Affairs and of Near Eastern Affairs, and with the work of select private research centers, particularly the Council on Foreign Relations.

Thereafter, several trends developed. Congressional and public partici- pation in Departmental postwar planning shrank rapidly, which was Hull's wish and plan. Consequently, some committees and subcommittees aborted; most, however, expanded and subdivided. The result was that a greatly enlarged annex of planners grew, seeming at times to rival, at least in terms of its paperwork and the number of its personnel, the De- partment's regular divisions.

By the end of the summer of 1943 expansion of the planning apparatus reached its limit as the hiring of outside specialists leveled off. By 1944 planning units were being integrated into the regular divisions, or being terminated. In contrast, the regular divisions, given the expectation that year of foreseeable Allied victory, were themselves devoting more and more time to postwar topics and to the increasingly operational postwar policy drafts made earlier by the planning apparatus.[18]

THE PLANNERS' MAIN CONCEPTIONS

Indirect evidence from diplomatic records indicates that frequently two types of interventionist attitudes tugged with each other in the discussions of the planning units during the period 1942–45. One attitude favored maximal, the other minimal, global interventionism and "involve- ment." That being said, it should be immediately noted that in this period minimalists were *not* in favor of returning to pre-Pearl Harbor pro-isolationist or neutralist positions; nor, at this time, were maximalists in favor of what maximal interventionism became after the war, namely, a position favoring America as a global foe of communism, with various regional alliances, pacts, and understandings.

Wartime maximalists, such as Assistant Secretary Adolph Berle, Jr., the area office directors in charge of Europe and the Middle East, and most Foreign Service Officers in the Middle East, wished to defeat the Axis utterly and to destroy the Axis mentality and Axis empires. This "abolitionist" spirit often spilled over onto America's allies as well. The attitude projected was that after handling the Axis, the Department would sanitize and decolonize the British, French, and Dutch empires.

Behind this ardor lay a uniquely American amalgam of feelings towards spheres of influence in general. Moral disapproval has already been noted. However, there was also envy of others' spheres; fear of being shut out by others' closed doors; fear of being exploited during the war as an innocent giant and New World adolescent who helps others (Allies) get their chestnuts (colonies) out of the fire but gets either burned fingers or nothing in return; *and* the latent hope for some American spheres of influence, such as China and the Middle East—as a just reward for America's war effort and as a deterrent against a third world war. These, of course, would never be called spheres of influence, nor would there be any annexation or crude colonialism involved. Rather, as Latin America was already, they would be "good neighbors," under a strong and friendly American influence.

Furthermore, maximalists assumed that despite all the uncertainties, including those concerning postwar Soviet policy, the postwar world would be a tired, worn, stagnant world, at the end of its tether, without any strong inner dynamic or any future. As such, the world would be in need of and ripe for American involvement and a "large" American policy. Moreover, the world would be manageable: it was not expected to break out with problems and new variables that had not been anticipated by the planners.[19]

The Department's second approach, which favored "safe" minimal involvement, was to some extent a carryover of the Department's traditional isolationism and fear of commitments. It was also the product of an inevitably slow bureaucracy, often drowning in its own paper. The influence of conservative personalities at the top, such as Hull, Long, and to a lesser extent, Acheson, gave added weight to this approach. Basically, minimalism represented a fear of going too far too fast, a fear that the United States, in its necessary repudiation of prewar isolationism, might overcommit itself before the war's end, particularly with regard to postwar territorial solutions. Overcommitment, it was forecast, would mean continued military expenditures, higher taxes, bigger government, and ultimately, the shedding of American blood on faraway shores, with the consequences of domestic outcry and a publicly forced reversion to pre-war isolationism.[20]

What holders of the maximalist attitude felt was bold was rash to holders of the minimalist attitude, and what the latter felt was prudent, the former felt was timid. Nonetheless, the interplay of the moods and assumptions of each side frequently led to pragmatic compromise and to what might even be called intellectual synthesis. Planners tended to choose the middle ground between the "extremes" as the wisest course, much as New Deal planners often had tried to fuse and compromise between the contrary pressures and views favoring socialism and capitalism in order to achieve a third and middle way. Holding to the axiom that the mean—as they perceived it—was always golden, Departmental officers and planners had the self-image of moderate and reasonable men, and they resented the American press's frequent aspersions to the contrary.

Thus, on implicitly asked key questions like how much pressure should the United States exert on the *internal political affairs* of a given state, and how much postwar "change" in those affairs should it espouse, the Department conventionally gravitated, certainly in the case of Middle Eastern states, toward ideas favoring gradualism and peaceful change. Indeed, in actual practice, the Department in many cases simply preferred a continuation of the political–social-economic mores and norms of the non-European indigenous population, notwithstanding the frequently nondemocratic character of those norms. Accordingly, any view, regardless of moral or other justifications, which might endorse "extreme" solutions like political revolution or large-scale demographic and boundary changes (such as the Jews were hoping for in Palestine, after World War II would end) was ipso facto undesirable.[21]

However, on the equally vital question of how the United States should react in the postwar period to the *external political affairs* of a given state, the Department's attitude was quite different. Here planners stressed not so much the virtues of moderation and gradualism, but those staunch American principles of national independence and political equality. Planners therefore usually preferred a solution which envisioned the leveling and transformation of states, and of the colonies and mandates of Axis and Allies alike, from spheres and dependencies to individual sovereignties. Indeed, the implementation of such transformations (which, to the planners, were hardly extreme, rather merely overdue) was in some cases (Syria, Lebanon) desired even before the war's end. Similarly, the Department was much concerned with the degree to which America's own foreign policy was "independent" from the influence of others, especially Britain and the Soviet Union.[22]

In sum, two themes of the planners were major: gradual, "golden-mean" reformism applied to states' internal affairs; and an accelerated rate of sovereignty applied to their external affairs. The two sometimes combined easily. One resisted British and Russian influence, not only because one wanted American policy to be independent, but because one preferred moderate American "reformism" as a mean between "a potentially expansionist Soviet policy and a rigid British policy."[23]

On the international plane the planners also favored an intermediate stance for America, and essentially for all states, between "selfish realism," nationalism, and unilateralism on the one hand, and "selfless idealism," internationalism, and multilateralism on the other. Thus, while the Department loathed the idea that the policy of America or any nation might be the creature of London or Moscow, it was as one in stressing the postwar need of every nation cooperating, and presumably compromising, with every other. By the same token, the Department urged the continuation into the postwar period of America's wartime cooperation (albeit as de facto senior partner) with the Russians and, in particular, the British.[24]

THE PLANNERS' MAIN PROPOSITIONS

These motifs, the golden mean and the sovereignty principle, were illustrated in the planners' approach to three major problems which were expected in the postwar period and which would have direct bearing on the Middle East: the structure of the peacetime United Nations Organization, the disposition of dependent areas, and the rectification of territorial and ethnic boundaries.

Like the rest of the Department, the planners were fully committed to the principle of a strong postwar United Nations Organization, with overt American participation and tacit American leadership. Indeed, figuring out how the United Nations wartime coalition ought to evolve into a permanent international organization for halting aggression—a League of Nations with teeth—was probably the most important and time-consuming task of the entire planning apparatus.

General commitment notwithstanding, the Department often felt that proposals entailing specific commitments were "extreme" or premature. For example, the planners opposed the possibility of a postwar U.N. based on regional councils composed of great powers and local states. They felt that such councils would be restrictive, hence injurious, on the precedent that in multilateral dealings the United States was strongest in "general collaboration" but weakest in "restricted arrangements."

What this apparently meant in part was that the Department feared that the Russians and the British, less publicly committed to moralistic-legalistic behavior and rhetoric than the Americans, might exploit their seats on regional councils and form closed-door spheres of influence. In the case of the Middle East, moreover, the Department opposed the council approach on the premise that the Arabs, of all the dependent peoples, did not need the great-power "tutelage" inherent in regional councils.

Finally, the Department did not want "restricted arrangements" out of fear that, as the world's leading great power, the United States would of necessity have a seat on most regional councils. The United States, therefore, would inevitably be dragged into various entangling commitments, necessitating the possible sacrifice of American soldiers' lives and producing adverse reaction in Congress and the public to America's over-commitments, for which the Department would be blamed.

One suspects that the Department to a degree hid behind these fears as an excuse for avoiding responsibility and keeping American policy ruggedly "independent." In any case, the planners, and the Department generally, felt the U.N. would better serve American interests if its structure were "loose," so that entangling commitments would be easier to evade. (Presumably, the U.N. would still have more teeth than the League—albeit "moderately" sized teeth.)[25]

On the issue of dependent areas (that is, mandates, protectorates, and colonies of the Allies), the Department, as noted, favored implementation with all deliberate speed of the Atlantic Charter's principles of self-determination and the economic open door. True, the Department did not wish to antagonize Prime Minister Churchill and the British military overtly by insisting on immediate across-the-board independence for British dependencies. Indeed, a few careerists and planners, but only a few, came to the realization that dismantling spheres was a complex affair which might jeopardize the economic rehabilitation of postwar Europe. On the other hand, no one, at least among the planners, wished to alienate nationalists in Arab lands and India (North African nationalists were less important to the Department, and Black African nationalists least of all) by failing to endorse postwar decolonization. Moreover, in order to rival both Soviet and Nazi anti-colonialist pronouncements aimed against the British in the Middle East and Asia, the Department periodically issued like pronouncements of its own.

The result emerging from these considerations was a compromise. The planners, far more than the British Foreign Office, insisted that the principles of the Atlantic Charter should apply to the postwar non-European world, and not only to lands under Axis domination. And yet that insistence was a few degrees less than an espousal of immediate and full sovereignty for all. By the midpoint of the war, the emerging Departmental norm on this issue was to emphasize temporarily delayed sovereignty, chiefly for British nonwhite dependencies—but with immediate native self-government and communal autonomy, and in the framework of short-run U.N. trusteeships instead of exclusive mandates.

With respect to the Axis empires, the Department's attitude was different. It stressed the need for immediate abolitionism rather than immediate gradualism. As shall be elaborated in Chapters 6 and 7, with respect to the French empire, too, the Department's view was increasingly in favor of abolitionism (except for Algeria, which was considered part of metropolitan France).[26]

On the question of border changes involving ethnic claims, the planners, with Departmental endorsement, again strove for the delicate balance of a middle way. They apparently hoped that in regions believed ready for independence—notably, Central and Eastern Europe and most of the Middle East—middle-sized states would emerge, that is, states which would be neither too large, and hence threatening, nor too small, and hence "unviable." Moreover, in their relations with their neighbors, these states, it was hoped, would be neither too united in political union nor too disunited by ethnic hostilities.

The planners tacitly feared that if disunity prevailed in these regions, the result would be a tangle of revanchism, autarky, and "balkanization." Furthermore, regional balkanization might produce political-military vacuums. Advantageous in theory to all great powers, such vacuums would mostly be to the advantage of the nearest great power. In the cases of all three regions under consideration, that meant the Soviet Union.

Conversely, the Department feared that too much regional unification or federation would create new "spheres," or political-economic blocs. Such blocs would represent new entities and variables, which would or could make planning more difficult. Furthermore, such blocs might jeopardize America's expected postwar prestige and leadership if used as instruments by America's rival "allies"—by Britain in the Arab world, or by the Soviet Union in Central and Eastern Europe. Finally, such blocs might strike a negatively independent course and legislate, in their own selfish regional interests, closed-door policies.

Through these uncertain crosswinds the planners veered, predictably, towards a course of "moderation"—which, however, had some rigid, even "extreme," implications of its own. On the question of postwar border rectifications, they stressed the principles of territorial integrity and national sovereignty, based largely on the pre-1939 status quo. Rectifications would thus be limited to changes produced by the war. Beyond that, changes would be held to a minimum and would be based only on pressing economic and security reasons. Changes based on historical reasons and ethnic claims, valid in the 1919 settlements, would no longer be honored.[27]

Regarding refugees and ethnic minorities expelled from or still living within a hostile majority, the planners favored turning back the clock to the pre-1939 status quo. This meant that the postwar norm would be "repatriation," that is, reabsorption of all populations dispersed by the war by their countries of origin. In some cases, exceptions seemed appropriate, and in the case of Jews the Department periodically considered in a positive light plans to establish refuge for them in various parts of Latin America and Africa (moreso than in Palestine or the United States). But even for Jews, Hitler's special victims, the "norm" was meant to apply, which would mean sending most European Jewish survivors of the war directly back to "motherlands" like Germany and Poland. Moreover, planners believed that once repatriated, refugees ought to be politically and socially assimilated. Yet they should be allowed religious–cultural autonomy—but without international guarantees. On the basis of League of Nations experience, such guarantees were considered too difficult and entangling to provide.[28]

The planners often turned to history to justify their preference for reabsorption as a solution to minority problems. Fancying themselves abler realpolitikers than the World War I generation of planners and peace makers, they regarded the territorial partitions and settlements made after 1918 as having led in a straight line to World War II. This was because the great sin of earlier planners, Wilson tacitly included, was an undue solicitousness born of ignorance and innocence towards ethnic pluralism and minority nationalisms, notably in the Austro-Hungarian empire. Those good intentions, it was now held, had fostered irredentist nationalism, fifth columns, and a receptivity to violence and fascism.[29]

Granted, it was too late to restore the Austro-Hungarian empire, but at least the "proven" folly of making radical changes in political frontiers, it was felt, need not be repeated. A major "lesson of history," therefore, was the necessity to minimize and discourage all pro-ethnic proposals—such as the creation of small ethnic states; or the legalization of ethnic pluralism and minority national "rights" within large states; or "radical surgery" solutions (such as those of Jewish Zionists, and modeled in part on the Greco-Turkish population exchanges in the 1920s), which proposed large-scale population transfers. Further, Departmental planners believed that not only would a minimalist territorial-demographic policy be maturer and safer than that which followed World War I; it would allegedly be cheaper to promote, at least in terms of American money and soldiers' blood.

Last but not least, it should be noted that during the war, the Department had another problem on its mind. Given its social background and patrician mentality, it often expressed anxiety over the hyphenated character of the United States' population and the ethnic nature of American politics. These traits, it felt, were potential sources of national weakness and wartime disunity—as indeed the enemy, Hitler, hoped they would prove to be. The planners' negative reaction to *domestic* pluralism seems clearly to have contributed to their negativism projected towards the "spectre" of postwar pluralism in Central and Eastern Europe and the Middle East.[30]

THE GLOBAL OUTLOOK NEAR THE END
OF THE WAR

By mid-1943, the conceptions and propositions examined above had achieved the status of consensus in the planning apparatus. By autumn, most of the apparatus' vast research on numerous other issues was also essentially finished. Concomitantly, plans for the postwar period were being drafted and discussed by the relevant hierarchy of planning committees and subcommittees. Many were in the redrafting stages and were already initialed by all relevant desks and echelons, on the operational as well as the planning side of the Department.

The overall result—approximately *two* years before the end of the war—was a formidable-appearing library of *final* statements and preferred solutions. These were framed in terms of the planners' two motifs (the golden mean, national sovereignty), as well as in terms of the Department's older desiderata and the by now fully revived Wilsonian principle of permanent collective security. Literally every geographic entity and most political-economic problems, real and potential, were "covered" and planned for.

The organizational and intellectual accomplishment that such speed and comprehensiveness represented was considerable. Even when the Foreign Service or the regular geographic and economic divisions of the Department were too occupied to seriously make use of the planners' massive research and analysis, the "backup" provided by the planners' output was always a tangible as well as a psychological asset. With that backup, the Department was confident in its vision of the morrow and felt that it knew what it wanted and how to get what it wanted in the postwar world with more certainty and detail than its counterparts in Britain, France, and the Soviet Union. Similarly, and with regard to the Middle East, its plans were worked out earlier and often in greater detail than counterpart plans of either the Arabs or the Jews.[31]

Even so, the planners themselves were relatively more certain of what they wanted the Department to pursue economically than politically, territorially, or militarily. As in the pre-1939 period, the Department's most important "concrete" desiderata were economic. Dealing with affairs of commerce and property was apparently easier and perhaps more natural and "American" than dealing with social and political affairs. Typifying this emphasis was the following summation of a major planning unit, the Policy Committee, in November 1944, when the war's end was already being anticipated. The list is also a significant summary of the Department's global priorities in terms of its short-run and long-run outlooks.

These priorities were to bolster Britain, and America's allies generally, during the war and at least three years thereafter; to restore and to increase American commercial relations worldwide; to articulate clearly, once and for all, American objectives, including lower foreign tariffs, global anti-cartel restrictions, public loans via the U.N. and the American Export-Import Bank, private loans and investments overseas, and repeal of the Johnson Act of 1934 which had forbidden private loans to states defaulting on World War I loans; and to revise prewar Anglo-American oil understandings.[32]

The motives behind these goals were implicit and will be amplified in succeeding chapters. The planners in essence wanted to prepare the way for a rapid and smooth transition from a war economy to a prosperous peace economy. Attaining new markets and rehabilitating Europe would serve these economic ends. Rehabilitation would also serve a political end by compensating Europe for the anticipated loss of colonies and influence. That loss in turn would be a necessary precondition for the success of America's global commercial and oil policies, as the Department wanted more access and freedom for Americans seeking trade relations, oil concessions and marketing rights, chiefly in the Middle East, than they had previously had.

NOTES

1. For deducing what were Departmental desiderata and basic beliefs before and during World War II, the most important collections of primary sources are the diplomatic correspondence in the volumes of the *Foreign Relations of the United States* series (henceforth *FR*) and the Departmental speeches in the volumes of the *Department of State Bulletins* (henceforth *Bulletin;* both printed by the U.S. Government Printing Office, Washington, D.C.); the postwar planning documentation in the Notter Papers; and the in-house articles and reports in the *Foreign Service Journal* (monthly, Washington, D.C.; in the 1930s called *American Foreign Service Journal*).

The most useful primary sources of book length on the Department of State as seen from Washington include Harley Notter, *Postwar Foreign Policy Preparation 1939–1945* (Washington, D.C.: GPO, 1949); Department of State, *Peace and War: United States Foreign Policy 1931–1941* (Washington, D.C.: GPO, 1942); Cordell Hull, *The Memoirs of Cordell Hull,* vol. 2 (New York: Macmillan, 1948), Sumner Welles, *The Time for Decision* (New York: Harper and Bros., 1944), *Where Are We Heading?* (New York: Harper and Bros., 1946), and *Seven Decisions That Shaped History* (New York: Harper and Bros., 1950); Henry Villard, *Affairs at State* (New York: Thomas Y. Crowell,

1965); and Dean Acheson, *Present at the Creation: My Years in the State Department* (New York: New American Library, 1969).

2. On the thesis that Department officers have been drawn from a narrow social base, see Robert Bendiner, *The Riddle of the State Department* (New York: Farrar and Rinehart, 1942); C. R. McKibbin, *The Career Structure and Success in the United States Foreign Service* (Ph.D. diss., Univ. of Kansas, 1968); D. C. Garnham, *Attitude and Personality Patterns of Foreign Service Officers and the Conduct of American Foreign Affairs* (Ph.D. diss., Univ. of Minnesota, 1971); and T. A. Krueger, "The Social Origins of Recent American Foreign Policy," *Journal of Social History* 7 (1973): 93–101. Yet cf. note 33, Chapter 4.

Wartime denials and charges of reverse snobbism are presented in reviews of Bendiner by Henry Villard, *Foreign Service Journal* 19 (20 August 1942): 543–44; and Orville Prescott, *New York Times*, 26 August 1942, p. 2. Also, see G. Howland Shaw, *Bulletin* 10 (1944): 73, 555.

3. On the Department's general unpreparedness for World War II, see Acheson, *Present at the Creation*, pp. 37–39, 64–67.

4. See Leo Pasvolsky, "The U.S. in the World Economy, 1940: Some Aspects of Our Foreign Economic Policy," 11 January 1941; Sumner Welles, "The U.S. and the World Crisis," 1 February 1941; Dean Acheson, "The Role of the Department of State in the Field of International Economic Operations," 25 October 1941; and Welles, Armistice Day address at tomb of Woodrow Wilson, 15 November 1941, all in *Bulletin* 4 and 5 (1941).

5. Acheson, *Present at the Creation*, p. 67.

6. Notter, *Postwar Foreign Policy Preparation*, p. 61.

7. Information collated from annual *U.S. Government Organization Manuals* (henceforth cited as *Government Manual*) and from *Foreign Service Lists* (both Washington, D.C.: GPO, 1939 through 1945).

8. Cf. Department rosters in *Government Manual* for 1944 and March 1945. Also, *Bulletin* 11 (1941): 778–81; Acheson, *Present at the Creation*, pp. 131–34; and R. L. Walker, "Edward R. Stettinius, Jr.," in S. F. Bemis, ed., *The American Secretaries of State and Their Diplomacy* (New York: Cooper Square, 1963), vol. 15, pp. 21–29.

9. See, e.g., Bendiner, *Riddle of the State Department;* Joseph M. Jones, *A Modern Foreign Policy for the United States* (New York: Macmillan, 1944), Chapter 2; and the debate between Professor R. B. Perry's "Harvard Group" and Welles, *New York Times*, 11 April 1943, p. 28.

10. See Acheson, *Present at the Creation*, p. 131; and note 18 below. On the economic origins of the Charter, note Welles (the drafter of the Charter), *Where Are We Heading?*, frontpiece; and L. L. Gardner, *Economic Aspects of New Deal Diplomacy* (Boston: Beacon, 1971), p. 173.

11. See Julius Pratt, "The Ordeal of Cordell Hull," *Review of Politics* 28 (1966): 76–98.

12. Ruth D. Russell, *A History of the United Nations Charter: The Role of the United States, 1940–1945* (Washington, D.C.: Brookings Institution, 1958), pp. 205, 211–12, 234.

13. See Welles, *Seven Decisions*, Chapter 5.

14. See *Register of the Department of State 1941* (Washington, D.C.: GPO, 1942), p. 33; and E. W. Spaulding, "Research Organization and Procedure Within the Department of State," *Bulletin* 4 (26 April 1941).

15. Information on Pasvolsky collated chiefly from: Notter, *Postwar Foreign Policy Preparation*, pp. 19, 58–59, passim; Pasvolsky to Hull, "Bases of Our

Program for International Economic Cooperation," 6 October 1943, E–I.O.1, Pasvolsky Papers, Box 1, Folder: "International Economic Relations 1943"; his co-authored book, *War Debts and World Prosperity* (Washington, D.C.: Brookings Institution, 1932); and his occasional speeches, e.g., in *Bulletin* 6 (7 March 1942).

16. On Bowman and the Council on Foreign Relations, see Notter, *Postwar Foreign Policy Preparation*, pp. 72, 86, passim; Council on Foreign Relations, *The War and Peace Studies of the Council on Foreign Relations 1939–1945* (New York: CFR, 1946); and Departmental reorganizational plans, in *Bulletin* 10 (15 January 1944). Other high-placed figures in the Council who were consulted, or entered Departmental planning at various stages included H. F. Armstrong, James Shotwell, Benjamin V. Cohen, William Westermann, Norman H. Davis, Philip Mosely, John Foster Dulles, and Russell Kirk. For a listing of other active private groups consulted, see Russell, *History of the U.N. Charter*, p. 215, n. 9. On the role of Bowman and others in the period of World War I, see Frank Manuel, *The Realities of American-Palestine Relations* (Washington, D.C.: Public Affairs Press, 1949), pp. 219, 222–23.

17. Notter, *Postwar Foreign Policy Preparation*, pp. 69–70, 163. My research in the Notter Papers confirmed that there were neither discussions nor plans contingent on American defeat or stalemate. Theoretically, such plans may have existed, then were removed or destroyed. I doubt this, if only because contingency discussion on another equally sensitive topic—the possibility of the postwar United Nations' failure—did occur and is documented. E.g., Minutes, 5th Meeting on UNO of SWNCC (State-War-Navy Coordinating Committee), 4 October 1945, Notter Papers, Box 79, Folder: "SWNCC (Ms UNO Min 1—)."

18. On administrative trends, see Notter, *Postwar Foreign Policy Preparation*, pp. 92–93, 101–8, 153–57, 207–8, 342–68; *Bulletin* 8 (1943): 43–58, and 10 (1944): 63–64; and W. Laves and F. Wilcox, "Reorganization of the Department of State," *American Political Science Review* 38 (1944): 289–301. On secrecy, see Notter, *Postwar Foreign Policy Preparation*, p. 117, and H. B. Westerfield, *Foreign Policy and Party Politics: Pearl Harbor to Korea* (New Haven: Yale Univ. Press, 1955), pp. 140–41.

19. For illustration of the "maximalist" view, see Notter, *Postwar Foreign Policy Preparation*, pp. 101–3, and the major position paper authored by Adolph Berle, Jr., "Report to the Policy Committee Regarding United States Interests and Policy in Eastern and Southeastern Europe and the Near East from the Subcommittee Comprised of Mr. Berle and the Directors of the Four Area Offices," PC-8 (second revision), 1 November 1944, and Annex J to PC-8 Revised, 4 November 1944, Stettinius Papers, Box 379, Folder: "S. D. Miscell.–Pol. Com. Docs. 1944."

20. Hull's cautious behavior, despite pugnacious words on imperialism, set the tone for a minimalist approach. See, e.g., his comment on British India in Hull, *Memoirs*, p. 1496, and Welles' counterpoint on Hull in *Seven Decisions*, Chapter 5. The "minimalist" view in the planning apparatus is mirrored in P-236, 2 July 1943, pp. 22, 36–38, Notter Papers, Box 3, Folder: "Doc.: Subcom. on Polit. Probs., Tent. View of Coms."

Acheson's famous quarrel with the maximalism of Roosevelt's special ambassador Patrick Hurley is also relevant here. For Acheson's (actually, his assistant Eugene Rostow's) remarks on Hurley's "messianic globaloney," see Acheson to Stettinius and Hull, 28 January 1944, p. 1, Stettinius Papers, Box 219, Folder: "U-Undersecretary of State 1/43"; Acheson, *Present at the Creation*, pp. 187–

89; and D. Lohbeck, *Patrick J. Hurley* (Chicago: Henry Regnery, 1956), p. 229.

21. See "Views of the Territorial Subcommittee," P 214-C, 10 March 1943, pp. 1–2, Notter Papers, Box 3, Folder: "Doc.: Subcom. on Polit. Probs., Tent. Views of Coms."; and notes 28 and 29 below.

22. On Syria and Lebanon, see note 17 in Chapter 6 and notes 1 and 16 in Chapter 7.

23. Berle, Annex J to PC-8 Revised, 4 November 1944, p. 1, Stettinius Papers, Box 379, Folder: "S. D. Miscell. Pol. Com. Docs. 1944."

24. Welles probably gave one of the earliest and clearest articulations of the golden mean approach, balancing the temptations of isolationism and globalism. See his speech to the *New York Herald Tribune* Forum, in *Bulletin* 7 (21 November 1942). Also, see Notter, *Postwar Foreign Policy Preparation*, pp. 101–3.

25. On the Department and the U.N., see cited works by Notter, *Postwar Foreign Policy Preparation*, passim, Russell, *History of the U.N. Charter*, passim, and Westerfield, *Foreign Policy and Party Politics*, pp. 143–45; also W. Edel, *The State Department, the Public and the United Nations Concept, 1939–1945* (Ph.D. diss., Columbia Univ. 1952).

On regional councils, see Welles, *Time for Decision*, pp. 377–81; Hull, *Memoirs*, pp. 1643–45; and P-236, p. 37, cited in note 20 above. On alleged contrasts between the postwar U.N. and the League of Nations, see Russell, *History of the U.N. Charter*, pp. 211–12, 231, 249; and speeches reprinted in *Bulletin* 12 (1945) of Green Hackworth, 28 January 1945; Joseph Grew and Alger Hiss, 4 March 1945; and James Dunn, 18 March 1945.

26. On the future of dependencies, material in the Notter Papers alone is very extensive. See E. Knight, "The Economic Importance of Colonies," E Doc. 84, T Doc. 314, 17 May 1943, Box 34, Folder: "T Docs. 310–19"; P-236, p. 22, cited in note 19 above; "British Policy in West Africa," CP-73, 17 November 1943, Box 114, Folder: "CDA Docs. 67–94"; a study on American and British attitudes toward dependent areas, CP-4, P-244, 29 September 1943, p. 2, Box 186, Folder: "Commitments: DA"; H-1064 Prelim., CTP-128, 24 February 1944, Box 175, Folder: "CDA (Committee on Dependent Areas), Docs. 121–42"; Post-War Committee, Minutes of 7th Meeting, 10 March 1944, Box 21, Folder: "PWC Com."; and PC-8 Revised, cited in note 19 above.

27. For references to fears of balkanization on one hand and hardening spheres on the other, see Notter, *Postwar Foreign Policy Preparation*, p. 86; Welles, *Time for Decision*, p. 265; Hull, *Memoirs*, pp. 1466–68; and Notter Papers, "Views of the Territorial Subcommittee," P 214-C, p. 5, cited in note 21 above; and P. Ireland in ST Minutes 13, 17 March 1943, p. 2, Box 79, Volume: "Minutes on Security Technical Problems (1–."

28. On questions of ethnic minorities and refugees, see Notter, *Postwar Foreign Policy Preparation*, p. 543 and Appendix 48, p. 642; and in Notter Papers, remarks of Berle, Bowman, and Harry Howard, in Post-War Committee, Minutes of 3rd Meeting, 18 February 1944, and of 46th Meeting, 8 June 1944, Box 21, Folder: "PWC Com.: Migration D 35, E-235," 16 December 1943, p. 3, Box 91, Folder: "E Docs. 216–34"; and PWC-320 and PWC-322, 22 November 1944, Box 20, Folder: "PWC Docs. 303–22."

On Jewish refugees, see Migration Memo 9, 6 March 1944, Box 106, Folder: "Migration Memos 1–9"; H-32a, 1 February 1944, and H-37b and H-37b Supplement, 1 March 1944, Box 57, Folder: "H Pol. Summaries 26–39"; and Chapters 13 and 14.

29. That Wilson actually helped to destroy ethnic pluralism (in the Austro-Hungarian "empire") and that discouraging the creation of small ethnic states could lead to *heightened* ethnicity were theses hardly contemplated by the planners.

On the Territorial subcommittee's negative attitude toward post-World War I territorial settlements, see Notter, *Postwar Foreign Policy Preparation,* pp. 86, 121, and with reference to League of Nations settlements, note 25 above.

As a rule, negative allusions to the "lessons" and failures of American policy makers in World War I, perhaps out of respect to Wilson, were not direct. E.g., Joseph Grew concurred with Welles' view (*Seven Decisions,* Chapter 5) that in contrast to the American practice during World War I plans, alliances and territorial adjustments should be made *before* World War II ended J. Grew, *Turbulent Era: A Diplomatic Record of Forty Years, 1904–1945* (Boston: Houghton Mifflin, 1952), p. 1450. (For all that, contradictions in the dense jungle of documents and memoirs are often rife. Thus cf. Grew's distinctly Hullian approach as Stettinius' Undersecretary: "I am convinced that no territorial problem can be solved by proclamations issued in the wake of an army on the march." Grew in *Bulletin* 12[2] (13 May 1945): 902.

30. On ethnic, or hyphenated, Americans, see the various speeches stressing mutual understanding, loyalty and unity addressed to Italian-Americans, Hungarian-Americans, Jewish-Americans, chiefly by Acheson and Berle, in, e.g., *Bulletin* 6, 7, 8 (6 June 1942, 14 November 1942, 6 February 1943, 8 May 1943) and *Bulletin* 11 (10 September 1944).

31. As indicated, *Postwar Foreign Policy Preparation* projects an image of a well-oiled planning apparatus finishing its labors ahead of all the competition. Similarly, Russell claims that plans for the postwar U.N. were so elaborate and detailed that if matters went well at Yalta, "the machinery for calling the [U.N.] conference could be put into motion immediately" (Russell, *History of the U.N. Charter,* p. 509).

There is certainly as much truth as hyperbole in these views, if only because non-American policy makers were more preoccupied with the war itself and were more polarized over what exactly to pursue after the war. Thus Director of European Affairs H. Freeman Matthews reported a British colleague's saying: "I think you in America have a much clearer idea of what you want our position to be in the world than we have of what we wish and expect of you. . . . We don't want you to return to isolationism and yet we are both surprised and resentful of any show of independent American policy." (Memorandum, Matthews to Stettinius and Grew, 6 January 1945, pp. 1–2, in Stettinius Papers, Box 622, Folder: "S-Sec. of State, 1–7 January 1945").

On the comparative state of unplanning and nonconsensus in the Jewish world, see, e.g., the Introduction by Ben Halpern, p. xvii, in *The Jewish National Home in Palestine: Reprint of Hearings before the Committee on Foreign Affairs of the House of Representatives, February 8, 9, 15, 16, 1944* (New York: Ktav, 1970).

32. Policy Committee's views (summary), Minutes of ECA-10, 4 November 1944, p. 1, Notter Papers, Box 14, Folder: "Pol. Com. Docs. ECA."

2

The Middle East:
An Overview

The Middle Eastern countries under examination in this book are Syria, Lebanon, Iraq, Egypt, Saudi Arabia, and Palestine (including Transjordan). This chapter offers useful and salient background material on each. Depending on the interests and expertise of the reader, this material may well be too little or too much. Nonetheless, its inclusion is surely necessary, on the principle that history, including the making of American foreign policy, does not exist in a vacuum.

The material covers key developments in each country to approximately 1939. Sections dealing with Saudi Arabia and Palestine are longer than those on other countries because of the overall importance and complexity of events in these two lands. Background information for each country for the period 1939–45 is incorporated in those subsequent chapters dealing with American relations with specific countries.

SYRIA AND LEBANON

French religious-cultural influence in Syria and Lebanon (the Levant) was strong and went back to the Crusades, although French mandatory rule dated back only to the 1920s. France's concern after World War I over its own future status as a European power, its desire to solidify and extend its influence in North Africa eastward, its antagonism toward British influence in the Middle East, its cultural and linguistic superiority complex—these were some of the factors which stimulated its pursuit of

25

predominance in the eastern Mediterranean. Still, in the total scheme of French foreign affairs and for most of the years before World War II, except for the period 1917–22, the Levant (unlike North Africa) was not a top priority.[1]

Paternalistic and often unpopular, France improved, yet exploited, the Levant's economy. Politically, it ruled by dividing the area into seven provinces, each distinguished by its own peculiar topography and local religious majority. Interestingly, some local majorities (for example, the Maronite Christians in Greater Lebanon and Moslem Alawite sect in Latakia) often preferred external French protection and internal communal autonomy to domination by the Levant's overall majority, the Sunni Moslems.

Even so, the Lebanese Maronites were basically unhappy with the French, as the French-designed borders of the new Greater Lebanon province-state had reduced the Maronites' majority percentage and had made them uncomfortably dependent on France. The Sunnis of the large province of Damascus were also hostile, indeed more so. To them it was perfectly clear that France was deliberately dividing the land and promoting particularism in order to destroy the impulse of pan-Arabism and to abort Sunni and Syrian hegemony in the Levant. All in all, from the 1920s on, provincial boundary disputes and the larger question of Levant independence constituted running sores on the Franco-Arab relationship.

The economic situation, whether good or bad, also fostered antagonisms. In the 1920s, increasing prosperity helped to encourage the thinking that dependence on France was unnecessary; but in the 1930s, the effects of the world depression led to local unemployment and anti-French riots. An additional catalyst of crisis was the Anglo-Iraqi Treaty of 1930, which terminated the British mandate. Incensed that a backward neighbor was getting more freedom while they seemed to be getting less, Damascus and Beirut both became more intransigent towards the French who, for their part, were incensed that Britain had gone as far as it did in Iraq and was thus undermining France's position.

After protracted negotiations, separate treaties were concluded with Lebanon and with Syria in 1936 (by this date, meaning the combined provinces of Damascus, Aleppo, Latakia, Jebel Druze, and Jezira, and including tentative control by Damascus of Hatay, the Turkish enclave surrounding Alexandretta). The treaty drafts were much like the Anglo-Iraqi and Anglo-Egyptian treaties. Syria and Lebanon were promised independence and sponsorship in the League of Nations within three years; in turn, each pledged to enter into a military alliance with France and to recognize the following: French diplomatic precedence; the acquired legal and economic rights of French nationals; the special interest of France in French-language institutions; and the semi-autonomy of non-Sunni Syrian provinces. In Lebanon, a provision was added allowing

French troops to be stationed without restrictions. Apart from the fact that there was always more pro-French sentiment in Lebanon than in Syria, a main purpose for the provision was to protect Lebanon's independence from possible Syrian irredentism.

However, the "new era" feelings of 1936 rapidly dissipated. Despite ratifications in the Syrian and Lebanese parliaments, the final negotiations with France broke down. A new conservative government in Paris, fearful of giving up external positions in the face of the Axis buildup and perennial British competition, did not act to ratify either treaty. The mandate continued; indeed, France's direct control increased. Moreover, France felt that in the coming lineup against Germany, it was more worthwhile to forge an entente with Turkey rather than with the allegedly unreliable Syrians. As a result, France took steps in 1937–39 through the League and through bilateral arrangements with Turkey which led to the cession of Hatay-Alexandretta to Turkey. France thus placated Turkish irredentism on the eve of World War II but fed the fires of Damascus' own irredentism and anti-French nationalism.[2]

"Greater Lebanon," or Lebanon, has always represented one of the smallest states of the Middle East. (It was considered by the French as a separate state, rather than province, as of the mid-1920s.) Lebanon's area, mostly mountainous, covered 3,470 square miles. In the late 1930s, its population, exclusive of those in the Lebanese diaspora, was approximately 860,000 mostly engaged in terrace farming and commerce. In the same period, Syria's overall population was 2.5 million, mostly agricultural and rural, in an area of approximately 72,500 square miles.[3]

As noted, the Levant contains historic mosaics of different Islamic and Christian groupings, the Sunni Moslems clearly predominating in Syria, the Maronite Christians until the 1960s slightly predominating in Lebanon. In some instances, a degree of political toleration and compromise was the result, as seen in the formerly well known Lebanese practice, begun in 1937, by which the republic's president was always a Maronite, the prime minister a Sunni Moslem, and the speaker of parliament a Shii Moslem. In most other instances, however, communal differences intensified personality clashes and political factionalism, leading, especially in Syria, to a history of parliamentary crises and dogmatic but weak leadership.

Factionalism sometimes derived from ideological differences, too. This was more the rule in Lebanon than in Syria. In Syria, uncompromising nationalism was the norm by the mid-1930s; there were no "factions" of minimalists versus maximalists. The great majority of Syria's elected representatives were Damascene Sunnis, belonging to the National Bloc, formed in the late 1920s. A group within the Bloc, more organized and for that reason seemingly more "radical," also took shape in the late 1920s.

Up to the 1950s, this group (Istiqlal) played the role of Syria's vanguard, comparable to the Wafd party in Egypt. (Its main leader, Shukri Kuwatli, was the first president of the Syrian republic as of 1944, and again, after returning from several years of exile in Egypt, as of 1955.) In 1928, the Istiqlal framed a constitution, the provisions of which most Syrian politicians would support for decades: Syria was to be a republic in the western sense; the official religion was to be Islam; and Lebanon and Palestine (and Transjordan) were to be annexed. As for France, it was ignored as if it did not exist.

In Lebanon, there was more substantive ideological divergence. A communist party was long active. However, the two significant focal points were the Unionist group, a major party in the 1920s, and the Constitutionalist group, which became the major party in the 1930s and 1940s. The former was led by Emile Eddé, the latter by Bishara Khuri. Though both were Maronites and culturally francophile, Eddé was more of an *assimilé* who viewed Lebanon as part of the Mediterranean world, facing seaward like its Phoenician progenitor. The Moslem religion and the Arab culture of the desert interior he saw as alien threats to Lebanon's national character. Eddé preferred a continuation of French protection and a territorially smaller, more Christian, Lebanon, freed from the danger of a large Moslem minority.

Khuri, however, felt Eddé was unpragmatic. A Lesser Lebanon would allegedly be less viable and defensible than a Greater Lebanon. And because he felt it harmful for Lebanon to become a foreign island in an Arab sea, Khuri believed it necessary to come to terms with pan-Arab nationalism. Furthermore, he wished to terminate the mandate, because it was, in his view, an obstacle to Moslem-Christian cooperation. Only thus would the larger Arab world come to recognize that Lebanon was not a French satellite, and only thus would that world forego insisting that Lebanon be ingested by ("united with") Syria.[4]

IRAQ

By decision of the Allied Supreme Council (San Remo, 1920) Britain was assigned the mandate for Iraq (Mesopotamia). In 1921, Iraq also became a constitutional hereditary (Hashemite) monarchy. For the following three decades, the tension implicit in these decisions led to constant friction and jockeying for power between Baghdad and London.

Iraq was the first Arab country where a mandate was officially (not actually) terminated (1930). Yet it was a large, underdeveloped, and underpopulated country; in 1934, there were 3.5 million inhabitants in an area of 116,000 square miles. Typically, the population was illiterate, poor, agricultural and rural. Eighty percent Arab Moslem, Iraq contained a large separatist Kurdish minority (16 percent) in the north, as well as smaller enclaves of Assyrians (Nestorian Christians), Turks, and Jews. Within the Arab Moslem majority, centrifugal forces were also strong, notably on the levels of religious sectarianism (Iraqis were almost equally split between Sunni and Shii) and socioeconomic animosities (among pastoral tribal bedouin, village farmers, and townsmen). Furthermore, Iraq's political life during the interwar and war years was characteristically unstable and mediocre, riven by querulous personality and party cleavages.[5]

For these and other reasons, Iraq was internally a divided and weak state. From the British strategic viewpoint, it was a peripheral state, being neither a direct vital link to British India, as was Egypt, nor a country positioned like Iran and Turkey, close to the immediate reach of Britain's great-power rivals, Nazi Germany and the Soviet Union.

Nonetheless, there were several factors which required the British to treat Iraq seriously. Iraq's oil fields and the direct interest of the British majority-owned, governmentally subsidized Iraq Petroleum Company (IPC) represented one such factor. (Mosul and Kirkuk in the Kurdish north, later Basra in the south, were the chief oil centers. Pipelines brought the northern oil to the Mediterranean coast via Haifa, Palestine, and until 1940, Tripoli, Lebanon.) Strong anti-British, anti-Zionist, pro-Nazi and later, pro-Soviet currents in Iraq's politics and media were another factor commanding British military and diplomatic concern, mainly after 1940. That Iraq became a depot and transit link for American Lend-Lease to the Soviet Union was a third factor.

A fourth factor was the leadership that Iraq lay claim to in the Arab world. Baghdad, as the center of the medieval Abbassid empire, felt it had clearer title to pan-Arab leadership than other claimants, like Egypt, Saudi Arabia, and Syria. A related consideration was the personality and status of Iraq's longtime leading politician, Nuri Said. One of the few men in the Arab world who qualified in the eyes of many Westerners as a potentially regional statesman, Nuri had the trust of the British Foreign Office. Before and during World War II Nuri was eager to be the founding father of a postwar Arab regional federation, under Iraq's Hashemite leadership and also under British aegis.

For all that, however, and for all the anxiety that Iraq would cause in the period of the Rashid Ali coup in April 1941, British interests in Iraq before the war were generally secondary.

EGYPT

The British interest in Egypt began earlier, and was consistently greater, than it was anywhere else in the Arab Middle East. The key reason was that through Egypt ran the Suez Canal which, within two decades of its inception in 1869, became Britain's famous imperial "lifeline" to India. Because of the high strategic and commercial value inhering in the Canal, Britain habitually sought to increase its influence throughout Egypt, making Egypt, as it were, a buffer zone around the Canal Zone. By 1914, several months after World War I began, a protectorate was formally established, confirming Egypt as an integral part of the British empire.[6]

However, nationalist violence erupted against the British presence at the close of the war. It was inspired in part by the feeling that Egypt was relatively the largest and most modern country of the region and therefore, that it particularly deserved to be the recipient of British wartime "promises" to the Arabs of imminent political independence. The Egyptians bolstered their case by invoking President Woodrow Wilson's celebrated principle of self-determination.

Taking the nationalist lead was a new upper- and middle-class political party, the Wafd, which in the 1920s was under a passionate Anglophobe and orator, Saad Zaghlul. Popular, militant, and in the political vanguard of native nationalism for the next three decades, the Wafd also became known for a high level of corruption, even for the Middle East.[7] When limited British military repression failed to stamp out the Wafd's agitations, the British sought to negotiate a treaty of alliance which would put a formal end to the protectorate but would maintain British military control in matters of external security. When the Wafd proved unwilling to accept the carrot, Britain by itself terminated the protectorate in 1922, but explicitly reserved for itself final authority over the Sudan and over the security of the Canal Zone, the Nile, and imperial communications generally. It also reserved the rights to intervene and defend Egypt from "aggression," and to protect minorities, foreigners, and the private interests of British nationals.

In theory, then, the protectorate ended and independence began in 1922—ten years before a comparable situation existed in any other Arab country (Iraq, in 1932). Despite this head start, Egypt's independence would be quite incomplete; indeed, British control in some ways increased in the 1920s and 1930s, even exclusive of the British presence in the Canal Zone and the Sudan. A Wafdist fanatic had touched off the process by assassinating a high British official in 1924. Without any half-measures or failures of nerve, the British severely clamped down. Indeed, as they usually did, the British treated Egypt "seriously," and also with a certain subjective contempt for the Egyptians. To some close observers, neither such seriousness nor such contempt were found in Iraq (the British liked the Iraqis) or in other Arab states.[8]

British power was also advanced by the fact that Zaghlul's death in 1927 weakened the Wafd even as the Wafd's principal internal rival, the

"Palace," was becoming stronger. The constitutional monarch, King Fuad I, who represented a coalition of landowners, merchants, and conservative Moslem leaders, succeeded in 1930 in dissolving the Wafd-controlled parliament. In the early 1930s, the Palace, and relatively harmonious Anglo-Egyptian relations, thus prevailed.

However, the king died in 1936, and other losses weakened the Palace. The Wafd, victorious in elections, returned to power, with the demand for a treaty relationship with Britain to supersede the 1922 declarations. The British, concerned at the time with Italian naval encroachments in the Red and Mediterranean Seas, were willing to placate the Wafd. In this context, the Anglo-Egyptian Treaty of 1936 emerged.

According to its terms, British control over the Canal and the Sudan continued; but in other areas concessions were extracted. Britain pledged to phase out its military presence in Egypt and to reduce its control over Egypt's army and police. It also agreed to replace its high commissioner with an ambassador and to support Egypt's entry into the League of Nations. Furthermore, it gave up its rights to protect minorities and foreigners and agreed to support the abolition of the old capitulatory system. This had given extraterritorial legal privileges to British and other Western nationals.[9]

By 1937, Egypt was a member of the League, and the Montreux Conference had abolished most of the capitulations. The Wafdist leader, Nahas Pasha, however, increasingly came into conflict with Fuad's young heir, Farouk, with the result that the old internal tug of war between Wafd and Palace was reactivated. As before, the Palace pressured its way to ascendancy and held on to it for the remainder of the 1930s.

In nonpolitical terms, too, Egypt by World War I was clearly emerging as the most important regional entity, not only because of the Canal but also because of its large population, resulting from a high birth rate and, to a lesser extent, from British hygienic efforts. (In gross figures and over random intervals, Egypt has increased its native population from 2.5 million in 1800 to 9 million in 1897, to 12.5 million in 1917, to 16 million in 1937, to 30 million in 1966, to 35 million in 1973.) However, as is well known, Egypt's arable land is restricted largely to the Delta and banks of the Nile (13,600 square miles in 1939, within a total area of 383,000 square miles). Not unlike Iraq, Egypt's population was and is characteristically illiterate, poor, rural, and agricultural.[10]

Egypt's chief minority has been the Christian Copts who, together with other Christian groups, represented approximately 8 percent of the population in the 1930s. In addition, there were about a half-million foreigners after World War I. In the sequence of their numerical weight, foreign enclaves consisted of Greeks, Italians, British, French, and with lesser numbers of Maltese, Jews, Armenians, and other European-descended

Levantines. Although illustrations of xenophobia, anti-Semitism, or the treatment of Copts as second-class citizens by Moslems were always to be found, it cannot be said that Egypt was a racial-minded and minority-riven society as was Iraq. That minorities and foreigners were few and that the latter were geographically removed, living mainly in Alexandria and Cairo, perhaps helped to account for this.

Among the Moslem majority, orthodox Sunniism predominated. Again, unlike the Iraqi case, Islam in Egypt was for the most part a unifying force (though not especially an intellectually progressive, tolerant, or humanizing force). Islam in Egypt was one of the taproots of Egyptian nationalism, fostering anti-Westernism, anti-secularism, and anti-Zionism. Moreover, because Egypt is on the geographic and racial periphery of the Arab heartland, Islam in Egypt was one of the few natural bridges (another was the Arabic language) to that heartland and to the regional cause of pan-Arab nationalism. Indeed, that El-Azhar, the world famous conservative Sunni "university," was located in Cairo was a factor which in itself gave Egypt a prestigeful connection to the Arab world.

Egypt had its centrifugal forces, too. There were cleavages in geography and class (landowner *vs. fellahin* share-cropper; city dweller *vs.* villager; the Delta of lower Egypt *vs.* upper Egypt and the western and eastern deserts). On the cultural level, there were antagonistic schools of thought (past-oriented Islam *vs.* future-oriented Western secularism; Egypt as part of the Occident and pluralistic Mediterranean civilization *vs.* Egypt as part of the Orient and the monistic pharaonic and Arab-Islamic cultures of the interior deserts). A fourth centrifugal force was politics, as indicated by the Palace-Wafd struggle—not to mention Egypt's smaller parties, the secessions within the Wafd, the rival ideologies and personalities under the rubric of Egyptian nationalism, or the influence of extremist groups like the Moslem Brotherhood (Ikwan), the communist party, and the fascist, youth-oriented Blue Shirts and Green Shirts.

Economically, Egypt's characteristic feature, its poverty, was both intensified and alleviated by the British. Alleviation was demonstrated by the "developmental" side of British imperialism—new infrastructure for transportation and industry, new spheres of employment and opportunity, better hygiene, improved agricultural and administrative efficiency, more education and modernization. Intensification was demonstrated by the "exploitative" side of imperialism—inflation, profiteering, visible economic gaps, social segregation, smoldering resentments and injured sensitiveness resulting from the mixture of Englishmen's superiority complexes and Egyptians' inferiority complexes. The biggest intensifier of poverty by far, however, was the combination of a too large, ever-expanding native population and a poor, almost resourceless land, most of which belonged to an elite of wealthy landowners.

In terms of external trade, Britain, the United States, and Chile were the main exporters to Egypt in the 1930s. Cotton, Egypt's chief money crop, was exported mainly to Britain, France, India, Burma, and Japan. If America was a relatively poor customer, it was due to Britain's mercantilistic controls; a lack of American business interest, knowledge, and communications regarding Egypt; the competition within the American market of Arizona Pima cotton; and the generally restricted conditions— in America due to the Great Depression, and in Egypt due to endemic poverty. Nonetheless, by the late 1930s there was a definite upturn, both in America's importation of Egyptian cotton (then cheaper than domestic cotton) and in Egypt's importation of American manufactured and luxury goods.[11]

SAUDI ARABIA

After a checkered career going back to 1901, Abdul Azziz Ibn Saud in 1926 became the most important monarch in the countries of the Arabian peninsula, and in 1932 assumed the title of King of Saudi Arabia. Still, he was, as previously, anxious over encirclement and revenge by enemies and rivals and by border problems, as well as the task of welding his realm, so large, isolated, and poor in population (less than four million), into one kingdom.

Nevertheless, the power of the monarchy steadily increased. One reason was the spirit of militant puritanism and tribal unity transmitted by Wahabism, an Islamic neo-orthodoxy adopted by the Saudis. A second reason was that Ibn Saud was the only ruler in the peninsula's interior under continuous British subsidy. Also, except for Yemen, all states bordering Saudi Arabia were in the British sphere and consequently were restrained from warring with or trying to overthrow the Saudis (and vice versa). A third reason for growing Saudi power derived from the fact that as protector of the holy cities of Islam and collector of pilgrimage fees and bequests, Ibn Saud automatically became a prestigious (and at least semi-solvent) figure, not only in the peninsula or the Arab world, but also in the larger Moslem world. A fourth reason was the fees, advances, and royalties from oil production, a process begun essentially in 1933.

A final reason for the monarchy's consolidation was the leadership of Ibn Saud himself. As king, he was physically impressive, politically dictatorial, religiously extremist (though not as much as some of his ultraorthodox countrymen), sexually prolific, with no shortage of male heirs (and concubine and family expenses), and diplomatically shrewd, manipulative, and often more tractable (for a fee) than he appeared. To some (more often to Anglo-Saxons than to Arabs, and among the Anglo-

Saxons, more often to Americans than to Englishmen), Ibn Saud was charismatic, the embodiment of the romanticized bedouin and archetypal noble savage, the long-last discovered fierce yet chivalrous desert warrior. In the Anglo-American stereotype, he would emerge by the 1940s as a presumed benevolent patriarch (but dangerous if his wrath was kindled), at the head of a potentially monolithic and fanatic horde of "Mohammedans," from Casablanca to the East Indies.[12]

Notwithstanding the 1927 Treaty of Jidda, by which Britain recognized the full independence of the Saudi kingdom, Britain was the predominant power in Saudi Arabia before World War II. However, other great powers were also interested. Indeed, the Soviet Union had been the first government to recognize Ibn Saud's sovereignty. Yet by 1938 the king terminated a Soviet proposal for a diplomatic mission in Jidda. Similarly, both before and after the start of World War II, he put off German, Italian, and Japanese expressions of interest in diplomatic and oil relations. While anti-communism was a factor, neither ideological belief nor Anglophilia were the reasons for the king's negative reactions. Concern over possible Soviet and Axis territorial motives, together with a willingness to continue benefiting from, and exploiting, the familiar British financial connection, were his chief reasons.[13]

With respect to Washington's efforts to pierce the British curtain, Ibn Saud was more receptive than he was towards Moscow or Berlin, though here, too, as shall be seen, he knew how to pit one power against the other. Pre-World War I Protestant medical missionaries in the Arabian peninsula represented in effect a first step towards eventual Saudi-American harmony. (Even so, after becoming king, Ibn Saud allowed such individuals into his realm for healing purposes only, and expelled them if they proselytized. The Department of State, for its part, was also averse to any Christian evangelism liable to diminish Arab-Moslem good will.)[14]

But a vastly larger step was taken when Standard Oil Company of California, in July 1933, won a 66-year concession in Hasa province to explore for and market Saudi oil—even though originally Ibn Saud and most of his advisers had favored a British-run concession. The reasons why Standard received it rather than the British contenders (the Eastern General Syndicate and the Iraqi Petroleum Company) have long been the object of interpretation. In essence, it appears that Standard was both readier and more generous in its initial offer of a down payment in gold coin (valued at £50,000).

The deal had actually begun in 1931 when Ibn Saud had met Charles R. Crane—American mining magnate from California, former minister to China, co-head of Woodrow Wilson's King-Crane Commission in the Middle East after World War I, and a man who was personally infatuated with the romance of Araby. The meeting resulted in permission for mineral surveys to be made by Crane's operative, Karl Twitchell, an engineer who was another adventurous and romantic Arabophile and who in years to come would be highly respected by Departmental officers dealing with Saudi Arabia.

It is interesting to note that when Ibn Saud agreed to the surveys, he was dubious about the discovery of oil, despite all the rumors about its existence, because a decade earlier a British firm had paid for a similar concession, prospected, and found nothing. If anything, the king in 1931 hoped for the discovery of water and gold, and hoped indirectly that since Americans were now involved, the American government would at last extend diplomatic recognition of his sovereignty. Twitchell, however, was looking primarily for oil (already discovered in the 1920s in nearby Bahrein Island, where Standard of California had a concession since 1928). When he had reason to suspect its existence in Hasa, he approached Standard, which, as noted, proved ready and willing.

Yet it appears the deal was finally consummated only when Ibn Saud went against his original preference for IPC—and not out of any particular suspicion of Britain or any particular fondness for faraway America, as both Standard and the Department of State were wont to believe in the 1940s. Rather, Ibn Saud accepted the advice of the remarkable Harry St. John B. Philby. Philby, formerly of the India Civil Service, a convert to Islam and an accomplished Arabist and writer, and in the early 1930s a businessman in Jidda and a trusted counselor to the king, was also apparently a man with personal grievances to settle against the British diplomatic establishment. Whether more for personal or business reasons, it was he who had first recommended the meeting between Ibn Saud and Crane, and it was he who persuaded the king to hold out for more money than IPC could then offer and to grant the concession to Standard. (The Depression had made Britain go off the gold standard, hence IPC could not offer gold; the United States would go off the gold standard, too, but within the year after Standard's deal.)

Accordingly, Ibn Saud received what he wanted most: much gold in hand to pay his bills and to offset the drop that the Depression had created in pilgrim revenue. However, generosity looks like parsimony over the distance of years, and early gratitude seems foolish: It would be a retrospective Saudi view in later years that the Hasa concession was settled far too much in America's favor, as a result of Saudi weakness.[15]

Withal, it was not until October 1938 that the operating company set up by Standard (CASOC, later called ARAMCO) was able to announce the large-scale discovery of oil.[16] And it was not until May 1939 that the first commercial exportation was made from the kingdom's Persian Gulf port of Ras Tanura. If 1933 had been a big step forward in Saudi-American relations, 1938–39 thus proved to be even bigger.[17]

What was also remarkable was the fact that despite its "backwardness," even relative to other Arab lands, Saudi Arabia never suffered the typical Arab sense of humiliation before Westerners. On the contrary, the imagery of remote, ancient "Arabia" as the home of the true Arab warrior untouched by time, the mystique of Ibn Saud as a Hero of the East, and of course the fact that his kingdom was floating on oil, led to the peculiar custom among occidentals—American businessmen and government officers, as a rule, more than their more imperious British counterparts—of kowtowing before the king to a degree which was rare in the twentieth century.[18]

PALESTINE (including Transjordan)

After centuries of political insignificance within the Ottoman empire, "Palestine" became relevant in the late nineteenth century as part of the imperial rivalry between Britain and France.[19] Each wanted to make Palestine a buffer zone against the other's sphere of influence in the eastern Mediterranean. When World War I broke out, friction only abated somewhat between the two, by now, "allies." According to the Sykes-Picot Agreement of May 1916, and with regard to Palestine, the French were to have postwar rule in the Galilee, the British in Haifa Bay.[20]

There were, moreover, two factors of which Britain, in particular, took cognizance: Arab and Jewish opinion worldwide. In part to woo the Arabs from following Sultan Mehmed V's call for holy war (*jihad*) against the Triple Entente (actually, the Arabs in the mass had no desire for *jihad*), and in part to woo the Jews from pacifism and/or sentiments against Czar Nicholas II and for Emperor Franz Joseph, Britain made overlapping wartime "pledges" to each side, relative to the postwar settlements in Palestine and the Middle East.[21]

Though it is outside the province of this book, it must at least be mentioned that these were, and are, controversial pledges with a long and disputatious history behind them. On behalf of the Arabs, the main documentation of pledges was the correspondence (eight letters, July 1915–January 1916) between Sir Henry McMahon, British High Commissioner in Cairo, and Hussein, Sharif of Mecca, of the Hashemite line, aspirant to the caliphate, and leader, with T. E. Lawrence, of the "Arab Revolt." On behalf of the Jews, Foreign Secretary Arthur Balfour's letter of 2 November 1917—a "declaration of sympathy with Jewish Zionist aspirations" sent to Lord Walter Rothschild—was the chief exhibit. When Britain became the mandatory power in both western and eastern Palestine, subsequent to General Allenby's conquests beginning in October 1917, and under the authority of the Allied Supreme Council in April 1920 (San Remo Conference) and of the League of Nations Council in July 1922, the Balfour Declaration was incorporated into the official League text and made part of the overall mandatory responsibility.[22]

In view of the Arab-Jewish confrontation over Palestine since World War I, it may be useful to take note of some demographic figures, even though estimates vary and are not reliable. In Palestine (east and west of the Jordan river), the Arab population at the turn of the century has been reported as about 570,000; the Jewish, about 80,000. Elsewhere in the Ottoman empire, the Jewish population was reportedly about 380,000, while in Egypt and North Africa it totaled slightly more than 190,000.

The Arab population in all instances was clearly larger than the Jewish. Yet it is significant to note that in broad terms the Arab majority was not overwhelming, nor was the Jewish minority minuscule. To be sure, there were other deeply rooted and substantial minorities in the Middle East also.[23]

Among the Arab population in western Palestine, the main religious-ethnic groupings were and would remain Moslem Sunnis of "native" pre-Arabic stock (Greco-Syrian, Israelite, Canaanite) and also Moroccan, South Arabian, Turcoman, and Circassian stocks; the Druses; and the Christians. Within the latter group, mostly native Arab, were more than two dozen denominations, represented chiefly by Greek Catholic and Greek Orthodox (the latter becoming the most anti-Zionist of all religious groups, Moslems included), Latin (Roman Catholic), and Maronite; also, Armenian Orthodox, Coptic, Ethiopian, and Syrian Orthodox.[24]

As in all other parts of the Middle East, Arab, or non-Jewish, society in early twentieth century western Palestine was largely "feudal." Typically, there were four classes—townsman; fellah (village peasant, often a sharecropper); effendi (landlord, stereotypically absentee and exploitative); and bedouin. Although the values of each were antagonistic, there was nonetheless a basic interaction among them of geographic and economic mobility, both upward and downward, and from desert to farm, and vice versa. Characteristic, too, were "interstate" Arab migrations to and from Palestine, and high birth and death rates. Such cities as Jaffa, Nablus, and Acre were the largest Moslem towns; Nazareth was Arab Christian. The Galilee and the West Bank were the main areas of village population.[25]

Within each religious-ethnic group of the Arab population, irrespective of class, there was typically a hierarchy, headed by male elders and bound together by an absolute clan-family loyalty. The next object of loyalty was one's particular home or village. A third degree of loyalty was more vague, pan-Islamic and pan-Arabic by turns, symbolized by the Koran among the religiously fundamentalist majority, by the history and myths of Arab power and splendor among the secular-minded. Palestine (*Filastin*), as a distinct political-national term, however, was rarely used before, during, or immediately after World War I.

While levels of patriotism and ethnicism existed, Arab Palestinian nationalism as such hardly existed in terms of group self-consciousness. Even the prewar layer of proto-nationalist intellectuals in Palestine did not yet think on this level; rather, they concentrated on the goal of a large, united Syria, with Damascus as capital. Furthermore, this layer was not large enough to ideologize the population or make Jerusalem or Nablus a center of renascent Arabism comparable to Cairo, Beirut, Damascus, Constantinople, or Paris.[26]

While there was, since antiquity, an unbroken (if often thin) thread of Jewish settlement in Palestine, and while there was a hoary history to Jewish interest in and contributions to immigration to Palestine, at the turn of the twentieth century most of world Jewry was preoccupied either with assimilation (in Western Europe), or immigration to the Americas (from Eastern Europe). Poor backward Palestine, the holy land with the graves of one's ancestors, did not seem a promising land for the living.[27]

Thus in 1914 there were, out of a total world Jewish population of 11.5 million, only some 80,000 in western Palestine, chiefly in the six cities of Jerusalem, Safed, Tiberias (where they were the majority), and Jaffa, Haifa, and Hebron. The Jews consisted essentially of three groups: the orthodox Sephardic and Ashkenazic communities (who formed the "Old Yishuv," or Settlement, and at the time represented the clear majority), and the secular Zionists. The eastern European Ashkenazim and Mediterranean Sephardim, despite their many differences, were, as well as very pious, very poor. The Ashkenazim were less self-sufficient than the Sephardim, often being dependent on Jewish charity from abroad, which was dispersed through a complicated and inefficient system called *haluka* (apportionment). For all their particularisms, which elicited both scorn and indifference on the part of the Ottoman officials and Arab majority, the religious Jews had neither national (as opposed to ethnic) consciousness nor political aspirations.[28]

The Zionist-minded minority was different. Starting in the early 1880s, a new kind of Jewish interest developed in the traditional motif of Return to Zion, chiefly in Russia and Rumania, and chiefly among student and lower middle-class circles affected by winds of nationalism, secularism, and socialism, not to speak of periodic storms of economic depression and of political and religious repressions. The Zionist thesis, in skeletal form, proposed that one could and should rebuild oneself while rebuilding one's ancestral fatherland, and that with their own land the Jews would no longer be a rootless, pariah people, in exile, dependent on others' sufferance. The old Jewish "Question" would thus be largely solved. To its adherents, the solution, with its dual emphasis on folk survival and cultural renascence, successfully synthesized pragmatism and idealism.[29]

The multi-faceted evolution of Zionism is largely outside the province of this book. Suffice to say that Zionism both vitalized and antagonized Jewish communities throughout the world; while demographically, the Zionist component of the Jewish settlement in Palestine grew, albeit in fits and starts, through periodic waves, or "ascents" (*aliyah*; pl., *aliyot*), of immigrants.

Palestinian Arab opposition to the Yishuv was, when articulated, continuous and uncompromising. Arab resentments had largely begun in the mid-nineteenth century when orthodox Jews had sought to acquire private property outside of Jerusalem, and had increased when the Zionists' First Aliyah (1880s) had begun establishing a "new Yishuv." From the Arab viewpoint, one basic reason for jealous hostility was and would increasingly be that Jews resisted assimilation and instead purchased land (often public and unfertile land, but land which as a rule they did not sell back to Arabs) in order to build an all-Jewish, that is, exclusive, society. In the language of Arab emotions and projections, Jewish behavior bespoke rejection of the Arabs and their culture, weakness (otherwise the Jews would not need to buy the land), and ambitions to dominate and expand. However, it was only after 1929 that the Arabs, under the leadership of Hajj Amin Husseini, the Mufti of Jerusalem, began organized violence and countermeasures.[30]

For their part, the British government, and especially British officers in the mandatory administration, reacted negatively to the Balfour Declaration from the beginning. Implementing the Declaration would, after all, create an economic and demographic change such that the Jews would become the majority, the Palestinian Arabs a hostile minority, and the Arab and Moslem worlds beyond also hostile and anti-British. Further, a large, modernized Jewish population (with presumed Bolshevik and also capitalistic leanings) would make a British presence in Palestine superfluous, and might make Britain feel ideologically threatened in the region as a whole.

Still, in the 1920s there was reason for some cautious British optimism on the possibilities of at least partial implementation of the Balfour Declaration, in the minimal sense of giving both Jews and Arabs assistance. If there were problems, as Arab-Jewish clashes in 1921–22 indicated, the British seemed willing to take the long view—empire had always presented its difficulties, and Palestine was not completely unique, as there were deep internal disputes in mandates like Iraq and Syria, too. The main thing was to get on with the job, the job being to rule fairly and prudently, befriend the established notables on both sides, enforce the law and centralize authority, impart British parliamentary procedures, survey land resources and fix the borders, develop the socio-economic infrastructure (though not too fast), set up schools (separate schools and languages for Jews and Arabs), and strengthen the ties with England so if the "inhabitants" ever took over, their loyalty and direction would be predetermined.[31]

One reason for Britain's cautious optimism was that the Churchill White Paper (1922) created out of the arid but very large eastern part of Palestine (34,740 square miles, as opposed to western Palestine's 10,100 square miles) a new Arab state, under a separate British mandatory regime. Nominally ruled by the Hashemite, Emir Abdullah, the new state of Transjordan was intended by the British (with the kingdom of Iraq) to compensate the Hashemites for their loss of the Hijaz to Ibn Saud and of Syria to the French. The partition of Palestine was also meant in part to fulfill Britain's dual wartime pledges to Jews and Arabs and its wish to be even-handed to the Jews and Arabs then in Palestine. Thus, while the Jews would have their national home "in Palestine" (meaning within), the Arabs of Palestine would have *their* due in Transjordan. It is worth noting that despite this partition, no Jews were to be allowed into Transjordan by the British; while the Zionists, having grudgingly given up eastern Palestine (except for a sizable minority which later formed the "Revisionist" wing of Zionism), were still required by the 1922 White Paper to share British favors in western Palestine with the Arabs.[32]

The second reason that a Palestine solution did not yet appear hopeless in the 1920s was the British view that the Balfour Declaration might not have to be implemented after all. Despite the Third Aliyah and Fourth Aliyah (between 1919 and 1928), net Jewish population gains were, while not insubstantial, not large in absolute terms. The depressed economy in 1926–27 also dampened communal politics. For their part, the Arabs did not appear anxious or violent. It thus appeared that the delicate experiment of making the Jewish minority into the majority need not have to be performed.[33]

However, serious communal tensions still existed; after outbreaks of violence and bloodshed in 1929, the British reassessed the Mandate. Although the Haycraft Commission of Inquiry (1921) and also the Churchill White Paper, as noted, had already reduced the pro-Zionist "obligations" of the Balfour Declaration, a series of new commissions and white papers furthered the process. The Shaw Commission of 1929, while singling out the Arabs' "racial animosity" and the Mufti's role, claimed that recent "excessive" Jewish immigration required review, it being the purported root cause of communal strife. The Hope-Simpson Report of 1930 asserted there was definitely no room for additional settlers, nor any extra cultivable Arab land for possible sale. The Passfield White Paper of the same year concurred with both reports, criticized the socialist Zionist principle of Jewish manual labor as exclusivist, stipulated that Jewish immigration was possible only if it did not conflict with Arab employment, and flatly rejected the view that references to the Jewish national home in the mandate represented the main purposes of the mandate.[34]

At the last minute, however, the Jewish case was reaffirmed, to the Arabs' chagrin, by Prime Minister Ramsay MacDonald in 1931, and the Passfield paper was shelved. Still, this Zionist victory did not last over the long run. Trends inside and outside Palestine would ultimately point in the other direction.

Yet in the short run the Zionists seemed to gather new strength after their 1931 victory. The institutional catalyst of the New Yishuv was the Jewish Agency. Authorized under Article Four of the mandate, the Agency acted as a combined fundraiser and government-in-preparation. Its luminaries were Dr. Chaim Weizmann, David Ben-Gurion, and Moshe Shertok (Sharett). By 1929 its governing board was enlarged. To gain greater Jewish unity and contributions, it now included prominent non-Zionist Jews as well as Zionist Jews. From the Agency's efforts and with the capital which Jews from Germany in 1933–36 (the Fifth Aliyah: about 165,000 Jews to 1936, and another 60,000 by 1939) were able to take with them, the Yishuv was enabled to make the largest socio-economic gains thus far. This, despite the Great Depression elsewhere and the general weakness in this period of the Zionist movement abroad.

In the early 1930s the Jewish militia (Haganah) and the Yishuv's trade-union complex (Histadrut) similarly expanded. Though rifts between Jewish rightist and leftist paramilitary groups and other segments of the Jewish population sometimes reached a critical stage, altogether the Yishuv seemed to justify the Zionist view that it was a "state-on-the-way." By 1936, it had a Jewish population of 400,000, or about one-third of the total in Western Palestine.[35]

On the Arab side, however, the Husseini clan had gained monopoly rule by 1937 in Palestine, via the Arab Higher Committee. Also, the Peel Commission that year had provoked Arab resentment by recommending that western Palestine be partitioned into a territorially and demographically small Jewish state and large Arab state. The result was a series of terroristic acts inspired by the Mufti against British, Jews, and anti-Husseini Arabs. This "Arab Revolt" of 1937–39, though put down with British martial law, led to a renewed train of British reassessments, reports, and white papers. In 1938, the Woodhead Commission decided that the recommendation of partition was impracticable. In November of the same year a White Paper accepted this latter decision and called for a round-table conference (the London, or St. James, Conference in February–March 1939) to confer about Palestine's future.[36]

The tide was fast shifting against the Jews, essentially for two reasons. First, although it had suppressed the Arab Revolt, the British government at last came around to accepting the mandatory administration's traditional view that the Arabs would never make peace with the thesis of a Jewish national home in Palestine. But since the Balfour Declaration was still a legal document, the trick was to turn it into a dead letter. With that in mind, the British argued in the late 1930s that they had fulfilled on behalf of the Jews the "spirit" of the Declaration, and would do no more. Thus did the Mufti's intransigence pay off.

Second, by the beginning of 1939 Prime Minister Neville Chamberlain and his military advisers were expecting war with Hitler. Final decisions had to be made to structure the conditions of war as much to Britain's advantage as possible. Out of a paradoxical sense of "resolve," and not "Munich weakness," the Chamberlain government felt that appeasing the Arabs, but being tough on the Jews, was imperative. The large Arab-Moslem world could make trouble; the Jews, so much smaller in the Middle East, under the heel of Hitler in Europe, walled in by Stalin, could not. In fact, the Jews, unlike 1914–17, had no choice but to support Britain as the world's chief adversary of Germany.[37]

When the London Conference convened, it was an interesting but futile affair, typified by Arab solidarity and refusal to have face-to-face negotiations with the Jews in the same room. The British played the honest broker; and when, as anticipated, the Conference foundered, the Colonial Office under Secretary Malcolm MacDonald published on 17 May 1939 a White Paper.

Its themes were that "His Majesty's Government now declares un-equivocally that it is not part of their policy that Palestine should become a Jewish state" and that "the objective of His Majesty's Government is the establishment within ten years of an independent Palestine state." Pursuant to this, Jewish (not Arab) immigration would be restricted by political, not economic, criteria. It would be held to a five-year quota of 75,000, thus making the Jewish population roughly one-third of the country's total. Immigration would not be continued after May 1944, "unless the Arabs of Palestine are prepared to acquiesce in it." Land purchase by Jews would also be under new regulations—strictly prohibited in 64 percent of western Palestine and restricted in 31 percent.

In Arthur Koestler's funereal words,

Thus, at the very moment when the extermination of the European Jews began, the doors of Palestine were slammed in their faces, while those already inside Palestine, who had come on the strength of the British undertaking that they would find there a National Home, found themselves trapped and condemned to live in "one more precarious oriental ghetto." It was the collapse of a dream and the beginning of a nightmare which was to last to the end of the British mandate.[38]

NOTES

1. On French policy in the Levant, 1919–1939, see, Gordon Wright, *France in Modern Times* (Chicago: Rand McNally, 1966), pp. 446–52; George Lenczowski, *The Middle East in World Affairs* (Ithaca: Cornell Univ. Press, 1958), pp. 266 ff.; Sydney Fisher, *The Middle East* (New York: Knopf, 1960), Chapters 28, 31; K. S. Salibi, *The Modern History of Lebanon* (New York: Praeger, 1965), pp. 164–82; and S. Joarder, "Syria Under the French Mandate: An Overview," *Journal of the Asiatic Society* (Pakistan) 14 (1969): 91–104. Good on great-power diplomacy before 1930 is H. I. Priestly, *France Overseas: A Study in Modern Imperialism* (New York: Appleton-Century, 1938), Chapter 17. Making use of the memoirs of key Frenchmen under the mandate is Stephen H. Longrigg, *Syria and Lebanon Under French Mandate* (New York: Octagon, 1972), Chapters 9 and 10.

Useful atlases on Syria, Lebanon, and other Middle Eastern states are R. C. Kingsbury and N. G. Pounds, *An Atlas of Middle Eastern Affairs* (New York: Praeger, 1963); and Central Intelligence Agency, *Issues in the Middle East* (Washington, D.C.: GPO, 1973). An important and highly useful source on issues and personalities in the Levant and elsewhere is Y. Shimoni, et al., eds., *Political Dictionary of the Middle East in the 20th Century* (New York: Quadrangle, 1974). For the reader with special interests in contemporary Middle Eastern history there are many bibliographic lists available. Two good annotated bibliographies, emphasizing sources bearing on American policy in the Middle East (chiefly since 1945), are John C. Campbell, *Defense of the Middle East: Problems of American Policy* (New York: Praeger, 1960), and Robert W. Stookey, *America and the Arab States: An Uneasy Encounter* (New York: John Wiley, 1975).

2. On France's treaty relations and the Hatay issue, see Lenczowski, *The Middle East in World Affairs*, pp. 271–75; Fisher, *The Middle East*, pp. 404–5, 416; and A. K. Sanjian, "The Sanjak of Alexandretta (Hatay): Its Impact on Turkish-Syrian Relations 1939–1956," *Middle East Journal* 10 (1956): 379–94.

3. Statistics come from the *Britannica Book of the Year: Omnibus for 1938–39–40–41–42* (Chicago: Encyclopedia Britannica Co., Annual); and *The New International Yearbook: Events of 1943–44–45* (New York: Dodd, Mead & Company, Annual).

4. On party and ideological differences, see, e.g., Salibi, *Modern History of Lebanon*, pp. 170–74. On the communist parties of Lebanon and Syria, note House Committee on Foreign Affairs, *The Strategy and Tactics of World Communism*, Report of Subcommittee No. 5, National and International Movements, 80th Congress, Suppl. III, Country Studies B: *Communism in the Middle East* (Washington, D.C.: GPO, 1949), pp. 15–20.

5. For background material on Iraq, see, e.g., Lenczowski, *The Middle East in World Affairs*, pp. 233–46; *Britannica Book of the Year: Omnibus for 1938–39–40–41–42*; Philip Ireland, *Iraq: A Study in Political Development* (New York: Macmillan, 1938); Abdul Raoof, "The Establishment of Statehood," in Tareq Ismael, ed., *Governments and Politics of the Contemporary Middle East* (Homewood, Ill.: Dorsey, 1970), pp. 181–97; and Eleanor Tejirian, *Iraq, 1932–1963: Politics in a Plural Society* (Ph.D. diss., Columbia Univ., 1972).

6. Detailed coverage of Egypt is found in P. J. Vatikiotis, *The Modern History of Egypt* (New York: Praeger, 1969); and John Marlowe, *Anglo-Egyptian Relations 1800–1956* (London: F. Cass, 1965). Focusing on Egypt's external

relations are Lenczowski, *The Middle East in World Affairs,* pp. 393–402, and Chapter 17; and Fisher, *The Middle East,* Chapter 33. Note also Ismael, *Governments and Politics,* pp. 304–10; George Kirk, *A Short History of the Middle East* (New York: Praeger, 1958), pp. 129, passim; and R. L. Tignor, "The 'Indianization' of the Egyptian Administration under British Rule, 1882–1914," *American Historical Review* 68 (1963): 636–61.

7. On the Wafd, see Vatikiotis, *Modern History of Egypt,* Chapter 15; and G. Kirk, "The Corruption of the Egyptian Wafd," *Middle East Affairs* 14 (1963): 296–302.

8. On British disdain of Egyptians, see Elizabeth Monroe, *Britain's Moment in the Middle East, 1914–1956* (Baltimore: Johns Hopkins Univ. Press, 1963), Chapter 3; and William Polk, *The United States and the Arab World* (Cambridge: Harvard Univ. Press, 1965), Chapter 10.

9. For the provisions of the 1936 Treaty, see Lenczowski, *The Middle East in World Affairs,* pp. 400–1.

10. *Britannica Book of the Year: Omnibus for 1938–39–40–41–42.*

11. Lloyd Gardner, *Economic Aspects of New Deal Diplomacy* (Boston: Beacon, 1971), p. 220; M. K. Issa, *Trade Between Egypt and the United States Since 1908* (Ph.D. diss., Univ. of Minnesota, 1969); and *The New International Yearbook: Events of 1943–44–45.*

12. For background details on Saudi Arabia, see Lenczowski, *The Middle East in World Affairs,* Chapter 12; S. Fisher, *The Middle East,* Chapter 38; Abdul Raoof, "The Kingdom of Saudi Arabia," in Tareq Ismael, ed., *Government and Politics of the Contemporary Middle East,* Chapter 15; and Karl S. Twitchell, *Saudi Arabia* (Princeton: Princeton Univ. Press, 1947), pp. 97. Also, *ARAMCO Handbook: Oil and the Middle East* (Dhahran, Saudi Arabia: Arabian American Oil Co., 1968), pp. 46–68; and *Britannica Book of the Year: Omnibus for 1938–39–40–41–42.*

13. On Ibn Saud's foreign policy before World War II, see Chapter 5; and Lenczowski, *The Middle East in World Affairs,* pp. 439, 524. Also, Departmental correspondence of G. S. Messersmith, et al, in period May 1939–February 1940, in *FR* 4 (1939): 824–31; and Department of State, "Saudi Arabia: Policy and Information Statement," 15 July 1946, pp. 12–14, James Byrnes Papers.

14. John DeNovo, *American Interests and Policies in the Middle East, 1900–1939* (Minneapolis: Univ. of Minnesota Press, 1963), pp. 355, 358.

15. The material on the origins of, and the personalities engaged in, the American concession is diverse and often polemical. For an interesting and very admiring portrait of Charles Crane, see J. Rives Childs, *Foreign Service Farewell: My Years in the Near East* (Charlottesville, Va.: Univ. of Virginia Press, 1969), p. 53. (George Antonius dedicated his book *The Arab Awakening* to Crane—"aptly nicknamed Harun al-Rashid, affectionately." Also, Twitchell's *Saudi Arabia* is dedicated to the memory of Crane.) On the role and personality of Philby, see his three works: *Arabian Days: An Autobiography* (London: Robert Hale, 1948), pp. 291–96; *Arabian Jubilee* (New York: John Day, 1953), Chapter 14; and *Saudi Arabia* (London: E. Benn, 1955), pp. 329–31.

On the competition among the oil companies, see G. de Gaury, *Feisal, King of Saudi Arabia* (New York: Praeger, 1966), p. 66; *ARAMCO Handbook,* pp. 107–12; Benjamin Shwadran, *The Middle East, Oil and the Great Powers* (New York: Praeger, 1955 edition), pp. 290 ff.; and Leonard Mosley, *Power Play: Oil in the Middle East* (Baltimore: Penguin, 1973), Chapter 5. On Saudi retrospection, see David Hirst, *Oil and Public Opinion in the Middle East* (New York: Praeger, 1966), p. 20.

16. The California Arabian Standard Oil Company (CASOC) was known after January 1944 as the Arabian American Oil Company (ARAMCO). CASOC-ARAMCO operated the American concessions in Saudi Arabia. The original parent companies owning all the stock of CASCO-ARAMCO were the Standard Oil Company of California (SOCAL) and the Texas Company.

17. As of 1 April 1939, there were 273 American citizens residing in Saudi Arabia: 263 were employed by CASOC; 10 by the Saudi Arabian Mining Syndicate. From William A. Williams, ed., *America and the Middle East: Open Door Imperialism or Enlightened Leadership?* (New York: Holt, Rinehart and Winston, 1958), p. 45.

18. See William Polk's comment that because Westerners came to Arabia chiefly as oil men, not soldiers, the heritage of "humiliation" was less than, e.g., in Egypt. "Far from refusing to let the Arabs in its posh clubs, the oil industry was delighted to sit as a guest in the bedouin tent or to build for the Arab Western, air-conditioned cities, railroads, schools, and hospitals in return for the privilege of being allowed to drill in the desert wastes for oil" (Polk, *The U.S. and the Arab World*, p. 160).

19. What after 1918 was sometimes called "eastern Palestine" (the land east of the Jordan River, or the East Bank, or Trans-Jordan) was, under the Turks, part of the *vilayet* of Damascus and ruled therefrom. What after 1918 was called "western Palestine" (the land west of the Jordan and extending to the Mediterranean) had boundaries closely approximating those of the state of Israel as of July 1967. Under the Turks, this latter area was divided into the *sanjaks* of Nablus and Acre (in the *vilayet* of Beirut and ruled therefrom) and the "independent" *sanjak* of Jerusalem (under the direct authority of Constantinople). The Jerusalem *sanjak* covered the Negev and extended (before 1906) to the port of Suez, but much of this desert area was in effect outside Ottoman jurisdiction.

On the boundaries and geopolitics of pre-1918 Palestine, see H. F. Frischwasser-Ra'anan, *Frontiers of a Nation: A Reexamination of the Forces Which Created the Palestine Mandate and Determined Its Territorial Shape* (London: Batchworth, 1955), Chapters 2, 3, 4; H. Z. Hirschberg et al., "Ottoman Period 1517–1917," in *Encyclopedia Judaica* (henceforth cited as *Ency. Jud.*) extracts, *History Until 1880* (Jerusalem: Keter, 1973), pp. 232, 236; M. Brawer, "Frontiers," in *Ency. Jud.* extracts, *History of 1880* (Jerusalem: Keter, 1973), pp. 262 ff.; *Facts About Israel* (Jerusalem: Israel Ministry of Information, 1974), p. 31; and Z. N. Zeine, *The Struggle for Arab Independence* (Beirut: Khayat's 1960), plate 5.

20. On Sykes-Picot, see E. Kedourie, *England and the Middle East* (London: Bowes & Bowes, 1956), Chapter 2 ff.; Zeine, *The Struggle for Arab Independence*, plate 6; W. Z. Laqueur, ed., *The Israel-Arab Reader* (New York: Bantam, 1969), document 5; and, on German initiatives which precipitated action by Sykes, et al., J. Kimche, *The Second Arab Awakening* (New York: Holt, Rinehart and Winston, 1970), Chapters 1, 2.

21. On the *jihad* factor, see George Antonius, *The Arab Awakening* (New York: Capricorn, 1965; first published, 1946), Chapter 7. On the Jews and British thinking, the literature is vast, as it is on all other related topics. See L. Stein, *The Balfour Declaration* (New York: Simon & Schuster, 1961); Isaiah Friedman, *The Question of Palestine, 1914–1918: British-Jewish-Arab Relations* (New York: Schocken, 1973), passim; C. Sykes, *Crossroads to Israel* (London: Collins, 1965), Chapters 1 and 2, and "Memories of My Father, Sir Mark Sykes," in Mendlin and Bermant, eds., *Explorations: An Annual on Jewish Themes* (Chicago: Quadrangle, 1968), p. 150.

22. Relative to the documentation and British interpretation of Sykes-Picot,

see note 20 above; also, C. Sykes, *Crossroads to Israel*, pp. 43–44; and Monroe, *Britain's Moment*, p. 51. Relative to McMahon-Husein, see Antonius, *The Arab Awakening*, Chapter 9 and Appendix A; Fisher, *The Middle East*, pp. 369 ff.; Kirk, *Short History*, Appendix 2; and Sykes, *Crossroads to Israel*, pp. 41–45, 84–86, 234–35. Also, R. John and S. Hadawi, *The Palestine Diary, 1914–1945* (New York: New World, 1970), vol. 1, p. 370; and Doreen Ingrams, ed., *Palestine Papers 1917–1922: Seeds of Conflict* (New York: Braziller, 1973), pp. 173–74.

Relative to Balfour, see note 21 above. On subtopics, e.g., Jewish anti-Zionism in 1917, see Lenczowski, *The Middle East in World Affairs*, pp. 314–16; and the anti-Zionist historiography of Alan R. Taylor, *Prelude to Israel: An Analysis of Zionist Diplomacy 1897–1947* (New York: Philosophical Library, 1959), Chapters 1, 2, and of A. Lilienthal's essay on the Balfour Declaration in G. L. Anderson, ed., *Issues and Conflicts: Studies in 20th Century American Diplomacy* (Lawrence, Kans.: Univ. of Kansas Press, 1959). On short lived Arab-Jewish amity (the Feisal-Weizmann connection), see works cited of Laqueur (document 8); Sykes (pp. 45–53); Antonius (pp. 394–98); and Kimche (pp. 179–83).

23. Figures compiled from census reports cited in *Encyclopedia Britannica*, 1910 edition, and *New International Yearbook: 1914*. Also see Hayyim Cohen, *The Jews in the Middle East, 1860–1972* (Jerusalem: John Wiley and Israel Univ. Press, 1973), p. 69.

24. J. Parkes, *Whose Land? A History of the Peoples of Palestine* (Harmondsworth, England: Penguin, 1970), Chapter 13; and Israel Ministry of Foreign Affairs, *The Arabs in Israel* (Jerusalem: The Government Printer, 1958).

After World War I, foreign "colonies" of Anglicans, Presbyterians, Baptists, Lutherans, and various evangelical sects from Europe and America would grow considerably and would, as a rule, be anti-Zionist and anti-Semitic. See Esco Foundation for Palestine, Inc., *Palestine: A Study of Jewish, Arab and British Policies* (New Haven: Yale Univ. Press, 1947), vol. 1, p. 547.

25. Psychologically, the non-Jewish population was often observed as tending toward a species of manic-depressive behavior: great apathy, followed by great bursts of volatility. While this may well be the norm for oppressed peasantry everywhere, what often struck observers was the extraordinary, often suicidal destructiveness, and not merely in terms of vivid oratory, expressed even during local intra-Arab quarrels: bloody vendettas for generations, uprooting of trees, burning of grain stocks, destroying of wells. Great envy, superstition, a talent for dissimulation mixed with ignorance and arrogance were the concomitants. The Moslems especially were noted for their faith, ignorance, and *hubris;* the Christian Arabs for their ikon worship, guile, and in the matter of Arab nationalism, for both ardor and insincerity. See W. Polk et al., *Backdrop to Tragedy: The Struggle for Palestine* (Boston: Beacon, 1957), pp. 302–4; Y. Allon, *Shield of David: The Story of Israel's Armed Forces* (New York: Random House, 1970), p. 81; Esco, *Palestine*, vol. 1, pp. 507–10, 522, passim; Parkes, *Whose Land?*, p. 267; and Kirk, *Short History*, pp. 148, 313, n. 2.

26. On Arab nationalism in this period and its qualities in Palestine, see Antonius, *The Arab Awakening*, Chapter 6; R. E. Gabbay, *A Political Study of the Arab-Jewish Conflict: The Arab Refugee Problem* (Geneva-Paris: n. p., 1959), p. 18; and A. M. Ghazaleh, *Arab Cultural Nationalism in Palestine 1919–1948* (Ph.D. diss., New York Univ., 1967).

Several recent revisionist studies, not to mention propagandistic ones, have concluded that strictly "Palestinian" Arab nationalism was older than heretofore assumed, as well as having been differentiated from pan-Arab and "South Syrian" nationalism [Y. Porath, *The Emergence of the Palestine-Arab National Movement 1918–1929* (London: Cass, 1975)].

27. Or, as one anti-Semitic American consul in Jerusalem, Seth Merill, put it pithily in 1891: "1. Palestine is not ready for the Jews. 2. The Jews are not ready for Palestine" (Frank Manual, *American-Palestine Relations*, p. 72). On Palestine's place in Jewish demography, see L. Hersch, "Jewish Migrations During the Last Hundred Years," in *The Jewish People, Past and Present* (New York: Jewish Encyclopedia Handbooks, 1946), vol. 1, pp. 407–30.

28. Clannish, litigious, unmannered and unwashed, the Ashkenazic *halukah* Jews were often the despair of "genteel" Western consuls, not to say of westernized Jews *and* secular East European Zionists who, having broken away from the ghettos and Orthodoxy of their youth, disliked seeing the reproduction thereof in Palestine. Unlike the equally parochial Arabs, the *halukah* Jews (in the eyes of western consuls) had piety and the Bible on their side, but no desert romance, masculinity, or work ethic to their credit. Indeed, it seems highly plausible that in the case of the American consuls at least, *halukah* Jewry unwittingly did much by its pitiful "first impressions" to fuel latent anti-Semitism and to sour the Department of State on all things Jewish. Even though Zionism would be patently anti-*halukah*, to the Department, Zionism, like the leopard which could not change its spots, would often seem merely a more secular and modern version of the old despised *halukah* system. These conclusions, it should be noted, are, while tenable, hypothetical. They are implicit in much of the documentation and in Manuel's spadework on this early period (*American-Palestine Relations*, Chapters 1, 2, and 3), though not expressed in extractable quotations.

On the Jewish Orthodox in Palestine, see J. Parkes, *Whose Land?*, Chapter 14; Manual, *American-Palestine Relations*, pp. 16–22 ff.; Esco, *Palestine*, vol. 1, p. 522; and Slutsky, "Under Ottoman Rule 1880–1917," in *Ency. Jud.* extracts, *History from 1880*, pp. 10–11.

29. On the intellectual and historical evolution of, and the diversities within Zionism, see A. Hertzberg, ed., *The Zionist Idea*, (New York: Meridan, 1960); B. Halpern, *The Idea of the Jewish State* (Cambridge: Harvard Univ. Press, 1961); and *Ency. Jud.* extracts, *Zionism* (Jerusalem: Keter, 1973), particularly the essay of M. Medzini, "Zionist Policy," pp. 80–129.

30. See Esco, *Palestine*, vol. 1, pp. 524, 529, 532, 560; and A. Hourani, "Palestine and Israel," in Majdia Khadduri, ed., *The Arab-Israeli Impasse* (Washington, D.C.: R. B. Luce, 1969), p. 158. On Jewish-Moslem relations in the Middle East as a whole at the turn of the century, see Cohen, *Jews in the Middle East*, Chapter 1.

31. On the norms of British-mandate governance, see Monroe, *Britian's Moment*, p. 80; and Polk, *The U.S. and the Arab World*, p. 134. On Palestine as experiment, see Parkes, *Whose Land?*, pp. 259 ff.; and Granott, *The Land System in Palestine: History and Structure* (London: Eyre and Spottiswood, 1952), pp. 291–314.

32. On the origins of Transjordan, see Kirk, *A Short History*, pp. 158–61, 323; Sykes, *Crossroads to Israel*, pp. 88, passim; and *Ency. Jud.* extracts, *History from 1880*, pp. 107–8 (for terms of the Churchill 1922 White Paper). Works on Transjordan through World War II include P. P. Graves, ed., *Memoirs of King Abdullah of Transjordan* (London: Jonathan Cape, 1950); J. Schechtman, *Jordan—A State That Never Was* (New York: Cultural Pub., 1968); and former Foreign Service Officer William Sands, "The Hashemite Kingdom of Jordan," in Ismael, ed., *Governments and Politics*, pp. 283–303.

33. The Third Aliyah (1919–23: 35,000 Jews, chiefly Russian) and the

Fourth Aliyah (1924–28: 34,000 Jews, chiefly Polish) often led, as in the cases of other *aliyot*, to considerable reemigration. Also, most of the Polish Jews settled in the Tel Aviv area, hence conflicts with the Arabs over agricultural land were minimal. Also to be noted is the fact that in the mid-1920s the Soviet Union banned further Jewish emigration, while restrictionist legislation in the United States sharply reduced Jewish immigration thereto. See Slutsky, "Under Ottoman Rule," pp. 53–55; and Sykes, *Crossroads to Israel*, pp. 110 ff.

34. For more information on the cited documents, see *Ency. Jud.* extracts, *History From 1880*, p. 101–2, 108–9.

35. On the Jewish Agency, see A. Zwergbaum, "Zionist Organization," in *Ency. Jud.* extracts, *Zionism*, pp. 141 ff. On the Yishuv's growth in the 1930s, see Slutsky, "Under Ottoman Rule," pp. 60–62; and A. Dorra, "Palestine and the Economic Development of the Middle East," in J. B. Hobman, ed., *Palestine's Economic Future* (London: Lund, Humphries, 1946), pp. 101 ff. Also see O. I. Janowsky, *Foundations of Israel: Emergence of a Welfare State* (Princeton: Van Nostrand, 1959), Chapters 4 and 5, and documents 8–10.

36. On the Arab Revolt, see the Mandate administration's *A Survey of Palestine* (prepared in December 1945 and January 1946 for the information of the Anglo-American Committee of Inquiry) (Jerusalem: His Majesty's Government Printer, 1946), vol. 1, pp. 38–42; and works cited by Kirk (p. 322); Sykes (pp. 174–87); Gabbay (p. 23); Allon (pp. 81 ff.). Also, M. Assaf, *The Arab Movement in Palestine* (New York: Hechalutz, 1937).

On the Peel plan the established Zionist leadership had reached, grudgingly, a consensus of acceptance (July 1937). Abdullah and a number of non-Palestinian Arab leaders also accepted partition—but they did not do so publicly, so as not to be any less loyal to the Arab cause than the Mufti's Higher Committee, which utterly negated the partition plan.

For synopses of the British documents, see *Ency. Jud.* extracts, *History From 1880*, pp. 102–4, 109–10. Also, see Y. Bauer, *From Diplomacy to Resistance: A History of Jewish Palestine 1939–1945* (New York: Atheneum, 1973), pp. 6 ff.; Sykes, *Crossroads to Israel*, Chapter 8; and Slutsky, "Under Ottoman Rule," pp. 68–69.

37. For other examples of the British practice of extending sword, then olive branch, to the Arabs, see text, Chapters 9 and 10. On British strategy with respect to Palestine, see Bauer, *From Diplomacy to Resistance*, Introduction and Chapter 1; Sykes, *Crossroads to Israel*, pp. 229–34; and D. Ben-Gurion, *Israel: Years of Challenge* (New York: Holt, Rinehart, 1963), pp. 15–16.

38. A. Koestler, *Promise and Fulfillment: Palestine 1917–1949* (New York: Macmillan, 1949), pp. 45–46 (incorporating Churchill's comment, delivered in the Parliamentary debate on the White Paper, May 1939). Quotations from the White Paper are from *Ency. Jud.* extracts, *History From 1880*, pp. 110–11. Also, see cited works by Lenczowski (pp. 323–25); Monroe (pp. 88–89); and Sykes (pp. 237–41).

One thesis, that Britain opted for the White Paper's clampdown of the Jews as a way of staying ahead of Nazi influence in the Arab world, has been disputed of late. Thus Kinche: "We know from the German documents that, so far as the Middle East was concerned, the British were under no particular pressure. On the contrary, it was the evidence of British uncertainty in acting on the Peel recommendations that prompted the Germans and the Italians to renew their encouragement of Arab opposition to the British" (*The Second Arab Awakening*, p. 186). For further documentation on German policy, see text, notes 8 and 9, Chapter 5.

3

Departmental Outlook and Expectations in the Middle East, 1919–45

During the interwar period in the Middle Eastern countries under review, three considerations were of chief importance to the Department of State: American national prestige; the influence and respectability of American noneconomic private interests; and the influence and profitability of American economic private interests. It is worth noting that even before 1914, American educational, philanthropic, missionary, and medical interests, mainly in Palestine, Syria and Lebanon, were already considerable by any standard. In the period 1919–39, and taking the region as a whole, American noneconomic and economic private interests were no less numerous than counterpart British or French interests.[1]

Accordingly, the Department kept watch lest any American interest be intruded upon. Directly charged with this responsibility were the Department's eyes and ears in the field, the Foreign Service Officers (FSOs). A priori, FSOs assumed that private American interests were in harmony with the Department's global principles and desiderata, and that these private interests, when added up, represented a national interest worthy of official protection. There were exceptions, notably the private interests of activist political Zionists and of activist Christian missionaries from America. Both groups, according to Departmental consensus, were the inevitable antagonists of the Arab Moslem majority and hindered the development of "good relations" between that majority and the American government. As such, both detracted from the national interest by jeopardizing national prestige.[2]

Despite America's private interests and despite the Department's

49

watchfulness over them, the American government nonetheless lacked the traditional and legal authority, and proximity, of the British and French in the Middle East. As a matter of course, the Middle East was universally regarded in the interwar period as a combined British and French (and, to a lesser extent, Italian) sphere of influence.[3]

This is not to say that powers other than Britain and France accepted their inferior influence as an unchangeable fact. Italy, Germany, and the United States, as the principal have-nots interested in the Middle East, did much to challenge and propagandize against British-French hegemony in the 1930s. Of the three, the United States engaged in less overt demagoguery and more quiet diplomatic maneuvering. The Department was also carefully eclectic in its reactions, acceding willfully to British-French hegemony when that hegemony suited the Department's purposes, and making a fuss when it was clear that hegemony was opposed to those purposes.

For example, whenever the Department was periodically urged by pro-Zionists, in the name of Congressional and Presidential support of the Balfour Declaration of 1917, to protest against British regulations in Palestine which restricted the immigration and investment rights of Jews, the Department would beg off. Basically hostile, it offered the rationale that Palestine, as a British mandate, was not America's legal responsibility. However, if requests for diplomatic intervention emanated from American oil interests, the Department, basically friendly, reacted differently. The usual result was a flurry of diplomatic notes insisting upon the open door and the rights of American nationals.[4]

Even when economic interests were not at stake, the Department often protested anyway. Throughout the interwar period it maintained a constant, though not high-pitched, resistance, on principle, both to the unmistakable reality of British-French hegemony and to Britain's and France's galling claims that their hegemony was fixed and legitimate. In a spirit of innocence wronged, combined with an angry mood of "pushiness," the Department repeatedly insisted on legal, linguistic, and educational rights (though not missionizing rights) for American nationals equal to counterpart rights of British and French nationals.

By the mid-1930s, when the Department increasingly viewed the Class-A mandates in the region as but temporary trusts (except for Palestine and Transjordan), Departmental protests took a more contentious, more patently "anti-imperialistic" tack. Britain and France, notwithstanding their loosening of the bonds of empire, were increasingly accused of trying to transform their mandates and spheres into exclusive and permanent fixtures. Concomitantly, Foreign Service Officers (FSOs) intensified their direct dealings with the strongly nationalist Arab elites so as to promote friendly contacts, quicken the decline of European hegemony, and put the United States in an advantageous position in the eventual post-imperialist period.[5]

The Department justified all of its watchful waiting, protests, and accusations on the fundamental and implicit premise that the United States was a great power which deserved to be consulted as a co-equal to the mandatory powers. The Department intimated that, though not a participant in the League of Nations from which the mandate system derived and to which the system was responsible, the United States nonetheless had been an indispensable power, both in the winning of World War I and in the formulation of international agreements at the Paris Peace Conference of 1919. As such, the Department felt that it had the legal right to assert what was tantamount to a veto over basic decisions of the mandatories.

This right was, in addition, presumed on the grounds that the United States had been a signatory in the early 1920s, with Britain and France, to bilateral conventions which covered the postwar mandates. These conventions had recognized the mandatory authority of Britain and France but also had expressed the point that Britain and France were to consult with and seek the approval of the American Department of State prior to making any significant changes in their mandates. Giving the consultation clauses a broad construction, the Department at times contended that Britain and France were legally *required* to receive prior Departmental approval for their mandatory policies.[6]

THE PRE-WORLD WAR II PROGNOSIS

There were other reasons, largely subjective, behind the Department's moderately active diplomacy in the region, particularly in the second half of the 1930s. Middle East experts in the Department were overtly sympathetic to the cause of Arab independence. Indeed, they felt, as the Arabs did themselves, that because Britain and France had "betrayed" the Arabs after World War I by reneging on promises of independence, independence for the Arabs must not be indefinitely deferred. The Department's subjective animus toward the French and their reputed anachronistic colonialism in the Levant was especially strong.[7]

Furthermore, the Department believed not only that spheres of influence were contrary to the American tradition, but also that their perpetuation was a distinct hazard to the world at large, even to the mandatories themselves. This was so because the anti-imperialist tide of nationalism in Arab lands, India, Burma, and southeast Asia seemed to be rising and was thus viewed by the Department as an inescapable wave of the future. Accommodation and preventive methods seemed necessary, lest war, power vacuums, and economic instability result. The Department conveyed the thought that it would be wise for all western powers, in their overseas colonies, mandates, and protectorates, to imitate the examples of America's own repudiation of the Roosevelt Corollary in Latin America and of its adoption of the good-neighbor policy instead.[8]

Finally, at the very end of the decade, the Department was coming to the conclusion that the United States, if it let nature take its course and did nothing rash, would almost *automatically* reap a profitable economic future in the Middle East. The preconditions for this opportunity seemed already established. The United States had a large reservoir of good will in the Arab world, nurtured by FSOs and generations of American Protestant missionaries, educators, and other such private ambassadors of good will. In contrast, the British, French, and Italians, in part because they were the victims of the truism that familiarity breeds contempt, were increasingly unpopular. (Parenthetically, German propaganda and influence, which, like America's, had the mystique of a faraway and friendly great power, were also quite popular.)[9]

The Department linked the future of the Middle East, and America's future therein, with the Arab Sunni-Moslem native majority, the natural inheritors of power when the mandate stage would pass. As indicated, the Department regarded it as essential to befriend that majority. Toward that end, the Department not only took pains not to side with private American interests, like Zionists and Christian proselytizers, who were felt to be inherently antagonistic to the Sunni majority. It also took care not to befriend members of ethnic or religious minorities who were long native in the region but were in chronic dispute with the Sunni majority. (Actually, if the Middle East were redefined so as to include Moslem countries like Iran, the Sunnis would not necessarily have formed the majority.)

Siding with the larger and ostensibly more important population, for all the American public's historic affection for small nations and underdogs, was the Department's normative attitude. In the period of World War I and the 1920s, the Department had discouraged any official endorsement of the minority cause of the Armenians relative to the Turkish majority in Anatolia, despite the popular sympathy for that cause in America. In like fashion, the Department discouraged in the interwar period any official endorsement of the Zionist cause and its political-territorial-demographic ambitions for rebuilding Palestine as a Jewish nation. Concurrently, the Department turned a deaf ear to the political-territorial problems and ambitions of other minorities—the Christian Assyrians and the Sunni Moslem Kurds in Iraq and the Maronite Arab Christians in the area of Mount Lebanon. With regard to political Zionists, the Department, as with regard to the French, had in addition a certain subjective animus which complemented its "objective" opposition to Zionism.[10]

In sum, the Department's "sensitivity" and degree of diplomatic activism in the Middle East steadily rose during the interwar period. This rise, it should be noted, was without benefit of special Departmental concern for Saudi Arabian oil, the region's geopolitical and air-communications value, the expectation of another world war or of German or Russian encroachments. Of course, when such new factors became relevant after 1939, the Department's sensitivity and activism increased commensurately.

Withal, it has to be borne in mind that in the three main periods considered in this work—1919–39, 1939–41, 1941–45—the Department's concern increased in other regions as well. In the global framework of America's national interests, the Middle East was always a secondary region. Individually, too, all the countries of the region (except Saudi Arabia after 1941) remained in each period in the secondary, or intermediate, category of "direct" American interest—that is, between "immediate" (primary) interest and "indirect" (tertiary) interest. More specifically, the American national interest in the Middle East throughout all three periods ranked an approximate fourth. In the eyes of the Department, the Middle East followed Europe, Latin America, and the Pacific; it was probably on a par with East Asia, though ahead of the Indian subcontinent, North Africa, and Tropical Africa.[11]

THE WARTIME OUTLOOK, 1939–45

In the months, let alone years, preceding September 1939, the possibility of large-scale world war, the possibility of the Middle East as a theatre of war, and the possibility of America as an active military participant in war did not figure seriously in the Department's thinking. Insofar as there were more instances of Departmental sensitivity, watchful waiting, and embryonic planning from the late 1930s to December 1941, these were mainly focused on Europe. As for the Middle East, the flow of events building up to war only engendered short-run and unrelated reactions.

Thus FSOs in the Middle East spoke in the spring of 1939 of German and Japanese approaches in Saudi Arabia and urged that the United States, in preventive and competitive reaction, strengthen its own diplomatic position there. Thus, too, the Division of Near Eastern Affairs (NEA) warned Secretary Hull to expect "problems" resulting from Nazi persecutions of Jews and from the forthcoming (May 1939) release of an anti-Zionist British White Paper (which was consented to in advance by the Department). Assistant Secretary Breckinridge Long also spoke direfully, yet, like the rest of the Department, insensitively, on the everlasting, ever-bothersome "Jewish Question." With regard to Jewish pressure to ease America's restrictive visa and immigration policies, Long felt it was "just part of a movement to place me and the Department in general in an embarrassing position." Moreover, giving in would allow radicals and undesirables to enter and would provide for Germany a "perfect opening . . . to load the U.S. with agents."[12]

Even when war did break out with the invasion of Poland, its significance as the start of a global war was not readily grasped, certainly not with regard to the Middle East. True, watchful waiting increased in the Department, as was the case on all levels of American society. Reports from FSOs in the Middle East on Axis influence and fifth columns in Iraq, Syria, and Egypt became lengthier and more frequent. "Concern" with Jewish pressure for rescue from Europe and immigration to Palestine and America continued. More sympathy for Britain and the survival of its empire and mandates, at least for the duration of the new "conflict," existed in the Department than previously. Still, the Department was reacting, not acting.[13]

Even in the aftermath of Pearl Harbor, uncoordinated reaction was the norm. Part of the reason was that the Middle East was less the object of America's new anti-isolationist, anti-Axis ardor than was Europe or the Far East. The Middle East remained a secondary theatre.

Nonetheless, there was a continuation, indeed, a slow increase, of Departmental demands for American "rights" in the Middle East in the months after Pearl Harbor. Such demands were more than carry-overs of prewar open-door, Wilsonian values. Nor was the general zeitgeist of pro-interventionism the main reason for the demands. Rather, Departmental demands were largely a reflection of the expanding scope of American military success.

Thus, between December 1941 and October 1941, a period when Axis arms and propaganda threatened to overrun North Africa and the Middle East, Departmental insistence on the open door and on the termination of the mandate system was minimal. Sympathy for Britain's lonely predicament was a factor, of course, but another was the realization that unless the United States could field an army and do better at war than Britain could, there was little point in protesting against British, and French, spheres and discriminations. However, when these two regions were liberated in October–November 1942, after the North African landings of mainly American forces in Operation TORCH, and subsequent to the British victory of El Alamein, the Department intensified its anti-colonial insistence, notably toward the weaker ally, France, and toward France's hegemony in Syria and Lebanon. Finally, after D–Day in June 1944, which presaged total American victory in war and an American peace, Departmental elan and anti-colonial demands grew further, directed now toward British as well as French hegemony in Arab countries.[14]

There was one special issue, however, which rapidly came to be viewed as so important that it was pressed without regard to the degree of American military successes at any given time. This was the issue of oil in eastern Saudi Arabia. Though the concessions to the Saudi oil fields had been a monopoly of the Arabian-American Oil Company (ARAMCO) since 1933, the gargantuan quantity and the usable quality of the fields' reserves had only been fully confirmed and accepted as a "vital interest" by the Departments of State, Interior, War, and Navy in 1942–43. In addition, the President and Congress were greatly interested in the "prize" represented by Saudi oil. The government as a whole, then, was eager to sustain at all costs, much as if the war and the expense of war were irrelevant, the close ties between ARAMCO and King Ibn Saud—so long as neither the company nor the king acted in such a way as to endanger the American government's interest in, and presumed first option to, the oil. However, in terms of the ultimate responsibility and "credit" for framing policy, it was, as shall be demonstrated in Chapters 11 and 12, due to the dexterity of the Department of State and its FSOs that Saudi oil, and ARAMCO's role as irreplacable middleman, became fixed national interests.[15]

For all that, the American momentum in the Middle East towards unilateralism and interventionism met with regular impediments. The State Department's own Eurocentrism was one. Probably more basic was the traditional prudence-timidity, compounded by fears of entanglement and expensive commitments. The old phobia of an official American commitment to a Zionist state—a phobia which predated both the establishment of Saudi oil as a national interest and the open hostility of Ibn Saud to Zionism—was the classic example of such fears. Yet at the other end of the scale, the Department was also loath to fully espouse an Arab federation in the region, despite long support for Sunni Arab national aspirations, among which was precisely that of pan-Arab union.

True, the Department would give a positive endorsement to the Arab League after the latter was finally formed in March 1945; and true, the Department long felt the Arab Middle East was the region of the colonial world most ready and deserving of postwar political independence, without benefit of United Nations overseers and regional councils. Nonetheless, wartime thinking in the Department on Arab union was often mixed, if not outright negative.

One reason, as noted in Chapter 1, was that the planning apparatus was anxious about new regional blocs generally, the uncertainty they posed to the planning process, and their potential for being too strong or too weak for the good of America's national interest. In the case of

Arab federation, while Arab sociocultural union had always been thought of as innocuous and acceptable to the Department as a "moderate" solution, every other type of Arab union seemed either nebulous or tended to conjure up possibilities of an extreme nature, like anarchy or xenophobia.

Typically, planners posed the following kinds of questions but rarely were able to answer them with consensus. Should Arab federation proceed before, after, or parallel to the settlement of the Palestine question and the question of Syrian-Lebanese interrelations? Should a federation have minimal or maximal geographic representation? Would federation result in lethargy or volatility? Would it fulfill pan-Arab longings, or would it but stimulate anti-Westernism and the old exclusivist concept of *dar-al-Islam* (the world of Islam)? Would the interest in federation expressed by the British Foreign Office promote among the Arabs a Western orientation advantageous to the United States, or an anti-American, pro-British affiliation? To what degree of seriousness would the Hashemite plans for federation, credited to Iraqi Premier Nuri Said and the Emir Abdullah of Transjordan, antagonize the rival house of Saud? Was the unprecedented interest in 1943 in leading a federation, on the part of both Egyptian King Farouk and his rival, Prime Minister Nahas Pasha, a new sign of Arab solidarity, inter-Arab political gamesmanship, or simply intra-Egyptian domestic politics?

Because too many of the answers were either uncertain or unpleasant, the planners' basic concerns were all the more anxious. To what extent would American support of the pan-Arab ideal of a regional federation entangle the United States in difficult political-military commitments? And more specifically, to what extent would such support undermine America's vital interest in Saudi Arabia? Given the fact that Ibn Saud's hostility to the pro-federationist and pro-British Hashemites showed no sign of waning, the Department apparently decided not to tilt toward federation and risk Saudi displeasure. It tacitly dropped the issue from further consideration in 1944–45, after having wrestled with it for two years.[16]

Toward the end of the war, the Department thus continued to see Arab unity, if expressed in sociocultural terms, as a desideratum and as a "direct interest" to the United States. In parallel fashion, however, it had come to see federation, if expressed in economic-political terms, as a complex, possibly hazardous "problem" which ought simply to wait for the long term, after the region's allegedly more pressing requirements were met.

In essence, and as succeeding chapters demonstrate, these requirements were by 1944–45 the *nullification* of French and Zionist claims, the less drastic *neutralization* of British claims, the *prevention* of possible future

Soviet claims, and the *encouragement* of individual Arab states to be free, sovereign, and pro-American.

ADDITIONAL FACTORS BEHIND MIDDLE EAST POLICY

There were other fears and assumptions impeding any Departmental tendencies towards bold and novel thinking in the Middle East. For example, because of the odium associated with Nazi geopolitics in the 1930s, even non-Nazi proposals, such as those of the Zionists, for altering a territorial-demographic status quo were automatically rejected. Planners tended to see such proposals as necessarily contaminated and as mere variations of Nazi-like *lebensraum*. As noted in Chapter 1, the putative "lessons" of World War I's history also instructed the Department in the unwisdom of tampering with territorial boundaries.[17]

In addition, because more of the area specialists among the planners were East Europeanists rather than Arabists, there was a tendency not to separate the two areas but rather to assume that the more fully explored problems and recommendations germane to Eastern Europe automatically applied to the Middle East, too. Because the realities of Eastern Europe made it very difficult to contemplate postwar initiatives such as large-scale border changes, schemes of economic regionalization, or population shifts, it was assumed that much the same reality and verdict applied to the Middle East. The assumption was probably in error, for the Middle East during and immediately after World War II was considerably more fluid and susceptible to revolution-from-above than Eastern Europe. In this connection, it is worth noting that the "reactionary" Churchill was far more radical in Eastern Europe and the Middle East than most high-ranking Americans, as is testified to by the many instances of his imperiously favoring shifting populations and redrawing boundaries.[18]

On another level, too, the planners, despite their admirable bulk of research, had a narrow view of the possibilities in the Middle East. In retrospect, it is apparent that they, and the rest of the Department, while aware of the collision course of Arab and Jewish nationalisms in Palestine, were superficial on the implications. They were intellectually prepared for neither long-run trends in the Arab world, such as the postwar population boom, class disorder, radicalization, and militarization—nor more immediate trends, such as the escalation in capability and urgency of Jewish determination for an independent state. While not entirely predictable, some of these trends should have been more visible by 1944, if not earlier, had the Department's research and analysis been more comprehensive and up-to-date and had its interpretations been freer from prejudgments and traditional perceptions.[19]

If, all considered, there were factors pushing toward, and others away from, a policy of assertiveness in the Middle East, which was the most decisive factor? It was a belief, already touched on, whose origin goes back to the late 1930s. This was the "golden mean" belief that if America maneuvered cautiously against Britain and France and at the same time watchfully let nature take its course in the Middle East, the mantle of regional power and status would *inevitably* pass to the United States. It was the belief that American influence and rights could best be won by avoiding extremes and the pitfalls of both pro-isolationism and pro-interventionism, and by taking a middle position of "active noninterventionism" (my phrase).

True, active noninterventionism was not completely a new species, and to a degree it was undoubtedly an excuse, as before 1941, for an absence or dilution of policy in the face of many fears and risks. In fact, from within the Department, Welles and Acheson accused Hull's noninterventionism of precisely that.[20]

Yet I submit that like the "positive neutralism" of a later period, Hull's active noninterventionism was more effective and less illogical and vacuous than it appeared. In the final analysis, it was the product less of his uncertainty or his desire to make a virtue out of the "necessity" of caution than of a fundamental belief that American success could be won with but little direct political-military involvement and, indeed, *was best ensured* by such a gradualist approach.[21]

By 1943–44, Hull's thesis and method proved generally acceptable to the Department, both to maximal interventionists, who wanted more American influence in the Middle East at all costs, and to minimal interventionists, who had been preoccupied with the expense and entangling commitments thought necessary for influence. The thesis was attractive not only because it represented a middle approach, but also because it seemed so timely. For at midwar, the Department saw that America's status in the Middle East was actually more favorable than ever before.

As a long-term result of a century of good works in the region, American citizens had built up "reservoirs" of good will and moral credit among the Arabs. Now, as short-term results of military success against the formidable Axis, the buildup of its military installations in the Middle East, and its propagandized image as a fabulously wealthy, friendly, freedom-loving giant, America had gained added prestige among all Middle Eastern peoples. As such, it was far ahead of all great-power rivals.

The fundamental implication was clear: the United States was no longer a parvenu, a new power knocking on the doors of Arabs, British, or French, demanding entrance or seeking changes in the internal structure of Arab society more favorable to Washington. Rather, the Department increasingly perceived the United States, and itself, as a confident veteran power, already inside Middle Eastern doors, there by right and might, not by sufferance or chance. Furthermore, by virtue of their patrician values and long familiarity with the Middle East, Departmental officers felt quite at home with Arabic-Islamic language and culture and with the generally stagnant, semi-feudal state of society found in most of the region. In sum, to capitalize on its assets, the Department felt it need only stay on its intermediate course.

However, by the spring of 1945 the Department did feel it necessary to accelerate its speed on this course in order to forestall end-of-war British retrenchment and Soviet inroads. To contain great-power competition and also to win the Arab world away, finally, from the deleterious influence and instability which direct British-Soviet competition would presumably produce, the Department espoused a big economic push. In effect, to crowd out the British and Russians, it wished to crusade for the open door, while dangling enormous loans and aid programs appetizingly.[22]

Still, except for this single desire for an economic offensive, Departmental consensus preferred traditional low-profile practices for the Middle East. Thus the Department continued to espouse, with respect to the internal problems of Arab states, strict noninterference (if it was talking with Arab leaders) or gradual reform (if it was planning and talking amongst itself).

On the other hand, and with respect to Arab states' external relations, the Department continued to give encouragement to the anti-British and anti-French inclinations of Arab leaders. The purpose was to force a change in the status of Arab states from dependency to sovereignty. Upon that achievement, the United States would be able, presumably, to establish solid bilateral relations with these states, and bypass once and for all the middleman obstructionism of the former colonial powers.

This two-handed approach was actually one and the same: a carefully-calibrated escalation of sympathetic Departmental endorsements, some public, most private, of Arab nationalism and its goal of political-territorial independence. As for the type of nationalists approved by the Department, they were the prospective post-colonial leaders who represented the traditional elites of the region's Sunni Arab population.

WARTIME DIPLOMACY TOWARD BRITISH-FRENCH HEGEMONY

Despite the Department's growing élan and its consensus which favored juggling activism with noninterventionism in the Middle East, the essential fact remained that during the war America exercised less direct authority there than did Britain, or even France. Furthermore, the Axis, at least until the very end of 1942, were still a threat to the Middle East. For these two overriding reasons, the Department's primary wartime goal in the region was working for the defeat of the Axis. The goal next in importance was planning the unseating of British and French hegemony, with careful attention to questions of how, when, where, and to what degree. Plans for actually profiting from Arab good will represented therefore a goal third in importance which, while already begun before the war, was projected for fullest activation to the immediate postwar period, after the first two goals were accomplished.

The first goal was direct and uncomplicated. As shall be shown in Chapter 5, removal of Axis political and ideological influence was more difficult. Nonetheless, at least the Department's will was unambiguous towards the goal of crushing Axis power. The second goal—unseating the British and French—was far more complex. In essence, the problem was to reconcile (1) the Department's prewar wish and postwar plans of sharply reducing British-French influence in the Arab world, (2) the wartime necessity of keeping on good terms with both British and French allies, and (3) the postwar need to keep both strong as trading partners and potential allies relative to the Soviet Union. The theoretical problem was exacerbated by the practical problem that, shortly after Pearl Harbor, two opposite tendencies developed in the Department. One favored reducing *immediately* American competition in the Middle East with the British and French, the other favored intensifying *immediately* that competition.

The argument of the "reducers" (usually Europeanists) was that Europe had undisputed priority over the Middle East, and that in order not to impede the war effort against the Axis in Europe, the United States should not simultaneously abet the Arab world's nationalistic demands and "flank attacks" on the British and French empires. Rather, Washington ought to strive "to keep the lid on" the Middle East for the war's duration. Through economic aid it should keep the region "stable." Through diplomatic finesse it should keep the Arabs, and the Jews, quiet and friendly, or at least neutral, toward Britain, France, and America and toward the military forces and economic interests in the region associated with the three powers.

The argument of the "intensifiers" (usually Arabists) was that the war represented a golden opportunity to displace the preeminence of the British and French, already weakened by Axis and Arab anti-imperialist pressures. As such, the fostering of regional stability and friendship should be done with an eye toward America's own postwar role, not toward the European war effort or the state of health of the British and French allies and their respective empires.[23]

Behind this argument were two significant suppositions: first, that if the United States did not exploit the opportunity and scramble *now* to become a great power in the region—primus inter pares, or, at the least, coequal to Britain—Britain and France, possibly in collusion, would later close the door and exploit whatever opportunities arose in order to prevent the United States from having a large postwar role. Second, if the United States did not act quickly to remove British-French imperialism, then anti-imperialist agitation in the postwar world, a worldwide phenomenon already exploited by the Axis, would rise in regions like the Middle East and India to dangerous levels. The result would be uncontrollable political-economic instability, a condition profitable only to a power with radical ideology, such as the Soviet Union. As instability and Soviet influence would be as undesirable to the British and French as to the Americans, the Department indeed tried to persuade British and French diplomats that, in the long run, "generosity" on their part toward their mandates and spheres would pay, and that their loss of direct influence in the short run was in the long run for their own good.[24]

As with maximal and minimal interventionists who eventually settled for Hull's make-haste-slowly policy of active noninterventionism, so the differences between those who favored reducing wartime competition in the Middle East, with Britain especially, and those who favored the opposite also leveled off. The result was a consensus neither strongly pro- nor anti-British, rather one which favored the intermediate position of revising the Anglo-American partnership in the Middle East so that in the postwar period Britain, not the United States, would be the junior partner. On another level of measured intervention, the Department increased efforts in the last two years of war to have the future peacetime U.N. take over the allegedly imperialistic mandate system—yet not so abruptly as to cause grave turmoil or long-lasting British enmity toward the United States. Once again, the Department's basic assumption was that if extremes could be identified and avoided, everything in the middle was by definition more sensible and realistic.[25]

NOTES

1. On prewar American private interests in the Middle East, the most important, and abundant, primary source is the official correspondence of the region's Foreign Service Officers with private citizens (bound volumes in Record Group 84, National Archives, Washington, D.C.) and with Department "headquarters" in Washington (State Department decimal file in Record Group 59, National Archives). For the wartime operational policies (not postwar plans as such) of the Division of Near Eastern Affairs (NEA) and the Foreign Service (FS), the most useful sections of the R.G. 59 files are the gen-

eral files and the internal political and economic files on Palestine (mainly 867N.01, also 767N.00), Egypt (883.00), Iraq (890G.00 and 890G.50), Syria (890E.00), Lebanon (890D.00), and Saudi Arabia (890F.00). The annual volumes on the Near East in the *FR* series, though somewhat abridged and dealing mainly with diplomatic, not consular affairs, are always indispensable, not to say easier to deal with.

For secondary sources, the widest and most authoritative coverage is found in DeNovo, *American Interests and Policies*. Also, see J. A. Field, Jr., *America and the Mediterranean World 1776–1882* (Princeton: Princeton Univ. Press, 1969); Ephraim A. Speiser, *The United States and the Near East* (Cambridge, Mass.: Harvard Univ. Press, 1952); and Polk, *The U.S. and the Arab World*. The missionary-philanthropic aspects are detailed in Robert L. Daniel, *American Philanthropy in the Near East 1829–1960* (Athens, Ohio: Ohio Univ. Press, 1970); Joseph L. Grabill, *Protestant Diplomacy in the Near East: Missionary Influence on American Policy 1810–1927* (Minneapolis: Univ. of Minnesota Press, 1971); and David Finnie, *Pioneers East: The Early American Experience in the Middle East* (Cambridge, Mass.: Harvard Univ. Press, 1967).

2. Historically, the Department did have cordial relations with American Protestant missions in the Middle East. By the 1930s, however, relations were better with those missionaries who were more socially involved, e.g., through the Y.M.C.A., than those who were evangelically involved. Indeed, in religious matters, the Department became willing not only to accept local restrictions on missionaries, but also to acquiesce fully, on the principle of noninterference, before Islamic theocracy which allowed slavery (Saudi Arabia), before restrictive French Catholic authority (in the Levant), and before overt acts of religious intolerance of native minorities (Jews in Vichy-controlled Morocco). On Saudi Arabia, see DeNovo, *American Interests and Policies*, p. 358; *FR* 3 (1928): 62 ff.; *FR* 2 (1930): 547. On the Levant, see *FR* 2 (1938): 1043. On Morocco, see *FR* 3 (1941): 592–95. In contrast, in Egypt the Department protested (to the British) on behalf of Christian missionaries, and as a result helped achieve there relative liberty of conscience [See *FR* 3 (1936): 20 ff].

For the Department's attitude toward American Zionists, see note 4 below, and text, Chapters 13 and 14. For a fuller discussion of "national interests," see Chapter 15.

3. Besides the works of DeNovo, Speiser, and Polk cited above, and others cited for the background material in Chapter 2, useful works which deal well with interwar British and French hegemony in the region are Richard Frye, ed., *The Near East and the Great Powers* (Cambridge, Mass.: Harvard Univ. Press, 1951); Philip Ireland, ed., *The Near East: Problems and Prospects* (Chicago: Univ. of Chicago Press, 1942); also Bernard Lewis, *The Middle East and the West* (New York: Harper & Row, 1964). Other sources are cited in Chapters 6–14.

4. On the "legalistic" aspects of the Department's interwar anti-Zionism and their "continuity" under Secretaries of State Lansing, Hughes, Kellogg, Stimson, Hull, Stettinius, and Byrnes, see Chapters 13 and 14.

On early Departmental protests over alleged British interference (mostly in Iraq) with American oil rights, see Herbert Feis, *The Diplomacy of the Dollar: First Era 1919–1932* (Baltimore: Johns Hopkins Univ. Press, 1950), pp. 49–60; *FR* 2 (1930): 607–11; *FR* 2 (1932): 673–85. On protests for oil rights in Palestine and the Persian Gulf, see *FR* 2 (1919): 258–59; *FR* 2 (1921): 102–3, passim; *FR* 3 (1932): 20. Also, text, Chapters 9, 11, and 12 (Iraq, Saudi Arabia).

5. On the Department's quickening pro-Arabism, see *FR* 3 (1936): 496–

502, and *FR 2* (1938): 1003–31 (on the Levant); and *FR 2* (1937): 622–23, 639–40 (on Egypt).

6. On American "veto" rights with respect to Britain's mandatory authority in Iraq, based on the Anglo-Iraqi Judicial Agreement of 1931, see the correspondence between the British Foreign Office and the Department, *FR 2* (1930): 602–8; and *FR 7* (1932): 672, 674, 684–85. On Syria and Lebanon, see note 7, Chapter 6. Yet cf. the Department's willingness to minimize its veto in Palestine (in section of Chapter 13 on Prewar Policy).

7. On the strong sympathy for the Arabs, "betrayed" by Europe, see, e.g., P. Ireland, "Regional Aspects of the Near and Middle East," 27 August 1942, P Doc. 47, Notter Papers, Box 63, Folder: "P Docs. 44–65"; also, Chapter 4. On the Department's special animus toward France, see Chapter 6.

8. For direct references to the presumed global applicability of the good neighbor thesis and the Monroe Doctrine, see *Bulletin* for speeches of Welles, 6 (24 January 1942); Berle, 6 (2 February 1942) and 10 (12 February 1944); Hull, 10 (15 April 1944); and H. Villard, 12 (28 January 1945).

9. On the expected American harvest, see "Summary of Views to Date," P-215, 19 March 1943, p. 3, Notter Papers, Box 63, Folder: "P Docs. 201–25"; and also the "passive" view of one-time territorial expert [Levant] in the planning apparatus, Wilbur White, Jr. In an interesting radio rebuttal to the advocacy of a "strong" Middle East policy by James Landis and Professor Carl Freidrich, White (essentially speaking for the Department) claimed that the U.S., by promoting independence and economic development and by letting Britain take responsibility in "primary" areas, was more successful than was generally appreciated. A more overt, "independent," and stronger policy, for all its superficial attractiveness, would be counterproductive, he claimed. See transcript of University of Chicago Round-Table Radio Discussion, 22 July 1945, in Landis Papers, Box 164, Folder: "The Middle East: Zone of Conflict?"

White's views are singled out here only because they spell out the Department's calculated easing-out-the-Europeans approach more directly than is done in most official papers—which, as any researcher knows, tend to be difficult to pin down, being written after all by careerists who have, to begin with, the agile verbal evasiveness of a host of Philadelphia lawyers and who also are often writing in the knowledge that their "private" memoranda will be seen by others and in due course will be made public.

10. On the Department's negativism, before and during the war, toward "troublesome" national minorities which did not fit into the Department's scheme of things, see n. a. (probably W. Westermann), "Near Eastern Peoples without a National Future: The Kurds," 1 December 1944, Council on Foreign Relations Territorial Series Memorandum, incorporated as T-298, Notter Papers, Box 69; and W. Westermann, "Near Eastern Peoples without a National Future: The Assyrians (Nestorial Christians)," 1 March 1943, incorporated as T-297, Notter Papers, Box 69.

On Zionism, see Chapters 13 and 14. On the Maronites, see Chapter 6, although it may be noted here that of all the non-Sunni Arab minorities, the Maronites were considered with slightly more sensitivity by the Department. This was due to a concern that if Lebanon were dominated by a Moslem Syria or Moslem Arab Federation, Christian churches in the West would react adversely.

11. The "secondary" ranking of the Middle East is implicit in the relatively low number of Middle East specialists and of meetings on Middle East topics in the planning apparatus generally, as noted in Notter, *Postwar Foreign Policy Preparation*, pp. 103–4, 149, and 520, Appendix 22. Perusal of the wartime volumes of periodical bibliographies like the *International Index* and

Reader's Guide (under War Aims, for example), offers similar, if more impressionistic, evidence of the region's secondary ranking. Also, see Memorandum of Territorial Subcommittee, 20 October 1942, Notter Papers, Box 2, Folder: "Work in SR" (Special Research division); and the section on postwar planning in Chapter 4.

12. On Saudi Arabia, see G. Messersmith to B. Fish (Cairo), 24 May 1939, *FR* 4 (1939): 824–25. On the White Paper, see Chapter 13 and W. Murray to C. Hull, 4 March 1939, *FR* 4 (1939): 723–25. Quotations from Long are from Israel, ed., *War Diary of Long*, pp. 161, 173.

13. See *FR* 3 (1940), for FSO reports from Egypt, pp. 465 ff.; Iraq, pp. 703 ff.; and the Levant, pp. 890 ff.

14. Thus would the Department seek new air and commercial rights, the elevation in rank of American diplomatic missions so as to neutralize and supersede British diplomatic seniority, the termination of the British-launched Middle East Supply Center, the total evacuation of *both* British and French troops from Syria, and more. See Chapters 6 et seq.

15. See Chapter 11 on Departmental relations with ARAMCO and Saudi Arabia.

16. On Arab federation—from the Arab, British, and Department points of view—the documentation is extensive. From the Notter Papers, see (all in Box 2, Folder: "Work in SR") Territorial Subcommittee Decisions and Directives" (n. d., probably July 1942); memo of 20 October 1942; and T-Staff Meeting notes, 12 December 1942. Also, see P 214-C, 10 March 1943, p. 5, and P-214, 12 March 1943, p. 15, both in Box 3, Folder: "Doc.: Subcom. on Polit. Probs., Tent. Views of Coms." Also, ST Minutes 13, 17 March 1943, p. 2, and ST Minutes 14, 2 April 1943, pp. 1–8, both in Box 79, volume: "Minutes on Security Technical Problems (1–." Also, H-71, 15 October 1943, pp. 6–7, Box 58, Folder: "H-Policy Summaries 56–74." For a roseate overview of federation, see Loy Henderson, Memorandum, "Attitude of the U.S. Toward the Question of Arab Union," 29 August 1945, *FR* 8 (1945): 25–29. Also, see "Development of the Arab League," *Bulletin* 163 (8 May 1947): 963–70.

17. For an eventual reaction to the simplistic view of geopolitics as a Nazi pseudo-science and "apology for theft," see R. H. Fifield, "Geopolitiks at Munich," *Bulletin* 122 (24 June 1945): 1152–62. (See S. Woodridge and W. East, *The Spirit and Purpose of Geography* (New York: Capricorn, 1967), pp. 122–23; and Frischwasser-Ra'anan, *Frontiers of a Nation*, pp. 141, passim, for insights into the potentially positive aspects of historical geography and geopolitics.)

On the distorted, albeit "sincere," equation of Zionist territorialism with Nazi lebensraum, see remarks of P. Ireland, Territorial Minutes T-19, 4 September 1942, Yale Papers, Box 1, Folder 7; and W. Yale, Memorandum on Zionism, 11 January 1943, Yale Papers, Box 2, Folder G/7.

As a rule, the Department did not accept this extreme coloration of Zionism, yet neither were Yale and Ireland, the planners' main experts on Palestine and the Jews, ever actually challenged or directly rebutted. (To be sure, respected "experts" like British Foreign Office adviser Arnold Toynbee and a number of prominent anti-Zionist Jews, such as Professor Hans Kohn, voiced similar views on "Zionist lebensraum"—not to mention the Arab-Moslem world, many Christian theologians, communist dialecticians, professional anti-Semites, dedicated internationalists, et al.) See text, Chapters 4, 13, and 14 on Zionism; and notes 24 and 28 in Chapter 1 on World War I lessons.

18. On the preponderance of Europeanists, see note 11 on Notter, *Postwar Foreign Policy Preparation*. For a vivid and rarely cited instance of Churchill's

map-carving approach—anathema to the Department—see his remarks (on Germany) at the Yalta Conference: "We have killed 5 or 6 million and probably another million before the end. There ought to be room in Germany for people transferred. They will be needed to fill vacancies. [So] we should [not] be afraid of problem of transferring population so long as it is proportioned" (from Alger Hiss notes, 7 February 1945, p. 6, Notter Papers, Box 285, Folder on A. Hiss' typed and handwritten notes).

19. In addition to inadequate data, there are in general at least two other problems attendant to any planning operation: wishful thinking and inability to correctly evaluate the available data. Dean Acheson described the former when he wrote that "the Department under Mr. Hull became absorbed in platonic planning of a utopia in a sort of mechanistic idealism" (Acheson, *Present at the Creation*, p. 131). For acute remarks on the second problem, though written with military intelligence and planning in mind, see Roberta Wohlstetter, "Pearl Harbor: A Failure to Anticipate," chiefly pp. 64–65, in R. Dallick, *The Roosevelt Diplomacy and World War II* (New York: Holt, Rinehart & Winston, 1970).

20. See the views of Acheson, Welles, also Grew and Berle, in notes 5, 19, 20, and 29 in Chapter 1.

21. See note 9.

22. On the desire for an economic offensive, see the position paper, "American Economic Policy in the Middle East," 2 May 1945, *FR* 8 (1945): 34–39; and NEA's August memorandum to Truman, ibid., pp. 45–48.

23. Hull, Grew, Welles, Acheson, Berle, H. F. Matthews were, so far as the Middle East was concerned, generally "reducers"; NEA and FSOs in the Middle East were almost invariably "intensifiers." For details on Departmental personnel and intradepartmental relations, see Chapter 4 and the last section of Chapter 7.

24. E. Foy Kohler, Memorandum of Conversation between Wallace Murray and British counselor Michael Wright, 4 October 1944, *FR* 5 (1944): 794.

25. For a lucid analysis of how pro- and anti-British positions neutralized each other and resulted in the third view that Britain, if in effect reduced to junior partner, could be useful to the U.S., see Frederick Winant's study on the Middle East Supply Center for the Policy Committee, 15 April 1944, Annex B to WEA-20, Stettinius Papers, Box 379, Folder: "Miscel. File Pol. Com. Doc. 1944."

The Department's tendency by 1945 to be more gradualist on decolonization not only was to avoid British enmity, but also was due to pressure from the Departments of War and Navy, both of which wanted the U.S. to retain formerly Japanese strategic areas in the Pacific. The State Department wanted to control the areas, too, although in a less conspicuous way, as it was quite aware of the contradiction of espousing independence for others' spheres while enlarging one's own. Its "solution" was to put somewhat new emphasis on mandate-style trusteeships for nonindependent areas generally; though toward the end of 1945 it preferred to defer the whole question of trusteeships, largely to keep Soviet interests in the question at bay. See Notter, *Postwar Foreign Policy Preparation*, pp. 432–33; Russell, *History of the U.N. Charter*, pp. 342–48, 510–14, 576–89; and Stettinius to Roosevelt, 10 April 1945, Notter Papers, Box 189, Folder: "Dependent Areas: General."

4

Departmental "Middle Management" and the Middle East

Critical to any large organization is middle management. Responsible to the board of directors, dominant over the workers, it is in a pivotal position. Its functions, which combine initiating and maintaining company policy, are similarly vital. Basically, if less rigorously, these truisms also apply to the Department of State and its middle echelons. Notwithstanding overlaps into the upper echelons, the middle echelons can be defined as the Department's directors, deputy directors, chiefs, assistant chiefs, ministers, and chairmen—in the Department's geographic, economic, and research divisions, in the Foreign Service, and in the postwar planning apparatus. Relative to Middle Eastern wartime issues, those representing middle management were quite small in number; and within that subgroup, those representing what could be called the "principals," or the most influential members, were more circumscribed still.

These principals numbered about a dozen. They were chiefly career diplomats, with a few hired academics; they represented the Division of Near Eastern Affairs, the Foreign Service in the Middle East, and the Middle East-oriented subcommittees of the planning apparatus. In the great majority of instances, their assumptions, interpretations, short-run and long-run decisions and nondecisions on the Middle East became in turn those of the Secretary and the upper echelons, and then of the President's administration as a whole. For these reasons, it is singularly important to examine the personnel of this core group and the history and function of the sections within the Department which they represented.

THE DIVISION OF NEAR EASTERN AFFAIRS AND PERSONNEL

The Near Eastern Division, as it was first called, was established in 1909 under Secretary Philander Knox. It, impressively, comprised the Ottoman, Russian, German and Austro-Hungarian empires, as well as Italy, Greece, the Balkans, Abyssinia, Persia, Egypt, and the Mediterranean colonies of Britain and France. Appropriately enough, the Division handled more correspondence annually than either the Far Eastern or Western European Division. Actually, however, the workload was not heavy, since American diplomatic involvement was, though wide, not very deep. As for the half-Ottoman-ruled, Arabic-speaking Near, or Middle, East, it was one of the least important areas under the Division's purview. And as for the pre-1914 "Eastern Question," that chiefly involved southeastern Europe, not the Arab world.

Three Departmental reorganizations between 1915 and 1921 shifted the Division's coverage away from Europe and toward the south and east. By September 1939, the countries covered by the renamed Division of Near Eastern Affairs (NEA) were Afghanistan, Burma, India, Greece, Turkey, Iran, Iraq, Palestine, Transjordan, Syria, Lebanon, Egypt, Saudi Arabia and all other countries of the Arabian peninsula, and all of Africa except Algeria and the Union of South Africa. Subsequently, as of January 1944, NEA, like the rest of the Department, was restructured once more and renamed the Office of Near Eastern and African Affairs. (However, it would also be referred to as the Office of Eastern and African Affairs. Its initials were never properly settled: EA & A, NE & A, and OEA were all used.) EA & A covered the same countries as the former NEA. At the same time, three geographic divisions were created under EA & A, because the workload for each country was getting larger and it was assumed that more compartmentalization would produce more specialization and efficiency.

One new division, though with old initials, was the Division of Near Eastern Affairs (NEA), this time covering only Greece, Turkey, Iraq, Palestine, Transjordan, Syria, Lebanon, Egypt, Saudi Arabia and all other countries of the Arabian peninsula. A second was the Division of Middle Eastern Affairs (MEA), covering Afghanistan, Burma, Ceylon, India, and Iran. A third, the Division of African Affairs (AFA), covered all of Africa, except Algeria, Egypt, and the Union of South Africa. These restructurings of 1944 remained unchanged during the rest of the war.[1]

Between 1909 and 1929 there were seven different chiefs of NEA. Most were generalists, not specialists, despite having spent early periods in their careers in a scattering of Near Eastern posts. Wallace Murray, who became the eighth chief in 1929, was also a careerist and generalist of the traditional mold. He was unique, however, in that the degree of his area expertise, and certainly his long tenure in NEA, surpassed those of his predecessors.

Murray had held secretarial posts in the early 1920s in the embassies at Budapest and Teheran and had been appointed assistant chief of NEA in 1927. Thereafter, although his titles changed, he remained the Department's senior expert and main policy initiator on the Arab Middle East and Palestine (not to mention the other countries under his purview), with scarcely any interruption, until after the Yalta Conference. At that point (spring 1945) he was appointed to a post he had looked forward to as a culmination of his career, the ambassadorship to Iran, where he served until June 1946. After retiring for health reasons, Murray was affiliated with American business interests in the Middle East as a director of the American Eastern Corporation. He also served on the board of the anti-Zionist American Council for Judaism. Murray died in 1965.[2]

Murray's closest prewar and wartime associate was Paul H. Alling, assistant chief of NEA from 1934 to 1942. Previously, Alling had held Foreign Service posts in Beirut, Aleppo, and Damascus. When Murray was elevated to adviser on political relations, a post equivalent to assistant secretary, from March 1942 to January 1944, Alling moved up to become the ninth chief of NEA. When, in January 1944, Murray became director of EA & A, Alling became deputy director. After the Yalta Conference, Alling served as an adviser to the American delegation to the San Francisco and other conferences. Desiring a post abroad, partly to get away from the ulcer-causing Palestine problem, he served as diplomatic agent and consul general at Tangier, and then as America's first ambassador to Pakistan. He died in 1949.[3]

Both in the long prewar and wartime periods, Alling and Murray appear to have worked harmoniously and to have shared the same views, though it has been said that Murray was often dependent on Alling for the finer points in a given policy's rationale. Alling seems to have been less outspoken than Murray and more the intellectual and proper gentleman who got on well with all. It may be added that Alling's personal friendships, like those of others in NEA, included Presbyterian missionaries and Y.M.C.A. officials active or once active in the Middle East. In contrast to Alling's temperament, Murray had an explosive temper which, with his clipped British accent, rankled some of his subordinates, not to speak of visiting Zionist delegations.[4]

From 1942 through 1945, the staff of both the old NEA and EA & A, exclusive of clerks, was nearly the same. The total number was usually about twelve, about half of whom were FSOs detailed to the Department in Washington as country specialists because, in some cases, wartime conditions had prevented them from returning overseas. The number of staff involved with the seven Middle Eastern countries under review was five, on the average, but the principals were usually three—Murray and

Alling until their respective appointments abroad in early 1945, and Gordon P. Merriam.[5]

Merriam had taught at Robert College (Constantinople) in the early 1920s and had been one of the first Departmental Arabic-language officers. He also had held vice consul posts in Beirut, Damascus, and Aleppo, and for a longer period, until 1935, in Cairo. Merriam became an assistant chief of the old NEA in May 1940 and was chief of the new, smaller Division of NEA at its inception in January 1944, when Alling became Murray's deputy director of EA & A. Merriam remained a principal in NEA until his retirement for health reasons in 1949. However, he had already expressed the desire three years previously to resign or be posted to Tunis, because he felt the Department's "battle" for Palestine was being lost to the Zionists. Loy Henderson, then director of EA & A, did not go along with Merriam's wish to leave Washington. Henderson approved of Merriam's work, his easygoing nature and experienced draftsmanship; moreover, Henderson did not want to risk getting a new associate whose qualities he could not be sure of in advance.

Like Alling, Merriam was a diligent low-key worker, though his wartime role in initiating proposals was smaller than Alling's. Indeed, Merriam was different from most of the key middle managers examined in this chapter precisely because he was not a "strong" personality with individualistic style or bold views. If he is included here, it is because of his rank, professional longevity, and bureaucratic competence. Furthermore, as an "organization man," Merriam was freer of the overt zeal and unprofessional argumentativeness sometimes generated in the Department by stronger personalities or by lateral entrants with ideological passions.[6]

Murray, Alling, Merriam, and their subordinates were all career officers of very similar social and intellectual background. When World War II began they were, moreover, in the prime of life, confident of themselves, their values, and their understanding of the American national interest in the Middle East. The negative corollary, however, of all this otherwise admirable permanence and esprit de corps was that the men of NEA were of like mind. Additionally, their collective mindset, despite individual differences in temperament, was already nearly completely and imperviously made up before the war with respect to positions the Department should or should not take on basic Middle Eastern questions, as subsequent chapters detail.

THE FOREIGN SERVICE

All foreign services have essentially two functions: consular and diplomatic. The former involves protecting and promoting the rights and private interests of nationals abroad. Typically, it entails much paperwork and covers a miscellany of time-consuming efforts, ranging from making burial arrangements for deceased nationals to facilitating large-scale private investments. The diplomatic function involves protecting and promoting the official national interest abroad. In essence, this function means cultivating friendly personal relations with local leadership, and more generally, conducting good public relations, possibly through economic and military understandings, so that all native elites in the society accept the image of the diplomat's country as a powerful friend. In addition, as authorized eyes and ears of the home office, a foreign service has as part of its diplomatic function the charge of gathering intelligence. So, for example, Foreign Service Officers traditionally sought to keep abreast in the Middle East of local street and palace rumors, newspaper headlines and editorials, and recondite statistics on agriculture and commerce. They then supplied NEA with periodic digests and evaluations.

As the business of the American government has historically been business, and because private enterprise has often been a species of national religion, the overlap between the United States Foreign Service's consular and diplomatic functions has traditionally been large. On the other hand, because of the limited nature of America's official interest in the Middle East, especially before World War I, diplomatic activity in the strict sense was often greatly outweighed by consular activity. During the 1920s and 1930s, the imbalance was lessened, but not greatly. Private interests still dominated official interests. As already noted, religious, educational, and philanthropic interests characterized American private interests in the region in the 1920s; archaeological, commercial, and petroleum interests came to the fore in the 1930s.[7]

Step by step, World War II changed much of that. During the period between September 1939 and December 1941, in addition to regular consular activity, Foreign Service work emphasized extensive reporting of local events and of Axis influence in a mood of watchful waiting. During subsequent months of active participation in war, consular activity region-wide decreased markedly (with the exception of consular activity on behalf of ARAMCO in Saudi Arabia). The decrease was technically due to wartime restrictions on shipping, trade, and currency exchange, and to the evacuations of American nationals. Conversely, diplomatic activity greatly increased, particularly in light of the fact that the initial Allied offensives were in the Middle Eastern theatre and that as of December 1942, the Middle East became the first "liberated," or "postwar," area of the war.

Parallel to the Department in Washington, FSOs thus emphasized diplomatic activity, variously consulting, cooperating, and competing with other Cabinet departments' missions to the area and of course with American, British, French, Arab, and Jewish diplomats. Because of America's increasing power and prestige, even routine conversations between, say, an American chargé in Damascus and a local nationalist or French administrator necessarily took on a new dimension of seriousness to everyone, local or not, interested in Syria's future.

By the closing months of the war, America's overall diplomatic activity and experience in the Middle East were considerable. FSOs fostered and exploited their opportunities whenever possible; and knowing that their views would be compromised and stalled back in bureaucratic Washington, they pushed their views on the Department all the harder.

If, in overview, diplomatic activity superseded consular activity, the job of the average FSO, regardless of time or place, seemed much the same. His work was by turns busy and dull, but never over or clear-cut; and if there were times when certain FSOs were much in the local public's eye, most FSOs were more often busily insulated in their offices. Another occupational hazard was that the diffuse nature of their functions scattered their energies and divided their attention; the breadth of the generalist, not the depth of the specialist, was the usual result. Moreover, if on the one hand they were frequently inundated by missives and directives from Washington, on the other they sometimes felt compelled to complain that they did not know what the Department in Washington was really doing or thinking. Even so, members of the Foreign Service, like members of any other exemplary organ of the civil service, were in most cases cited by observers both in and out of the Department for a high degree of personal competence and dedication (though not necessarily for administrative efficiency). Yet for all their professionalism, esprit de corps and, as noted elsewhere, clubbiness and shared values, FSOs were also often engaged in sharp rivalries for individual career advancement.[8]

Turning to the Foreign Service posts themselves, one notes that early in the 1930s there was already a moderately sized network of American posts in the region. In Egypt, there was a legation in Cairo and consulates in Alexandria and Port Said (and by 1943 in Suez). In Iraq, there was a legation in Baghdad (and by 1943 a consulate in Basra). In Palestine and Transjordan, there was a single consulate general for both, in Jerusalem. In Lebanon, there was a consulate general in Beirut (elevated to legation in 1942). The minister resident in Beirut also oversaw American interests in Syria (in 1945, a separate legation was established in Damascus). For Saudi Arabia, the minister resident in Cairo had traditionally overseen American interests, and in 1939, as noted, a separate legation was established in Jidda, in reaction to Japanese and German diplomatic initiatives and in sympathetic response to the wishes of American oil interests. (In 1945, a consulate was also established at Dhahran.)

In terms of staff numbers, the strength of these posts in the war years varied. While to some degree increments provide a clue as to which posts gained in importance, it is well to remember that more important was the status within the Department of the chief of mission in any given post. Also, it is fair to surmise that the Department, in some cases of public controversy (e.g., Saudi Arabia), kept staff figures to a minimum to avoid the possibility of adverse publicity at home. Furthermore, the Department did not have the manpower or budget to spare and besides, was loath to use non-FSOs abroad, even if they were already lateral entrants in the Department. In terms of style and method, Secretary Hull seemed to prefer a small, unostentatious Foreign Service fraternity that he could oversee and which was made up of a few well-connected and experienced generalists, rather than a large bureaucracy made up, potentially, of heterogeneous, quickly-rotating specialists.

Nonetheless, it is appropriate to note that Foreign Service posts in Egypt, over the span of 1942–45, saw the single largest increase in staff. Saudi Arabia also saw an increase, though the full scope of the Department's role and the size of contingents assigned do not show on the official Foreign Service records, ostensibly on the grounds that most of the official American personnel were on temporary and special missions—military, petroleum, mining, water, agriculture, public works, and the like. In Iraq, Syria, and Lebanon, there were similar, if smaller, increments, together with the elevation in rank of posts and FS titles.[9]

In contrast, the staff size of the Jerusalem consulate, which dealt with Palestine and Transjordan, hardly changed, consisting throughout the war years of a consul general, two consuls, and two to three vice consuls. Also symptomatic of the low priority of the Jerusalem post was the fact that the Foreign Service had by the war years a number of junior and senior officers fluent in Arabic, but none fluent in Hebrew or Yiddish. Similarly, on its planning committees, the Department in Washington had, as shall be seen, a number of experts on Arabic studies, Orientalia and Islamica, but none in any serious sense of the word on Judaism or Zionism—this despite the fact that the Department, and the media, considered Palestine a critical area and despite the fact that (with the exception ultimately of Saudi Arabia) more American private capital, not to speak of American citizens, was concentrated in Palestine from the 1920s onward than in all the other countries under review *combined*.[10]

In terms of middle echelon personalities at the helm, what was already said of the principals of NEA can be applied to the principal FSOs in the Middle East during World War Two: they were a small group of intelligent professional careerists dedicated to the American flag *and* to their Arab "constituency," among whose Western-educated upper classes they had lived for long periods. Interacting smoothly with each other and with Murray, Alling, Merriam, and later Loy Henderson, in Washington they knew each other on a first-name basis, rotated posts periodically, were fully acquainted with all local leaders and foreign diplomats, and by the outbreak of war were generally in the prime of life, with their values, convictions, self-confidence, and biases well established.

FOREIGN SERVICE PERSONNEL IN THE MIDDLE EAST

In terms of status, long-term influence, and intensity of personal involvement, the most important FSOs in the region were Alexander Kirk, George Wadsworth, Harold B. Hoskins, William Eddy, and Loy Henderson.[11]

Kirk, a pre-World War I graduate of Yale and the Harvard Law School, held secretarial posts between 1915–40 in Berlin, Tokyo, Peking, Moscow, and for a longer period, Rome. From February 1941 to December 1943 he was envoy extraordinary and minister plenipotentiary (E.E. & M.P.) to Cairo, holding the same rank, until July 1943, in Saudi Arabia too. From June to December 1943, Kirk was also minister to the Greek government-in-exile in Cairo. As of March 1944, he was on the Allied Advisory Council dealing with Italian and Mediterranean problems and he subsequently was the first American ambassador to liberated Italy.

Partly due to his background in the world's major capitals, and to his intimacy (though not as an Arabist) from 1941 to 1943 with Egypt and Saudi Arabia, Kirk was ever the realpolitiker concerned with large strategic questions, like how the State Department should proceed in order to secure a monopoly on Saudi oil and to replace British economic hegemony in Egypt. His advocacy of a strong policy was, role and background apart, a direct projection of his character as well. His "values" included jaundiced views of the British, viewed as incompetent and out to hoodwink the Americans, and also of the Zionists and Russians; and an aggressive devotion to the open door which probably outdid that of anyone else on the Middle East scene, including Secretary Hull. Kirk, of course, was "pro-Arab," but he does not appear to have been as much an Arabophile as other FSOs. There was the exception in the person of Ibn Saud, before whom Kirk, like everyone else in the Department, did obeisance. Oil, and the mystique built up around the king, had much to do with that.[12]

George Wadsworth as a young man was an instructor at the American University of Beirut, from 1914 to 1917. For his entire life thereafter he was affectionately connected with that institution. Wadsworth entered the Foreign Service in 1919. From 1935 to 1941 he was consul general in Jerusalem, where, though he had minimal direct contact with them, he cultivated an already developed abhorrence for East European Jewish immigrants to Palestine. As of October 1942, he was the diplomatic agent and consul general in both Syria and Lebanon; in September 1944, his rank was raised to E.E. & M.P. After the war, his posts included the ambassadorships to Iraq, Turkey, and Saudi Arabia. In 1952, as a member of the Department's Policy Planning Staff, he was a proponent of the Eisenhower Doctrine and of active resistance to communism in the Middle East.

Like Kirk, Wadsworth was responsible for two Arab capitals, and like Kirk again, he was a strong personality, though more blustery and something of a maverick according to the prep school and corporation standards of the Service. Addicted to bridge and golf, he kept odd office hours and rarely delegated authority to his subordinates. Wadsworth particularly kept tight rein on (and assisted in transferring) one of his consuls, William Gwynn, who ironically happened to be the only FSO in the entire region who was pro-DeGaulle and also unsympathetic with what he felt was the fraudulent and blackmail quality of Arab nationalist demands. Wadsworth was the precise opposite. Indeed, he periodically embarrassed NEA, Secretary Hull, and, later, Acting Secretary Joseph Grew by going beyond instructions in his zealous and open espousal of independence for the Levant and in his diatribes against the French and the Zionists—both of whom tried, unsuccessfully, to get Hull and Grew to remove him. The British Foreign Office, in contrast, was exceedingly pleased with Wadsworth's appointment; and during a 1943 showdown between the ranking British and French representatives, Sir Edward Spears and General George Catroux, Wadsworth worked especially closely with his bridge partner, Spears, both as sympathetic listener and as advocate, urging the British to take action.[13]

Harold B. Hoskins,[14] born in Beirut of Presbyterian missionary parents and one of the few members of the Department who knew Arabic from childhood, graduated from Princeton in 1917 and saw service with the U.S. Marines. At the start of World War II he worked for the Department's Foreign Activity Correlation Division and as executive assistant to Assistant Secretary Adolph Berle, Jr. Holding the military rank of lieutenant colonel, Hoskins subsequently was, at various intervals, head of several special missions to the Middle East related to organizing propaganda for the Office of War Information (OWI), surveying the moods in various capitals, and sounding out Ibn Saud on the possibility of a meeting with Zionist leader, Dr. Chaim Weizmann.[15]

Furthermore, Hoskins was the last chief American representative to the Middle East Supply Center, appointed in May 1944. Stationed mainly in Cairo, he was in roving liaison, as economic adviser, with most other regional Foreign Service posts. (In September 1945 he resigned from his Cairo post, largely because MESC by then was rapidly being dismantled, though partly, it appears, because of his frustration in not seeing his advocacy of bolder American moves realized.) In between these wartime assignments, Hoskins was, as it were, a freelance: at various times he was on military duty, lobbied on Capitol Hill for pro-Arab, anti-British, anti-Zionist support, and participated as adviser in Departmental operational and planning meetings. He also served as a Departmental liaison to the President and to the Joint Chiefs of Staff. Later, in private life, he was active as a trustee for the American University of Beirut.

Hoskins was not typical of the principals of NEA and the Foreign Service; and he never had a key post or tangible influence for long. Nonetheless, while neither a careerist nor a gray eminence, he was a constant presence whose views carried weight. From another angle, while he was a de facto FSO who shared much of the social background of regular FSOs and who was on excellent personal terms with Welles and Roosevelt, Hoskins was also an outsider who was always chafing at what he felt were NEA's bureaucratic timidity and its personnel's overconcern for their careers. He appreciated the fact that most FSOs were not, as he was, independently wealthy and therefore were not independent-minded. Still, he felt that wartime made it incumbent to break out of the mold and take new risks. For its part, NEA felt Hoskins was too pushy. Temperament apart, he and the Division were in agreement on most positions.

There were two exceptions, however. NEA disagreed with Hoskins' repeated thesis that the Department should view the Middle East the way the British supposedly did, as a dynamic *whole*, rather than as—in his interpretation of the Department's viewpoint—a static collection of separate nation-states. Also, earlier than anyone else in the Department, Hoskins had recommended another "bold" approach, namely, that some 500,000 Jews be brought into Palestine in due course, in order to bring the Jewish total into parity with the Arab total (Jews and Arabs to number approximately one million each). Thereafter, Palestine would be off-limits to Jewish immigrants who, suggested Hoskins, should be steered towards the scarcely populated, ex-Italian colonial area of northern Cyrenaica (Libya) for their possibly Jewish state. The Allies would presumably oversee the entire procedure. As for Palestine, it was assumed that the Arabs' high birth rate was a guarantee that Palestine would remain an Arab country.

It is probably fair to say that over the span of the war years, NEA, and the Department generally, inched toward accepting Hoskins' somewhat Churchillian cut-the-Gordian-knot approach to Palestine. That is, NEA did not recoil completely in aversion. Still, it never really accepted Hoskins' large view as a policy which the Department should support and take responsibility for implementing.[16]

Hoskins' cousin, Colonel William Eddy, had much the same kind of temperament and background: boldness, missionary parents, Princeton, the Marines in World War I (both had almost died from gassings in the trenches). In the interwar period, however, while Hoskins had entered business (becoming an executive with Cannon Towels Co.), Eddy had become an academic (chairman of the English department at the American University, Cairo, 1923–28, and president of Hobart College, New York, in the late 1930s). Then, having left an unsatisfying college presidency and having reenlisted in the Marines in 1941, Eddy became prominent in the Office of Coordination of Information (COI), and in COI's successor, the Office of Strategic Services (OSS).

While stationed in Tangier, one of Eddy's dashing plans included "going to the natives" to try to stir Arabs and Berbers into anti-Vichy acts of sabotage. His superiors, the Joint Chiefs of Staff, disapproved, preferring to put their faith in the projected Operation TORCH. Nonetheless, toward the end of the war Eddy in effect did in Saudi Arabia what he had been unable to do in North Africa, namely, secure a tacit Arab-American alliance. Succeeding FSO James Moose, Jr., in September 1944, he became minister to Jidda and developed a closer personal rapport—which of course was the Department's object in assigning him—with Ibn Saud and his advisers and minions than any previous American diplomat had.

Eddy remained in Jidda until succeeded by an old-Middle-East-hand of the prewar NEA, J. Rives Childs, in mid-1946; thereafter, Eddy rejoined the OSS as a special assistant to Secretary of State James Byrnes, in the capacity as head of the Department's research and intelligence branch (R & I), succeeding Professor William Langer. (R & I was the interim successor of the OSS, which had been partly terminated, partly integrated into the Department by Truman in September 1945.) Eddy also gained brief fame as Arabic-English translator at the post-Yalta meeting of President Roosevelt and Ibn Saud at Great Bitter Lake in the Suez Canal, about which he wrote a book published by the pro-Arab lobby (and CIA-subsidized), American Friends of the Middle East, Inc., in 1954. From 1947 to 1952, Eddy in addition was a consultant for ARAMCO and in 1955, for ARAMCO's subsidiary, Trans-Arabian Pipeline Company (Tapline).

Eddy was probably the nearest thing the United States had to a Lawrence of Arabia. He was *the* great and personal friend of the Arabs and expressed their point of view, especially Ibn Saud's, with unceasing advocacy, the premise being of course that American and Arab interests were one and the same. His dispatches from Jidda—particularly from June to September 1945, the twilight period of the war and crucial formative period of the postwar—were ever urging immediate and massive aid to the king, predicting dire consequences otherwise (that the king would become bankrupt and politically weak, that the king would deliberately bait and bleed ARAMCO for money, and/or that the king would return to the British fold).

Eddy's interest was more than keeping Ibn Saud on the American side for oil or Anglophobic reasons; it was far more dramatic and historically symbolic than that. Suggesting a monumental rapprochement à la Saladin and Richard the Lion-Hearted, Eddy wrote of the Ibn Saud-Roosevelt meeting, 13–14 February 1945, that it represented a "moral alliance," "cemented" between the modern world's equivalent of a Defender of the Moslem Faith and the Arabian Holy Cities, sacred to 300 million people, and the head of a great Western and Christian nation. Moreover, the meeting, he said, represented a mutual breakthrough, Saudi Arabia emerging from its isolation, the United States asserting itself unilaterally and manfully in the Arab world, without looking over its shoulder at the British or the Jews.

Roosevelt's death shortly after the meeting was thus a grave setback to Eddy and to the bilateralism he had helped to nurse on both sides of the water. Another setback occurred later, when Truman accepted the partition of Palestine; symbolically, Eddy resigned (October 1947) from the Department in protest. Living or dead, Eddy's heart was always in the East. In 1962, when he died, he was, at his request, buried in his birthplace in Lebanon (Sidon), and with only the words "U.S. Marines" on his tombstone.[17]

Loy Wesley Henderson, in the interwar period an FSO in the Baltic region and the Soviet Union who shared his Estonian wife's anti-Soviet attitude, had become persona non grata in Moscow in 1938. According to Henderson's own version, Commissar for Foreign Affairs Maxim Litvinov had successfully urged Eleanor Roosevelt to have Henderson removed, as he was alleged to be a bar to Soviet-American amity. Thereafter, from 1938 to 1943, Henderson was a principal in the Department's European Division. Wishing to advance, but not, in his phrase, desiring to jump over other FSOs, he took advantage of an ambassadorial opportunity in Baghdad which no one else apparently wanted. Though Iraq was outside his area of experience, he became ambassador in October 1943. In due course he became directly familiar with the Arab world and increased his reputation as a model FSO known for dedicated work and quality of reporting. On the bases of these high marks and his friendships with fellow southerner and contemporary, Wallace Murray, and also with Undersecretary Grew, Henderson became Murray's successor as director of the Office of Near Eastern and African Affairs in April 1945.[18]

Henderson's prominence, in terms of the Department's Middle East policy making, thus began very late in the war years and is essentially postwar. Even so, he is included here as a principal wartime FSO in the Middle East because his short wartime role was a large one and because his personal and ideological closeness to Murray highlights the nearly unmodified continuity of policy in old NEA and new EA & A.

However, in his personal manner, if nothing else, Henderson was somewhat less anti-Zionist than Murray had been, and somewhat more opposed to Britain, France and Russia. On the first point, Henderson expressed "great respect" (as invariably have most FSOs interviewed and researched) for Zionist "moderates" like Stephen Wise and Chaim Weizmann and of course the noted "spiritual" Zionist, Judah Magnes.[19]

In addition, Henderson's objections to the proposition of a Jewish state appear to have been less sweeping than those of other FSOs, not that his views were any less intense for these reasons. In brief, he felt that a Zionist state in a partitioned Palestine would be impractical—economically unviable and militarily indefensible, requiring American intervention and blood to protect it—and that in any case such a state would be a liability to American interests because it would alienate the Arab-Moslem world and would introduce into the conduct of foreign policy the presumably dangerous and inappropriate precedent of domestic ethnic politics.[20]

Some three years later, when Truman was supposedly forced by American Jewish voters to recognize the state of Israel, the evil ways of domestic ethnic politics seemed confirmed to Henderson. Nonetheless, it is worth noting that Henderson and his staff drafted Truman's famous letter of instant recognition in May 1948, notwithstanding the conventional view that the Department was surprised and chagrined at Truman's rash action. As a model FSO, Henderson apparently felt that loyalty to the Chief overrode one's own wishes and values. And Henderson was apparently concerned that alleged Jewish power and privilege in America (an absolute Departmental fixation in the 1940s which the realities of European death camps and later displaced refugee camps did nothing to offset) would hurt the Department. That is, if the battle royal in the "Jewish influenced" media especially, between Zionist sympathizers and the Department became too intense, his career and health, and the careers and health of his colleagues, might well be ruined.[21]

THE POSTWAR PLANNING APPARATUS

Within the postwar planning apparatus created after Pearl Harbor were several divisions and committees which concentrated on American long-run plans, chiefly for Eastern and Central Europe and the Middle East. Working with the veteran middle managers of NEA, and to a lesser extent with the Foreign Service, these consisted of, in 1942–43, the Territorial subcommittee, the Political subcommittee, and the Division of Special Research. In the period after August 1943, the first two planning units were fused and then reorganized, without any real change except in name, into several interdivisional country-and-area committees. The research unit was divided, then expanded into separate divisions of economic studies and of political studies. This latter division was segmented into several new research units, the most important on Middle Eastern problems being the Division of Territorial Studies.

The guiding principles and main attitudes of the postwar planners have already been discussed in Chapter 1. What follows here are the specific methods and procedures of the Middle Eastern planning units. For the Territorial subcommittee, the procedure was to hypothesize problems likely to arise at the end of the war, to draft a list of alternate "solutions" or at least responses, to weigh the advantages and disadvantages of each, and to indicate or suggest preferences and the "objective" reasons why, based on the Department's past and present statements on the national interest. The subcommittee held fifty-nine informal biweekly meetings—minutes were rarely kept—from March 1942 to December 1943. These meetings usually alternated with technical meetings with NEA, other divisions, and outside specialists. As earlier noted, however, most of the staff and time of the Territorial subcommittee were devoted to Eastern Europe, not to the Middle East.

The Political subcommittee included all members of the Territorial subcommittee, among others, and met regularly for sixty sessions between February 1942 and June 1943, with Undersecretary Welles in the chair until January 1943 and Secretary Hull in the chair thereafter. Of all the early subcommittees in 1942 and 1943—those on territorial problems, political problems, security problems, economic reconstruction and policy—the Political subcommittee was the single most important one in the entire planning apparatus. It also became known simply as the Political Committee. Hull favored it, and according to Departmental historian Harley Notter, it exerted "appreciable" influence on all other subcommittees.

Preliminary and ad hoc committee studies occupied the Political subcommittee's first eight months. Then from October to December 1942 there was a "first round," that is, a general survey of all major active and potential political problems in the world. This was followed by a "second round" during which specific positions and preferred solutions were offered, along the lines of the Territorial subcommittee's procedure. As with other committees, in both rounds of the Political subcommittee, Middle Eastern problems were of relatively secondary importance. When the Middle East was discussed, it was usually in connection with the obstreperous Palestine problem.[22]

For its expertise on the Middle East, the Political subcommittee drew on the Territorial subcommittee, which in turn was dependent on the studies of the Special Research division. As noted in Chapter 1, this division predated the war; in the late 1930s its chief was Leo Pasvolsky, and it consisted of ten specialists. By the middle of 1942, its staff had expanded considerably, drawn chiefly from university faculties and research foundations. As a rule, these lateral entrants were already familiar with the Department through family-social connections or previous work experience. They were a kind of available reserve, already known to the regulars in the Department. Most entrants were older men who were above the age of military conscription yet were patriotically desirous of doing something lasting for the nation.

By December 1942 the Special Research division had a total of fifteen researchers on the economic side; while under Pasvolsky's assistant, Harley Notter, on the political side there were six researchers on international organization; eight for security, armaments, and law; seven for Western Europe's territorial problems; six for the Far East's; four for Eastern Europe's; three for Central Europe's; and three for the Middle East's. These three were Philip Ireland, William Yale, and Halford L. Hoskins. Again, the relative quantities indicate the Middle East's secondary status in the total scheme of things.[23]

The Special Research division's earliest wartime function was to prepare a study of all public and confidentially expressed commitments and views on the postwar period that had emanated from both Allies and neutrals. Thereafter, it produced reams of political, economic, and geographic memoranda, both descriptive and analytic, the latter of which were supposed to test the feasibility and desirability of alternate solutions. The Territorial and Political subcommittees in turn would discuss these more elaborately and then send them back to the researchers for revision. In brief, the division's research was not only copious, it was often academically competent and shows, as noted elsewhere, that the Department's postwar plans were worked out early in the war, often considerably ahead of those of other interested parties and nations.

Such "success" partly derived from the fact that the Middle East planners, like their counterparts in NEA and the Foreign Service, were a group of like background, with considerable rapport, which fact, given the constant press of time, was conducive towards quick consensus. On the other hand, their research on the Middle East was also defective. It was very inbred, with impressionisms and biases rarely acknowledged, with self-congratulating references to the research's completeness and "dispassionate objectivity," and without any self-testing adversary system or checks by a disinterested third party, or even first-hand, fresh sources. In the case of Palestine, there was a tendency to over-rely on those British royal commission reports of the 1930s which were least optimistic on the Zionist enterprise and on partition.[24]

It should be noted that the geopolitical or economic value of a Middle Eastern country was not necessarily proportional to the quantity of time and research spent on it. The degree of potential obstructiveness to the national interest was also a raison d'être of much research. In quantitative terms, the countries which received the most "planning" attention were, in descending order of "importance": Palestine, Syria and Lebanon, Arab federation, the Suez Canal, Saudi Arabia, Transjordan, Egypt, and Iraq. (Saudi oil within the planning apparatus was handled mainly by economists, not Middle East experts and Arabists.)

However, in opposition to this rule that obstructionism begets attention, there was one topic bearing on the Middle East which was almost avoided. As noted in Chapter 1, the need of a "home" for surviving European Jewish refugees was only inconsistently considered within the planning apparatus. When it was, planners generally lumped Jewish refugees with all other refugees (otherwise the Jews would be "privileged" characters) and as a rule advocated repatriation for the whole lot. Planners specializing in the Middle East hardly considered the Jewish refugee problem, in terms of territorial solutions, at all. True, they were fully aware of the problem, had their own theories as to what caused it (basically, Jewish particularism) and how assimilation could solve it. But the only connection they saw between the problem and "their" region was that immigration of refugees to Palestine would engorge the land, inflame the Arabs, and make things "difficult" for themselves, for their plans for postwar Arab-American comity, as well as for Britain and the general war effort. Beyond that, they refused to deal with the topic, first because it was not strictly in their assigned "province," but more deeply, because they adamantly refused to accept what they felt was mere Zionist propaganda, namely, that there was a connection between Jewish suffering and the lack of a Jewish national home.

By the middle of 1943, the pace of the war and the creation of postwar liberated zones after the Allied victories of Stalingrad, North Africa, and Sicily quickened the pace of the Department as a whole. The fact that the Political subcommittee had completed its second round that summer was also a stimulus. One result was that the meetings of the Territorial and Political subcommittees were temporarily suspended, which gave the researchers opportunity to refine, summarize, and disseminate their memoranda on alternate solutions to all sectors of the Department and Foreign Service. Another result was the establishment of several interdivisional country-and-area committees. For the Middle East, area experts from the planning side and representatives from NEA sat together on the "interdivisional country committee on the Arab countries" (subsuming Palestine as well). As of December 1943, Philip Ireland, sitting in for NEA chief Wallace Murray, presided. In the months ahead, this committee was the main postwar planning authority on the Middle East.[25]

The purpose of the committee was to coordinate current and postwar policy more closely by narrowing the gap between the short-run work of the geographic division (NEA) and the long-run work of the planning units. Actually, very little new coordination had to be done, or was. Ireland's committee was only a new home for the views and bodies of the Middle East experts of the former Territorial and Political sub-committees and former Special Research division. Contributing to this heremetic situation was the fact that the number of experts from the planning side was as small as from NEA's side. Also, the planners were even more hidden from the public eye than was NEA. Ivory tower immolation and secrecy were the planners' antidotes to the possibly infectious winds of public scrutiny or of ethnic demands, such as had buffeted postwar planners during World War I.

THE PERSONNEL IN MIDDLE EAST PLANNING

The planners who were most closely and continuously involved in the wartime research, drafting, initiating, and follow-up advocacy of postwar solutions for the region were but two in number: Dr. Philip W. Ireland and Professor William Yale. Smaller and briefer roles were played by others, like Wilbur White, Jr. (on Syria and Lebanon), Christina P. Grant (on Syria, Lebanon, and Saudi Arabia) and Halford L. Hoskins (on the Suez Canal). On the top of the planning apparatus were people who also had expertise on the Middle East—notably Isaiah Bowman. Also, at planning meetings on the Middle East were Territorial subcommittee members from NEA like Paul Alling and Foy Kohler. But it was Ireland and Yale whose province was Middle East planning and who therefore were the principal middle managers for the region within the planning apparatus.

Ireland had been an instructor at the American University of Beirut in the 1920s; and after receiving graduate degrees from Oxford, Cambridge, and the London School of Economics, he taught Middle Eastern history at Harvard, Johns Hopkins, and the University of Chicago. In July 1942 he entered the Department as an assistant in the Special Research division, under Notter and Pasvolsky, soon becoming an active participant in Territorial and Political subcommittee meetings. Subsequently, he was acting chairman of the interdivisional country committee of the Arab countries, assistant chief under Philip Mosely of the Division of Territorial Studies (heir to the divisions of Special Research and of Political Studies), special assistant to Director of Eastern and African Affairs, Loy Henderson, and assistant to the American delegation to the San Francisco Conference in the spring of 1945.

Ireland directed the research and analysis on the Middle East and was the main spokesman for Middle East researchers, serving as their liaison to the planning subcommittees and to NEA. His own personal research focused on Libya, Syria, Lebanon, Arab federation, together with inter-mittent studies of a historical or advisory nature, usually co-authored with Yale, on a diversity of topics, such as the roots of the Middle East's problems, Zionist pressures, and the desirability of sending American "advisors" to the region after the war.

While academically and linguistically qualified, Ireland, somewhat of a dandified and Anglicized personality, was always quite abrasive and dogmatic. He had a reputation for being an overly sensitive and officious autocrat and an "odd duck," to use one former FSO's phrase. Another former colleague, while fully sharing Ireland's views, including his abso-lute anti-Zionism, expressed the view that although practically everyone in the Department treating the Middle East was an anti-Zionist, Ireland was one of the Department's few anti-Semites. However, evidence for this opinion is not apparent in Ireland's published writings. Yet his tendency during planning meetings to equate Zionism with Nazi *lebens-raum* does suggest that his anti-Zionism was a passion, perhaps a mania, not simply an intellectual thesis.[26]

On the Levant, Ireland regularly affirmed the need to end French influence once and for all and to separate Syria and Lebanon into two states. However, like all others in the Department, he favored separation in political affairs only. (The word "partition" could just as well have been used, but that word, somehow, was only used for Palestine.) He preferred a final solution that would include economic union between Beirut and Damascus and a common membership in a larger Arab federation. On federation, his view was that though the idea was "nebu-lous," it deserved serious consideration, if only because the British might promote it to their own advantage.

As for the postwar disposition of Libya, Ireland was open to several alternatives, including regional-council supervision under the United Nations organization or border rectifications in favor of Egypt. Ulti-mately, however, he seems to have preferred a British trusteeship in eastern Libya (Cyrenaica), while Italy would retain the western part (Tripolitania). In any case, he did not express himself in favor of the idea, bruited about by Harold B. Hoskins, of using part of Libya as a Jewish asylum. Ireland also was clearly opposed to any exclusive great-power interest in Libya, by which he meant the Soviet Union, lest air power be some day massed against the British-guarded Suez Canal. Basic to all these individual viewpoints was the thesis that Ireland regularly advanced, namely, that the United States should adopt a larger and more active role in the postwar Middle East.[27]

With Wallace Murray, William Yale (born in 1887, the same year as Murray) was the oldest Middle East expert in the Department. (He had, in fact, begun Departmental service earlier than Murray.) The son of a wealthy upstate New York family, Yale went to the Lawrenceville

School and Yale University. After having briefly worked in Panama and Palestine for the Socony Vacuum Oil Company (Mobil), he was hired by the State Department during World War I as special agent on the Middle East and liaison to General Allenby's British forces; as a technical adviser in Lebanon, Syria, and Palestine to the King-Crane Commission; and then as an assistant to the American delegation at the Paris Peace Conference of 1919. Though quite young and not an Arabist or political scientist by training, Yale achieved these glamorous if distinctly peripheral roles largely by a combination of school ties, family connections, and plain happenstance. After the Peace Conference, Yale entered small business ventures in Egypt and New Hampshire. From 1928 to 1942, he served as an assistant professor of History (mainly Russian and Near Eastern) at the University of New Hampshire.

In the interwar period, Yale cultivated what was, as he himself recognized, a strong emotional and intellectual interest in Jews (anthropological and historical more than religious). It was an interest which fluctuated between strong sympathies (for "gentle" Sephardic Jews, for assimilationist and liberal German-American Jews, for socialist Bundist Jews) and strong antipathies (for "arrogant" East European Jews, for capitalist Jews, for political Zionists of all stripes and for American Zionist lobbyists especially). Psychologically, he seems to have acquired some of the dislike of Jews which his father, as Yale acknowledged, had—although social environment doubtlessly helped, given the anti-semitic pseudo-anthropology and discriminatory practices so pervasive at schools like Yale University, circa 1910, when he graduated.[28]

During 1941 Yale sent several lengthy and unsolicited memoranda from New Hampshire to then Assistant Secretary Berle, admonishing the Department to beware of Zionist machinations. Whether these were factors in his reemployment by the Department is hard to say; in any case, his World War I activities were familiar to the Department, and at the end of 1942 he was recruited to come to Washington by Philip Ireland. Once ensconced in the planning apparatus and put in charge of planning for Palestine, Yale always spoke as the elder expert who "knew" Jews and Zionists like nobody else. His tone was always Catonian, his attitude that of the watchful bulldog. His abiding thesis was that if the Department did not watch out, the Zionists would manipulate American foreign policy during and after World War II—as they had allegedly done during and after World War I, when they supposedly managed to cement American support for the Balfour Declaration into a fixed American foreign policy.[29]

Besides Palestine, Yale also did occasional planning for Transjordan and Saudi Arabia. Moreover, unlike other researchers, he was a regular and vocal member of the Territorial and Political subcommittees and the interdivisional committee on the Arab countries. At such meetings, his Zionophobia was unsurpassed, even by Ireland and Wadsworth. As researcher and drafter, his written output was also extraordinary. Put otherwise, there is far more from Yale's pen on Palestine in the documentation of postwar planning than there is by any other author on any other Middle Eastern country or combination of countries.

It is also noteworthy that with Ireland and Harold B. Hoskins, Yale was one of the few Department officers who was willing to fight fire with fire and engage in extra-Departmental covert maneuverings and lobbying against Zionists. For example, one of Yale's brainstorms (endorsed by NEA) was to contact prominent Jewish anti-Zionists, be they ultra-orthodox, socialist, or assimilationist. (Yale was especially fond of the latter two, and he was in periodic personal contact with Reform officers of the American Council for Judaism like Lessing Rosenwald and Rabbi Morris Lazaron.) Yale's purpose was to generate a domestic Jewish "popular front" against the efforts of the Zionist Organization of America which was seeking, apparently successfully, to convert American Jewry to the cause of Zionism. His effort did not get very far, however; as explained in Chapter 13, the risks of exposure from such Departmental activity were too great.

Ardent Zionophobia notwithstanding, Yale was not an Arabist or as much an Arabophile as other FSOs. After World War I, he had dissented to a degree from the overtly pro-Arab findings of the majority on the King-Crane Commission (findings which were in any case shelved by Woodrow Wilson). Similarly, during his World War II service, he did not, as a rule, favor an Arab state in Palestine. What he personally favored—and, fitting facts to theory, felt was objectively realistic—was a certain type of political binational state. That is, after an initial period of U.N. trusteeship administered by the British, Palestine would politically be a binational state, but would economically and socially remain Arabized, rural, and agricultural. Such a state would thus be safe not only from the chimera of Jewish nationalism, but also from the modern capitalism, urban industrialism, and the traumas of rural dislocation which Yale felt were the real dangers inherent in the value system Zionist Jews would impose in Palestine.

Indeed, like Philip Ireland, Yale saw Zionism as a pathological system which he equated with Nazism (much as, in reverse, the Nazis saw Jewry as a pathological race which *they* equated with Americanism). To Yale, Zionism *was* Nazism because both were nationalistic, racist, and territorialist, and manifested a fascistic mix of socialism and capitalism.

In sum, as well as his turn-of-the-century upper-class anti-Semitic snobbism and anxiety about capitalistic Jews, à la Henry Adams, there was a 1930s-vintage populism, agrarian sentimentalism, and academic

Marxism à la Charles Beard in Yale's outlook. These, more than pro-Arabism or any Biblical romanticism about the Holy Land, were the fuel which fed his Zionophobia.

As before the war, Yale's "philo-Semitism" and anti-Zionism went hand in hand during the war. He expressed positive admiration for non-Zionist Jewish leaders, as well as earnest sympathy for the age-old Jewish problem and for Jewish suffering under Nazism; and he ardently detested Nazism. Yet he also stoutly resisted the occasional plan that came to the Department's attention for the rescue of Jewish children from the crematoria by, for example, transshipping them via Iran and Iraq to Palestine. His "objective" view was that to call such efforts humanitarian was to play into the hands of the Zionists, since it was clear that the more Jews in Palestine, whether children or adult, the more Zionists; and the more Zionists, the more probable the emergence of a Jewish state.

Immigration into Palestine, except in token amounts, was thus anathema to Yale. When Truman rejected this position, of which Yale was drafting officer and which every echelon and relevant Department division had accepted as policy and had initialed, and when he (Truman) urged that the British give 100,000 Jewish Displaced Persons entry certificates in April 1945 on humanitarian grounds, Yale resigned in pique and frustration. He returned to his wife and to the University of New Hampshire, later becoming professor emeritus—and thereafter a lecturer at Boston University. He died in 1975.[30]

Finally, and as was mentioned, Yale, in a minor way, was a planning officer for two other Middle Eastern countries—Transjordan and Saudi Arabia. About the first he had little to recommend except that it should be separated from the Palestine question and from the possibility of establishing agricultural settlements of Jewish refugees there. Furthermore, it should remain an enclave under British control. About Saudi Arabia he had more to say. In fact he, with Ireland, authored in the summer of 1944 a rapid succession of memoranda for NEA and the upper echelons, urging a large policy of permanent financial support for Ibn Saud, above and beyond Lend-Lease and the like. Both also urged the systematic dispatch of "advisors" and technicians to Saudi Arabia—and to Syria, Lebanon, Iran, Ethiopia, and Afghanistan. The main goals were securing oil, preempting British and Russian ambitions, and stabilizing local political conditions by unprecedentedly vast economic transfusions.[31]

CONCLUSIONS

Superficially seen, the prewar and wartime responsibility of NEA, FSOs in the Middle East, and Middle East planners consisted of fulfilling merely a moderate level of middle-management functions, namely, researching and interpreting the facts, presenting drafts of prospective trends, policy alternatives, and recommendations to the upper echelons, after which NEA would convey the upper echelons' ultimate decisions and advice back to FSOs in the field. *De facto*, however, middle management's role was larger. NEA was one of the oldest divisions, with a staff of great continuity and longevity. Its seniority and respectability were high, as instanced by the fact that NEA people were prominent in the management of the in-house *Foreign Service Journal*. The upper echelons had confidence in, and many friendships with, NEA. Furthermore, because the upper echelons were usually preoccupied with other matters, they tended to accept the views of NEA (and in turn of NEA's colleagues in Middle Eastern Foreign Service posts and in the Departmental planning apparatus) as the last word in unbiased reporting and expertise.

Seen from close up, therefore, NEA and these colleagues were architects of Middle East policy. They were, moreover, typically "pushy" advocates of the economic open door in the Middle East, of full self-determination for the Sunni Arab majority, *and* of postwar American hegemony and indirect, nonannexationist *imperium*. (Such loaded words were not used, for the very reason that they were loaded, but the intent was there all the same.) On the surface, of course, NEA, et al, were merely intelligence-gatherers and "middle managers," akin to humble draftsmen and messenger boys.

Interestingly, these men had difficulty coping with American political life. Insulated and inbred, elitist and of the upper middle class, the officers and colleagues of NEA viewed Congress and public opinion in general (and the growing public approval of the idea of a Jewish state in Palestine in particular) with consistent disdain. This negativism toward the American hoi polloi is paradoxical, because abroad, as noted, the Department was usually beating the drums for anti-imperialism, majority self-rule, and other democratic principles. For example, whenever the Arab "world" seemed to talk violently or hold street demonstrations on a non-local issue, NEA and its Foreign Service liasions, "alarmed" and "impressed" (and at times personally anxious over their own safety), acted as if that world were a democratic electorate and they, the Americans, were its messengers and representatives. Regardless of the merits of the issue agitated over, they would instinctively urge the Secretary to placate the clamor for the sake of the American national interest and (left unsaid) for their own peace of mind and body. The truism that Americans abroad have had a need to be liked certainly applied to the Arab Middle East.

However, if *American* public opinion seemed to clamor for some object, NEA's instinctive reaction was to turn a politely attentive but deaf ear. It did this out of the conviction that not only was Congressional and domestic opinion ephemeral, "uninformed," divided, and corrupted by special pleading and election "politics"—but that even if it were none of these things, public opinion, as a political science abstraction, did not and should not have a tangible role in the formulating of American foreign policy.[32]

Finally, it should be underlined that despite the wartime increase in Departmental staffing and the growing attention paid to the Middle East within the Department, the pilots, so to speak, at the controls of the Division of Near Eastern Affairs remained remarkably continuous and homogeneous. It has been said that while presidents come and go, the Department, and therefore foreign policy, remains the same. By the same token, one could add that while Departmental secretaries and upper echelons come and go, the middle echelons, and therefore foreign policy, remain the same. Certainly this was true of NEA, where throughout the prewar and wartime periods, and only to a somewhat lesser extent the immediate postwar period, too, the *same* very small group of middle managers held sway.[33]

NOTES

1. Information on NEA's evolution collated from Graham Stuart, *The Department of State: A History of Its Organization, Procedure, and Personnel* (New York: Macmillan, 1949), p. 216; *American Foreign Service Journal* 10 (1933): 16; *Register of the Department of State 1941* (Washington, D.C.: GPO, 1942, renamed *Biographic Register* as of 1943), p. 24; and *Bulletin* 10 (15 January 1944): 57.

Of the many studies of the Department in general, those most useful on the period under review include Graham Stuart, *American Diplomatic and Consular Practice* (New York: Appleton-Century, 1936); W. Laves and F. Wilcox, "Reorganization of the Department of State," *American Political Science Review,* 1944, v. 38, pp. 289–301; N. Graebner, ed., *An Uncertain Tradition: American Secretaries of State in the Twentieth Century* (New York: McGraw-Hill, 1961); and A. DeConde, *The American Secretary of State: An Interpretation* (New York: Praeger, 1962).

Although they deal mainly with the postwar Department, the following also proved useful: R. E. Elder, *The Policy Machine: The Department of State and American Foreign Policy* (Syracuse, N.Y.: Syracuse Univ. Press, 1960; D. K. Price, ed., *The Secretary of State* (Englewood Cliffs, N.J.: Prentice-Hall, 1960); B. M. Sapin, *The Making of United States Foreign Policy* (New York: Praeger, 1966); and I. M. Destler, *Presidents, Bureaucrats and Foreign Policy: The Politics of Organizational Reform* (Princeton: Princeton Univ. Press, 1972).

2. *Biographic Register of the Department of State 1945;* Obituary, *New York Times,* 28 April 1965, p. 45. Murray's affinity for the American Council for Judaism's thesis that American Jews had no interest, and ought not to have any interest, in Palestine was expressed often. Thus: "If the establishment of a Jewish State in Palestine would solve the Jewish question, there might still be some justification for a continuance of Zionist agitation. It is, however, open to grave doubt that the majority of American Jewry has any such belief." The

latter had come to the United States voluntarily to become good American citizens and did not like movements like Zionism, which, said Murray, "involves primary loyalty to a foreign political cause" (Murray to Sumner Welles, 27 November 1942, 867N. 01/11–2342, p. 3).

3. *Biographic Register of the Department of State 1945;* Obituary, *New York Times,* 19 January 1949, p. 27.

4. Information on Murray and Alling collated from interviews with former Departmental postwar planner William Yale, 10 June 1971 and 29 July 1971; former FSO Loy W. Henderson, 28 July 1972; former FSO Gordon Mattison, 31 July 1972; former FSO Evan M. Wilson, 8 August 1972; former FSO Gordon P. Merriam, 23 August 1972; Lt. Col. Harold B. Hoskins, 31 August 1972; Dr. Emmanuel Neumann of the Zionist Organization of America, 21 October 1972. (Note: The views and interpretations expressed here and throughout this and subsequent chapters are my own and do not necessarily reflect those of any of the interviewees, unless so specified.) Information also collated from the memoranda of Murray and Alling and their correspondence with FSOs in the field and with their superiors in the Department, as found mainly in the *FR* series from the late twenties to 1945; and to a lesser degree, from the postwar planning documentation in the Notter and Stettinius papers. Also see Chapters 11–14.

5. Of lesser import, though actively engaged in some of the policy problems of the region, were Foy D. Kohler (Merriam's assistant chief in the new NEA), John D. Jernegan, William L. Parker, and Evan M. Wilson, who in the approximate last two years of the war was the desk officer for Palestine. George V. Allen and Henry Villard, though dealing with northern tier countries and Africa respectively and, as of January 1944, functioning as divisional chiefs of MEA and AFA, also had periodic influence in NEA. When Loy Henderson became director of EA & A, as of April 1945, he became a new principal in matters of the Arab world. For a description of his role and views, see below, under FSO principals.

6. Information on Merriam collated from *Biographic Register of the Department of State 1945;* from interviews with Loy Henderson, 28 July 1972; Evan M. Wilson, 8 August 1972; Gordon P. Merriam, 23 August 1972; and from the wartime memoranda and correspondence of Merriam that appear in the *FR* series.

7. See note 1, Chapter 3.

8. On internal problems, e.g., envy of the very close liaison the British Foreign Service had with the Foreign Office and Colonial Office, see P. Blanchard, CT P-95, 25 January 1944, Notter Papers, Box 114, Folder: "CDA Docs, 95–120"; and P. Jester to NEA, 13 July 1943, 111.23/128. Interviews (4 August 1972 and 7 August 1972) with retired FSOs Ray Hare (formerly stationed in Cairo) and Joseph Satterthwaite (Damascus) also revealed that communication between FSOs and the Department, especially the postwar planning apparatus, left something to be desired.

On Foreign Service efforts to correct its problems and rebut accusations of inefficiencies, poor reporting, discriminatory practices against women, etc., see *Bulletin* 10, 11, and 13 (17 June 1944, 24 June 1944, 17 December 1944, 5 August 1945, and 30 December 1945); and also in-house editorials and articles in wartime issues of the *Foreign Service Journal,* e.g., H. S. Villard's report on sagging FSO morale, *FSJ* 22 (1945): 10–11. Furthermore, the Service was often poorly regarded by the very people it sought to aid. Said one corporation executive, "The American foreign service in the Near and Middle East is understaffed and hopelessly inadequate for the task of helping American exporters and improve their position" [T. L. Gillis (Johnston & Johnston, International), *New York Times*, 7 Feburary 1945, p. 27].

For other relevant studies of the Foreign Service, note J. McCamy and A. Corradini, "People in the State Department and Foreign Service," *American Political Science Review* 48 (1954): 1067–82; Z. S. Steiner, *Present Problems of the Foreign Service* (Princeton: Princeton Univ. Press, 1961); R. L. Brown, *The Personnel System of the United States Foreign Service: Design and Practice* (Ph.D. diss., Harvard Univ., 1967); B. Halpern, "The Making of United States Middle East Policy," in *The Anatomy of Peace in the Middle East* (Conference proceedings of American Academic Association for Peace in the Middle East, New York, 1969), pp. 54 ff.; and W. W. Blanke, *The Foreign Service of the United States* (New York: Praeger, 1969). Also see note 1 above and notes 2, 8, and 9 in Chapter 1.

9. Rank and content of FS posts collated from *Register of the Department of State 1941* and *Foreign Service Lists*, volumes for January 1943, January 1944, and April 1945 (Washington, D.C.: GPO).

Regarding Egypt, in 1943 the Cairo legation included a minister, a consul general, three second and three third secretaries, one commercial, three military and five naval attachés, and three temporary specialists, including one economic analyst and one communications officer. By April 1945, the staff saw its military and naval attachés reduced by three, but enhanced by a second economic analyst, one agricultural attaché, one civil air attaché, one special assistant, and several vice consuls and third secretaries. (These figures, which were augumented in the second half of 1945 and in following years, do not include Department staff detailed to special temporary missions in Egypt, or to the Middle East Supply Center.)

Regarding Saudi Arabia, by the middle of 1944 the Jidda legation had its own resident minister and was no longer dependent on the minister resident in Cairo. By April 1945, besides several third secretaries and attachés, the Jidda post had one permanent economic analyst and one civil air attaché. In that month the Dhahran consulate began its functions.

10. For capital investments and nationals from the U.S., see sections on Departmental prewar policy in Chapters 6 and 13.

11. Also important during the war, though less so in my view, were Lowell Pinkerton, consul general in Jerusalem; James Moose, Jr., chargé and minister in Jidda, also consul in Damascus; and Ray Hare, chargé in Cairo and Jidda. There were other "important" FSOs detailed to NEA and abroad, too, some of whom, like Foy Kohler, Parker Hart, and William Porter, became rather prominent in the Department after the war. Indeed, all these lesser principals had more of a role, if only in terms of making the first drafts of the dispatches signed by their chiefs of mission, than the formal sources give them credit for.

12. Information on Kirk collated from *Biographic Register of the Department of State 1945*; interview with Ray Hare, former chargé under Kirk, 4 August 1972; and the correspondence in 1941–43 between Kirk and the Department, in the *FR* series. For instances of obeisance to Ibn Saud, see Kirk to Hull, *FR* 4 (19 May 1942): 570; and Chapter 12.

13. Information on Wadsworth collated from *Biographic Register 1945*; Obituary, *New York Times*, 6 March 1958, p. 27; interviews with Ray Hare, 4 August 1972, and with former FSOs under Wadsworth in the Levant, Gordon Mattison, 31 July 1972, and (by telephone) Joseph Satterthwaite, 7 August 1972; and the correspondence between Wadsworth and the Department in the *FR* series, much of which is singled out in Chapter 6.

For an illustration of the affection, or "localitis," of Wadsworth regarding the Levant, see his remarks, "Friendship in American-Levant Relations," at a dinner in his honor given at a New York Syro-Lebanese Club, printed in *Bulletin* 13 (9 December 1945): 940–41. On the Department's efforts to periodically restrain him, see Murray to Wadsworth, 15 September 1944, 890E.00/9–1544 OS/D; also Grew to Wadsworth, 11 May 1945, *FR* 8 (1945): 1073.

14. Not to be confused with Dr. Halford L. Hoskins from the Fletcher School of Law and Diplomacy, another Middle East expert and Departmental consultant (e.g., to the Division of Territorial Studies), both in the wartime and postwar periods.

15. In this last instance, Hoskins was a sort of rival to Ibn Saud's senior English adviser, H. St. John B. Philby. Although the evidence is contradictory, Philby had apparently broached the idea of a meeting to Weizmann and to Churchill, who in turn recommended it to Roosevelt and to the Department of State (which, like the Foreign Office, and the Jewish Agency, too, was highly dubious from the start). The basic idea was to arrange a tradeoff between Weizmann and Ibn Saud—Jewish financial assistance in return for Arab non-interference in Palestine, with in addition Britain's grooming of Ibn Saud as a "boss of bosses" in the Arab world.

On the Hoskins-Philby-Ibn Saud affair, see the first section of Chapter 14; also, correspondence of Hoskins, *FR* 4 (July–August 1943): 800–801, 807–10, 811–14; Chaim Weizmann, *Trial and Error* (New York: Harper and Bros., 1949), pp. 427, 432–33; Y. Bauer, *From Diplomacy to Resistance: A History of Jewish Palestine 1939–1945*, pp. 224–27, 250–52; and Philby, *Arabian Jubilee*, pp. 213–17.

Hoskins' report that Ibn Saud treated the idea of a meeting with Weizmann with contempt subsequently puzzled Weizmann and led Philby, who developed a great animus toward Hoskins, to believe that Hoskins, out of maladroitness before Ibn Saud, exaggerated the latter's negativism. Twenty-nine years later, Hoskins related to this interviewer the following account. After ritualistic small talk, Hoskins had asked Ibn Saud if he would see Weizmann. The king said no. Hoskins said that he did not pursue the matter—though he thought that given his financial problems, the king would have been amenable to pressure. But he (Hoskins) did not feel it was appropriate for him to apply that pressure.

This struck me as ironic, in view of Hoskins' outspokenness on all other occasions. I asked if he conveyed the impression that the king would be amenable to pressure, upon his (Hoskins') reporting back to the Department and the President. Hoskins' clear reply was that he did not, but his stated reasons to me were not definite. He said to me that he was not sure at the time of Ibn Saud's amenability; and that his view of the king being amenable was partly a judgment in hindsight. Personally, I think that Philby knew his Ibn Saud better than Hoskins or anyone else in the Department.

16. Information on Hoskins collated from *Biographic Register 1945;* interviews with Loy Henderson, 28 July 1972; Ray Hare, 4 August 1972; Evan Wilson, 8 August 1972; Gordon P. Merriam, 23 August 1972; and Hoskins, 31 August 1972. Also, from Hoskins' correspondence with Roosevelt and the Department, particularly Welles, 1941–45, in the *FR* series, and also in the Notter Papers and Long Papers. References to his regional approach and to his Libyan plan are in Hoskins' two memoranda to Welles, "Suggestions for Appointment of Ambassador-at-large to the Middle East," 8 March 1943, and "Plan for Peace in Near East," 20 March 1943, p. 8, Notter Papers, Box 43, Folder:

"Near East." Also, brief descriptions of Hoskins and other FSOs can be found in Freya Stark, *Dust in the Lion's Paw: Autobiography 1939–1946* (New York: Harcourt, Brace, 1961), pp. 182 ff.

Several more things should be said about Hoskins. Though an Arabist, he was neither an emotional Arabophile nor Zionophobe. As he said in the interview (half-seriously, half-facetiously, I assume), "I hate them both." Nonetheless, he was one of the Department's most assiduous lobbyists among Congressmen and public figures for a pro-Arab line. He did it not only because he believed that it was essential for the U.S. to have the Moslem world on its side, but as well because he was independent, because he always saw himself as a derring-do marine rather than a "civilian bureaucrat." And also, because unlike the deskmen in the Department who shunned anything imprudent, he enjoyed the intrigues and cat-and-mouse games of wartime. Rather than smolder like the rest of the Department because pro-Zionists were lobbying, he played the game, too, and then some.

17. Information on Eddy collated from Obituary, *New York Times,* 5 May 1962, p. 27; interviews with Evan Wilson, 8 August 1972, and Harold Hoskins, 31 August 1972. Also, R. H. Smith, *OSS, The Secret History of America's First Central Intelligence Agency* (New York: Delta, 1972), p. 46; William A. Eddy, *FDR Meets Ibn Saud* (New York: American Friends of the Middle East, Inc., 1954), pp. 42–43, passim; and Eddy's correspondence with the Department in the *FR* series for 1944–1946. Also see Chapters 12 and 14.

18. Theoretically, assistant chief of the old NEA, G. P. Merriam, was the logical successor, but Merriam was not as senior or as "dynamic" as Henderson, and moreover, had a serious deafness which impaired his ability to run conferences.

19. It may be noted that this respect was based on empathy for Weizmann and Wise's "style," and not on their ideological objectives. Both Zionist leaders, being somewhat Anglicized gentlemen of the old school, struck a more responsible chord with very proper gentlemen like Henderson. In contrast, FSO vitriol was typically reserved for "activists"—who were in addition, "ungentlemanly"—like Abba Hillel Silver and David Ben-Gurion; and later, for the so-called Jewish grey eminence at the White House, Truman adviser David Niles. See Chapters 13 and 14 on Department-Zionist relations.

20. While this summary would certainly typify the wartime and postwar views of all Middle East experts in the Department, there are two qualities of Henderson's mind imbedded in this summary not found to the same degree in others. One, Henderson was—as model FSO class-one, "Mr. Foreign Service," etc.—a highly "principled" individual who in the case of Palestine felt to an extraordinary degree that it was "wrong," impracticalities apart, to contemplate a Jewish state in an Arab region. Such a state would run counter to the doxology of the Atlantic Charter and the principles of refugee repatriation and self-determination for native majorities living under European mandates. Two, the fact that the Baltic countries to which Henderson has been emotionally attached were taken over in 1939 by the Soviet Union and the fact that the Department was never able to reverse those annexations made it appear to Henderson—it is my impression—that for the United States to support a Jewish state was playing ethnic favorites and, again, "unfair."

21. Information on Henderson collated from *Biographic Registers of the Department of State;* from interviews with Henderson, 28 July 1972; Gordon Mattison, 31 July 1972; Evan Wilson, 8 August 1972; Gordon Merriam, 23 August 1972; Dr. Emmanuel Neumann, 31 October 1972; from Herbert Feis, *The Birth of Israel: The Tousled Diplomatic Bed* (New York: Norton, 1969),

pp. 45, 61; and from Henderson's correspondence as minister in Baghdad and director of EA & A in the *FR* series, from 1944 on.

On the closeness of Murray and Henderson and the praise and grooming extended by the former to the latter, see Henderson to Murray ("Dear Wallace" letter), 4 November 1944, *FR* 5 (1944): 631–33; and Murray's personal and confidential ("Dear Loy") reply, 4 November 1944, 867N.01/11–1644, in which Murray wrote that Henderson's "telegrams provide us with exactly the ammunition which we needed to drive the point home of Arab anti-Zionism and the danger to America's stake in the Arab world." Also, note Murray's extraordinary praise, in Murray to Stettinius, 7 November 1944, Stettinius Papers, Box 217, Folder: "NEA (Mr. Murray) January 1944—."

For additional examples of Henderson's foreign policy thinking, see his comments in the radio transcription, "Our International Information Policy," *Bulletin* 13 (16 December 1945): 948–53; his "Foreign Policies: Their Formulations and Enforcement," *Bulletin* 15 (29 September 1946): 594–95; and his "American Political and Strategic Interests in Southeastern Europe," *Academy of Political Science Proceedings* 22 (1948): 451–59.

As of the summer of 1972, when he was interviewed, Henderson, then in his eightieth year, was writing his memoirs for publication. Henderson has also been known in these twilight years to be more pro-Israel and anti-Arab than in the 1940s. One reason is his disdain for radical Arab politics and perhaps especially for its brutality, as was instanced when Henderson's old friend Nuri Said was cruelly murdered and impaled by a radical coup in Baghdad, 1958.

22. On the composition, evolution, and interaction of the Territorial and Political subcommittees, see Notter, *Postwar Foreign Policy Preparation,* pp. 92–108, 117–22, passim.

23. On the research aspects of the planning apparatus, see ibid., pp. 151–53, 520, Appendix 22, passim; and notes 15, 16, and 18 in Chapter 1.

24. On the extensiveness of planning, see note 31 in Chapter 1 and the citations in all subsequent chapters relative to Departmental policy in individual countries. On the "objectivity" of the planners, see Acheson's view in note 19 of Chapter 3, and the illuminating admission of William Yale in note 67, Chapter 14.

25. Notter, *Postwar Foreign Policy Preparation,* p. 178.

26. Ireland's publications include *Iraq: A Study in Political Development;* "The Near East and the European War," in *Foreign Policy Reports* 16 (15 March 1940): 2–16; and Ireland, ed., *The Near East: Problems and Prospects.*

Of the Jews in Iraq, Ireland had written in his book on Iraq prior to 1938 that they were "perhaps the most progressive single element in the land" (p. 227). On his lebensraum fixation, see note 17, Chapter 3.

When I tried to speak to Ireland to arrange an interview (Bethesda, Maryland, July 1972), he was still as shrill as he apparently was in the war years. He refused to be interviewed, assuming that I was a "revisionist" historian.

27. Information on Ireland collated from *Biographic Register 1945,* and from interviews with William Yale, 20 August 1971; Loy Henderson, 28 July 1972; Gordon H. Mattison, 31 July 1972; Harry Howard, 3 August 1972; Ray Hare, 4 August 1972; Evan Wilson, 8 August 1972; Gordon P. Merriam, 23 August 1972; and from my abortive conversation with Ireland, 30 July 1972.

Ireland's thesis on Syria and Lebanon can be seen in his "Preliminary Draft: Maintenance of Independent Status for the Lebanon," 4 September 1942, T-62, Notter Papers, Box 300, Folder: "Post-War Problems Studies: Near East." Ireland's views on Arab federation are expressed in the documentation cited in note 16, Chapter 3. For his views on Libya and the Soviet Union, see T-Doc.

209, 8 January 1943, Notter Papers, Box 32, Folder: "T. Docs. 199–210;" H-5a, 20 May 1943, Notter Papers, Box 57, Folder: "H-Pol. Summaries 1–15;" and also his article, "The Near East and the European War," p. 13. Many additional memoranda written by Ireland are found in the Notter Papers and the Yale Papers.

28. Illustrative of this background and spirit of the times was his essay, "Non-Assimilation of Israel," *Atlantic Monthly* 130 (1922): 276–78. Its pseudo-anthropological theme was that the "Jewish" attitude toward women was gross and indelicate compared with the chivalrous "Christian" attitude.

29. Two instances of Professor Yale's historiography are worth singling out. In the course of his interviews, Yale held to the remarkable view that Germany had been historically a happy haven for Jews and that Hitler's intense hatred, supposedly contrary to German tradition, could therefore only be explained by the Jews' having done something awful to arouse his intense ire. That "something" was the creation of the Balfour Declaration of 1917 which, he theorized, made Jewry world wide rally around Britain, in Germany desert the Kaiser en masse, and as such "stab Germany in the back." To Yale, the Declaration therefore was not only a major blunder for the course of Middle Eastern history, but also a direct cause of Jewish suffering and punishment under Hitler.

On Dr. Chaim Weizmann, Yale always felt that he had the real lowdown, that he was no moderate, as many foolishly believed, but was as "ruthless" and "passionate" in his nationalistic zeal as all political Zionists. As Yale has recounted numerous times in his papers, marginalia and interviews, he supposedly remembered "seeing" Weizmann in 1919, privately, in London, bang on a table menacingly with his fist and saying that if Britain did not live up to its promise to the Jews in the Balfour Declaration, then the Jews would bring down the British empire, much as they had toppled the czarist empire! How Yale received such a private performance has never been made clear. In any event, although Yale found out later that the Jews were not really the main factor in bringing down czarism, he remained forever fixated, after this alleged illumination, that Zionism was evil and that there was no such thing as moderate Zionism.

(In going through Yale's papers at Mugar Library, Boston University, I found a fine letter of recommendation that Weizmann had written in the 1930s for Yale when he applied for a Guggenheim Fellowship. Weizmann had known Yale briefly in the period of the Paris Peace Conference, and had responded with delicacy and courtesy when Yale, a nonentity in New Hampshire, was trying to contact big names on his own behalf. When I brought this deed of a man that Yale has ever maligned to Yale's attention, his reaction was a short flush, then a remark that he had forgotten about that letter; but nothing more. Yale did not get the fellowship.)

30. Another reason for his resignation was that, as Yale told me, there were strains in the working relations between Ireland and himself. This, despite their identical views on Zionism and most other issues, despite the fact that Ireland had hired Yale, and despite the fact that both felt, and would continue to feel, intensely bitter toward Presidents Roosevelt and Truman and particularly toward Jewish White House advisers Samuel Rosenman and David Niles. Presumably due to these advisers' efforts at obstructionism and un-American sabotaging, all the postwar planning on the Middle East, especially on Palestine, (in Ireland's words to me) had "no impact and was all in vain."

Nonetheless, there was one topic on which Ireland and Yale did differ, though I have no evidence that it was significant or produced strain between them. The topic was the Soviet Union. Ireland, as indicated, was hostile toward the Soviet Union. Yale minimized Soviet ambition and Soviet potential. In memoranda on other issues which touched on the Soviet Union, he was often complimentary. My impression is that this pro-Soviet attitude was due to Yale's admiration of the Soviet war against Nazism, to his "Beardian"-style anticapitalist orientation, and to the humanitarian and antinationalistic aspects of communist ideology which appealed to him, including his belief that under communism there was no anti-Semitism or Jewish Question and therefore no justification for Jewish separatism.

While I have no evidence that Yale's wartime sympathies towards Russia went beyond this, there is evidence of his "fellow traveler" sympathies in the late 1940s and 1950s. As he told me, he once defended himself by lying to, and by trying to ridicule, the House Un-American Activities Committee. Abetted by zealous anticommunist publisher William Loeb of Manchester, New Hampshire, the committee had investigated him as a "radical professor" preaching the need to admit Communist China into the U.N. and other views then considered subversive.

31. The information on Yale included in this chapter is more copious than on any other middle manager. Obviously, he was not as important as someone like Wallace Murray; but then, Murray left no papers and his surviving wife refused with heat to be interviewed, while Yale has been free with interviews and has left no less than five (!) manuscript collections covering his career. True, his papers are often of inflated value; still, something is better than nothing, presumably, and they do often contain, if not valuable, then "interesting," information. For such reasons—in addition to the fact that Yale was the Department's postwar planner for Palestine (a remarkable choice which is of course a direct reflection on the wartime Department)—Yale has received disproportionate attention.

Information on Yale has been collated from interviews with him, 10 June 1971, 29 July 1971, 25 August 1971, 26 August 1971; with Ireland, briefly, 30 July 1972; from Yale Papers, Mugar Library, Boston University (folios since 1945; marginalia in Yale's book collection on Jews, the Middle East, etc.); from Yale Papers, Houghton Library, Harvard University (mainly originals of his drafts and memoranda, as postwar planner 1942–45; also, correspondence, planning committee minutes, etc.); and from Yale's memoranda on Palestine in the Notter Papers, National Archives. (Information on his Departmental experience in World War I is found in the Yale Papers, Sterling Library, Yale University, the Yale Papers at the National Archives, and in the Oral History Collection, Columbia University. Also, regarding the 1919 period of Yale's career, see Kedourie, *England and the Middle East,* passim; and Manuel, *American-Palestine Relations,* passim.) Yale's published works include several articles and his opus, *The Near East: A Modern History* (Ann Arbor: Univ. of Michigan Press, 1958).

On Yale's prewar memoranda to the Department, see, e.g., Yale to Berle, 12 March 1942 and 23 March 1942, 867.01/1800. For an example of Yale's counterlobbying (trying to block the publication of a pro-Zionist ecological study, Walter Clay Lowdermilk, *Palestine: Its Decay and Restoration,* published as *Palestine, Land of Promise* (New York: Harper & Bros., 1944), see Yale Papers (Harvard), Box 2, Folder 8/H; and Lowdermilk, Transcript, vol. 1, pp. 187–92, Oral History Collection, Columbia University. For his communications with Jewish anti-Zionists, see Yale Papers (Harvard), Box 3, Folder: "Personal Correspondence and Related Matters." On his equation of Zionism with Nazism, see note 17, Chapter 3).

On Jewish immigration, see Yale, "Basic Factors in the Palestine Problem,"

T-309, 20 April 1943, pp. 10–11, Notter Papers, Box 34, Folder: "T Docs. 290–309." On the U.S.S.R. and Jews, see Yale, "Statement of the Palestine Problem: Today's Realities (Part IA, II)," n. d. (probably 1944), p. 1, Yale Papers (Harvard), Box 1, Folder: "7, PSP folder 5." On Transjordan and Saudi Arabia, see Transjordan #2, Yale Papers (Harvard), Box 4, Folder: "Transjordan #2"; Yale and Ireland, "An American Advisor System for the Near East," 12 August 1944, Yale Papers (Harvard), Box 3, Folder: "Am. Policy Folder #1"; also, Chapters 12 and 14. For more details on Yale and the Jewish Question, see Chapters 13 and 14.

32. Instances of the Department's positive response to Arab views and threats are many, as this book makes clear. Instances of the Department's negativism toward American politics and public opinion are also many. See J. Rives Childs' disdain for Roosevelt, and for Hull, too, who supposedly played politics on Palestine to get Jewish support, in Childs, *Foreign Service Farewell*, pp. 104–9, passim. For Hull's own irritation with Rooseveltian politics, see Hull, *Memoirs*, vol. 2, pp. 1536–37, passim. Also, see Breckinridge Long's watchdog efforts to keep Congress and the newspapers out of any Departmental decision on Palestine and oil, notably in February–April 1944, in Long Papers, contents of Box 200, Folder: "Palestine 1944," and Box 201, Folder: 'Petroleum 1944." The Department's tendency to ignore public opinion when possible was confirmed in interview with Merrian, 23 August 1972, and from a letter of 15 October 1971 from H. Schuyler Foster, former Public Opinion Studies officer in the Department.

To all the above, cf. Harry Truman's famous rebuttal: "The difficulty with many career officials in the government is that they regard themselves as the men who really make policy and run the government. They look upon elected officials as just temporary occupants." Truman, *Memoirs* (Garden City, N.Y.: Doubleday, 1956), vol. 2, p. 165.

33. The point, several times made, that Departmental principals (upper-middle-class white Protestant males) shared a remarkable homogeneity and common mindset does not necessarily imply a uniformity of academic or geographic origin. Thus, Paul Alling originally graduated from Trinity College, Loy Henderson from Northwestern University, George Wadsworth from Union College (in electrical engineering!); thus too, Wallace Murray came from Kentucky, G. P. Merrian from New England, Philip Ireland from the Midwest. Still, it may be worth pointing out that most of the principals discussed in this chapter had a private school background, and many were from the South (e.g., Henderson, Murray, also R. Hare, J. R. Childs). Also, on the Department's planning side, there were generally more academic degrees than on the operational side.

II

Policy Toward the Axis, the Soviet Union and the French Sphere of Influence

5

The Axis and the Soviet Union

Whether the Middle East has been perceived by great powers primarily as a means to an end—Europe's southern flank, gateway to India—or as an end in itself—Arab markets, oil—it has been a perennial, predictable stage upon which aspiring dominators of adjacent Europe have played their roles as rivals. In this vein, one reflects on the continuities in the region, linking the nineteenth-century conflict between Victorian England and Czarist Russia; the conflict in the early stages of World War II between Britain and the Axis; and the post-World War II conflict between the "successor" states of Britain and Germany, the United States, and the Soviet Union. Nicolas Spykman's paraphrase of the iron law of British geopolitical thinker Halford MacKinder is apposite in this context: "Who controls the Rimland [mainly, the Middle East] rules Eurasia; who rules Eurasia controls the destinies of the world." For all the continuities and iron laws, however, the Middle East has often been a changeable, indeed quixotic and irrational region, with numerous rises and falls of regimes, alliances, and ideologies.[1]

With these deterministic and nondeterministic thoughts in mind, it may be pertinent to examine, side by side, Axis and Soviet policies and influence through 1945 in the Middle East and to examine also the reactions to them, particularly on the part of American policy makers in the Department of State. In this study I have developed no models for current predictive purposes or for extracting "lessons" from history. But I think the study is useful, and not only for its intrinsic historical interest or for its suggestiveness as to which factors in great-power relations with the

Middle East may be constants and which may be variables. Such a study, after all, has bearing on that larger, ever relevant question—What were the recent origins and motivations behind the United States' assumption of a great-power role in the Middle East?

AXIS INFLUENCE IN THE MIDDLE EAST

In the second half of the 1930s, Axis propaganda and diplomatic offensives and Arab collaboration steadily increased. Receptivity in the Arab world was considerable in light of the psychological appeal to many Moslems of fascism's authoritarianism and romantic-militant nationalism and in light of the fact that Germany was the implacable foe of the Arabs' chief enemies, the British, the French, and the Jews. True, Germany was associated with Italy, which had imperialist ambitions in the Arab world and which was not widely considered a friend of the Arabs. Still, Germany's "virtues" outweighed its vices; moreover, it was considered—rather like America and also the U.S.S.R.—as a faraway, friendly great power without selfish ambitions in the region. Indeed, it is the retrospective view of a number of historians that Germany actually underplayed its hand in the Middle East and that it could have been much more "successful" if its propaganda and military efforts had been even a little greater than they in fact were. Insofar as Germany did have postwar territorial plans outside of Europe and Russia, these related not to the Middle East but toward restoring Germany's pre-1918 African colonies and then expanding them into a "middle colonial African empire."[2]

In any event, the Axis momentum in the Middle East reached its height between the fall of France in June 1940 and the Allied counter-offensives in the Mediterranean theatre toward the end of 1942. After the British victory at El Alamein and the chiefly American Operation TORCH in North Africa, the military threat of the Axis taking over the region was averted, along with a deflation of local pro-Axis emotion. Nonetheless, Axis propaganda continued to sow the winds (stressing hatred of the Jews and the British more than pro-Arab nationalism as such) throughout the war, and significant remnants of Axis influence and ideology outlasted the war. The three countries where Axis wartime influence was strongest were Iraq, Syria, and Egypt.

Iraq's oil development and political status had long been dependent on Britain. Partly for that reason, Iraq led the Arab world in the early 1940s in anti-British fervor. Friendly German relations with the Baghdad government (and also with the Kurdish dissidents in northern Iraq) had previously been established, special diplomatic agents and ambassadors like Dr. and Frau Fritz Grobba were active, and with a precedent of internal coups d'état, Iraq thus had the ingredients for a fifth-column takeover. The latter occurred in April 1941. At that time, the relatively pro-British Hashemite monarchy was overthrown by a conspiratorial coup led by pro-Axis politician Rashid Ali Kilani and four colonels known as the "Golden Square."

However, shortly thereafter, British troops were sent to Iraq from India and later from Palestine and Transjordan on orders of the British War Cabinet and Foreign Office (though such action was not counseled by British commanders in the field). Ostensibly, the purpose was to ensure the security of British military and air bases, pursuant to the general war emergency and the Anglo-Iraqi treaty of alliance of 1932. More basic were the political-diplomatic objectives of restoring the Hashemite regime and pro-British politicians like Nuri Said, restoring as well British prestige with a great show of force, and keeping not only Germany but also Russia out of Iraqi affairs.[3]

Finally, it was the overarching British thesis that taking a strong stand in Iraq would prevent Vichy-controlled Syria, to the west of Iraq, from sliding further into the Axis camp. That possibility in turn would endanger Palestine and the eastern border of Egypt at a time when Egypt's western border with Italian-held Libya was in periodic jeopardy. Similarly, repression of Rashid Ali would presumably prevent dominoes under unsteady British influence to the east of Iraq, namely, Iran and Afghanistan, from falling under either Axis or Soviet influence. The British therefore provoked Rashid Ali into confrontation, then crushed his military "rebellion," which, as intended, resulted in the restoration of a friendly regime and the general restoration of British prestige.[4]

In Syria, anti-French sentiment stimulated Axis influence among segments of the Arab population, while it was anti-British sentiment that built up Axis influence among the French personnel of the Vichy administration. In the case of the Arabs, pro-Axis sentiment was an amalgam of old resentments recently inflamed; a feeling of humiliation, particularly after France's Debacle of June 1940, at being subjected to a defeated and weak nation; and a rather blind admiration of the military strength, foreign policy, and authoritarian and anti-Semitic ideology of Germany. As for the local French authorities, when the Third Republic fell, most sided with the successor Vichy regime rather than with the Free French or other resistance groups. Generally, these authorities stayed in their Levant posts, trying to preserve the integrity of the French empire. However, they were apprehensive over Britain's hostility in Europe toward the Vichy government and felt that perfidious Albion was conspiring to take over the Levant mandate for itself.

Though ostensibly neutral, the Vichy administration in the Levant, under high commissioner General Henry Dentz, veered toward direct collaboration with Germany. Dentz allowed freer rein to both Nazi propaganda and infiltration from November 1940 on. He also placated the Arabs by restoring a measure of self-government in Syria and Lebanon. The denouement arrived when it became apparent to the British that the Germans seemed poised in the Balkans for a strike against the Middle East, that French airfields in Syria were being utilized by German aircraft for bringing war material to Rashid Ali's rebellion in Iraq, and that the Rashid Ali rebellion was igniting a profound anti-Western mood throughout the region. With the Free French, the British coordinated, as it were, these three points on the graph and prepared for action.[5]

But there were some factors which militated against intervention: the low repute of Free French military prowess, and the fact that the Vichy government in Europe wanted German planes removed from Aleppo precisely so as to avoid a pretext for a British invasion. Moreover, some observed that ideologically Germany would not, and logistically it could not, fully assist the Arab cause. To support Arab independence would antagonize Italy and Vichy France, both of which had imperialist claims in the Middle East. Such factors notwithstanding, the British and Free French decided to invade Syria; and in July 1941, they defeated the Vichy "defenders." As in Iraq two months previously, the imminence of Axis military-political control was thwarted by a decisive use of British arms.[6]

In the case of Egypt, anti-British sentiment was also a main reason for popular receptivity to Axis propaganda. In fact, Egypt's receptivity was older—though probably less widespread or politically effective—than that of Iraq or Syria. It went back to the mid-1930s, prior to the Anglo-Egyptian treaty of 1936. This was a period when Britain, concerned with Italian naval interests in the Mediterranean and Red Seas, was increasingly willing to conciliate the Wafd, the most prominent and anti-British political party in Egypt. In general, Egyptian sentiment at that time seemed divided: on the one hand, native pro-fascism grew, as Britain appeared threatened and weakened; yet on the other, awareness of what Italian fascism had wrought in Ethiopia in 1935 made others more eager for a protective relationship with Britain.

After 1939, receptivity to Axis propaganda against "Anglo-Jewish imperialism" and for "Egypt for the Egyptians" reappeared. But ambivalence and divisions of opinion again clouded the will to actually rebel or stage a coup as in Iraq, especially as the British military were stationed in force in Egypt and the Canal Zone. Short of that, however, Egypt resisted and obstructed Britain whenever it could. In September 1939, Egypt was prompted by Britain to break relations with Germany and Italy, but it did not declare war. In April 1940, a time when the Axis was very much on the offensive in western Europe, the out-of-power but still powerful Wafd was pushing for the abrogation of the 1936 Anglo-Egyptian treaty and the evacuation of British troops. (This, despite the fact that both countries had agreed that the treaty would have a minimal twenty-year duration before revisions could be negotiated.) When Italy attacked Egypt from Libya in September 1940, the "Palace" government of King Farouk also showed itself increasingly hostile to the British. It continued to resist Britain's wish that it declare war, having accepted Rome's declarations that the invasion was aimed at Britain, not at Egypt.

Passive toward Italy, the friendly invader-liberator, Egypt was thus ever on the edge of rioting against Britain, the enemy protector-conqueror. But the British succeeded in both beating back the Italian attack and maintaining martial law. In April 1941, when Rommel's German troops crossed into western Egypt, the Egyptian government took no action, despite occasional rhetorical flourishes promising "resistance." Ambivalence again was the rule during these invasions of the western border and the air attacks on the Suez Canal in the early 1940s. "Strangely enough the public was both terrified at the possible coming of the Axis occupation and at the same time pro-Axis in their sympathies."[7]

Axis efforts to woo the Arabs were not limited to Iraq, Syria, and Egypt, and they did not cease after 1942. Nonetheless, Axis objectives in the region, even in the most promising of times, were often less sweeping and portentous than appeared at first sight. First, as ideologues of Aryan imperialism, the Germans often had contempt for the non-Aryan Arabs and had little genuine sympathy for the cause of Arabism. Second, the Eastern and Western fronts were strategically and tactically always more important to Hitler than the Mediterranean. Furthermore, when Operation BARBAROSSA bogged down in December 1941 and when Mussolini was unseated in July 1943, operations in the Middle East— which Hitler originally had wanted to undertake after swiftly dealing with Russia—were too unrealistic to consider. Third, the policy-making organs in Germany were at various stages in the 1930s and 1940s divided as to the degree of Axis activism desirable in the Arab world. Overall, the result was limited interventionism (an ironic counterpart to Secretary Hull's own "active noninterventionism," as detailed in Chapter 3). By and large, the Nazi party apparatus and the Reich's propaganda organs were ardently in favor of interventionism and a large German policy in the region, while the German Foreign Office and the military were more conservative and "noninterventionist."[8]

There were several compelling reasons for the latter position, relative to Italy, Vichy France, and Britain. As noted above, Germany was restrained by consideration of Italian and Vichy interests from full commitment to Arab independence. Such commitment might also alarm other friendly powers, like Franco Spain and non-Arab Turkey and Iran. As for the British presence in the Middle East, it is worth noting that Germany's hostility was significant only in the period from the 1938 Munich crisis to El Alamein, in October 1942. Before this period, German military strength was still forming; and German foreign policy, pre-occupied with *Mitteleuropa,* sought to avoid open provocation of Britain. Germany therefore did not usurp or even challenge British hegemony in the Middle East, and its pro-Arab propaganda was not yet systematic. After this period, however, desertion by Italy and absorption in Russia hobbled Germany's anti-imperialistic, anti-British efforts in the Middle East, except in the realm of propaganda warfare.[9]

POLICIES TOWARD AXIS INFLUENCE

The Department of State's view of Axis influence in the region was hostile, though the actual Departmental response divided along several levels. On one level, there was watchful waiting. FSOs filed reports on rumors, fifth-column activities, Axis diplomatic demarches to Arab states; and NEA drafted memoranda on the difficulty represented by Jewish immigration to Palestine and on like issues, as instanced in Chapter 3.[10]

On another level, the Departments of State and War in 1942 began contingency plans—though they never finished them—in case of Axis success in the Middle East and in case Saudi oil fields lay open to inva-sion. One such plan was to seal and blow up the wells, as the British had already done in the Kirkuk fields of Iraq, thus "denying" them to the enemy. Objections were made by CASOC, but conflict over the plan among company, king, and the Department never became critical, as the Axis military threat to the region aborted. Another contingency plan involved collaboration between the Department and the OSS in estab-lishing an Arab Bureau in Beirut so as to wage "political warfare," mean-ing counter-subversion and counter-propaganda against Axis elements, particularly in Syria and Iraq. This plan was never implemented either.[11]

On a third level, the Department was supportive of Britain's exer-cising its "military responsibility" in the region—not only supportive in the general sense of sending Lend-Lease to Britain and joining the British-founded Middle East Supply Center, in July 1942, but also in the specific sense of tacitly endorsing British military intentions in Iraq and Syria in 1941 and of performing local acts of friendship. For example, the American minister at Baghdad, Paul Knabenshue, though an old-time FSO highly critical of Britain, nonetheless turned the American legation into a refuge for British civilians and deposed Iraqis in danger of their lives during the tumultuous days of the Rashid Ali coup.[12]

Beyond these levels, however, the Department refused to go. In the case of Iraq, any inclination toward some form of American unilateral-ism, even rhetorical, in the period of Rashid Ali was deterred, not only by the generalized noninterventionist climate in America, but also by the Department's realization that the Iraqi situation called for a substantial Western military presence there for the rest of the war. It was an unwritten Departmental law, after as well as before Pearl Harbor made America go to war, that in places like Iraq it would be "better" for Britain to shoulder such "military responsibility" than the United States. The Department felt the same toward Palestine and the Suez Canal. Officially, the Department took this position on the grounds that America was busy elsewhere militarily and that Iraq was a traditional British sphere anyway. Moreover, though Iraq was important to the United States as a transit depot of Lend-Lease to the Soviet Union, it was not as directly vital as Saudi Arabia.

But there was another motive, more cynical about Britain and more selfishly protective of America than was apparent. Basically, the Department neither supplemented nor opposed Britain's military role because that role meant that *Britain* would perform the necessary dirty work of controlling the population; Britain would receive the great measure of pan-Arab abuse and the small measure of praise and profit that such a policing role would produce; and British, not American, soldiers would shed their blood if need be. Still, despite accepting British military responsibility, the Department never ceased trying to reduce Britain's claim of political-economic responsibility in Iraq. To the British, the latter responsibility was a logical quid pro quo for the former responsibility. To the Department, there was no connection between the two; and political-economic responsibility was simply a euphemism for imperialistic privilege.[13]

The case of Syria was similar. Although the Department approved of Britain's invasion of Vichy Syria, it refused Britain's subsequent wish that the United States cut off relations with the collaborationist Vichy regime in France and, as Britain did, recognize the "independence" of Syria and Lebanon. There were broad strategic and intelligence reasons behind the Department's Vichy "gamble," as shall be noted in Chapter 6. Relevant here, however, is that some of the Department's reluctance was due to an anxiety that if independence did not materialize or succeed, the United States might find itself entangled in commitments to the Lebanese and Syrian governments. Furthermore, there existed the fear that too much close association with British policy positions would, in Arab eyes, tarnish America's image as an "independent" and anti-imperialistic power without ulterior motives.[14]

For like reasons, NEA was opposed to fully accepting British martial law repressions in Egypt. To NEA, these were sometimes acts of straightout British imperialistic interference in Egypt's internal political affairs. Though Undersecretary Welles, on at least one occasion, restrained NEA from protesting, in general the Department made its disassociation from British policy clear to Egyptian diplomats.[15]

Basically, it was NEA's assumption, accepted by Hull, that so long as pro-Axis feeling in the Arab world remained passively diffuse (albeit widespread), there was no reason for the United States to express either any overt approval of British interventions or any disapproval towards pro-Axis Arab proponents. One result of this thinking was that Departmental officers were, on the whole, much more critical of the British and French in the presence of Arab leaders than they were critical of pro-Axis Arabs in the presence of the British and French.

This unwillingness to be critical of pro-Axis Arabs was buttressed by the fact that the Department did not really believe the Arab world had pro-Axis segments. This wish not to believe was grounded on the assumptions that Arab-Axis ties were neither strong nor irreversible where they did exist, and that the popularity of Axis propaganda was superficial, due merely to Axis military successes against the British, French, and Jews—not to any basic attractiveness of fascism's authoritarianism and racism.

Hence the Department never actually accepted the documentable fact that with few exceptions (Emir Abdullah of Transjordan, some Maronite politicians in Lebanon), *all* Arab leaders were at times drawn to fascism and hopeful for an Axis humiliation of the West in general, and of the British, French, and Jews in the Middle East in particular. The Department tended to ignore or explain away as ungenuine and circumstantial this pan-Arab hopefulness: thus, when pro-Axis sentiments flared up at the time of the Rashid Ali coup but seemed to die down when the British counteracted, the Department assumed that the fire was permanently out. It did not appreciate that the sentiments largely went underground— to reappear in the future as part of the independent Arab states' attraction to intolerant, authoritarian regimes. Periodically sharing these pro-Axis sentiments were America's "great and good friend" Abdul Azziz Ibn Saud, Britain's similarly good friend Nuri Said of Iraq, also Shukri Kuwatli of Syria, Farouk of Egypt, and future leaders there like Gamal Nasser and Anwar Sadat, not to speak of the more well-known pro-Axis personalities like the Mufti of Jerusalem, Hajj Amin Husseini, and the Iraqi, Rashid Ali Kilani.[16]

SOVIET INFLUENCE IN THE MIDDLE EAST

The Soviet Union's demarches and communist propaganda were known in the Middle East earlier than Germany's counterpart efforts, and because of the outcome of World War II, these would expand and succeed more than Germany's. Yet before the 1950s the Arabs, as a whole, were not demonstrably receptive to Soviet communist activity. The reasons were that the Arabs were more feudal-minded or bourgeois-minded than proletarian-minded; they were still steeped in Islam, which meant that to a large degree, their minds were closed to Russian influence (and *not* that Islam is necessarily antithetical to communism). Some Arabs had heard of Soviet ill-treatment of Moslem subjects. Censorship of communist literature by the mandatory authorities and the mythical connection of Bolshevism with Zionism were additional factors. Furthermore, communist weakness in the region was due to Stalin's relative lack of personal interest in the non-European world beyond Russia's southern borders—though the Comintern, for its part, was consistently and highly active after 1929 in trying to propagandize all levels of Arab society.

Insofar as the Middle East *was* a traditional "great-power" concern to Russia, that concern lay chiefly in the non-Arab parts. Thus Turkey, Iran, and Armenia had always been significant because they were by definition strategic border states, often associated, moreover, with British influence. Palestine was also significant, if less consistently so, because of its Christian holy places, its central location, and its potential—as in the Crimean War of the 1850s or in the second half of the 1940s—for giving Russia a small wedge of influence with which to crack the regional power of France, Britain, or America.[17]

Withal, the Soviet Union increasingly asserted itself directly in the Arab world. It was the first government to recognize Ibn Saud's Hejazi state in 1926; and in 1932 Crown Prince Feisal visited Moscow, meeting Stalin and Molotov and familiarizing himself with aspects of Soviet Moslem life. By the mid-1930s, Moscow was moving "ideologically" toward a popular front phase and regarded figures like Ibn Saud (and the *imam* of Yemen, also recognized by Moscow) not as obscurantist feudal tyrants, but as "objectively progressive" forces of national liberation. Indeed, much as Roosevelt and Churchill came to believe, the Soviets felt that future Arab leadership would logically come from the two main kingdoms of the putative Arab "heartland," Saudi Arabia and Yemen—both of which, in addition, straddled the strategic Red Sea gateway to the Indian Ocean.[18]

In this period the Soviet Union was interested in piercing the British-French curtain in the region for the added purpose of checking the growing German influence there, notably in Iraq, Iran, and Turkey. Subsequently, however, in the period between the Molotov-Ribbentrop Pact of August 1939 and the surprise German invasion of Russia in June 1941, Soviet policy veered toward appeasing Germany while still maintaining its older position against British imperialism. Both motives were in operation when the Soviet Union praised the "revolutionary act" of Rashid Ali's coup in Iraq in 1941 and when, concurrently, it expressed the view that the anti-British Wafd party in Egypt was insufficiently anti-British.

With respect to the Pact itself and those clauses in it which carved out postwar Soviet and Axis spheres of influence, it has sometimes been regarded as significant that the Soviet Union was allotted not only a sphere in Eastern Europe but also one in the direction of the Persian Gulf (Turkey, Iran, and perhaps Iraq). However, it should be noted that this allotment was *not* a symptom of Soviet expansionism in the Middle East. In order to distract the Soviets from their concern that German troops were stationed in Finland and Rumania, Germany had tried to lure the Soviet Union into pipe dreams of controlling the Persian Gulf. When Soviet Foreign Minister Vyacheslav Molotov realized that Germany would not withdraw the troops under question, he nonetheless signed the Pact, with its German-initiated references to the Persian Gulf, in order to get as much out of the agreement with Germany as possible.[19]

However, after June 1941, the Soviet Union changed direction. Hostile to Germany and all its associates, it now contended that Rashid Ali was a fascist hireling and that the Wafd was too defeatist and insufficiently pro-Allies. One may note that in the cases of Iraq and Egypt, the U.S.S.R. was more overtly anti-British before June, and more anti-fascist *and* pro-British in the immediate months after June than was the United States.

Still, June 1941 did not actually mark a full diplomatic revolution. Even in the earlier period of active Moscow-Berlin rapprochement, the Soviet Union was displeased when Arab nationalists made *their* rapprochement towards Berlin and Rome. For this reason, the Mufti of Jerusalem, whose leadership of the Palestinian Arabs and religious Moslems generally had long been approved by the Soviet Union, was viewed negatively by late 1938 and for the duration of the war (though after World War II the Mufti's extraordinary collaboration with the Nazis would be forgotten and he would again be supported by Moscow.[20]

Concurrent with their disapproval of the Mufti, the Soviets intensified their anti-Zionism. (There was no automatic see-saw diplomacy in Moscow towards Arabs and Jews as there was in London.) Generally, in the period between 1933 and 1939, the Soviet regime tended to see a connection between Nazism and Zionism on the basis of their alleged reactionary racism and on the basis that Hitler Germany was "stimulating" German Jews to emigrate to Palestine. Zionism was also condemned as pro-British and, after 1939, it was condemned for warmongering. Soviet-Palestine relations were further complicated by the fact that there was a large, latently pro-Zionist Jewish population in the U.S.S.R. and by the fact that the subjective, personal conflict was long and deep between Zionist ideologues and Soviet ideologues. (A number of the latter were Jewish-born Bolsheviks who intensely hated Judaism as reactionary clericalism and Zionism as a form of bourgeois capitalism.)

Thus anti-Zionism was as much a domestic-policy issue as a foreign-policy issue. It was largely to fight the domestic appeal of Zionism in Eastern Europe, on grounds of being anti-Soviet, that Soviet propaganda drastically down played Nazi anti-Semitism and harped on so-called Zionist-Nazi collaboration. In fact, the Soviet government hid the news of Nazi persecutions to such a degree that when the Nazis invaded in June 1941, many Soviet Jews did not flee.[21]

For all that, the communist party in Jewish Palestine—along with those in the (substantially Christian) Levant states—was numerically the largest in the Arab Middle East. Indeed, although Soviet foreign policy, like America's, basically favored the nationalist leadership of the Sunni Arab majority—the side presumably with the biggest battalions, and markets— communist ideology was typically most attractive to non-Sunni minorities. Hence the phenomenon in non-Sunni-Arab enclaves and strata of energetic communist parties—though with scant influence either locally or on Stalin and his policy makers.[22]

By 1943, when the Red Army was beginning its counter-offensive, Soviet policy also took something of a diplomatic offensive in the Middle East. Diplomatic ties were resumed with Cairo in August, and vice foreign commissar Ivan Maisky toured the region and held friendly talks with Arab leaders. The U.S.S.R. resumed its propaganda against British imperialism and its solicitude for Arab independence. In the period between July and September 1944, unqualified diplomatic recognition was extended to Syria, Lebanon, and Iraq, in that order. In January 1945, the Soviet Union was reported to be setting up a special region-wide ministry, resident at Teheran, similar to Britain's region-wide ministry, resident at Cairo. The U.S.S.R. also began an assiduous cultivation of Moslem and Orthodox Christian leaders in the Middle East and promoted ties with their counterparts in the Soviet Union. On another level of propaganda, the image in the Arab world of the Soviet Union as a faraway but friendly great military power supplanted, to some degree, the like image of formerly invincible Nazi Germany and also competed, to some degree, with the like image of the United States.[23]

As for Palestine in the second half of the war, there were indications that, despite the Kremlin's visceral anti-Zionism, despite the quantitative insignificance of Palestinian Jewry, and despite the demarches Soviet diplomats made to Arab capitals, the Palestinian Jewish community of approximately one-half million was not looked upon with actual enmity. From time to time, the Soviet media would even lapse into half-friendly praise of Palestinian Jewry's socialism or anti-fascist military efforts; contacts would be made between "progressives" on both sides; and officials like Maisky would make a friendly tour of Jewish agricultural settlements.

Insofar as such Soviet nonenmity was a policy, rather than a temporary absence of policy, it can in part be attributed to several pragmatic considerations. To cover themselves in case their pro-Sunni-Arab-majority policy failed due to its being preempted by Britain and/or America, the

Russians considered it important to have backup pro-Soviet support among non-Sunni minorities, such as the Jews, Armenians (including Jews and Armenians in their respective diasporas), Kurds, and Orthodox Christian Arabs. Indeed, to create fissures in the British empire and possibly to gain actual footholds in the region, it was always necessary to be prepared to befriend those opposed to British policy, even if the anti-British elements were as ideologically impure and diverse as the Zionists or the Wahhabi monarchy of Saudi Arabia.[24]

Region-wide probes and pressures accumulated during 1945. Thus the Soviet Union expressed the desire—though not in an insistent or belligerent fashion during diplomatic exchanges—to join Britain and America in determining the future dispositions of Tangier, Tripolitania, and northern Iran. Ostensibly, its grounds were "legalistic"—that the U.S.S.R., as both a great power and regional state, had a legitimate interest in the entire Mediterranean area. The State Department and the British Foreign Office did not as a rule welcome Soviet interest and, for all their own competition in the region, closed ranks. As shall be seen, they did their best diplomatically to evade and cold-shoulder Soviet "intrusions." In sum, by mid-1945, the Soviet Union's influence and interest in the Middle East were clearly growing—but were clearly still slight, compared to those of either Britain or America.

POLICIES TOWARD SOVIET INFLUENCE

Up to early 1944 there was hardly any formally articulated Departmental policy addressed to the issue of influence, real and potential, of either the communist ideology or the Soviet government in the Middle East. American diplomatic papers on the topic are largely blank, first and foremost because neither influence was yet serious or even discernible. A second reason was because in the spirit of keeping the region restricted to the competition and cooperation of two powers only (Britain and America), it was understood by both that it was Britain's military and intelligence-gathering responsibility to keep prospective interlopers, like the Axis or the U.S.S.R., at bay. A third reason was because anxious as the word "communism" might inwardly make the men of the Department, it was the outward policy of the Department to be "unflappable" and accordingly to say as little as possible about the Middle East to Soviet diplomats—lest Soviet obstructionism increase or appetites be whetted. True, there were times when the Department's outward tactics were the opposite—in the Levant and Palestine, as will be noted. But usually the norm was the less broached the better. To that extent, then, the diplomatic record's silence was "golden," and deliberate.

Even so, the first trickle of stated concern in the Department came in early 1943, within discussions by planning subcommittees of postwar Libya and the eastern Mediterranean generally. It was theorized that the U.S.S.R. might prove to be a threat to the Dardenelles and the Suez Canal. Beyond that, however, the planners did not go, except tacitly to conclude that Britain should not be expected to give up its rights of controlling the Canal; nor could Russia be expected to give up its ambitions of having rights of untrammeled merchant and naval passage, and of fortification, in the Turkish straits.[25]

It was only by the spring of 1944 that Soviet silence, and the Department's let-sleeping-dogs-lie approach, began to fade. Concern was expressed that the Soviet-recognized Free French under Charles DeGaulle, in order to resist Arab, British, and American efforts to terminate the French mandate in Syria and Lebanon, would make friendly gestures to Moscow and seek to split the working British-American-Russian alliance. However, the concern was never critical, as it was presumed that the Soviet Union would not endorse France's "imperialistic" designs in the Levant. Indeed, Departmental policy later in the year "welcomed" the Soviet Union's increasing interest in Syrian and Lebanese independence. It was believed that mutual anti-imperialism would put Moscow and Washington on the same side of the barricades against the French. That position in turn stood to enhance Soviet-American cooperation on other problems, such as the Polish question, where, because of potentially acrimonious deadlock, mutual good will was counted valuable.[26]

Still, the Department did not want to be upstaged or embarrassed by Soviet demarches with the Levant. Thus, while there were other factors involved, the main reason the Department finally recognized, on 19 September 1944, the independence from France of the Syrian and Lebanese republics was to prevent just such upstaging by the U.S.S.R. Shortly before (21 July–3 August), Moscow had recognized "without reservations" and had established diplomatic relations with Damascus and Beirut. Further, on September 15, the Department was informed that President Kuwatli of Syria was openly appealing not only to Churchill and Roosevelt to help oust the French, but to Stalin, too.[27]

To be sure, the race to recognize was over short-run prestige and did not reflect any serious fear on the part of the Department that it would in the long run be displaced or undermined by Soviet communist infiltration. At this juncture, the Department felt certain that America's chances for influence in the Arab world were overall much better than Russia's, despite the fact that the Department *did* accept as a general proposition that mutual Soviet-Arab interests would probably increase. This increase would be as a result of Soviet wartime successes and traditional interests in the Mediterranean and as a result of the Arabs' residue of anti-Westernism. It was also anticipated that the Arabs would search for friendly great powers and, to maximize their momentum, would try to play one power against the other.

The Department, however, was confident it could handle the situations as they might arise. In a similar spirit, though it kept abreast of the local activities and propaganda of the Middle East's communist parties, it saw no reasons to become seriously concerned.[28]

More portentous than the Department's attitude toward the Soviet-Levant connection was its attitude towards the connection between the U.S.S.R. and Middle Eastern oil. In April 1944, the Department's oil policy crystalized. That policy endorsed expanding the region's oil production, and America's role therein, for postwar marketing worldwide; simultaneously the Department would seek to confine Latin American postwar production to United States producers and consumer and military markets in the United States. Among the major objectives were (1) the demotion of Britain's role from senior partnership in developing and controlling Middle Eastern oil to junior partnership with the United States; and (2) together with Britain, the prevention of a postwar scramble for Middle Eastern oil, a scramble which would predictably include the U.S.S.R.[29]

By the autumn of 1944 enough signals of Soviet interest, real and potential, in the Middle East had accumulated—as did signals of Arab interest in promoting Soviet interest—that the Department finally felt required to articulate an overall policy position, with Russia clearly in mind. Another motive was that by the autumn the planning apparatus was winding up its affairs, prior to Hull's resignation (late November).

The Department's position, in essence, was a reaffirmation of the Atlantic Charter, with the customary emphasis on the economic open door and political self-determination for native majorities as the two best avenues to end the "ferment" in the Arab Middle East (and also, Eastern Europe). Strict adherence was regarded as the best way to assert American foreign policy "independence" from London and Moscow. Implementation of the Charter would also counter British ideological conservatism and British economic control of the region. Implementation would at the same time presumably buttress Britain's waning economic power in the region and strengthen the "Western" or Anglo-American economic position. A final presumption was that implementation would head off the possible attractiveness of communist propaganda and also the temptation to the U.S.S.R. to take advantage of British weakness. In sum, the Department's position of November 1944, in self-conscious pursuit of rugged independence and gradual postwar reform American-style, established anew the direction which American foreign policy would take at the conferences at Malta, Yalta, San Francisco, and Potsdam, not to speak of subsequent meetings.[30]

Long-term projections notwithstanding, Departmental short-run policies toward Soviet probes in the Middle East, as of late 1944 and through 1945, related chiefly to three areas (the Levant states, Palestine, and Saudi Arabia) and two issues (oil and postwar trusteeships). In all cases there were Departmental forebodings, with the result that the Department's initial reaction was to try to think of ways to keep the Russian bear away from the honey.[31]

That reaction changed, however, with respect to the Levant states and Palestine. Though it remained anxious, the Department adopted the tactic that, under certain conditions, if one cannot or will not beat the opposition, one ought to join it.

In Syria and Lebanon, therefore, once Soviet diplomatic demarches were made, they were, as noted, "welcomed" and capitalized on by the Department, with an eye to reinforcing pressure on the French to withdraw. In the case of Palestine, the Department hardly waited for overt Soviet expressions of interest. Indeed, the Department both anticipated *and* to a degree solicited Soviet expressions of interest—once it had become clear that Soviet interest in the Middle East as a whole was not a temporary affair, and once it had become clear that Stalin was not only an anti-Zionist in theory, but more to the point, was also opposed to the creation of a Jewish state.[32]

The purpose of NEA's special interest in the Soviet position on Palestine was to initiate a policy of "consultation" and cooperation with the U.S.S.R. on Palestine. The object was not to oust the British—the way America and Russia each wanted to oust the French from the Levant. Rather, NEA's object was to use Stalin's negativism as reinforcement to the Department's and the British Foreign Office's own negativism towards political Zionism. Conversely, Stalin's position might strengthen "progressives" and "moderates" in both the Palestinian Jewish and Arab communities. With Jewish and Arab "extremists" having no postwar great power to turn to, and with the moderates thus strengthened, the eventual result might be a non-Zionist binational Palestinian state, the State Department's own preferred postwar "solution" to the Palestine imbroglio.

As in the case of the Levant, the Department also saw advantage in a policy of consultation on Palestine for wider purposes. It wished to head off Russia's upstaging America as the more pro-Arab great power; and it apparently wished to reduce all unnecessary points of friction between the two allies so as to maintain cooperation into the closing months of the war and beyond, too, in the projected framework of the United Nations Security Council.[33]

However, while Roosevelt did raise the Palestine issue at Yalta with Stalin, and Truman did the same at Potsdam, the discussions, from all the evidence, seem to have been fragmentary, and their conclusions are in dispute. In part, the failure to co-opt Russia was the Department's own doing. Hull's successor, Edward Stettinius, Jr., did not wish to pester the President further on Palestine and did not send NEA's proposal to solicit Soviet interest to Roosevelt who, in any case, wanted to conduct his own diplomacy when he met with Stalin. Moreover, the Department, NEA included, seemed to lack full confidence in the wisdom of the proposal; it feared public reactions; and it was sometimes tired enough to believe that, even if it did stick its neck out, the effort would be futile, as the Palestine question could only be resolved as a political question, and on the Presidential, not Departmental, level. It therefore did not push for Russian-American-British solidarity on Palestine with its customary drive. Basic British reluctance to approve of even limited consultations on Palestine with the U.S.S.R. also served to blunt NEA's will.[34]

However, with respect to Saudi Arabia and oil generally, the Department's tacit rule of nonconsultation with the Soviet Union was fully adhered to. In the crisp words of the Department's Briefing Book for the Yalta conference: "Soviet Russia has no direct interest in Saudi Arabia. It is considered, therefore, that it would not be either appropriate or desirable to discuss Saudi Arabia during the forthcoming tripartite conversations." The self-assurance of this pronouncement was reinforced by the fact that Ibn Saud, so dependent on British and American funds, seemed unalterably on the West's side. Furthermore, he seemed the most zealously anti-communist Arab leader of all (which, however, did not mean, as the Department was wont to believe, that he was necessarily a Russophobe or a pro-Western ideologue).

It should be further noted that if Russia went unconsulted, the Department similarly avoided taking Britain into basic consultations over Saudi Arabia. This was demonstrated by the surprise and vagueness with which Roosevelt broached to both Churchill and Stalin, at the end of the Yalta Conference, his Departmentally planned and imminent meeting at the Suez Canal with Ibn Saud. However, on Middle Eastern oil matters unrelated to Saudi Arabia, the Department did try (unsuccessfully), from 1944 on to forge a formal Anglo-American accord and "partnership" against the possible encroachments of the U.S.S.R. and other European nations.[35]

Held at arm's length by either American or British containment in most of the eastern Mediterranean and the Arabian peninsula (before that word, containment, became the Department's postwar policy—a case therefore of the deed preceding the concept), the Soviet Union, in the post-Yalta months of 1945, began to push for influence in the Levant states. It also expressed interest, apparently for the first time, in the western Mediterranean (Libya, Tangier, also the Dodecanese Islands and Italy). In essence, the U.S.S.R. wanted DeGaulle out of the Levant, Franco out of Tangier, and a role in Libya's trusteeship now that Italian control was void in Libya. Met, however, with Anglo-American evasion and unresponsiveness, and given the fact that American and British, not Russian, troops prevailed in the Mediterranean theatre, the U.S.S.R. again shifted tactics. It tried to undermine both the rules of the game and the Anglo-American front by, for example, urging open discussion at the San Francisco Conference of the entire question of postwar mandates and dependencies. A similar sequence of stratagems was apparent with respect to Soviet interest in the Dardenelles. At the Potsdam Conference in July Stalin pushed for greater Soviet naval control in the Dardenelles. When the Anglo-American reply proved evasive, Stalin riposted that if Russia could not get the same hegemony over the Straits that Britain had over the Suez Canal and the United States had over the Panama Canal, then all three waterways should be demilitarized and internationalized.[36]

CONCLUSIONS

The fact is, however, the Soviet Union was unable in 1945, and for about a decade following that date, to achieve either its specific desire for footholds or its general desire to erode the Anglo-American front in the Middle East. While the weakness of Soviet naval strength in the region was a key factor, as was the U.S.S.R.'s comparative concentration on Turkey and Iran rather than on the Arab countries, "credit" must also be given to the State Department for its talents in the years 1944–45. Without seriously alienating the U.S.S.R., the Department side-stepped and postponed Soviet efforts to be admitted as trustee and regional power in the Mediterranean, neutralized Soviet interest in Syria, Lebanon, and Palestine, kept the U.S.S.R. away from the Persian Gulf, had more skill and influence in dealing with Arab leadership than had Soviet diplomats, and matched Moscow in the anti-imperialist, pro-nationalist propaganda war. Furthermore—and without seriously alienating Britain—the Department increasingly weakened Britain's ability to act unilaterally, yet made Britain a junior partner in a solid-appearing Anglo-American regional front designed to contain Soviet, French, or any other power's penetration. For all the belittling stereotypes of America winning the war but losing the peace, due to presumed diplomatic innocence before Old World schemers, the reality was that the Department's skill at the diplomatic balancing game was second to none.

NOTES

1. On continuities, see Bernard Lewis, "Russia in the Middle East: Reflections on Some Historical Parallels," *Roundtable* (London: 1970), vol. 60, pp.

257–63. The quotation is from John W. Spanier, *American Foreign Policy Since World War II* (New York: Praeger, 1968), p. 3.

2. On Arab receptivity to Nazi Germany, see "Assets of Axis Propaganda in the Moslem World," OSS Report, R & A #508, 21 November 1941, in Department of State files. On the wider topic of the attractiveness of authoritarian and military leadership in the Arab world, there exists a substantial body of historical and theoretical literature. See, e.g., Majid Khadduri, "The Role of the Military in Middle East Politics," *American Political Science Review* 47 (1953): 511–24; Sir John Glubb, "The Role of the Army in the Traditional Arab State," *Journal of International Affairs* 19 (1965): 8–15; and note 17 below.

On Germany's "circumspection" in the Arab world, see Howard M. Sachar, *Europe Leaves the Middle East, 1936–1954* (New York: Knopf, 1972), pp. 47 ff.; Circular of the Foreign Ministry (Berlin), 20 August 1940, in R. E. Herzstein, ed., *Adolf Hitler and the Third Reich* (Boston: Houghton Mifflin, 1971), pp. 213–14; and note 5 below. On Germany's postwar plans in Africa, see James V. Compton, *The Swastika and the Eagle* (Boston: Houghton Mifflin, 1967), p. 257.

3. The Soviet Union, to Britain's chagrin, had recognized and appointed an ambassador to the Rashid Ali government. However, Stalin's purpose may have been less to embarrass Britain than to appease Hitler. Russia's situation was precarious vis-à-vis Germany, and Stalin had in this period tried to appease Hitler by "derecognizing" the Norwegian, Greek, and Belgian governments-in-exile, based in London.

4. On the Rashid Ali coup and British strategy, see Lenczowski *The Middle East in World Affairs*, p. 247; Kimche, *The Second Arab Awakening*, pp. 147–53; Llewellyn Woodward, *British Foreign Policy in the Second World War* (London: Her Majesty's Government Stationery Office, 1970), vol. 1, pp. 577 ff.; *Britannica Book of the Year Omnibus for 1938–39–40–41–42;* and Anthony Eden, *The Memoirs of Anthony Eden, Earl of Avon: The Reckoning* (Boston: Houghton Mifflin, 1965), vol. 3, pp. 28, 308–14. Note, too, Franz van Papen, *Memoirs* (New York: Dutton, 1953, translated from German), p. 476. Rashid Ali's treaty arrangements with the Axis, not merely his profascism, are shown in E. Kedourie, "Pan Arabism and British Policy," pp. 107–8, in W. Laqueur, ed., *The Middle East in Transition* (New York: Praeger, 1958). A recent monograph tries to be the most comprehensive of all: Geoffrey Warner, *Iraq and Syria 1941* (London: David Poynter, 1974), passim. Also, see Chapter 9.

5. Actually, the Axis in the Balkans was but securing its right flank preparatory to attacking the U.S.S.R. See, e.g., D. A. Rustow, "Foreign Policy of the Turkish Republic," in R. C. Macridis, ed., *Foreign Policy in World Politics* (Englewood Cliffs, N.J.: Prentice Hall, 1958 edition), pp. 303 ff.; and George Kirk, *The Middle East in the War: Survey of International Affairs 1939–1946* (London: Oxford Univ. Press, 1952), p. 20, n. 1.

6. On the British-Vichy French-Arab tangle in the Levant, see Lenczowski, *The Middle East in World Affairs*, pp. 275–76; Woodward, *British Foreign Policy*, pp. 567, 580–81; Albert Hourani, *Syria and Lebanon: A Political Essay* (London: Oxford Univ. Press, 1946), pp. 233–46; "Henricus," "Patterns of Power in the Arab Middle East," *Political Quarterly* 17 (1946): 93–112; and Eden, *Memoirs*, pp. 283–88. Also, Chapter 6.

7. On Egypt, the Axis, and the British, see Michael Howard, "The Mediterranean in British Strategy in the Second World War," in Howard, *Studies in War and Peace* (New York: Viking, 1959), pp. 122–40; Monroe, *Britain's*

Moment, pp. 89 ff.; Louis E. Frechtling, "War in the Eastern Mediterranean," *Foreign Policy Reports* 16 (1 February 1941): 271–80; H. P. Whidden, Jr. "Rommel's Drive Precipitates Allied Military Crisis," *Foreign Policy Bulletin* 21 (3 July 1942): 3. The quotation is from Vatikiotis, *Modern History of Egypt,* p. 351. Also, see Chapter 10.

8. The most thorough examination of Axis strategy and problems in the Middle East and of the Arab-Axis tie, enormously researched and based largely on Nazi documents, is Lukasz Hirszowicz, *The Third Reich and the Arab East* (London: Routledge & Kegan Paul, 1966, translated from Polish). On conflicts among German foreign policy makers, see Gordon A. Craig, "The German Foreign Office from Neurath to Ribbentrop," in G. Craig and F. Gilbert, ed., *The Diplomats 1919–1939* (New York: Atheneum, 1968), vol. 1, pp. 406–36; R. Melka, "Nazi Germany and the Palestine Question," *Middle Eastern Studies* 5 (1969): 221–33; and David Yisraeli, "The Third Reich and Palestine," *Middle Eastern Studies* 7 (1971): 343–54. A famous account of Axis inroads in the Middle East, now very dated but interesting for its projections and anxious tone, is Robert L. Baker, *Oil, Blood and Sand* (New York: Appleton-Century, 1942).

9. Next to Hirszowicz, an excellent source on inter-Axis and intra-Axis policy making on the Middle East is Sachar, *Europe Leaves the Middle East,* pp. 44–50, passim (on Germany); pp. 109–18; passim (on Vichy France); and pp. 118–25, passim (on Italy). Also, on German-Italian policy, see H. Stuart Hughes, *The United States and Italy* (New York: Norton, 1968), pp. 107–9; and F. Gilbert, "Ciano and His Ambassadors," in Craig and Gilbert, *The Diplomats,* pp. 512–36. On the tangled Germany-Vichy relations, see William Langer, *Our Vichy Gamble* (New York: Norton, 1966, originally published 1947), pp. 148, 160; and Sumner Welles, "The Decision to Recognize the Vichy Government," in Welles, *Seven Decisions,* Chapter 2. On German-Spanish relations, see Richard Herr, *Spain* (Englewood Cliffs, N.J.: Prentice-Hall, 1971), pp. 228–31. On German-British relations with respect to the Middle East, see Kimche, *The Second Arab Awakening,* pp. 185–87; and Hirszowicz, *The Third Reich and the Arab East,* pp. 314, passim.

On German propaganda, it is worth noting that even at its wartime height most of it was aimed, in quantitative terms, not toward the Middle East but toward America, Britain, Europe, East Asia, and Russia. See Chief of Propaganda Mengele's Directive No. 27, originally dated 12 May 1943, reprinted in *Bulletin* 141 (3 March 1946): 311 ff. For illustrations of German propaganda policy in the Middle East, see "Adolf Hitler and the 'Third World': Documents Relating to the Arab World and India," in Herzstein, ed., *Hitler and the Third Reich,* pp. 211–21; Eliahu Ben-Horin, *The Middle East: Crossroads of History* (New York: Norton, 1943), pp. 164–74; and "Sample Axis Broadcasts in Arabic to the Near East," 28 July 1942, F.W. 867N.01/8124/5 PS/LBC.

10. See notes 12 and 13 in Chapter 3; also, on Iraq, P. Knabenshue to Hull, 10 April 1941, *FR* 3 (1941): 498; and British Foreign Office telegram, 17 April 1941, *FR* 3 (1941): 501. On Syria, Hull to ambassador in Vichy, W. Leahy, 14 May 1941, *FR* 3 (1941): 709–10. On Egypt, Murray to Welles, 5 February 1942, *FR* 4 (1942): 68–69.

11. On the possibility of denying Saudi oil wells, see *FR* 4 (1942): 576–85. On the idea of an Arab Bureau, see Assistant Secretary Berle to Roosevelt, 13 July 1942, in Hopkins Papers, Official File 3500: Arabia.

12. On the activities of the American legation in Baghdad, see *FR* 4 (1941): 486 ff.; and William J. Porter, "The Ides of May—Baghdad, 1941," in *Foreign Service Journal* 49 (June 1972): 23 ff.

13. For instances of the Department's low-key, though consistent, efforts to reduce Britain's preeminence, see Hull to consul Farrell, 14 September 1942, *FR* 4 (1942): 351; W. Murray, Memorandum, 26 January 1942, 890G.00/ 613.3; and Department of State Aide-Memoire to Iraqi Legation, 9 August 1943, *FR* 4 (1943): 643–44.

14. On the Department's reluctance to coordinate with Britain a policy of recognition of Levant independence, see *FR* 3 (1941): 785 ff.; also Welles, Memorandum, 23 March 1942, and Engert to Hull, 1 May 1942, p. 595, both in *FR* 4 (1932). Also, see Chapter 6.

15. See the exchanges between Murray and Welles, 5 February 1942, *FR* 4 (1942): 69–71, and text, Chapter 10.

16. On the Department's kid-glove approach toward native Arab leadership in Iraq, Syria, and Egypt, see Hull to Knabenshue, 7 April 1941, *FR* 3 (1941): 496; Departmental press release of 29 November 1941, *FR* 3 (1941): 807–8; and memoranda by Murray, 10 July 1942 and 14 July 1942, *FR* 4 (1942): 24–25. On the "abnormal" pro-Ally alignment of the Maronites and Abdullah, see Wadsworth (Beirut) to Hull, 20 November 1942, *FR* 4 (1942): 668; and Graves, ed., *Memoirs of King Abdullah*, pp. 240–42.

Illustration of the positive connections with the Axis of specific Arab leaders is evidenced in Hirszowicz, *The Third Reich and the Arab East*, on Ibn Saud (pp. 47–50, 59–61, 313), on Kuwatli (pp. 184, passim), on Egyptian leadership (pp. 232 ff.), and on the Mufti and Rashid Ali extensively throughout the book. On Ibn Saud again, note Melka, "Nazi Germany," pp. 225–26. On Nuri Said, see Majid Khadduri, "General Nuri's Flirtations with the Axis Powers," *Middle East Journal* 16 (1962): 328–36; and Kimche, *The Second Arab Awakening*, pp. 145–46. On Iraq in general, note L. Henderson's report, 24 January 1945, 890G.00/1–245. On Egypt, see Eliezer Be'eri, *Arab Officers in Arab Politics and Society* (New York: Praeger, 1970), Chapter 2; and Anwar Sadat, *Revolt on the Nile* (New York: John Day, 1957), pp. 38–39, passim.

Note, too, Saul Friedman, "Arab Complicity in the Holocaust," *Jewish Frontier* 42 (1975): 9–17; Record of Conversation (Hitler and the Mufti), 30 November 1941, in W. Z. Laqueur, ed., *The Israel-Arab Reader* (New York: Bantam, 1969), document 20; R. Melka, *The Axis and the Arab Middle East 1930–1945* (Ph.D. diss., Univ. of Minnesota, 1966). On the record of anti-Jewish disabilities in Arab lands, see Jewish Agency, *The Jewish Case before the Anglo-American Committee of Inquiry on Palestine* (Jerusalem: Jewish Agency, 1947); and on Iraq especially, H. J. Cohen, *The Jews of the Middle East*, pp. 26–32. On the attractiveness of authoritarian ideology, see note 2 above.

17. The most useful sources on Russia's traditional policies in the Middle East are Walter Z. Laqueur, *The Soviet Union and the Middle East* (New York: Praeger, 1959); John C. Campbell, "Soviet Union and the Middle East," *Russian Review* 29 (1970): 143–53, 247–61; Lewis, "Russia in the Middle East" and "The Middle East in International Affairs" (in Lewis, *The Middle East and the West*, pp. 115–41); L. I. Strakhovsky, "The Nature of Soviet Propaganda in the Near East," in R. Frye, ed., *The Near East and the Great Powers*, pp. 65–69; and Kirk, *A Short History of the Middle East*, Chapter 9, passim.

On communism in the Middle East, the literature by now is considerable. See, e.g., Laqueur, *Communism and Nationalism in the Middle East* (New York: Praeger, 1956) and essays by W. Z. Laqueur, A. V. Sherman, N. A. Faris, and B. Lewis, in Laqueur, ed., *The Middle East in Transition*.

18. Gerald deGaury, *Feisal, King of Saudi Arabia*, pp. 74–75; and Laqueur, *The Soviet Union and the Middle East*, p. 55. Also see Chapter 11.

19. On shifting Soviet ideological analyses, see Laqueur, *The Soviet Union and the Middle East*, pp. 16, 20, 38, 66, 68; and Vernon Aspaturian, "Soviet Foreign Policy," in R. C. Macridis, ed., *Foreign Policy in World Politics* (1972 edition), pp. 226 ff. On the Soviet views of the Wafd and Rashid Ali, see Laqueur, *The Soviet Union and the Middle East*, p. 124. On the Molotov-Ribbentrop Pact, sources included Louis Snyder, *The War: A Concise History 1939–1945* (New York: Dell, 1968), pp. 91–94; John C. Campbell, *Defense of the Middle East*, pp. 149–51; Aaron S. Klieman, *Soviet Russia and the Middle East* (Baltimore: Johns Hopkins Univ. Press, 1970), p. 34; and discussions with Professor Uri Ra'anan, Fletcher School of Law and Diplomacy.

20. Laqueur, *The Soviet Union and the Middle East*, p. 119.

21. Ibid., pp. 32, 86, 101, 124–27, passim. Also, Salo W. Baron, *The Russian Jew Under Tsars and Soviets* (New York: Macmillan, 1964), pp. 290–312; and Joseph B. Schechtman, *Zionism and Zionists in Soviet Russia* (New York: Zionist Organization of America, 1966). On the so-called Nazi-Zionist connection, see Sachar, *Europe Leaves the Middle East*, pp. 67 ff.; Gerhard Weinberg, *The Foreign Policy of Hitler's Germany: Diplomatic Revolution in Europe, 1933–1936* (Chicago: Univ. of Chicago Press, 1970), pp. 329–30; and Circular of the Foreign Ministry (Berlin), "The Jewish Question as a Factor in Foreign Policy in 1938," in Herzstein, *Adolf Hitler and the Third Reich*, pp. 92–93. On the Nazi concept that Zionism and Bolshevism were synonymous, see, e.g., Walter Z. Laqueur, *Russia and Germany: A Century of Conflict* (Boston: Little, Brown, 1965), pp. 192–95.

22. See House Committee on Foreign Affairs, *World Communism*, pp. 1–28. Also, Y. Porat, "The Origins, Nature and Disintegration of the National Liberation League 1943–1948," *Hamizrach Hechadash* (Jerusalem: 1964), vol. 14, pp. 354–66.

23. On the Soviet diplomatic offensive, see Laqueur, *The Soviet Union and the Middle East*, p. 132; *New York Times*, 8 September 1943, p. 5; 30 October 1943, p. 3; 2 January 1944, p. 17; 6 August 1944, p. 27; 20 September 1944, p. 11; 9 January 1945, p. 5; 15 January 1945, p. 3. Also, see Sachar, *Europe Leaves the Middle East*, pp. 335–50, passim; Lenczowski, *The Middle East in World Affairs*, pp. 522–28, passim; David Dallin, "Soviet Policy in the Middle East," in G. S. McClellan, ed., *The Middle East in the Cold War* (New York: H. Wilson, 1956), pp. 36–41; John C. Campbell, "A New Area of Diplomacy: The Middle East," in Kertesz and Fitzsimmons, ed., *Diplomacy in a Changing World* (South Bend, Ind.: Notre Dame Univ. Press, 1959), pp. 327–38; and E. L. Crowley, ed., *The Soviet Diplomatic Corps 1917–1967* (Metuchen, N.J.: Scarecrow Press, 1970).

Probably the most important official document attesting to Russia's stepped-up interest in the Middle East is Francis Stevens (Secretary of American embassy at Moscow), "Soviet Attitude Toward the Near and Middle East," a memorandum sent to Hull's successor, Edward Stettinius, Jr., with cover letter by George Kennan, 20 December 1944, 867N.01/12–2044. Cf. E. M. Wilson, Memorandum of Conversation (N. Goldmann, W. Murray, et al.), 13 September 1944, pp. 2–3, 867N.01/9–1344.

24. These considerations also offer a partial explanation of Soviet conduct in the period 1945–1948, when Moscow permitted refugee immigration from Eastern Europe to Palestine, was the first power to grant Israel de jure recognition in May 1948, and allowed Czechoslovakia to supply arms to Israel that year. See Laqueur, *The Soviet Union and the Middle East*, pp. 146–47;

Yaacov Ro'i, "Soviet-Israeli Relations, 1947–1954," in Confino and Shamir, ed., *The U.S.S.R. and the Middle East* (Jerusalem: Israel Univ. Press & John Wiley, 1973), pp. 123 ff.; Avigdor Dagan, *Moscow and Jerusalem: Twenty Years of Relations between Israel and the Soviet Union* (New York: Abelard-Schuman, 1970), pp. 20–26; A. Krammer, "Soviet Motives in the Partition of Palestine, 1947–1948," *Journal of Palestine Studies* 2 (1973): 102–19; and Nadav Safran, "The Soviet Union and Israel: 1947–1969," in Lederer and Vucinich, ed., *The Soviet Union and the Middle East* (Stanford: Hoover Institution, 1972), pp. 159–62. But cf. Baron, *The Russian Jew under Tsars and Soviets*, p. 312.

25. ST Minutes 10, 24 February 1943, and ST Minutes 13, 17 March 1943, Notter Papers, Box 70: Bound volume: "Minutes on Security Technical Problems (1—." Although no decision was made, the very existence of Soviet interest in Libya strengthened the Department's prewar tendency to support the continued presence of the British in the Canal Zone into the postwar period. Also see Chapter 10.

26. *The Complete War Memoirs of Charles DeGaulle* (New York: Simon & Schuster, 1964), pp. 893–94; G. Wadsworth to Hull, 11 October 1943, *FR* 4 (1943): 997; and Policy Committee Memorandum, "Near and Middle East Beyond Immediate Periphery of Russia," Annex J to PC-8 (Revised), 4 November 1944, Stettinius Papers, Box 379, Folder: "S. D. Miscell.–Pol. Com. Docs. 1944." A significant position paper, Annex J refers to the U.S.S.R. as follows: "[Though British influence remains strong] there have recently been evidence of ferments working in this area which in due course may radically change the existing situation. These new elements have taken inter alia the form (1) of an apparent disposition of the semi-independent Arab peoples to discard their previously strong anti-Soviet prejudices and to begin thinking in terms of possible Russian assistance in the event that they are unable to obtain from the Western Powers the assurances which they desire in respect of achieving their nationalist aspiration, (2) of intimations by the French that they would be prepared to turn to Moscow in the event that the British sought to root the French out of their special position in the Levant States, (3) of the recent establishment of Soviet relations with Egypt, Syria, Lebanon and Iraq." On Stalin's general unwillingness to side with DeGaulle, see Ministry of Foreign Affairs of the U.S.S.R., *Stalin's Correspondence with Roosevelt and Truman 1941–1945* (New York: Capricorn, 1965), pp. 170–72. On the willingness of the Department of State to side with Stalin against the French in the Levant, see Yalta Papers, p. 208, in Notter Papers, Box 3, Folder: "Briefing Book for Yalta Conference—1945." Note also P. Alling, Memorandum (on history of U.S. relations with Levant), 10 March 1945, *FR* 8 (1945): 1054–55.

27. On Syria's appeal to Stalin, see Wadsworth to Hull, 15 September 1944, *FR* 5 (1944): 778. Parenthetically, for insight into the attraction Russia has traditionally had toward segments of the Syrian population, note the concluding chapter of Derek Hopwood, *The Russian Presence in Syria and Palestine 1843–1914* (London: Clarendon, 1969). Soon after Kuwatli's appeal to Stalin, the Department was informed by American and British military attachés in the Levant that Moscow was also being appealed to on the grounds that London and Washington were selling the Arabs out to the Zionists. Dispatch of 30 September 1944, *FR* 5 (1944): 615.

28. For the inference that Russia's role would not be decisive with respect to Syria's future, see Wadsworth to Hull, 17 October 1944, *FR* 5 (1944): 801. On the expected increase and expected manageability of communist activity

in the Levant, see F. A. Kuhn, "Communism in Syria and Lebanon," Memorandum prepared for NEA synthesizing various OSS and MID (British intelligence) reports, 14 November 1944, 890D.00B/11–1444. Furthermore, Soviet diplomats sent to the Levant were unfamiliar with the Arab world and appeared to FSOs as greenhorns. Interview with former FSO Gordon H. Mattison, 31 July 1972; also William Porter (Damascus) to Byrnes, 24 September 1945, 890G.00/9–2445.

When Loy Henderson became director of EA & A, his strong anticommunism became a factor that made the Department's treatment of Soviet interest in the Levant more serious. Despite that, Syria's request for American arms and money in the second half of 1945 was turned down by the Department, even though it was considered likely that Syria might turn to Russia as an alternative. See *FR* 8 (1945): 1201–16; and Chapter 7.

29. "Foreign Petroleum Policy of the United States," 11 April 1944, *FR* 5 (1944): 27–32. This position paper, originating in the Department's Interdivision Petroleum Committee and redrafted by the Intradepartmental Petroleum Committee and the Post-War Program Committee, was and would remain until 1947 "the only official statement of foreign petroleum policy" [Comment of *FR* editors, ibid., p. 28, n. 32].

30. The position papers, authored essentially by Assistant Secretary Berle, are cited in note 19 in Chapter 1. Also, see note 26 of this chapter.

31. References to forebodings over Soviet designs are numerous, even in 1944. Thus, "The Russians are in effective occupation of a considerable portion of Iran, and we have recently received reports to show that they would like to expand their influence and gain some sort of long-term foothold, through the concession of a free port or by other means, upon the shores of the Persian Gulf. This, of course, would place the Russians within a very short distance not only of the oil fields in southern Iran, Iraq, and Kuwait, but also of those in Bahrein and eastern Saudi Arabia" (Murray to Stettinius, 27 October 1944, *FR* 5 [1944]: 626). "If Britain and America alienate the Arabs over Palestine we run the risk of throwing the whole Arab world into the arms of Soviet Russia" (Murray to Stettinius, 1 December 1944, 867N.01/12–144, p. 12).

32. On Soviet anti-Jewish-state attitudes, see report conveyed to the Department from Ankara by Ira Hirschmann of the War Refugees Board, in Murray to Stettinius, 3 October 1944, *FR* 5 (1944): 623–24. Also, Stevens and Kennan, "Soviet Attitude toward the Near and Middle East," p. 3.

33. On the need to have a more "positive" policy leaning towards consultation with the U.S.S.R., see Annex and Sub-annex, "Suggested Procedure Regarding the Palestine Question," (n. d.) in Stettinius to Murray, 23 December 1944, *FR* 5 (1944): 655–57. (This document, actually drafted by E. M. Wilson and G. P. Merriam, 8 January 1945, is also found in Departmental files, 867N.01/1–845, and also as part of the Yalta Briefing Papers.)

NEA's thesis was that making the Russian outlaw into a legal partner would head off unilateralist Soviet bids to the Arabs: "It would be inadvisable for the United States and Great Britain to undertake any long-range settlement for Palestine without the approval of the Soviet Government. We should not give the Soviet Government an opportunity to augment its influence in the Near East by championing the cause of the Arabs at the expense of the United States or at the expense of both the United States and Great Britain" (ibid., p. 656).

On the buildup of concern lest Soviet pro-Arabism outshine America's and Britain's because of the Palestine obstacle, see the anxious correspondence in the period September–December 1944 among Murray, Henderson, A. Harriman (Moscow) and Stettinius: *FR* 5 (1944): 615, 623–24, 625–26, 629, 632, 633, 641, 646–48.

On the postwar planner's preferred solution for Palestine, see Chapter 14.

34. "No record has been found of discussion regarding Palestine at the [Yalta] Conference" [Editors, *FR* 5 (1944): 655, n. 82]. However, see *FR* volume on Malta and Yalta Conferences 1945, p. 924 (and note the ellipsis). Former Departmental researcher Harry Howard, in an interview on 3 August 1972, said he recalled that in the original Yalta file, Roosevelt (in reply to Stalin's query about his imminent talk with Ibn Saud) said that he (Roosevelt) was going to ask for the admission (to Palestine) of some seven million Jews! One assumes that the ellipsis in the *FR* volume refers to the removal of that exchange. It is of course possible that Roosevelt's remark was in the form of banter, as was perhaps his remark (printed) that he as a Zionist—to which Stalin said he was one, too, in principle. [Stalin allegedly repeated this to Truman at Potsdam. See L. Pinkerton (Jerusalem) to Byrnes, 10 August 1945, 867N.01/8–1045.] One regrets that the insufficiency of further documentation makes it impossible to analyze these glimpses in depth. Cf. too Joseph Heller, "Roosevelt, Stalin and the Palestine Problem of Yalta," *Wiener Library Bulletin* 30 (1977): 25–35.

35. The quotation relative to Saudi oil is from comments on Saudi Arabia, dated 6 January 1945, in Yalta Papers, in Notter Papers, Box 3, Folder: "Briefing Book for Yalta Conference—1945," p. 220. Similarly, note William Clayton to Roosevelt, 19 January 1945, *FR* 5 (1944): 36. Also on Saudi Arabia, oil, and the British, see Chapters 11 and 12. On Churchill's reaction to Roosevelt's informing him of his meeting with Ibn Saud, see Robert Sherwood, *Roosevelt and Hopkins, An Intimate History*, pp. 871–72.

36. On Soviet interest in the trusteeships and the western Mediterranean, see Anthony Eden, *Memoirs*, pp. 633–34; notation of 24 July 1945, Joseph Grew Papers, MS Am 1687.3, vol. 7 (37); exchange between Stettinius and Andre Gromyko, 20 June 1945, Notter Papers, Box 218, Folder: "Stettinius—General;" and Russell, *History of the U.N. Charter*, pp. 343–48, passim. On Soviet tactics regarding the Straits, see *FR* volume on Malta and Yalta Conferences 1945, p. 328; Conference Proceedings, 23 July 1945 and 24 July 1945, *FR* (volume on Potsdam Conference) 2 (1945): 303–4, 365–66, 372; Sachar, *Europe Leaves the Middle East*, pp. 364–74; and text, Chapter 10.

6

Syria and Lebanon Through 1942

THE DEPARTMENT AND FRANCE

France, easily as much as the Soviet Union, was America's uncertain ally during World War II; and in Syria and Lebanon, in fact, France was regarded by the State Department as an adversary. The Department opposed it with nearly as much conviction as it did the Axis. More paradoxically, the Department opposed the Gaullist Free French administration in the Levant more than it opposed that of the Vichy French. However, America's interference in the Levant was not direct. Instead, it often initiated from afar the sequence of pressures which eventuated in direct constraint being put on the French, to Arab satisfaction, by the (for the most part, willing) British government and British military. The Department's object was elemental: to remove the French and French influence.

PREWAR POLICIES

In 1938, United States exports to both Syria and Lebanon approximated $3.5 million in value; American imports were $1.5 million. In the same year there were thirteen American business firms in the Levant with a total investment of about $7 million. The amounts involved were comparatively small. France and Britain were the chief economic traders and investors in the Levant, not the United States. Nonetheless, the

123

State Department was future-minded and accordingly, it pushed for the open door, even though the potential wealth and markets of Syria and Lebanon seemed clearly limited.

In contrast, on the noneconomic level the Department was very present- and past-minded. Monetarily, private American investment in educational, missionary, medical, and philanthropic institutions in the Levant was not awesome: in 1938 the total was about $4.5 million. Yet the sum was large for the times and, except for American Jewish investment in Palestine, it represented the largest private noneconomic investment of Americans in any part of the Middle East. In fact, in 1940 there were 71 American schools in Syria and Lebanon, with 11,000 students enrolled, more than 2000 of which attended the regionally influential American University of Beirut.[1]

There was a century-old continuity behind such good works which, in the Department's perception, had produced a fund of Arab good will. Indeed, immediately after World War I, there had existed a popular desire in Syria and Lebanon for an American mandate rather than a British or French one. In the late 1930s, the Levant's attitude was still pro-American: America's cultural investments—second only to France's and far more extensive than Britain's—were not stigmatized as imperialist blandishments the way France's were.

For its part, the Department consistently felt that France violated the spirit and letter of its mandate by overt economic discriminations. The Department also shared the fears of American Protestant missionaries and educators that French cultural and Catholic interests in the Levant would hurt American interests. Though such concern proved to be exaggerated, concern over economic discrimination remained.

Overall, the Department's negativism towards France and its fears that American goodwill investments might be jeopardized—either directly by France or indirectly by America's support of Zionism—were the motor forces behind Departmental policy in the Levant prior to World War II. As yet, there was *no* Departmental concern or anticipation with respect to the Levant's geopolitical potential, the effects of oil production in adjacent states, or the coming influence of Axis and communist ideologies.

An additional, if distinctly lesser, factor behind Departmental policy was the interest of American citizens resident in the Levant. Generally, there were two groups of citizen involved: naturalized, or first-generation ("hyphenated"), American citizens of Syrian or Lebanese extraction; and "unhyphenated" American citizens of Anglo-Saxon extraction, long resident in the Middle East. The first group, the Syrian- and Lebanese-Americans, was part of one of America's smallest immigrant-ethnic communities: there were less than 100,000 Syrians and Lebanese in the United States in the 1930s. Interested in their homelands, some had returned, and once returned, they often required consular assistance from the American Foreign Service. They represented the majority of American citizens living in the Levant. (In 1938 there was a total of nearly 1,700 American citizens of all provenances in Syria and Lebanon, the largest such figure—again, excepting Palestine—in the Middle East. In 1939, the figure fell to about 1,400, and in the war years thereafter it fell much more sharply.)[2]

As in the case of other ethnic groups in America, the concern of Syrian- and Lebanese-Americans, whether they resided in America or in the Levant, for their homeland was duly noted by the Department. As a professional bureaucracy, the Department replied to any and all such concern with formal courtesy. But that concern was not seriously considered a legitimate component of the national "interest." Nor were Levantine-Americans regarded as a significant pressure group, real or potential, necessary for the Department to contend with.

In contrast, the interests and views of "unhyphenated" American nationals long resident in the Levant—educators and supporters of the American University of Beirut, Presbyterian missionaries, the American expatriate "colonies" in the larger cities—were more important to the Department. These nationals represented wealth and prestige and were of the same social background as, and were often personally acquainted with, Departmental officers. Largely for such reasons, the private interests of these American nationals and their anxieties about the French and the Jews simply seemed more "American" and more "in the national interest" than the private and parochial interests of the hyphenated Americans. Curiously, the unhyphenated Americans endorsed Arab nationalism more than most Americans of Levantine extraction did. One reason was that the latter, mostly Christians, had originally fled from Moslem pressures at home and were not eager to support the nationalist principle in full, out of fear of refueling those same pressures.

Overall, Syria and Lebanon in the 1930s were second only to Iraq as the chief locus of the Department's demands for American rights, mainly in matters of tariff and language discrimination. As noted in Chapter 3, such legalistic-moralistic anti-French protests were colored by Departmental animus toward France. The animus was more than mere petulance: it was deep and long-standing and in fact was in itself a factor which, since both Americans and Arabs shared it so acutely, went a long way in cementing American-Levant friendship.

Illustrative was the fact that in the 1920s Paul Knabenshue, then consul in Beirut, urged the Department to approach Britain for the purpose of having Britain take over from France as mandatory in the Levant. (The Department, however, did not accept Knabenshue's proposal.) Moreover, in a number of instances after the Franco-American Treaty was signed in 1924, the Department adopted a strident tone, insisting on its treaty rights to the maximum letter. (In essence, the treaty had noted that the United States granted recognition to France as mandatory power in the Levant, while France granted the United States consultative rights in the event that significant changes were contemplated by France.) More than it did with respect to similar treaties with Britain in the mandates of Iraq and Palestine, the Department insisted on being closely consulted and also on having the right to give prior approval or disapproval, with veto power, to French policy changes contemplated for the Levant.

Similarly, the Department insisted on receiving a most-favored-nation status. In the period 1936–38, it presented itself as an interested party to the hoped-for termination of the Levant mandate by the socialist Blum government in Paris. The Department was on record as "sympathetic" and "favoring" independence for Syria and Lebanon.[3]

SYRIA AND LEBANON DURING THE WAR

Before and during the initial phase of World War II, incessant French conflict with Syria's leadership combined with French fears of defeat by Germany and of imperial dismemberment by Germany, Italy, and/or Britain. The result made the Third Republic adopt a policy of dictatorial martial law within Syria and Lebanon and declare that the mandates were henceforth belligerents on the side of France. In reaction, existing native pro-Axis sentiments spread. Their exact quality and quantity, however, have always been subject to debate. As noted in the previous chapter, when France underwent its Debacle in June 1940 Arab resentment was intensified at the thought of being subject to a defeated and weak power.[4]

The Third Republic's successor, the Vichy regime, was aware of the Levant's mood, and to gain support it restored a measure of self-government in Syria and Lebanon. It also created an ideological bridge, to some degree, with pro-Axis Arabs with its own record of anti-Jewish repressions in France and North Africa and with its own propaganda against "Anglo-Jewish imperialism." However, the Vichy-British tangle in the Levant was short-lived as a result of the successful takeover of Syria by the British Ninth Army, assisted by the Gaullist Free French, in July 1941.

Syria and Lebanon were thereafter "protected" by British troops but were under the mandatory authority of the Free French. This triangular relationship, which became a quadruple one with America's growing participation in the Mediterranean Theatre, was not a happy one. Basically, the Free French, exactly as the Vichy French had before them, deeply distrusted British motives and tried to preserve all French mandatory prerogatives. Although De Gaulle in June 1941 had been pressured by Britain to pledge independence for the Levant, he subsequently argued that full implementation of the pledge would have to wait until the postwar United Nations Organization took up the question of mandates from where the defunct League of Nations had left off. Later in the war he also tried to argue that the shift of fighting to the Far Eastern theatre necessitated continued French control of the Levant, as a way-station vital to the war effort.[5]

The British (until the end of 1944) were usually quite willing to placate anti-French, pro-nationalist feelings in the Arab world, and in the Department and the White House. In addition to its hostility to Vichy France, Britain basically wanted a Levant, not in the British sphere as such, but merely free of turmoil—and free from France's or any other power's sphere. Its political and economic interests in the Levant were thus not "direct." Yet Britain observed that its troops seemed constantly bogged down in the Levant. Such a state of affairs was exasperating, for costly troop deployment in the Levant did not really help the British national interest, as bogged down British troops in Iraq, Egypt, and Palestine could at least claim.

Even so, Britain's position was constantly wavering in the Levant. The reason was due largely to the division of opinion among British policy makers on the long-run question of which should be Britain's priority in the Middle East—good Anglo-American, Anglo-(Free) French, or Anglo-Arab relations? For its part, the British military was not keen on the possibility of a continued French military presence in the Levant after the war. On the other hand, the Foreign Office increasingly wanted a continued French presence. Despite its polished appearance of cooperation with the State Department, the British Foreign Office was always interested in limiting long-term American influence. Since shoring up the French seemed to be one way of keeping America at bay, the Foreign Office would tilt toward the French, mainly in 1945, if only by *not* pushing France to terminate its Levant mandate quickly, as the State Department wanted.

In part, the Foreign Office's mild friendliness towards France can also be explained by the fact that Foreign Secretary Anthony Eden was both more sympathetic toward De Gaulle and less the Americanophile than Prime Minister Winston Churchill. Furthermore, the Foreign Office realized that if it and America, like "sorcerers' apprentices" (De Gaulle's phrase), helped to eliminate France's Middle Eastern sphere entirely, Britain's Middle Eastern sphere would be the only one left and would logically be the next to go.[6]

Withal, pressures from the Department, the Arab world, and Britain's ardent anti-Gaullist minister to the Levant, Sir Edward Spears, combined to make the British, vacillations and divergent views notwithstanding, into watchdogs over the Free French for the duration of the war. From

1943 to 1946, it was the British Ninth Army which almost regularly stepped in under orders by Churchill, who was under pressure from America, to threaten and restrain De Gaulle's administration in the Levant. That administration wished to repress the increasing outbursts of Arab protests and strikes, which were aimed at France's alleged privileges, inertia, and in particular France's local military units, the *troupes speciales* (often Senegalese). Such protests, as will be noted, were abetted by American FSOs' diplomatic counsel to Arab leaders. Protests were also encouraged by the high visibility of France's great-power weakness before Britain and America, just as earlier in the war France's weakness and nakedness had been "exposed" by the Axis.

Internally, the struggle against De Gaulle's administration was both a frustration and a stimulus to Levant nationalism. Syria wanted to precipitate a crisis with France and thereby force Britain to intervene—lest Britain withdraw as it did after World War I and leave the field to France. Yet Syria, still nursing its own ambitions of leading pan-Arabism, was also suspicious of British policy. It was anxious over the Foreign Office's endorsements in the first half of the war of Nuri Said's Fertile Crescent plan, which had proposed the annexation of republican Syria to the Hashemite realms of Iraq and Transjordan.[7]

In Lebanon, politicians took pride in the fact that many of them had been under wartime political arrest and that their minuscule state therefore was, presumably, an example of stout resistance to European domination. However, compared with Syria, Lebanon was quiet and its leadership was moderate. Under Bishara Khuri's government, Lebanon pursued cooperation with both France and the pan-Arab movement, even as it vocally defended its territorial integrity and separation from Syria. It thus succeeded in having its independence recognized by the Alexandria Protocol in 1944, and it subsequently became a member of the Arab League. Apprehension over projects of pan-Arab unity continued to trouble Lebanon, however.[8]

In March 1945, Syria and Lebanon both announced adherence to the Declaration of the United Nations and declared war on the Axis. They were the last of the Arab states to do so, although Lebanon had been known to be probably more genuinely pro-Allies than any other Arab state but Transjordan. At the behest of America, Britain, Russia, and China, France reluctantly accepted Syria's and Lebanon's participation in U.N. deliberations. In these, both states were fully assertive, especially on the Palestine question.[9]

However, if both Syria and Lebanon were practicing the arts of high politics at the end of the war, within their respective domains it was often a case of "the more things change, the more they remain the same." Internally, political-religious factionalism, nepotism, inertia, and demagoguery continued to plague the political process of each state.

WARTIME POLICIES

In the period between September 1939 and June 1942, the two questions in the Levant which most preoccupied the State Department were the question of the mandates' neutrality and belligerency and the question of the utility and legitimacy of American diplomatic relations with the Vichy government.

Toward the end of 1939, Britain and France had brought "into the status of war with Germany" Syria, Lebanon, Palestine, and mandated regions in sub-Saharan Africa and Australasia. Germany protested on the grounds that France and Britain, lacking sovereignty over the mandates, were unjustified in making the mandates belligerents. The Department agreed with Germany, though its tone was less strident. The Department argued that changing the status of Syria, Lebanon, and Palestine to belligerents would introduce naval prize courts and import and exchange controls that were "inconsistent" with the purposes of the mandate system.

The Department deemed it inadvisable to make a full and formal protest, however—not so much out of commiseration that Britain and France might become weakened relative to the Axis as out of several minor pragmatic considerations. The Department felt informal conversations generally to be more efficacious than formal protests. And, in view of the state of emergency in Britain and France, it believed that formal protests would not only fail but would also backfire. Protests would intensify British and French controls, thus making matters worse for American nationals. To some degree the Department feared, too, that American ships in the Mediterranean would be endangered by possible German submarine attack; on that assumption, it seemed temporarily irrelevant whether the unneutral and "closed door" status of the mandates was ultimately legal or not.

In the period 1939–42, the Department thus marked time and kept a very low profile. The only actual policy adopted was unilaterally to define the mandates as nonbelligerents, notwithstanding opposite declarations by London and Paris, in order to justify American ships' carrying, for example, cargoes of arms and small weapons. To the Department such limited commerce was permissible and innocuous, on the premise that these small arms were destined for local purchase, and not for the use of third-party belligerents like the British or French.

When, however, the Axis threat in the Middle East began to subside by late 1942, the Department began to revive its traditional insistence upon the open door for the Levant—though it did not revive its insistence that the mandates resume the status of nonbelligerents vis à vis the Axis.

The Department's approach, in summary, was and would be consistent with the philosophy of "try to have your cake and eat it, too": the Levant must have its door open, in theory, to everyone; in practice, to America; but certainly not to America's enemies.[10]

With respect to the Vichy regime, the Department opposed antagonizing Vichy rule in the Levant; it did not therefore press for the termination of the French mandate there. The British Foreign Office felt otherwise, its thesis being that Vichy's reluctance to grant independence to Syria and Lebanon—and after July 1941, De Gaulle's identical reluctance—destabilized the Arab world, tied up Allied troops, and hurt the war effort. The Department was sympathetic to the British view, yet even after the British military abolished Vichy control of the Levant in July 1941, the Department maintained diplomatic relations with the Vichy regime in metropolitan France and refrained from accepting continuous British proposals that Washington, like London, recognize Syrian and Lebanese independence.

The Department believed that, pending the implementation of secret plans to invade Vichy-administered North Africa in November 1942 (Operation TORCH), there were more advantages than disadvantages in having direct dealings with the Vichy government in France. Presumably America's intelligence-gathering and general influence were enhanced by virtue of maintaining diplomatic ties. For its part, the Vichy government, though under the Nazi shadow and ever oscillating in the penumbra between collaborationism and neutralism, wanted diplomatic relations with Washington as a means of expressing its putative sovereignty. It also wanted recognition in order to be qualified for receiving American economic aid. Vichy contended and the Department believed that aid would make Vichy less dependent on the Nazis.

Because Vichy wanted American aid and recognition, therefore, at least as much as the Department wanted to contain Nazism, the Department had some leverage as creditor. When in 1942 it believed that Vichy was swerving too much towards collaborationism, the Department began to feel that it need not constantly appease, but could risk exercising a more punitive carrot-and-stick policy. Still, until approximately mid-1942, the Department usually preferred to appease Vichy and extend the carrot.[11]

In the Levant itself in 1940–42, the policy of NEA and the Foreign Service was also essentially to behave prudently, with activities confined to tactfully discouraging Vichy-German collaboration and to conciliating British-French and Arab-French antagonisms in order to expedite the general war effort. Indeed, mediating British-French differences was a practiced chore of the then American consul general in Beirut, Cornelius van Engert. In 1941, he helped to arrange the armistice between the Vichy and British forces.[12]

When the Free French succeeded the Vichy French as mandatory in the Levant, Engert continued his good works, as when, for example, in March 1942 the rupture between Britain's minister to the Levant, General Edward Spears, and French High Commissioner, General Raoul Catroux, became severe, mirroring, even outlasting, the bad feelings between Churchill and De Gaulle. Each general was accusing the other of trying to oust him from the Levant, as indeed each of them fervently (if privately) wished to do.

Engert emphasized in his mediations the need to "forget all personal ambitions and petty political rivalries in order to defeat [the] common foe as quickly as possible." He personally agreed that the British were justified in believing that popular unrest was due and would be due to De Gaulle's defaulting on his independence pledges. Yet he felt, and Hull concurred, that it would be unwise for the United States to commit itself publicly to the British side, lest Washington be blamed for future complications. Besides, it was accepted in the Department that too close an association with Britain was intrinsically unwise. In the Middle East, such an association might have a contaminating effect, given the abiding dislike many Arabs had toward Britain, a fact which Britain, the Department believed, failed to see.[13]

On Arab-French tensions, the Department, in the period before TORCH, also took an indirect approach, indeed, more cautiously so than before the war, when it had been overtly tilting towards anti-French Arab nationalism. The Department now opposed the Arab (and British) wish for immediate American recognition of Syrian and Lebanese independence, yet also opposed the French wish for an American stance against recognition. Instead, the Department expressed itself in favor of American recognition, but in the short-run future. It thus seemed to alienate no one. Apart from its traditional gravitation toward such intermediate, "moderate" solutions, the Department particularly did not want to alienate Vichy France. Even after Vichy forces lost control of Syria in mid-1941, the Department still had, as noted, reasons for keeping intact its bilateral ties with the Vichy regime in Europe.[14]

Besides Consul General Engert, several other FSOs and planners preferred a noninterventionist approach in the period 1939–42. Indeed, the then consul at Beirut, William Gwynn, considered even the Department's gradualism as too much. When, as a gesture toward future recognition, the status of the chief American diplomatic post in the Levant was raised in June 1942 from "consul general" to "diplomatic agent and consul general," Gwynn said that the change was not only premature but pointless. At the end of July he wrote to Secretary Hull, "I can see no great advantage in changing now the present status of this post. The disadvantage of becoming implicated in any way in the Franco-British jockeying for position must be apparent." A month later his remonstrance was sharper:

It is my conviction that the Arabs here have little use for the Allies and from what I can learn the situation would not appear to be very different in other countries. They will like us when we have proved our strength and fall on us if we show any weakness. If our policy is based on seeking their favor it is, I fear, ill-inspired.[15]

Gwynn's anti-Arab nationalist (and pro-Gaullist) views were most unusual and represented the most strongly expressed dissent, to the point of alienation, within the Department's entire circle of Middle East experts during the entire wartime and prewar periods. For their atypicality, his views are thus highlighted here. In contrast to Gwynn's views, Departmental policy in the region was based squarely on currying Arab favor.

One other dissenter, on the planning side of the Department, was Professor William Westermann, a scholar on the Middle East with Departmental planning experience in World War I. Westermann was the planners' main outside expert on the Levant during 1941 and most of 1942. He proposed American friendship and sympathy, but beyond that a studious avoidance of promises of recognition to Syria and Lebanon. He also urged the Department not to alienate the Maronites. Though they were a minority in the Levant as a whole, he regarded them favorably, as reliable and pro-Allies as well as pro-French and opposed to Islamic pan-Arab nationalism. The pro-Axis Syrians, Westermann viewed negatively. He also urged that America abide strictly by the 1924 convention with France and not try to promote American interests at French expense; or Levant independence from France's mandate; or a separation of Syria and Lebanon as two distinct states. Separated from each other and divorced from France, he alleged, they would be economically unviable.[16]

These voices of dissent slowed rather than changed the direction of American policy in the Levant. Even so, by the autumn of 1942 they were voices no longer heard from. Gwynn was muzzled by the new consul general, George Wadsworth, and would soon be reassigned out of the region; and Westermann was increasingly supplanted as a result of Philip Ireland's use of full-time in-house specialists on the Levant (Wilbur White, Jr., Christina Grant, and Ireland himself).

For other, more substantive, reasons, too, the Department made a half-turn between April and November 1942 toward endorsing independence for the Levant and toward dropping the Vichy-Washington connection. The reasons were diverse. They included the operational shaping-up of the North African landing plans; the danger represented by Axis offensive plans; new German diplomatic probes in French North Africa which, ominously, were not met with protests from Vichy; and the apparent imminence of Japanese expansion in French island-and-coastal territory adjacent to already occupied French Indo-China. In April 1942 the pro-collaborationist Pierre Laval replaced Admiral Darlan as Marshal Petain's number-two man in the Vichy regime. As an ostensible protest,

American ambassador William Leahy was recalled to Washington the following month.

These reasons fed into other reasons for reappraisal. Vichy's utility as an intelligence source within Axis Europe and as a wall against Nazi encroachments across the western Mediterranean into North Africa was declining. The publicity which America's liberal press directed at the Department's policy of "appeasement" of Vichy was becoming more adverse. The Department anticipated that diplomatic relations with France in the coming month would be ruptured anyway, following the surprise of TORCH's invasion of Vichy-controlled North Africa. Psychologically, Department officers felt an itching need to act more decisively against any French presence in the Levant before it was too late, that is, before the obstreperous De Gaulle, cordially disliked by the Department, entrenched himself in the Levant in Vichy's stead. When TORCH succeeded in November, another factor entered the picture: a new élan and a confidence in unilateral American action.

Finally, as indicated, two very pro-Arab-nationalist Departmental officers came to the fore at this time: George Wadsworth, former consul general for Palestine and Transjordan, became consul general for Syria and Lebanon; while Philip Ireland, as head of Middle Eastern research in the Division of Special Research, finished consolidating his staff and became the chief spokesman on Middle Eastern issues in the Territorial and Political subcommittees. Indeed, at least four months before TORCH, Ireland had already overridden Westermann's demurrals; and the two postwar planning subcommittees under Ireland had begun "leaning toward" preferred solutions of independence of Syria and Lebanon from France and partial separation thereafter between the two states.

The activist mood intensified in the fall. In harmony with this process of tilting decisively away from mediation with the French and toward pro-Arabism, it was the planners' new consensus, by October 1942, that in fact the United States had a "direct interest" in Syria and Lebanon— that is, an interest which was not merely an "indirect interest," although it was not yet an "immediate interest."[17]

NOTES

1. DeNovo, *American Interests and Policies*, pp. 322 ff.; and W. White, Jr., "Syria and Lebanon: Interests and Position of the United States," T-308, p. 1, 14 April 1943, Notter Papers, Box 34, Folder: "T Docs. 300–309."

2. DeNovo, *American Interests and Policies*, p. 337; Department of Commerce, *Historical Statistics of the United States, Colonial Times to 1957* (Washington, D.C.: GPO, 1960), p. 66.

3. On the Department's relations with the mandatory, see DeNovo, *Amer-*

ican Interests and Policies, p. 336, and the correspondence in *FR* 8 (1936): 460 ff., and *FR* 2 (1938): 1003 ff.

4. On French-Arab tensions in the Levant at the start of the war, see Lenczowski, *The Middle East in World Affairs,* pp. 275–76; Hourani, *Syria and Lebanon,* pp. 233–34; and Chapter 5.

5. On the Far Eastern connection, see *New York Times,* 15 May 1945, p. 11.

6. Thus DeGaulle: "Of course, and in any case, our troops would not leave the area so long as the British forces remained there. As for what would happen then, I did not doubt the agitation supported in the Levant by our former allies would spread through the entire Middle East to the detriment of these sorcerers' apprentices, and that eventually the British and Americans would pay dearly for the enterprise they had launched against France." DeGaulle, *Memoirs,* p. 894.

On other aspects of British-French relations, with emphasis on the Levant, see ibid., pp. 183, 206–7, 878–80, 885–93; Winston Churchill, *Closing the Ring* (Boston: Houghton Mifflin, 1951), pp. 185–86, passim; Anthony Eden, *The Reckoning,* pp. 290–91; Woodward, *British Foreign Policy,* vol. 1, pp. 561–69; Lenczowski, *The Middle East in World Affairs,* pp. 277–83; Guy de Carmoy, *The Foreign Policies of France 1944–1968* (Chicago: Univ. of Chicago Press, 1970, trans. from French), pp. 16–20; and R. Loir, "Comment Finit le Mandat de la France en Syrie," *Ecrits de Paris* 3 (1971): 46–54.

On the wider background of Anglo-French tension, see J. C. Cairns, "Great Britain and the Fall of France: A Study in Allied Disunity," *Journal of Modern History* 27 (1955): 365–409; and Dorothy White, *Seeds of Discord: DeGaulle, Free France and the Allies* (Syracuse, N.Y.: Syracuse Univ. Press, 1964).

7. On Syrian nationalism during the war, as well as basic secondary sources like Lenczowski and Fisher, see Hourani, *Syria and Lebanon,* pp. 254, 268–70; Gordon Torrey, *Syrian Politics and the Military, 1945–1958* (Columbus: Ohio State Univ. Press, 1964), Chapter 1; and Patrick Seale, *The Struggle for Syria: A Study of Postwar Arab Politics 1945–1958* (London: Oxford Univ. Press, 1965), pp. 25–27.

8. On Lebanese nationalism during the war, see Salibi, *Modern History of Lebanon,* pp. 186–97; and M. Z. Yakan, *Lebanon's Politics in Inter-Arab Relations 1943–1964* (Ph.D. diss., Univ. of Michigan, 1965).

9. On Syria's and Lebanon's admission to the U.N. and the San Francisco Conference, and their approach to the Palestine question, see Russell, *History of the U.N. Charter,* pp. 626–28, 828.

10. See NEA's J. Rives Childs, "Status of Palestine and Syria in the Light of the Belligerency of Great Britain and France," 26 January 1940; Childs to H. Wilson, 8 February 1940; Judge Moore to Wilson, 21 February 1940; and Wilson to Hull, 19 February 1940 and 23 February 1940, all in Department of State file 640.0011, "European War 1939," 1572 1/2.

11. On Washington-Vichy relations, see note 14 in Chapter 5 above and this author's unpublished paper, "The Role and Character of Admiral William D. Leahy as American Ambassador to Vichy France." On these relations the chief primary source material in English is found, passim, in *FR* 1, 2 (1940); *FR* 1, 2, 3, 4 (1941); *FR* 2 (1942); William Leahy, *I Was There: The Personal Story of the Chief of Staff to Presidents Roosevelt and Truman* (New York: Whittlesey House, 1950); Robert Murphy, *Diplomat Among Warriors* (Garden City, N.Y.: Doubleday, 1964); Welles, *The Time for Decision;* Hull, *Memoirs,* vol. 2; Sherwood, *Roosevelt and Hopkins;* and Samuel Rosenman,

ed., *The Public Papers and Addresses of Franklin D. Roosevelt*, vol. 10, *The Call to Battle Stations* (New York: Harper, 1950).

Also, see Hull's defense of his Vichy policy, 7 June 1941, pp. 681–82, and 13 June 1941, pp. 715–16, in *Bulletin* 4 (1941); and Sumner Welles' defense of accommodationist policies in North Africa and Franco Spain, in "Public Understanding of the Issues of the War," *Bulletin* 8 (17 April 1943): 319–21. Also, cf. Langer, *Our Vichy Gamble,* and Louis Gottschalk, "Our Vichy Fumble," *Journal of Modern History* 2 (1948): 47–56.

On TORCH, note L. J. Meyer, "The Decision to Invade North Africa," in K. R. Greenfield, ed., *Command Decisions* (New York: Harcourt, Brace, 1959), pp. 129–53; and A. L. Funk, *The Politics of TORCH: The Allied Landings and the Algiers Putsch* (Lawrence, Kans.: Univ. of Kansas Press, 1974).

12. On Engert's mediations, see his exchanges with Hull, *FR* 3 (1941): 725–84.

13. See Engert, dispatches of 1 May 1942 and 6 May 1942, in *FR* 4 (1942): 595–96. Parenthetically, it is interesting to note here that as the Department *and* the Free French were both firmly anti-Zionist, their shared animosity would provide a small bridge of agreement that made it easier for each side to address the other. Thus Catroux, who otherwise detested Engert's successor, George Wadsworth, would build up a semblance of friendship with him, for example, on one occasion asking Wadsworth, of all people, "could not something be done to discourage university professors and others [in the United States] from publicly voicing pro-Zionist views?" (Wadsworth to Hull, 12 March 1943, *FR* 4 (1943): 958).

14. On an elaboration of the Department's principle of "moderation," see Chapter 1.

15. Gwynn to Hull, 26 July 1942 and 21 August 1942, *FR* 4 (1942): 653–58.

16. W. Westermann, "The United States and Syria–Lebanon" (n. d., probably December 1941), originally written for the Council on Foreign Relations and incorporated as a Departmental territorial paper (T-4), Notter Papers, Box 31, Folder: "Docs 1–36." Also, see Westermann's opposition to the planners' increasingly anti-French position in the Levant, in P Minutes 24, 29 August 1949, p. 1, MacLeish Papers, Box 41, Folder: "Secret File: Political Subcommittee, Department of State."

17. On the planners' tilting, see in the Notter Papers: Territorial Subcommittee: Decisions and Directives (n. d., probably July 1942) and T-Subcommittee Memorandum, 20 October 1942, both in Box 2, Folder: "Work in SR" (Special Research Division); and P. Ireland, Preliminary Draft: "Maintenance of Independent Status for the Lebanon," 4 September 1942, T-62, Box 300, Folder: "Post-War Problems Studies: Near East."

7

Syria and Lebanon, 1943-45

WARTIME POLICIES, 1943

Having moved toward a recognition policy and toward viewing the Levant as a direct interest of the United States, in a series of meetings in the spring of 1943 the planners wrestled with the question of what would happen after France's withdrawal. Throughout, there was considerable division of opinion in the three relevant planning circles—the Security, Political, and Territorial subcommittees. The tone of most opinions, however, was pessimistic. Would Syria and Lebanon "fly at each other's throats"? To enhance Syria's stability, should a plebiscite be held—or would a plebiscite turn into a staged farce? As French interests went down, would British interests go up, and if so, was that in America's interest?

In essence, the Security subcommittee could only reach agreement that France should be forced to vacate and that an imposed union between Syria and Lebanon would not work. The Political subcommittee concluded that the maintenance of the Levant's independence should "rest with" the United Nations Organization. The Territorial subcommittee held that while independence was better than the restoration of the mandate, the issue of a united or separated Levant could not yet be dealt with. The Territorial subcommittee also saw the issue as contingent on the prior settlement of questions such as what Arab regional federation would be like, whether or not the Zionist movement would finally be curtailed by the British through the White Paper of 1939, and whether or not Palestine would also become part of a federation. Tentatively summing up, the Political subcommittee recommended Levant independence from France, approved the idea of a regional federation with Levant membership, *and* advocated building closer political and commercial relations between and among Syria, Lebanon, and the United States.[1]

Because the interests and rights in the Levant of the United States, Britain, and France still seemed to require clarification, Wilbur White, Jr., of the Territorial subcommittee prepared three studies detailing this information in April 1943. On America's interests, White underlined the Department's established overview of the region, contending that if Washington but behaved prudently, it would reap an abundant harvest in the Arab world. On the Levant specifically, private American missionary, educational, and philanthropic activity had established a necessary precondition for success, namely, a "reputation relatively above reproach." Added White, "There is reason to believe that an investment of a million dollars in education creates more goodwill and no less interest in the United States than a million-dollar business investment." America's reputation and Arab good will were "currently threatened, however, by suspicions of American support of Zionism."[2]

As for the British and French, White suggested that the former were starting to drag their feet, while the latter were still deceiving themselves into thinking that their economic-cultural preeminence in the Levant was simply one of right. He concluded in essence that Washington should continue to push London to push Paris to withdraw French troops. At the same time, the continuation of a British military presence in the Levant after a French withdrawal and the emerging leniency and ambivalence of Britain's Foreign Office with regard to France's claim of a sphere of influence ought to be opposed.

On the post-withdrawal period, White felt that complete separation of Syria and Lebanon would be economically difficult; yet a binational or federated Levant would make the Lebanese Christians an endangered minority. Unlike Philip Ireland and the rest of the planners, White did not opt for a compromise of loose confederation. He preferred instead a pro-Maronite solution: division of the Levant into two separate independent states, each operating under voluntarily chosen advisers. (Separation was also recommended on the assumption that the Christian world would oppose a united binational state in which Christians would be a minority subordinate to Moslems.) In the case of Lebanon, foreign advisers, White postulated, would doubtless be French. Thus, France would retain a minimal influence, the expectation of which, he concluded, might make France more tractable in the current discussions dealing with the termination of the mandate.[3]

While the planners were trying to sort out their differences and inching towards consensus, reports from the Levant in 1943 made the Departmental state of mind increasingly anxious and impatient. Spearheading, nudging, cajoling, alarming, and embarrassing the deskmen in Washington was FSO Wadsworth. Full recognition now of Syrian and Lebanese independence, he urged, would be an important and timely act of identification with Arab nationalism, the wave of the future. American prestige would instantly surpass Britain's or France's, and Arabs everywhere would see that America was moving neither towards isolationism nor pro-Zionism (the latter being the same as unmitigated anti-Arabism, in the minds of Arabs and Departmental FSOs).[4]

Although NEA's own recommendation of early recognition fell short of Wadsworth's in intensity, NEA too very much felt that Secretary Hull should put teeth into the Department's Levant policy. NEA became particularly annoyed by reported French heavyhandedness in the census and parliamentary elections of Syria and Lebanon in the summer of 1943. It was also disturbed by Arab agitations from North Africa eastward, which Foreign Service and Office of War Information reports attributed to pro-Zionist petitions in Congress and to pro-Zionist speeches by former Presidential candidate Wendell Willkie.[5]

Moreover, the British Foreign Office was renewing pressure for a closing of Anglo-American ranks and for an early extension of American recognition of Syrian and Lebanese independence. It was Britain's fear, at this particular juncture, that if France succeeded in holding onto Lebanon, French advisers and the French language would displace the buildup of British influence. Furthermore, if the French succeeded, Arab regional union would be frustrated because the Levant either would not participate at all or would be an obstreperous participant. Hopes for a British-sponsored federation, led either by Iraq or Egypt, would thus be aborted.[6]

Pressure on the Department for greater American involvement also came from segments within Syria and Lebanon. With regard to their quarrels with the Moslems, the Maronite bishop of Beirut and his Greek Orthodox counterpart actually approached the Department, through Wadsworth, and "petitioned American intervention." Concurrently, Shukri Kuwatli, after he was inaugurated as Syria's president, told Wadsworth that "he [Kuwatli] knew he could count on continuing American support" vis à vis the French.[7]

Hull and the upper echelons took a cooler view of the Levant imbroglio. They resisted being pressured by the Foreign Service, NEA, the British, or local parties into going beyond traditional expressions of sympathy for the aspirations of Syria and Lebanon. Accordingly, Wadsworth was restrained periodically by the upper echelons and, to a degree, by NEA from making promises and building expectations.[8]

Despite Hull's apparent braking of FSO enthusiasm, and despite the apparently stationary and hands-off nature of his policy of benevolent neutrality, the momentum and accumulation of small bits of Foreign Service activism had moved the Department closer to involvement than Hull realized. Furthermore, it seems that Hull did not fully grasp the point that American neutrality, rather than being an absence of influence, could be a considerable influence, capable of tilting the scales and shaping the future.

A relevant example of such influence-by-default occurred in November 1943, when post-election conflicts in Lebanon between France and Bishara Khuri's victorious Constitutionalist (pro-Arab federation) party led to riots, Free French repressions, and the appointment of Francophile Emile Eddé as caretaker president. To Wadsworth, Eddé was "chief French stooge," and he requested that the Department have no official relations with the Eddé regime. Hull concurred, out of dislike towards the Free French and a basic desire to stay uninvolved. Partly as a result of such American nonaction, however, the Eddé regime was isolated and lost any credibility it might have had. In turn, the cycle of Arab agitations and French repressions was renewed. British minister Spears and the British Ninth Army stepped in. With Departmental assent, the British served the French with an ultimatum. The French backed down, the high commissioner was replaced, Eddé was removed.[9]

If Hull thus backed into involvement, the middle managers of NEA and the Foreign Service moved forward into involvement, particularly after the aforementioned "last straw" of Lebanon's parliamentary conflict with France. One keynote of this forward momentum would be greater independence from what minister Alexander Kirk in Cairo called the "continuous tortuousness" of Anglo-French relations in the Middle East. Thus, for example, when Eddé was removed and the British Foreign Office pushed France to reinstate all ministers previously removed, the Department now vigorously entered the fray from the sidelines and went one better than the British. Under Hull's signature, the Department pushed for a *complete* restoration of the status quo ante constitutional situation in Lebanon "consistent with the French promises of independence."[10]

Such affirmative actions were not only the result of middle management's exasperation with the French, who seemed to mess up even their best claim to preeminence, Maronite Lebanon. They were also the result of Hull's phobia toward the possibilities of an Anglo-French deal in the Levant and a closed-door policy toward American influence and economic interests, notwithstanding the fact that to all appearances British policy in the Levant was still far more wedded to the United States than to France.

Finally, such steps were due to the fact that even before the Lebanese crisis, Departmental planners, as of August 1943, had at last produced a long-run policy toward the Levant. It is noteworthy that in this policy position, earlier doubts about the ability of Syria and Lebanon to deal fairly with each other and with their respective minorities and foreign nationals, and earlier questions on the effects of federation and of Palestine on the Levant's future, were not answered. They were simply noted and then, in effect, dismissed as immaterial. Among the three subcommittees involved, the Political subcommittee did hold out the longest in favor of dealing concretely with the Levant's minority-majority problems. It persisted into the last stages of deliberation in advocacy of a program of aid, advisorship, and limited trusteeship for protecting minorities. But the Territorial and Security subcommittees did not pursue such problems, mainly on the grounds that Syria would object to such interference with its sovereignty and would become hostile to the United States.[11]

In general, a facile optimism—and perhaps a certain weariness with the Levant—prevailed as the planners discarded doubt and dissent and arrived at consensus: France must go; Lebanese autonomy and Syrian-Lebanese economic cooperation and confederation would—hopefully—develop naturally; beyond that, Syria and Lebanon would simply have to acquire political experience by themselves. It is noteworthy that, all in all, if elsewhere in the world America's adherence to the emancipationist principles of the Atlantic Charter became toned down as the war progressed, in Syria and Lebanon the reverse was true.

WARTIME POLICIES, 1944

By 1944, the planners were well into the process of intellectually solidifying and buttressing their Levant policy. Indeed, like a wedge in the door, that policy was now being used to help discredit French rule in North Africa, too. Prior to 1944, Departmental policy had countenanced an at least minimal postwar continuation of French hegemony in North and West Africa. In theory, this policy had been "based upon the maintenance of the integrity of France and of the French empire." By January 1944 that policy was being reversed. As a result of the French "fiasco" in the Levant, presumed to be symptomatic of French ineptitude everywhere, it was now felt that postwar changes in the status of Morocco and Tunisia would be necessary. Also, it was hoped that the failure of France's rigidity in the Levant would provide a lesson to France, namely, that wisdom counseled withdrawal, flexibility, and a good neighbor approach for North Africa.[12]

It was also postulated in early 1944, by a new planning expert on the Levant (Christina Grant, replacing Wilbur White, Jr.), that a main reason the United States favored Levant independence was not merely because the idea was consonant with America's longstanding principles or because the French and British were doing a poor job. Rather, it was because America was now perceived, by the planners and by the Arabs, as already directly committed to the success of, and not just the idea of, Arab independence. Thus it was held that American prestige and interests would be seriously reduced if the Department failed to assure the various pledges of independence and if the Department failed to keep Syria and Lebanon, in the aftermath of independence, stable.[13]

This stepped-up sense of responsibility for the Levant was both a cause and effect of the increasingly polarized relations by mid-1944 between De Gaulle on the one hand and Roosevelt and Churchill on the other. If, for example, in mid-1942 the Territorial subcommittee had but "leaned toward" independence for Syria and Lebanon, though with the stated stipulation of not wishing to offend French sensibilities, in mid-1944 the gloves were off. Even Wilbur White's suggestion—that as a token gesture towards France, the Department should accept the likelihood that Lebanon would prefer French advisors—was dropped from any further consideration. Instead, the interdivisional committee on Arab countries advocated that British and American advisors from the Cairo-based Middle East Supply Center (MESC) be "made available" to the Levant and to other countries of the region. It even recommended that key French financial interests be nationalized by Syria and Lebanon![14]

In reaction to the Department's increasingly obvious treatment of French mandatory authority as null and void, De Gaulle's government insisted that its mandate was still judicially in force. Concurrently, the French tried to persuade Syria and Lebanon that great powers other than France were not true friends (in America's case, because of its basic isolationism and economic greed). Such French propaganda in turn hardened the Department's position a few degrees more.

Finally, the impasse ended. The Department formally recognized the independence from France of the Syrian and Lebanese republics on 19 September 1944. The main factor, as noted in Chapter 5, was the Soviet Union's full recognition policy in July–August 1944. (Adjacent Arab countries, China, Brazil, and several Eastern European governments-in-exile were also in the process of recognizing Damascus and Beirut.)[15]

Clearly, the Department felt that the United States might lose some points of prestige by the upstaging performances of the Soviet Union. The Department was also disgusted with De Gaulle, while being constantly nagged by its FSOs in the region to grant recognition. There were, moreover, other considerations which led to the September decision.

First, it was felt that an angry nationalism was heating up in Syria, partly in reaction to French truculence and partly manufactured by Syria's politicians, their object being to retrieve Syria's pre-mandate status in the Arab world as founder and leader of pan-Arabism. Second, it was felt that it was militarily unnecessary, as well as psychologically impossible, to defer any longer to De Gaulle and his great-power pretenses. And third, it was the Departmental consensus that the United States, already

Britain's senior partner in most respects, would and should continue after the war to maintain a regional predominance which would also embrace the Levant. While it was expected that this de facto hegemony, overall, would not be difficult or expensive, success was not expected to be so automatic that no effort would be required. Minimal action to keep the ground moist and fertile was necessary; hence the extension of recognition in September 1944.[16]

On the local level there were two other catalysts. One was Syria's anger over pre-election party platforms and speeches in America favorable to Zionism; the other was Syria's desire for cordial relations with Washington and for recognition and aid. (Interestingly, it was apparent to FSO William Porter in Damascus that to achieve the latter desire, Syria was willing to mute the former anger somewhat.[17] However, neither Porter nor the Department drew any moral from this observation, such as that the United States had a potentially good opportunity, as a victorious great power, to offer the Syrians support, provided they compromised their absolute anti-Zionism.) To void French claims and to cement good relations with America, Syria also wanted to declare war against the Axis and have United Nations forces use its territory for the "common" war effort.

Finally, an American recognition policy was precipitated by a surprise British Foreign Office reversal of its Levant policy. Prior to the September decision, the Foreign Office pulled back from its three years of trying to persuade the Department to extend recognition. Partly in reflexive reaction to suspected British chicanery, Hull deliberately went ahead.

Even so, the Foreign Office did not quit. It now tried to offset the Arabs' negativism toward France, which British and American diplomats had been encouraging for decades; and it came out in favor of French hegemony. Toward that end it charged General Spears, though personally an avid Francophobe, to persuade the independent states of Syria and Lebanon to make a treaty with France that would acknowledge France's basic preeminence and rights of militarily defending the Levant. Britain's treaty relations with Iraq were to be the model, as these presumably showed that great-power preeminence and native independence were not necessarily incompatible.

The British explained their move to the Department as a continuation rather than a reversal of policy. They were merely trying to "get things ironed out" regarding French-Levant relations. More broadly, they wanted to maintain good relations with France by demonstrating that neither in the Middle East nor in Europe was London conspiring to supplant Paris. They also said that they wished finally to withdraw British troops from the Levant in view of the fact that the progress of the war made it needless to stay in Syria and protect it for the sake of the war effort. Too, the British claimed that the French under De Gaulle were getting stronger. It would therefore be wise for Syria and Lebanon to negotiate a treaty with France now, as they "might not be able to obtain later the same favorable terms they could expect at present."[18]

The Department disagreed, Hull and the planners taking particular umbrage. The British stance was viewed as another illustration of Albion's manipulative deceit and stubborn rivalry toward its American benefactor. On the personal level, the planners felt that if it were successful, British policy would frustrate and undermine their own long and wearisome labors of deliberating and drafting America's Levant policy.[19] NEA and the FS also dissented, but with less pique and disappointment.

Withal, the Department adopted what in effect was a two-level approach towards the subject of treaty negotiations between France and the Levant states. On one level, Hull and Roosevelt, in the final months of 1944, expressed a seemingly benign and laissez-faire attitude. As long as American interests in the Levant were not injured, as long as the open door would be affirmed there, the United States would be neutral on the treaty issue relative to French cultural and military preeminence. Of course, in the event that a treaty was negotiated and it discriminated against Americans, the Department, said Hull, would refuse to approve it.[20]

On a second level, however, the Department was actively involved in aligning all the interested parties so as to discourage the emergence of any treaty with teeth. It sought to keep the British from taking an active role on France's behalf; and indeed, Wadsworth reported to the Department with apparent satisfaction that both he and Syrian President Kuwatli disbelieved that the British, particularly in their army circles, were really all that desirous of a Franco-Syrian treaty.[21]

Similarly, the Department tried to convert the French from their waywardness, and it periodically preached the gospel that generosity, concessions, and flexibility paid. Wallace Murray, speaking in the posture of a friend, tried to impress on French diplomats that Russia would capitalize on the troubles of the Levant and would be the only one to gain, to the collective detriment of the American-British-French alliance. He also suggested that France revive the slogans of the French Revolution and thus evoke native enthusiasm in Syria and Lebanon![22]

However, toward the Arabs of the Levant the Department preached absolutely nothing about the virtues of moderation and flexibility. As with the effects of American "neutrality" in other instances, the Department's hands-off attitude toward Syria's demands of the French buttressed even more the Syrian disposition of intransigence and self-righteousness. Wadsworth, the man on the scene, was as usual irrepressible with good will and friendship toward Syria's Francophobic leadership. Nor did Roosevelt say or do anything to lay to rest Syria's fixation that making even a minimal treaty with France would automatically void its sovereignty and its participation in the United Nations Organization.[23]

By the end of 1944, the Department's pressure and persuasion directed toward the British had proved successful. The British relented and dropped back from pressing for Paris-Beirut and Paris-Damascus treaty negotiations precisely when the French were becoming confident of achieving a treaty with Syria. Toward the French, however, Departmental sermons proved unavailing. The French would thus persist in their alleged folly, in what Murray considered to be their "insistence upon a legalistic and dictatorial approach." And toward the Syrians, the Department's policy of conveying expressions of continuous and open-ended good will showed Damascus that it could completely reject any terms France might offer, knowing that Washington would be supportive.[24]

WARTIME POLICIES, 1945

Because neither the French nor the Arabs changed their views, the conflict between the two escalated. Intermittently from December 1944 to June 1945, and more sporadically thereafter until the end of 1946, the French risked the world's displeasure by using force, including sending warships to Beirut and bombarding Damascus. Yet before 1945 France had already turned over to both Levant governments all the functions of the mandate except control of the *troupes speciales*. In the winter and spring of 1945 it revealed that it was willing to transfer these, too, if the British first withdrew the Ninth Army and if France received treaty rights for naval bases in Lebanon and air bases in Syria.

The British answered that they would withdraw only when a treaty was made. Actually, however, it was immaterial to the British, at this juncture, whether France did or did not get its bases. London was now less concerned with Anglo-French harmony than with long-run stability in the Arab world and an end to the war without Middle Eastern distractions. For these reasons, Britain, in mid-1945, once more intervened against French military measures, Churchill's rationalization being the military necessity of preserving communications to the Far Eastern theatre. Out of the same concern over instability, and because he was unafraid of speaking his mind to Arab leaders, Churchill earlier in the year had also urged Kuwatli of Syria to sign a treaty with France and not to fear that loss of sovereignty would result. Along the same lines, the Foreign Office was hopeful that the Department and Roosevelt would also try to soften the Syrians.[25]

Indeed, several within the Department itself—for example, Foy Kohler of NEA and Joseph Grew, veteran ambassador and undersecretary to

Edward Stettinius, Jr., Hull's successor after November 1944—for the first time began to articulate the thought that Syrian and Lebanese intransigence was becoming indefensible. Grew, who was in effect the Department's main policy maker in the first half of 1945, stood for moderation on all sides. Though hardly pro-French, he nonetheless steered the ship of state a few degrees away from Hull's one-sided hostility to De Gaulle and a few miles toward greater activism and mediation. In this connection, he several times requested George Wadsworth—as Hull had done before him and as Dean Acheson would do after, though Grew did it more often—to restrain his well-known enthusiasm.

Unlike the Department's Middle East experts, Grew believed that it was both right and necessary to deal with De Gaulle's France as one of the great powers, and that De Gaulle was amenable to reason. Grew tended to deal with De Gaulle's rule in the Levant more by way of the Department's Europeanists and FSOs in France than by way of its Arabists. This was partly because the Europeanists shared his view that, in the interests of the postwar Atlantic alliance, America should not alienate France on secondary issues like the Levant. Grew's modus was to have the Europeanists and Ambassador Jefferson Caffery in Paris work on French Foreign Minister Georges Bidault, who, while he spoke for De Gaulle, was personally more tractable. The hope was that De Gaulle, approached as the head of a great power and in the name of the Western alliance, would be persuaded of the necessity to change France's counterproductive methods on several fronts, the Levant and the Franco-Italian border particularly.

Grew was willing, moreover, to practice an overt form of carrot-and-stick pressure against France. Though France never received Lend-Lease for Syria and Lebanon, it did receive military supplies on a bilateral basis. These were suspended through the Department's doing—until Grew recommended to Truman that they be renewed in mid-1945, after De Gaulle had withdrawn from confrontation on the Italian border.[26]

For all that, Grew was no Francophile; and while it is often not clear from the diplomatic record to what degree the middle managers for the Middle East in NEA and the Foreign Service influenced Grew, the fact was that their efforts to persuade never ceased. The effect of such input was to limit Grew's own limited policy of working for moderation on all sides. FSO dispatches from Jidda and Baghdad, which reported Arab anger and hopes that America would forcibly restrain France, served to keep alive the Department's fundamental anxiety about alienating the vast and presumably monolithic Arab-Moslem world. George Wadsworth continued to meddle—here, agreeing with Syria and Lebanon that a good way to avoid France's wish for a special treaty was to offer identical treaties to other powers; there, suggesting that Britain physically prevent French troops from disembarking at Beirut's port—and while his wrist was occasionally slapped, he went his merry way. In fact, he was defended orally by Grew when France several times sought his removal as persona non grata. Moreover, although Wadsworth as a reporter editorialized in his dispatches more than any other FSO in the region, he was never corrected.[27]

Loy Henderson, when he became director of a reorganized Office of Eastern and African Affairs (EA & A) in the spring of 1945, also turned out to be a vociferous foe of France in the Levant. His frequent memoranda were presented as dire and urgent philippics. French tactics, he inveighed, "are similar to those used by the Japanese in Manchukuo and by the Italians in Ethiopia," as well as to those "pursued by Russia in Eastern Europe." France disgraced the Allies, destroyed the confidence of little countries in great powers, and dealt a blow to the prestige of the infant UN Organization and the recently convened San Francisco Conference. As for France's wish for preeminence in the Levant, none at all should be countenanced, said Henderson, even on the level of education, language, and culture. The French have no rights in the Levant, indeed had none even when the mandate was legal. Any influence they might have in the future must be secured on a nondiscriminatory basis and by the free consent of the Levant states.[28]

To Henderson, the Levant problem boiled down to narrow French opportunism versus idealistic American principles. Paul Alling, Henderson's associate, had an identical view. When a French diplomat asked whether the open-door principle, sponsored by a colossal America, did not create an unfair and weighted competition against war-scarred powers like France, Alling "vigorously" disagreed. He went on to sermonize with sincerity that "equality of opportunity was high on our list of war aims and that we had no intention of fighting this war and then abandoning our objectives."[29]

In sum, relative to France, some mediation with the French on the part of the upper echelons and more confrontation on the part of the middle echelons were the two main currents in the Department, both before and after Hull's departure in November 1944. Relative to Syria and Lebanon in particular, the pattern was similar: the upper echelons hesitated to accede to the Levant's requests for active American involvement; and the middle managers pressed forward precisely for "more action, less words."

On all levels, however, the Department invariably sympathized with Syria's posture as victim and with its grievances against the French. These grievances were many. For example, at various times in 1945 Syria was hesitating about joining the war against the Axis alongside a French "ally" whom it despised; and Syria was pointing out that the French were inciting Syria's minorities, dragging their feet about withdrawal, and massacring civilians.

At the same time, Syria was ever eager to compete with adjacent states for prestige and power, specifically, to seek recognition as pan-Arab leader. Toward the satisfaction of all these grievances and desires, therefore, Syrians held numerous public demonstrations, and their government repeatedly asked for American political intervention. Syria also sought military supplies and an American military-training mission. It even hinted at the desirability of sending American troops.[30]

Even if its sincere sympathy for Syria was discounted, the Department never really needed Damascus' special pleading in order to protest against the French presence in the Levant. Self-interest was enough. It was therefore easy for the upper echelons to comply with the identical requests of Syria, on the one hand, and of NEA and the Foreign Service, on the other, for diplomatic pressure against De Gaulle.

However, the upper echelons drew the line when it came to converting American diplomatic sympathy and protests into concrete actions, such as employing sustained sanctions against France or shipping American arms and loans to Syria. Thus, and even with Departmental sympathy considered as an important input in the making of foreign policy, the upper echelons rebuffed the middle managers, and Syria's leaders, on the topic of military aid requests.

This rebuff, in the period August–November 1945, presents an interesting revelation of intradepartmental conflict in early postwar tactics and viewpoints. The middle managers for the Middle East felt that to assist Syria tangibly was an absolutely incontrovertible and desirable objective. Accordingly, Henderson and his colleagues, notwithstanding their usual aversion to opportunism when practiced by others, were wholly enthusiastic over the fact that "the present request from the Syrian government [for military assistance] constitutes an excellent opportunity which we should seize at once." Pressing their case, they used every argument conceivable, from the tremendous benefits that would spontaneously accrue region-wide if American leapfrogged over the French and British by responding favorably to Syria's "easily granted" requests, to the tremendous loss of face and status that would accrue if America failed to respond.[31]

To the Middle East managers, the opportunity provided by Syria's request for a military mission seemed especially bright because of Britain's weak domestic economy. In the period August–October, the Atlee-Bevin Labor government complained of the strain imposed by the Levant crisis: hence the British were agreeable to an American military role there. It may be noted that this was an early sign of a British trend which, two years later, culminated when the Foreign Office asked the Department to fill the breach in Greece and Turkey and the Department responded with what became the Truman Doctrine and a policy of global containment.

Even when, by November–December 1945, divisions among British policy makers became apparent and it seemed that the Foreign Office was once again tilting away from America toward France, the Office of Eastern and African Affairs was confident that it could make the British reconsent to a future American military presence in Syria. Like the tail that wags the dog, EA & A felt its will, largely unseen by the public, could control the very visible and, to all appearances, powerful British presence in the Levant.[32]

However, Grew, Acheson, and the middle managers of the Office of European Affairs, while opposed neither to EA & A's principle of a larger policy in the Middle East nor to the specific desirability of direct aid to Syria, felt that there existed militating factors. Uncertainties about legal precedents, about Congressional approval, and about the Department of War's ability to spare material freely represented one cluster of factors. Another was the external uncertainty about the chances of success of an American military mission, given Syria's backwardness and given its volatility in the event that the Truman government veered favorably toward pro-Zionism. Finally, the Department's Europeanists did not wish to rub salt in France's wounds, which would be how the sending of an American military mission would be perceived.

All in all, to the upper echelons and to the middle managers for Europe, the opportunity in Syria was not all that clear and bright, at least not yet, for an active American role. Indeed, in rebuttal to EA & A, it was contended that activism at that time might well be a "disruptive factor" with regard to (1) the joint Franco-British discussions on withdrawal from the Levant then taking place, and (2) the broader negotiations towards a European Franco-British alliance, which the Department's Europeanists wished to see achieved.[33]

CONCLUSIONS

Unsuccessful regarding the military mission to Syria, the Middle East middle managers were nonetheless not seriously in retreat for long. Made up of strong-willed and senior men, they would continue to press their views. The wartime research and analysis of the postwar planners on the Middle East also served to strengthen the belief that to be anti-Gaullist and pro-Arab was to be "objective." Likewise, in the postwar period pressures against France's presence in the Middle East (and North Africa) emanated chiefly from NEA and the Foreign Service. The Middle East experts would thus in effect weaken the resolve and ability of the upper echelons and of the Department's Europeanists to establish an Atlantic alliance with strong and willing French participation.[34]

The arguments used by NEA and FSOs in favor of Arab sovereignty in the Middle East invariably stressed the policy's moralism and realism. However, the other reality, that Arab nationalism was and would often be authoritarian, uncompromising, and brutal, and moreover was chauvinistic, irredentist, and imperialistic in a number of its aspirations, was considered immaterial. That most Arab nationalist leaders had respect neither for treaties they signed with former mandatories nor for the desire of political self-determination on the part of minorities in their midst, such as Jews, Maronites, Kurds, and Assyrians, were additional realities which were also immaterial and of no moral consequence to the Department. As noted in Chapter 1, the Department, after all, had a similar lack of respect toward, and fear of, too much ethnic-religious pluralism ("balkanization"), whether in Eastern Europe, the Middle East, or the United States itself.

In brief, the Department's "realism" and "moralism" were ever selective and opportunistic. To be sure, such selectivity based on selfish interest is a normal phenomenon. The Department would not have agreed with these views, however. Its self-deceiving self-image of being more objective and principled than everyone else would have prevented it from seeing itself as anything less than a beacon to all mankind.

NOTES

1. The relevant subcommittee papers are, in the Notter Papers, the following: ST Minutes 11, 3 March 1943, pp. 9–10; ST Minutes 12, 10 March 1943, pp. 4–6; and ST Minutes 13, 17 March 1943, p. 2, all in Box 49, volume: "Minutes of Security Technical Problems (1—." Also, "Tentative Views of the Subcommittee on Political Problems," P-214, 12 March 1943, p. 15; and "Views of the Territorial Subcommittee," P-214c, 10 March 1943, p. 5, both in Box 3, Folder: "Doc.: Subcom. on Polit. Probs., Tent. Views of Coms." Also, P-215, 19 March 1943, p. 3, Box 63, Folder: "P Docs 201–225." In the MacLeish Papers, see P Min 48, 20 March 1943, p. 3, Box 41, Folder: "Secret File—Polit. Subcom., Dept. of State."
2. Wilbur White, Jr., "Syria and Lebanon: Interests and Positions of the United States," T-308, 14 April 1943, p. 1, Notter Papers, Box 34, Folder: "T Docs. 300–309."
3. White, "Syria and Lebanon: British Interests and Commitments," T-306, 19 April 1943; and "Syria and Lebanon: French Interests and Commitments," T-307, 19 April 1943, both in Notter Papers, Box 34, Folder: "T Docs 300–309." Also, White, "Syria and Lebanon: Degree of Unification," T-331, 3 June 1943; "Syria and Lebanon: Degree of Independence," T-332, 3 June 1943; and "Syria and Lebanon: Economic Foundations," T-335, 14 June 1943, all in Box 34, Folder: "T Docs 326–336."
4. On Wadsworth, see the section on FSOs in Chapter 4 above; also, e.g., Wadsworth to Hull, 23 March 1943, *FR* 4 (1943): 963–65; and Wadsworth to Hull, 1 May 1943, 890D.00/956.
5. Wallace Murray to Hull, 1 January 1943, FW 890D.00/928.
6. For the British view, see Wadsworth to Hull, 25 May 1943, p. 973;

British embassy secretary M. Wright to P. Alling, 28 June 1943, p. 979; and Aide-Memoire from the British embassy to the Department, 10 September 1943, p. 991, all in *FR* 4 (1943). Also, on the British views in the Levant, see Woodward, *British Foreign Policy*, vol. 4, Chapter 54. This volume, an excellent if official study based on Foreign Office documents, became available too late for me to use and incorporate in my own study, much as I would have liked to. Volume 4 is also germane on British and British-American policy in Saudi Arabia and Palestine.

7. Wadsworth to Hull, 2 August 1943, *FR* 4 (1943): 982. The bishops' approach was apparently a reaction to the fact that the French authorities, the Maronites' traditional "protectors," had acceded to Moslem insistence on restructuring the Moslem-Christian ratios, to the detriment of Christian representation and power. Wadsworth wrote, relating his reply to the bishops, "I was politely discouraging; diplomatic practice precluded my interfering in internal political matters." On Kuwatli, see Wadsworth to Hull, 18 August 1943, *FR* 4 (1943): 986.

8. See note 26 below; and note 13 in Chapter 4.

9. Wadsworth to Hull, 11 November 1943, p. 1016; Wadsworth to Hull, #310, 11 November 1943, p. 1012; and Hull to Wadsworth, #269, 12 November 1943, p. 1022, all in *FR* 4 (1943).

10. Kirk to Hull, 11 November 1943, p. 1021; Hull to Wiley (consul general, Algiers), 23 November 1943, p. 1045; and Paul Alling, Memorandum, 25 November 1943, p. 1049, all in *FR* 4 (1943). In the latter, Alling expressed the wish of Roosevelt that "we should support the British position in Lebanon and even try to make it more positive."

11. The planners' discussions, and omissions, are found, in the Notter Papers, in W. White, Jr., H-35, 20 August 1943, p. 2; and H-36, 20 August 1943, pp. 2–5, both in Box 57, Folder: "H-Policy Summaries 26–39."

12. In addition, it was believed on general principles that America's long-run interest in decolonization made the "ultimate liberation" of Morocco, and possibly Tunisia, a major American interest. This was the view of Departmental legal advisor, Green Hackworth, and implicitly of the planners' Policy Committee and of the Office of Economic Affairs, although FSOs in North Africa dissented somewhat. It should be noted that Algeria was excluded from the discussion. It was not considered a French colony to be liberated, but was seen as part of metropolitan France.

In the Notter Papers, see "Summary of Official Policy With Respect to the Post-War Administration of Dependent Areas," P-244a, 15 March 1944, pp. 6–7, Box 186, Folder: "Commitments: Dependent Areas"; and Minutes of 5th meeting, Policy Committee, 28 January 1944, Box 15, Folder: "Pol. Com. Min. 1–22." The quotation on 1943 Departmental policy is from P-240, 12 July 1944, p. 12, Box 186, Folder: "Commitments: Dependent Areas." Another typically simplistic analysis on the theme that if only the French were removed, instability in North Africa would cease, is in OSS Report, R & A Branch, #1693, 20 May 1944, Box 38, Folder: "T Docs 484–90." On the historical precedents of American policy, see Charles F. Gallagher, *The United States and North Africa: Morocco, Algeria, and Tunisia* (Cambridge, Mass.: Harvard Univ. Press, 1963), pp. 101–2, 232–37.

13. C. P. Grant, "Syria and Lebanon: Future Status," H-170 Prelim. 25 April 1944, pp. 4–5, 8–10, Notter Papers, Box 60, Folder: "H-Pol. Sum., 166–79."

14. The relevant planning papers are, in the Notter Papers, ibid., p. 5; C.

P. Grant, H-170, 25 May 1944; and H-170 Supplement, 8 June 1944, p. 3, all in Box 60, Folder: "H-Pol. Sum., 166–79."

It is interesting to note that the planners also justified sending American advisors to the Levant on the grounds that the United States had many citizens of Syrian-Lebanese background; and that there were other American citizens interested in the Iraqi Petroleum Company and the American University of Beirut. C. P. Grant and W. Yale, Paper on U.S. Advisers for Middle East, H-186 Prelim., 3 August 1944, p. 4, Notter Papers, Box 60, Folder: "H Pol. Sum. 180–80." Departmental sympathy for the rising Arab nationalism of Syrian-Lebanese Americans was occasionally expressed. Thus Grew, on the Arab-American lobby, the Institute for Arab American Affairs: "[It made] the interesting point that numbers of Americans of Syrian and Lebanese origin had died while serving in the U.S. armed forces in the liberation of France" [Memorandum, 1 June 1945, Grew Papers, MS Am 1687.3, vol. 7(22)]. Of course when ethnic feeling was *not* seen as pro bono publico, the Departmental criticized it as an un-American example of dual loyalty. Cf. Chapters 13 and 14, text; also, notes 2, 7 and 8, Chapter 6, and notes 28 and 30 in Chapter 1.

15. See "Official Statement and Views Pertaining to the Administration of Dependent Areas After the War," P-2406, 31 August 1944, pp. 65–66, Notter Papers, Box 186, Folder: "Commitments: Dependent Areas."

16. The relevant Departmental reports, for the pivotal month of September 1944, are in *FR* 5 (1944): 774–91. For Hull's first recognition statement, on 19 September 1944, see p. 782.

Despite the twists and turns after the Vichy period, it is important to realize that the Department always intended to recognize the independence of Syria and Lebanon but was ever waiting for the most opportune and necessary moment. See Hull's earlier press release of 29 November 1941 on the Question of Recognition of Syrian and Lebanese Independence, in *Bulletin* 5 (1941): 440.

17. "It had been apparent for some time that only the desire of the Syrian Government to maintain the most cordial relations with the United States restrained the smoking editorial pens of this city from making hot rebuttals to Mr. [Thomas] Dewey's statement [on Palestine]." From William Porter, "Monthly Review," 10 November 1944, p. 5, 890D.001/11–1044. See also Porter, "Monthly Review," 4 October 1944, p. 3, 890D.00/10–444.

18. On the British reversal, see Wadsworth to Hull, 15 September 1944, p. 777; and Foy Kohler, Memorandum of Conversation (NEA and M. Wright of British embassy), 28 September 1944, p. 792, both in *FR* 5 (1944).

19. "It is an effort by the British to predetermine post-war settlements with respect to Syria and the Lebanon without taking into consideration the wishes of the U.S." (W. Yale to P. Ireland, Memorandum, 25 September 1944, p. 1, Yale Papers, Box 4, Folder: "Syria, #3").

20. Hull to Wadsworth, 7 October 1944, p. 789, and 14 October 1944, p. 802, both in *FR* 5 (1944).

21. Wadsworth to Hull, 20 October 1944, *FR* 5 (1944): 805.

22. F. Kohler, Memorandum of Conversation (W. Murray of NEA and French delegation), 10 October 1944, *FR* 5 (1944): 799–800.

23. Roosevelt to Kuwatli, 7 December 1944, *FR* 5 (1944): 812–13.

24. The quotation is from an exchange between Murray and British counselor M. Wright, 4 October 1944, *FR* 5 (1944): 794.

25. A critical and complicated month was February 1945; all official and Departmental interest in Syria and Lebanon, if only on the level of quantity of communications, was increasing by leaps. On French "belligerence" and Churchill's reactions, see *FR* 8 (1945): 1034–50.

26. On Grew's Europeanist approach to France, see Grew to Caffery (ambassador, Paris), 23 May 1945, *FR* 8 (1945): 1092–93; memoranda, 2 June 1945, 8 June 1945, and 13 June 1945, Grew Papers, MS Am 1687.3, vol. 7 (22, 27, 30); and Grew, *Turbulent Era,* vol. 2, pp. 1508, 1515. One of Grew's most significant acts, though trivial on the surface, was to persuade Truman to deal with DeGaulle by means of a friendly and personal letter. *FR* 8 (26 May 1946): 1104. On Grew's intermittent restraining of FSO Wadsworth, see *FR* 8 (1945): 1042–43, 1073, 1117.

27. Wadsworth to Hull, 20 October 1944, *FR* 5 (1944): 805; Wadsworth to Grew, 9 January 1945, *FR* 8 (1945): 1034–35; Wadsworth to Grew, 2 February 1945, ibid., p. 1038; Wadsworth to Grew, 8 May 1945, ibid., p. 107; and Chapter 4 on FSOs. Wadsworth's irrepressibility extended after the war, too. See Memoranda, 4 February 1946 and 9 February 1946, Pasvolsky Papers, Box 7, Folder: "Security Council Feb. 1946."

It is worth noting that Wadsworth in effect misled his Arab hearers with his constant maximal pledges of American support and with his concomitant downgrading of any American interest in Zionism. Thus, whenever an American political leader endorsed a Jewish homeland in Palestine the Arabs felt, variously, that it was mere electioneering, or that they were being "betrayed" by America, and/or that a Jewish conspiracy of wealth and the media in America had caused a reversal. For had not Departmental officers like Wadsworth conditioned and assured them for years that American foreign policy was anti-Zionist? I would submit that the Department's practice of such self-deception and deception of the Arabs—as if, in the making of American foreign policy, Presidential, Congressional, and domestic opinion counted for naught—was as much a cause of the Arabs' evolving hostility to the U.S. as of the substantive fact that after the war American Presidents did support the right of a Jewish state to exist. On the Department's insular and "elitist" approach to foreign policy making, see note 7, Chapter 4. For an example of postwar Arab frustration (Feisal of Saudi Arabia) as a result of Wadsworth's rhetorical overkill, see de Gaury, *Feisal,* pp. 73–74.

28. Quotations are from L. Henderson, Memorandum, 23 May 1945, *FR* 8 (1945): 1093–94. Also, note Henderson, Memorandum, 15 May 1945, ibid., pp. 1075–78; and the section on FSOs that treats Henderson in Chapter 4.

29. F. Kohler, Memorandum of Conversation (P. Alling, Fr. counselor F. Lacoste), 10 March 1945, *FR* 8 (1945): 1054.

30. On Syria's emotions, as perceived by the Foreign Service, see the references in *FR* 8 (1945): 1047–49, 1062, 1095, 1122, 1125; also, J. Grew, Memorandum, 3 August 1945, Grew Papers, MS Am 1687.3, vol. 7(43).

With regard to the turbulent wartime Arab street demonstrations, of which Damascus' demonstrations were the archtype, the Syrian leadership often alluded ominously, and sincerely, to the negative effects anti-Western, anti-Zionist demonstrations could have. Syria might veer away from the United States. The United States might lose prestige and influence. However, it seems that part of the emotional anxiety felt by Arab political elites in general derived from personal fears of political displacement and bodily injury, either from the very street masses they had long whipped up or from a conclusive clash with the British Ninth Army, if it should move in. To keep one step ahead of the crowd, they therefore spoke, and with great emotion, of dire consequences to the Allies if France, or the Jews, were not expelled. It is my conjecture that the Foreign Service tended, or preferred, to see this purple emotionalism of Arab leaders solely as evidence of a grave threat to the Allies (and perhaps to the FSOs personally), rather than as a partial projection of the Arab leaders' own defensiveness and fear of the masses' violence. For allusion to these fears, see Wadsworth to Hull, 17 November 1943, *FR* 4 (1943): 1035.

31. Henderson to Assistant Secretary James Dunn, 17 August 1945, pp. 1201–3; Henderson to H. Freeman Matthews (Office of European Affairs), 13 November 1945, pp. 1208–9; and Adrian Colquitt, NEA Memorandum, 6 November 1945, pp. 1209–13, all in *FR* 8 (1945).

Interestingly, however, Henderson, together with the Department's economic consultants, was negative to Syria's request in September for a $20 million loan; and in fact he encouraged Syria to avail itself of French funds. Implicit was the view that important as it was for the United States to assist Syria, it was also important not to throw dollars away, given Congress's monetary stringency and its animus toward the Department, and given Syria's lack of oil and exploitable resources, its general poverty, and its inability to repay. (Better to let France bear the economic responsibility—though of course without giving the French any economic privileges.) L. Henderson, Memorandum, 10 September 1945, *FR* 8 (1945): 1215–16.

32. Thus Colquitt, NEA Memorandum, p. 1211: "NEA is aware that lack of British support might impair—or contribute to the impairment of—the success of the [military] mission. It seems highly probable, however, that the British will support us if we show that we mean business."

33. Acheson to Wadsworth, 15 September 1945, pp. 1203–4, and Matthews to Henderson, 17 November 1945, pp. 1214–15, both in *FR* 8 (1945). Also on the Europeanist-Arabist contrast, see G. P. Merriam, Memorandum, 15 June 1945, 867N.01/G–1545.

34. That France has never forgiven the U.S. for forcing it out of the Mediterranean is a truism revealed repeatedly in the decades after 1945, e.g., after the Yom Kippur War of October 1973 in the form of the Franco-American dispute over Western consumer policy toward Arab oil producers. To Americans, the French are often narrow, intriguing, and obstreperous; but to the French, Americans are often placed among the biggest imperialists of all. The dialogue of the deaf has been long between the two, as evidenced in the following comments by Anne O'Hare McCormick, at the 1945 San Francisco Conference: "France, on her side, is tortured by defeat into an excess of self-assertiveness which clouds her judgment. She is inclined to be more than ever suspicious of Britain and even of the United States, *for strange as it may seem to Americans, fear of 'American imperialism' is real in many French minds*" (Emphasis added. *New York Times*, 30 May 1945, p. 18).

III

Policy Toward the British Sphere of Influence

8

Britain and the Middle East
Supply Center

THE DEPARTMENT AND BRITAIN

During World War II, Departmental policy toward the British in the Middle East was deliberately bifocal: As shall be demonstrated in this and subsequent chapters, the Department was supportive in the short run, for the sake of the combined war effort, and was competitive in the long run, for the sake of solidifying America's postwar economic hegemony. Essentially, the Department's regional objective was to reverse roles with the British: if Washington had been a junior partner to London in the region before the war and in its first phases, the Department sought to make sure that thereafter Washington would be senior partner, or if not that, at least co-equal to London.

Within these general objectives, Departmental tactics were eclectic, depending on a complex of factors at any given moment, such as the "mood" of Washington, the phase of the war, the state of Allied arms, and the particular Middle Eastern country and interest involved. Thus, in oil-rich Saudi Arabia the Department was determined by the last third of the war to replace completely British political-economic-military influence with a monopoly of American influence. In British spheres like Egypt and, after July 1941, Syria and Lebanon—without oil, but with strategic and commercial potentials—the Department was more interested in simply leveling but not necessarily eliminating British influence. The object here was economic access and open-door competition, not monopoly.

However, in Palestine, Transjordan, and the Suez Canal Zone (though not in the rest of Egypt) the Department wanted a continuation of Britain's "primary military responsibility." The Department wanted the British to police and keep the lid on Arab-Jewish tensions over Palestine and on Arab-Arab tensions over Transjordan (where there was competition between the Hashemite and Saudi dynasties). The Department also wished to keep the strategic Suez Canal Zone under Western control, out of the reach of any Soviet probes into the region. The Department wanted the British to pursue these ends at their own expense and without reaping any special rights or privileges from their labors.

The Department was least interested in the British-run emirates and states on the periphery of the Arabian peninsula, and in "independent" Iraq. In these areas it preferred a continuation of Britain's predominance to that of other powers; and despite protestations it did not seriously, or consistently, object when Britain tended to arrogate to itself political, economic, and military rights. This aloofness obtained during most of World War II—in marked contrast to the early 1920s, when the loudest Departmental protests against British privilege dealt with the Persian Gulf area and Iraq.

It appears that the Department tacitly endorsed British continuity in these latter cases as a tradeoff for the British loss of Saudi Arabia. Endorsement was also understood by the Department as representing an act of regional "partnership," as well as furnishing evidence that the United States was not desirous of forcing the British out of the region. Furthermore, the Department trusted that British influence would prevent instability or local interstate encroachments, which were definite possibilities, given the internal weaknesses and slender populations of Britain's feudal client states. That too much American unilateralism would be costly and entangling and that too much American anti-imperialism would do harm to the British home islands and reduce their utility to the United States as an Atlantic trading partner and military associate were also fundamental considerations in the formulation of tactics toward the British presence in the Middle East.

Clearly, the Department's relations with Britain were the most widespread, continuous, and crucial, not to say complex, of all America's great-power relations in the region. Understanding Anglo-American relations is, in addition, an essential prerequisite for understanding America's bilateral policies with the individual countries of the Middle East. However, because America's bilateral relations with Egypt, et al, were so entwined with relations with England, it is best to leave to the chapters on individual countries the full, if localized, examination of Anglo-American relations. There is at least one exception, a case in which Anglo-American relations were not entwined with any single Middle Eastern state. This exception also represents a good case study on a regional scale of great-power economic initiative and diplomacy, typified by surface cooperation and subsurface competition. As an introduction to Anglo-American Middle East diplomacy, it is appropriate therefore to examine Departmental policy towards the British-founded Middle East Supply Center (MESC).

THE RISE OF DEPARTMENTAL APPROVAL OF MESC

In April 1941 the British established a Middle East Supply Council in London and a Middle East Supply Center in Cairo. The general purpose was to make up for the war-caused shortages of civilian imports, food supplies, and shipping transport in the Middle East. The British believed that they could achieve this purpose by husbanding local resources, developing agriculture and local industries, and rationing those commercial imports which continued in spite of the war. The instrumentality would be the Center in Cairo, assisted by a regional network of British-staffed ration boards and outlets.[1]

MESC's objective was more than philanthropy and relief. Rather, MESC was meant to maintain British regional hegemony by "stabilizing" economic conditions. Hence, in the early phase of the war, when the Axis powers were presenting themselves to the Arab world as alternatives preferable to Britain, MESC saw to it that regional shortages did not get out of hand and lead to Arab agitation. Such a situation, the British felt, could easily have impeded the war effort, intensified Axis influence, and alienated the Arabs completely from the British.

In the second half of the war, MESC became important to the British for different reasons. By this time, it had successfully stimulated the growth of industry and modernization, notably in the Jewish part of Palestine and in Egypt. In the British view, MESC thus proved to be a successful model of etatism and economic planning. Its continuation into the postwar period seemed desirable on both counts: not only would it strengthen the Middle Eastern economy; MESC's organization and rationing system would also presumably provide guidance in solving Britain's own expected postwar shortages in the home islands.

By 1944 MESC had emerged as an instrument which had cemented, under British aegis, the wartime economic relations of most Middle Eastern states. The British felt that if it were continued, MESC would be capable of checking America's expected economic and political advances in the region. MESC was also viewed by the Foreign Office as a likely stepping-stone to a postwar federation of Arab states under British sponsorship.[2]

For all that, the British wanted American support for MESC. The idea was first broached by the Foreign Office to the Department early in 1942, when Britain was facing the Axis with its back to the wall and therefore needed help badly. The stated reasons for the overture were that Britain felt efficiency and friendship would be furthered if American collaboration would be more direct and involved than the liaisons the Department thus far had maintained with MESC through the American legation in Cairo. The Foreign Office spoke of "showing joint decision and full cooperation."

At bottom, however, the Foreign Office, under Foreign Secretary Eden, wanted and needed a marriage of convenience with a rich junior partner. It was the British ambition to continue to make the major decisions while obtaining more Lend-Lease supplies for its Middle Eastern sphere of influence. Concurrently, Washington, through direct participation, would gain coveted prestige as co-author and "great power," would be weaned yet farther away from its ever-present isolationist tendencies, would clearly help the British pull their "chestnuts" out of the fire by taking on financial responsibilities for the Middle East—but not to the point of having more than the illusion of being a regional power equal to Britain.[3]

In Washington, Herbert Feis, the Department's Economic Adviser, together with Undersecretary Sumner Welles and Frederick Winant of the Division of Exports and Defense Aid, reacted favorably to the idea of American participation in MESC. Winant, who in May 1942 would be chosen as first American representative to MESC, expatiated on the advantages of participation to the war effort and to America's self-interest, even though he sensed that Britain would try to reap the advantages and keep the actual American role small.[4]

Winant claimed that participation would cut down on waste, duplication and a "collision" of viewpoints, in short, that participation would enhance the war effort by promoting an "optimum correlation." Also, participation would provide the United States with "complete information on country and area requirements" of the Middle East and would promote this country's "strong political influence over the affairs of the Near East as a sphere, in addition to the influence now exerted on the individual countries." Winant concluded that the advantages of wartime participation were possibly stepping-stones to a stronger postwar American role as well.[5]

Ironically, FSOs seemed less eager and somewhat defensive. Minister Alexander Kirk in Cairo expressed objection at first to the idea of American participation. He claimed that his own bailiwick, the American legation, was doing a fully satisfactory job as liaison with the British MESC. He also intimated that full participation would open the door to new and ignorant Lend-Lease people who would come into his preserve and override the views of established American and British experts. In this vein, he feared that such a change in the status quo might interfere with the legation's "easy access to these experts as well as to those connected with the Egyptian Government and certain private organizations here."[6]

However, Kirk did not press his point; and regardless, by June 1942 the deal had gone through in London and Washington. Secretary Hull informed Kirk that General R. L. Maxwell, already on a military mission in Cairo, would be America's military representative to MESC, and Winant would be "United States Civilian Representative on the MESC," attached also to the Foreign Service missions at Cairo, Teheran, and Jidda.[7]

Hull's positive decision on participation had significant implications. By the end of 1942, one school of thought in the Department was projecting from MESC's success in the pooling of wartime supplies a large-scale solution for the expected postwar problems of global shortages and reconstruction. This school, represented by Assistant Secretary Adolph Berle, Jr., theorized that because such problems would have to be solved before peace and free trade could be fully restored, and since the whole process of restoration might take years to complete after the war ended, the spirit of wartime cooperation and the machinery of the Allies' vast pooling efforts ought to continue after the war for as long as necessary.

Moreover, Berle felt that the continuity of the principle of governmental economic planning, so well epitomized by MESC, was important from the standpoint of "lessons" to be learned from history. After World War I, Washington had not only withdrawn from its wartime associates into political isolation and a cessation of governmental foreign aid; it had also dismantled its domestic economic planning and pooling boards. This "back to normalcy" approach—which, he argued, had also prevailed after the Civil War, leading to the period of the robber barons—had left the field free to unchecked private enterprise in the 1920s. Berle, a political economist of long standing, felt that this license, at home and abroad, had led to uneven postwar reconstruction, bitter interstate economic rivalries, vast domestic speculation followed by the Great Depression—in short, to much of the chaos which "caused" World War II. To avoid repeating this situation after World War II, MESC and like arrangements were thus deemed necessary.[8]

This school of thought was soon countered by a second one that was negatively disposed toward MESC and American participation, and that ultimately superseded the first school and became Departmental and Presidential policy. In essence, the second viewpoint argued that because MESC was a British creation and political instrument, and also an etatist-socialist economic model, it should be regarded as inherently contrary to American national interests: political, economic, and ideological. Hence MESC should be deprived of American financial support and then should be scuttled entirely at the earliest opportunity, even before the end of the war.

As for the anxieties that early termination would lead to shortages, poverty, and political instability, adherents of the second school felt these anxieties were groundless. Between the ever-increasing quantities of

American unilateral aid and Lend-Lease exported during the war, and the large-scale, pent-up American trading, shipping, and investing activities anticipated as soon as the final shots of the war were over, problems of shortages would be, it was believed, nipped in the bud.

There were a number of mutations and contrasting assumptions within this second school of thought. For that reason it is appropriate to take a closer look at its evolution, particularly in 1944. This was a watershed year because the Department, judging the war more than half over, gave more attention to postwar considerations than it had previously.

THE DECLINE OF DEPARTMENTAL APPROVAL OF MESC

In January 1944, Dean Acheson, Assistant Secretary for economic affairs—and a personal antagonist of Berle—intimated his opposition toward increasing America's staff personnel in, and supplies to, MESC. At the same time, Acheson explicitly advised against bypassing MESC and moving into the Middle East unilaterally, in the fashion advocated by Roosevelt's special ambassador, and an arch-critic of the Department, Patrick Hurley. Acheson's fear was that in *either* case a "large" American policy would carry the taint of imperialism, would breed bureaucratic bungling, and would create unnecessary suspicions and conflicts with America's chief allies, Britain and the Soviet Union.[9]

Acheson preferred a policy of reverse gradualism. He was optimistic that the Middle East's supply problems could be taken care of by the process, already begun, of restoring trade to private channels. Such a return to the status quo ante, he believed, was the best way not only to advance America's economic interests but, of equal concern to Acheson, to avoid political problems with allies and natives.

Somewhat less sanguine was the view of NEA. In March 1944, for example, NEA's W. L. Parker argued that the British might be correct after all in their contention that disruption of MESC would produce economic dislocations. Two things were therefore necessary, according to NEA: continued American support of MESC in the short run; and also new American pressure on Britain to give the Arab states more responsibility and rights in the management of MESC. The objective was to have MESC tutor the Arab states for postwar independence and therefore to transform MESC into more of an Arab and American, and a less exclusively British, tool. Like Acheson, NEA thus did not want to bypass MESC; unlike Acheson, it wanted to increase American representation in MESC.[10]

But exactly how far should Washington push London, and how much responsibility did the Department really wish to take? In April, Frederick Winant, chairman of the Middle East Supply Committee and former

MESC director, sought to analyze these questions at length. He concluded that in view of America's growing economic involvement in the region, America could not and should not accept a future role second to Britain's; but because of risks and costs, neither should it seek to displace Britain by outright competition. It would be best, implied Winant, if the United States pursued the middle way of a partnership role, provided that there was to be "equality of economic opportunity without any discrimination" and that "scarcity controls not be perpetuated beyond the period of a war economy."

Winant wished to see more quality, not more quantity, in the American staff, and more efficient use of existing administrative and supply offices in MESC under American supervision. Such improvements would produce a stronger American voice and participatory role in the making of MESC policy. "Decisions so reached will of necessity include protection of American interests."[11]

Parallel to Winant's formulation was that of Wallace Murray, the Department's chief Middle East expert, then in London with Undersecretary Edward Stettinius, Jr., for consultations with the British Foreign Office. On the future of MESC, Murray reiterated NEA's view favoring greater Arab participation. In response, the Foreign Office appeared cooperative and went out of its way to present the British position in a manner which could hardly be labeled imperialistic or contrary to the American principles of native self-determination and free trade. The Foreign Office dwelled on MESC's attempts to get local peoples to actively cooperate. It said that MESC was eager to persuade the Arabs that there were many long-run benefits to be gained from the improvement of local production methods, and in fact it wished to draw "them into the over-all picture through regional conferences."

But then the Foreign Office subtly tried to twist the Department's arm. These worthy efforts, concluded the Foreign Office, might be undermined—and with them the possibility of postwar regional development and mature, pro-Western native leadership—if American participation in MESC should falter. Thus did the British position of April 1944 come out strongly in favor (as it had in the more difficult days before El Alamein) of a continued American presence in, and continued economic support of, MESC—for postwar Anglo-American and native benefit, and not for Britain's exclusive gain.[12]

Murray generally acceded to his British colleagues' descriptions of MESC's present and future prospects, though he reiterated the Department's standard opposition "to the use of the MESC to perpetuate wartime controls and artificial trade barriers" and the Department's desire that "local [political] autonomy should be developed as rapidly as possible." The British, however, felt to the contrary, that regional and economic development should be the chief priority. As noted, the Foreign

Office hoped that MESC would be a stepping-stone, leading to the pro-British economic regionalism necessary for a future pro-British Arab federation.[13]

Apparent differences over priorities notwithstanding, both Murray and his counterpart, Sir Maurice Peterson, "emphasized . . . that it would be disastrous if American and British support were withdrawn too soon and the MESC allowed to deteriorate." And both agreed that the "ultimate ideal was an organization run by the native peoples with appropriate British and American advisers." Even so, like a fold in a rug that will not go away no matter how much the rug is bent and flattened, the Anglo-American "friendly rivalry" was still visible. In that regard, the Foreign Office probably won a minor delay, at least on paper, despite the Department's insistence on accelerated Arab participation in MESC. According to the final Agreed Minute's reference to MESC, "it was agreed that the Middle Eastern Governments should *if possible* be drawn *gradually* into closer association with the Centre so that they could be aided to cooperate with each other on social and economic problems."[14]

Agreement, however, did not last. Basically, the typical American attitude towards economic "controls" clashed with the typical British attitude. Americans only

saw in the MESC system a maze of detailed controls which outraged every American conception of free trade and free enterprise. Where the British saw a glorious opportunity the Americans saw a hateful necessity, to be abolished at the first possible moment.[15]

What brought the conflict into the open was a combination of American impatience over British foot-dragging in restructuring MESC, together with growing American élan over the fact that the war's outcome was becoming more definite and more of a distinctly "American" military victory. Thus the Department, never totally enthusiastic over MESC, moved increasingly toward quitting MESC once and for all. James Landis, Winant's successor as chief American civilian representative to MESC, catalyzed the downward process in June 1944, on a return visit to Washington. Within the Departmental planners' Policy Committee he intimated that Winant's earlier thesis of partnership in MESC was impossible, as MESC's very framework of controls and restrictions was and would remain inherently discriminatory and to America's disadvantage.

In this connection, Landis changed his own earlier view—he had favored more American manpower in MESC. He now differed from NEA, and also from the division of Wartime Economic Affairs (WEA) under Charles Taft. NEA and WEA still wanted at this juncture to increase America's manpower in MESC. In opposing that move, Landis joined Winant (whose concern had been quality, not quantity) and Acheson (whose fear was Hurleyesque crusading).

But it should be noted that Landis's opposition to larger representation bore only a superficial resemblance to Acheson's opposition. Acheson wanted a *conservative* role for the United States in the postwar Middle East. Insofar as there was to be any emphasis within that limited role, it was to be a *military-security* one, not an economic or political one. A small American MESC staff would be in keeping with limited economic activity. Landis, however, wanted larger *economic* activity and implied that a *small* American MESC staff could, in practice, promote that end more ably than a large staff.[16]

Subsequent arguments by others added to the negative judgment of MESC: British policy in MESC, while ostensibly serving emergency needs, was believed to be, both in effect and by design, predetermining the future of the Middle East to Britain's advantage. Yet British postwar plans on the ministerial level with respect to the disposition of war surplus by MESC were woefully incomplete, leaving the impression that much wasteful expense would have to be borne by the United States. Taken all together, these views, and the moods of impatience with Britain and élan over American victories, led the Department to view the British (on MESC and on most other issues, too) as right-thinking and fairly sincere in their wish for Anglo-American comity—yet grasping for the main chance and deceptive toward American innocents—and finally, as slothful in planning as they were inept in battle.[17]

By the end of 1944, the Departmental intention to dismantle MESC—and also Lend-Lease in general—became more certain. This was a result of the Department's acceptance of the November 1944 report of former ambassador William S. Culbertson's Special Economic Mission. The findings of this wide-ranging report—specifically alluded to thereafter by the Department as a "major document" of American economic policy—was based on visits that Culbertson and his "government-business team" had made to Italy, North Africa, and the Middle East. Given their a priori ideas about the beneficence of free trade and given the pressures imposed on them by sectors of American business, the mission found several predictable needs. It saw a need to relax MESC's and all other wartime controls, on the grounds that the emergency in the Mediterranean area was rapidly abating. And it saw a need to restore trade to private channels and implicitly to expand it, too, by exploiting America's new prestige and power and by propagandizing the open-door thesis.[18]

CONCLUSIONS

The Culbertson Report not only hardened intentions; it also led to a stepped-up effort by the Department to prepare the American public for imminent decisions affecting wartime controls. Thus, if MESC had once served, in 1942, as an example of the thesis that pooling efforts should be continued after the war, by the beginning of 1945 MESC served as an example of the opposite. An attitude of "good riddance to MESC" replaced the attitude that MESC could be the wave of the future. Indeed, the Department was in a hurry; the last chief American representative to MESC, Lt. Col. Harold Hoskins, was urging that the date of expiration of American participation and funding, and hence of MESC's existence, be advanced, from the designated date of 1 January 1946, to 1 November 1945.[19]

Patently eager to write MESC's obituary even before MESC was officially terminated (in November 1945), the Department also wished to have the public believe that MESC's termination was not a matter of any controversy within the Department, or between the Department and the Foreign Office, but was a natural and irreversible fact desired by all sides. Departmental speeches and releases spread the falsehood that MESC's apparatus, from the inception of American participation, was always uniformly regarded by the Department as for war use only. After all, "its controlling functions were hardly consistent with the American government's peacetime commercial policy."[20]

For its part, the Foreign Office sought delays on the grounds of MESC's administrative complexity. Finally, however, it acquiesced, and in September 1945 a joint Anglo-American statement on termination was released. One reason Britain acquiesced was because apparently it was loath to let America announce the termination unilaterally, as this would embarrass the British before the Arabs. More basic was the new Bevin-Atlee government's hope for postwar American loans, together with anxieties over possible American alienation and America's undermining traditional British markets. Also, the Arab League was already six months old, and the role of MESC as stepping stone to regional unity was apparently no longer considered necessary by the Foreign Office.[21]

In retrospect, British predictions of economic dislocations in the Middle East proved partly true. In October 1945, the Department noted that termination of MESC on the decreed date of November 1 would cause some hardships because of the inadequacy of private trade. It thus decided to continue for the indefinite future its MESC office and staff in Cairo. However, the term "MESC" was no longer to be used, and the office and staff were simply to be under a "regional economic counselor."[22]

All in all, the Department's concluding measures on MESC offer indirect proof that if MESC was hurried to the grave in 1944 and 1945, it was not because its economic functions were unnecessary. It was because the Department had decided that MESC gave Britain too much advantage, that it was a bad ideological precedent, that it was an obstacle to America's progress in the region, and that it must be thwarted.

NOTES

1. On MESC's birth, and the context thereof, see early chapters in Martin W. Wilmington, *The Middle East Supply Center,* ed. Lawrence Evans (Albany: State Univ. of New York, 1971); also Fisher, *The Middle East,* pp. 490–91.

2. See Guy Hunter, "Economic Problems: The MESC," in Kirk, *The Middle East in the War,* pp. 169–93; M. W. Wilmington, "MESC: A Reappraisal," *Middle East Journal* 6 (1952): 144–66, and addendum, pp. 366–67; and Sachar, *Europe Leaves the Middle East,* pp. 408–9. For a contemporary account, see H. P. Whidden, Jr., "MESC Holds Promise for Future of Middle East," *Foreign Policy Bulletin* 2 (24 September 1943): 4.

3. On the British "selling" of MESC to the Department in the period February–June 1942, see Herbert Feis, Memorandum of Conversation (Feis and G. Thorold, British embassy secretary), 24 February 1942, *FR* 4 (1942): 1; and other dispatches, pp. 2–17.

4. "Whether the British envisage the participation as a full partnership is not known, but the chances are that they think of the move as considerably less." Winant to Acheson, 17 April 1942, *FR* 4 (1942): 9.

5. "It may be that the Near East will become a focal point in the present world conflict, and that the United States forces will play an increasingly prominent part in the probable campaigns of the future. Gaining authority in the area for the current administration of *civilian* supplies would pave the way for similar authority in the *general* affairs of the area in the future." Emphasis added. Ibid., pp. 11–12.

6. Kirk to Hull, 19 March 1942, *FR* 4 (1942): 3.

7. Hull to Kirk, 18 June 1942, *FR* 4 (1942): 17. As of January 1943 MESC would consist of two headquarters. The first was that of the executive (operational) committee in Cairo, under Frederick Winant and, after August 1943, James Landis. Also attached were two American army representatives. In the main, Americans worked out of, and in liaison with, the legation in Cairo under FSO Alexander Kirk. According to one researcher (Wilmington), the total staff of MESC at its maximum was about 500, mainly of British and Commonwealth nationalities; and American personnel never exceeded 50, or 10%, of this total—although these latter figures seem contravened by Winant's 15 April 1944 report to the Departmental Policy committee, cited in note 11.

The second MESC headquarters was that of the policy making committee—i.e., the Middle East Supplies Committee, or Council, based in London. The U.S. representative was the Lend-Lease Coordinator, W. A. Harriman, Jr., with several alternates from the American embassy. See press release on MESC, *Bulletin* 8 (16 January 1943): 76 ff.; Wilmington, *MESC,* pp. 366–67; and F. Winant, "The Combined Middle East Supply Program," *Bulletin* 10 (26 February 1944): 204.

8. For an erudite and history-minded defense of MESC, see Adolph Berle, Jr., "The Realist Base of American Foreign Policy," *Bulletin* 7 (17 October 1942): 831–35. For more of his "Hamiltonian" ideology, see, *The Twentieth Century Capitalist Revolution* (New York: Harcourt, Brace, 1954).

9. "A distributing organization to perform all the functions of the United Kingdom Commercial Corporation might well require a staff of several thousand men, comparable to the staff of the United Kingdom Commercial Corporation. Anything like an organization on that scale, if our experience so far is

a guide, could easily destroy our prestige in the Middle East, and create endless, unnecessary and potentially disastrous conflict both with the British and the Russians, between whom we would be caught" (Acheson to Stettinius and Hull, 28 January 1944, p. 2, Stettinius Papers, Box 216, Folder: "U-Undersecretary of State, October 1943—"). Also, see note 20 in Chapter 1.

10. W. L. Parker, Memorandum on MESC, 16 March 1944, Stettinius Papers, Box 249, Folder: "London Mission—Background Material." Also, see Annex A to Supplement to NEA-1 (n. d., probably March 1944), Stettinius Papers, Box 378, Folder: "S. D. Miscell. File, Pol. Com. Docs. 1944."

11. Quotations are from F. Winant, Memorandum to Policy Committee on MESC, Annex B to WEA-20, 15 April 1944, pp. 1–2, Stettinius Papers, Box 379, Folder: "Miscell. File, Pol. Com. Docs. 1944."

12. According to Foy Kohler's report, the Foreign Office "emphasized that the real aim of the British as far as the MESC is concerned is to rationalize and coordinate the economic activities of the Middle Eastern countries and not in any sense to further British trade interests." Furthermore, the Foreign Office said that, "the British were concerned that the United States' participation in the MESC should be reinforced . . . that the Middle East cries out for leadership, particularly native leadership, being the first area to develop a post-war mood. There were a number of outstanding local economists and technicians throughout the region. Many were trained by the Rockefeller Foundation or trained in the United States on Rockefeller scholarships. However, if the matter were left to the local governments there was no assurance, in view of the prevailing nepotism and political favoritism, that these trained people would be usefully employed. On the other hand, their employment by outside powers was also disadvantageous. Consequently, the solution seemed to reside in the development of the MESC as an autonomous Middle Eastern economic organization, and the British are thinking along these lines" [F. Kohler (NEA), Memorandum of Conversation on MESC (W. Murray, et al.), 18 April 1944, p. 2, Stettinius Papers, Box 251, Folder: "London Mission—Murray"]. Other quotations in the text above, relative to the Stettinius mission, are also from Kohler's report, pp. 1–2.

13. Ibid., pp. 2–3.

14. In their sequence, quotations are from ibid., p. 3; ibid., p. 3; and "Agreed Minute, Anglo-American Discussions Regarding the Near and Middle East: April, 1944," 28 April 1944, p. 4, Stettinius Papers, Box 251, Folder: "London Mission—Conversations (Murray)." (Emphasis added.)

The faith in the MESC as Anglo-American developer and hence stabilizer was also echoed at this date outside the Department and the Foreign Office, e.g., in the Foreign Economic Administration. Memorandum on MESC, FEA, Special Areas Branch, M. E. Division, May 1944, Yale Papers, Box 2, Folder: "14/N."

15. Quotation is from Hunter, "Economic Problems: The MESC." See also Wilmington, *MESC*, pp. 161–62.

Hunter suggests that the Foreign Office, reflecting popular wartime feeling, preferred the continuation of MESC for etatist, antidepression reasons rather than for traditional imperialist reasons. This impresses me as exaggerated, but with a core of truth. If so, it implies that the Department's stereotype of Britain's interest in MESC as purely imperialistic was off the mark.

Hunter also makes the point that the Foreign Office saw from the MESC experiment the need in the future for *more* British commercial and scientific experts, advisors, etc. It was the Foreign Office's view, he suggests, that the British had hardly tapped the potential wealth of the Middle East, despite their long presence there. He thus implies another disortion in America's perception of British policy. Conventionally, the Department viewed Britain as a reactionary, bent only on holding onto its prewar predominance; the corollary was that it was only the Department of State which had a dynamic, economically expansive program for the Middle East. To Hunter, however, the Foreign Office also had a self-image as progressive innovators, eager to develop and exploit the region (Hunter, "Economic Problems: The MESC," p. 192).

16. Replying to Taft, Landis said he felt it was "more effective, even though somewhat unwelcome to the British, to have a small group which can roam at will through the MESC rather than large numbers in subordinate positions not concerned with policy making" (Policy committee, Minutes of 65th meeting, 28 June 1944, p. 6, Notter Papers, Box 15, Folder: "Pol. Col. Minutes, 50–80").

For an expansion of Landis' criticisms of MESC and his formulation of a large postwar economic policy, see Landis, "Anglo-American Cooperation in the Middle East," *The Annals of the American Academy of Political and Social Science*, E. M. Patterson, ed., *Our Muddled World* [*Annals* 240 (July 1945): 64–72]; and Landis, "Middle East Challenge," *Fortune*, September 1945, pp. 161 ff.

For the attitude of WEA, see Charles Taft, "Wartime Economic Problems and Post-War Trade," 20 May 1944, *Bulletin* 10 (1944): 469.

17. See Notter Papers: Memorandum, WEA-19, 12 June 1944, Box 15, Folder: "Pol. Com. Docs. WEA"; Summary of Policy Committee, 67th Meeting, 3 July 1944, Box 16, Folder: "Policy Committee—Agenda"; and Policy Committee, Minutes of 72nd meeting, 17 July 1944, p. 3, Box 15, Folder: "Pol. Com. Minutes 50–80." Also, see "Report to the Secretary of State the Hon. Cordell Hull (Submitted by Undersecretary Stettinius, On Conversations in London, 7–29 April 1944)," p. 33, Box 87, bound volume of same title. Also, Departmental aide-memoire to British embassy (Washington), 28 September 1944, *FR* 5 (1944): 41–42.

18. On the importance attached to the Culbertson Report, see *FR* 5 (1944): 39, n. 6. On Culbertson's views and the report itself, see D. S. Gilpatrick, "Resumption of Private Trade in Liberated Areas: A Progress Report on the Work of the Special Economic Mission," 10 December 1944, *Bulletin* 11 (1944): 720–22; W. S. Culbertson, "The Work of the Special Economic Mission," 14 January 1945, *Bulletin* 12¹ (1945): 62–63; F. Winant, "Trade Controls Today in the Middle East," 21 January 1945, *Bulletin* 12¹ (1945): 81; and W. S. Culbertson, "Principles of Economic Policy," 25 February 1945, *Bulletin* 12¹ (1945): 299–301. Also, John DeNovo, "The Culbertson Economic Mission and Anglo-American Tensions in the Middle East, 1944–1945," *Journal of American History* 63 (1977): 913–36.

It is worth noting that Gilpatrick (a secretary of the Culbertson Mission and assistant chief of WEA) singled out in his report the "terrific [business] pressure on our Government to relax trade controls on the assumption that private enterprise could take care of itself.... The Mission is giving its particular attention to the possible need for collaboration between government and business in restoring and protecting private trade and, if such is desirable, also to the nature of what that collaboration should be."

With an eye to the probability of the Mission and its ideas being a precedent for bigger things to come, he added: "In view of the current and substantial interest of private business in learning of economic conditions in liberated areas and in sponsoring independent analyses of these conditions, the advice of the Mission members in this respect should furnish a cogent argument as to the desirability of sponsoring other special economic missions as the war in Europe progresses."

Ironically, the author (speaking only for himself) also hoped that the Mission would serve to dissuade "businesses in this country who have been previously urging a program of removal of restrictions—a removal which seems impractical to most Government representatives who have actually faced supply problems in the field."

Overall, one gets the following image: the Department was with one hand forcing the British to relax controls, yet with the other it was holding at bay American businessmen eager for free trade, or persuading them, for their own good, to collaborate with the Department, as controls could not be easily removed.

[For an effort to synthesize the thesis of the Culbertson Report with the thesis that the postwar U.S. should possess a strong public investment policy, see Charles Bunn (Office of Economic Affairs), "Legal Policy for Trade," 28 January 1945, *Bulletin* 12¹ (1945): 142–44. For the Culbertson Mission's and the Department's anxiety that Zionism would jeopardize the Mission and its promotion of American business, see (relative to the Palestine Arab boycott of the mission), *FR* 5 (1945): 616 ff.]

19. On the push for early expiration, see reference to Departmental telegrams of 3 August 1945 and 20 August 1945, *FR* 8 (1945): 85, n. 3. On the related push for termination of the Lend-Lease program, see Statement of Joseph Grew, 20 May 1945, *Bulletin* 12² (1945): 940–41; and Acheson, *Present at the Creation,* pp. 172, passim.

On the drive toward indoctrinating the public of the wisdom of a larger postwar free trade policy, see, in *Bulletins,* F. W. Fetter, "Anglo-American Cooperation For Expansion of World Trade," 12¹ (25 March 1945): 503; W. Clayton, "Relations Between Foreign Trade and the Welfare of Small Business," 12² (22 April 1945): 762; Charles Taft's detailed rebuttal of the American Tariff League, "Renewal of Trade Agreements Act," 12² (10 June 1945): 1079; and Statement by Secretary James Byrnes on Full Employment Bill of 1945, 13 (26 August 1945): 279–80. Also, see Position Paper, "American Economic Policy in the Middle East," 2 May 1945, *FR* 8 (1945): 34–39.

20. Francis Boardman, "Civilian Requirements From War to Peace: The MESC," *Bulletin* 8 (23 December 1945): 998. (Boardman was with the Far and Middle East Branch, in the Division of Commercial Policy, in the Office of International Trade Policy.)

21. Note joint Anglo-American Statement on the Dissolution of the MESC, *Bulletin* 13 (30 September 1945): 493–94; and *FR* 8 (1945): 85–87. Also in this connection, see George Soule, "The United States and Britain's Economic Policy," pp. 55–63, and Michael Wright (British counselor, Washington), "British Foreign Policy in Europe," pp. 73–78, both in E. M. Patterson, ed., *Our Muddled World* (Special issue of *The Annals of the American Academy of Political and Social Science,* July 1975).

22. See Statement on U.S. Supply Arrangements for the Middle East, 4 November 1945, *Bulletin* 13 (1945): 727.

9

Iraq

PREWAR POLICIES

Of all the Arab countries, it was Iraq with which the Department was most concerned and periodically assertive in the 1920s and early 1930s. The problem was the oil fields, in Iraq and the Persian Gulf, where American companies were having difficulties gaining concessionary rights in competition with British companies. The subsidies granted to the latter by the British government, taken together with the prejudices of British officials, reportedly made the competition unfair, unfree, and disadvantageous to American oil interests.

Given the facts that in the 1920s free trade was an American national credo, the "business of government was business," and the Department was eager that the United States be everywhere respected as a great power, the reaction to British action was inevitably strong. The tone of Departmental protests was simultaneously defensive and aggressive. The protests themselves, drafted in NEA and with the advice of the Foreign Service, took the form of legal admonitions. These guarded to the maximum letter the Department's right to be "consulted" on all matters relative to Iraqi oil, a right which, it was presumed, derived from America's role as Britain's benefactor during and right after World War I.

Moralism-legalism also came to the fore when the Department made its claims to the right of consultation and to the implicit right of exerting a veto power on a second basis, namely, that the United States had

171

been an "assenting" power to British mandatory agreements (for example, the Anglo-Iraqi Judicial Agreement of 1931).[1]

Later, in 1936, the Department tried to breach British hegemony with a third argument—that Iraq, officially sovereign and no longer a subservient ward of the British, should be able to negotiate bilaterally with America. The Department's object was a nondiscriminatory, most-favored commercial status for the United States. (Parenthetically, in negotiating for such a treaty, the Department insisted that total reciprocity would not be granted; that is, the Department stipulated to Iraq, as it did to other nations, that foreign trade would not be permitted with *America's* specially protected wards—Cuba, the Philippines, and the Panama Canal Zone.)[2]

The Department's arguments and protests tapered off sharply by the mid-1930s, subsiding almost to the point of nonexistence in the period 1937–1944. In part this trend is evidenced by the extremely thin correspondence relative to Iraq in the Departmental files. Secretary Hull's generally "prudent" and passive approach was undoubtedly one reason for the trend. Another was that American oil interests (in the consortium called the Near East Development Corporation, the key members of which were to be Standard Oil of New Jersey and Mobil Oil Company) did have since 1928 an approximate 25 percent share of the stock in the Iraq Petroleum Company (IPC, which before 1929 had been called the Turkish Petroleum Company, or TPC). The American firms, working always in very close consultation with the Department, had come to accept and to a degree even prefer collaboration with Britain and IPC's famous "Red Line" Agreement which, *inter alia,* closed the door to other companies wishing to explore in Iraq. In the immediate context, therefore, to push for the open-door doctrine would have been inexpedient.[3]

Also contributing to the lack of American interest was the fact that the profitability and market potential of commercial trade with Iraq turned out to be very limited. As the British themselves had come to be negatively impressed by the weakness and poverty of Iraq, so had the Department. (Indeed, Baghdad seemed an unusually stagnant backwater to many FSOs, as witnessed by the fact that even in the "exciting" war year of 1943 there were no takers for the temporarily vacant ambassadorial post to Iraq—until Loy Henderson, as noted in Chapter 4 above, chose to switch his career field from Eastern Europe to the Middle East and requested the post.)

Furthermore, Saudi Arabia was being wrested away from British influence and was becoming the locus of the Department's regional oil interest. As a result, the Department did not have the time or the wish to pursue advantages in Iraq. Moreover, pursuit would have added difficulties to the oil needs of Britain and its military and to the special Anglo-American relationship being built up in the late 1930s and early 1940s.

Finally, another deterrent to active American unilateralism was the increasingly obvious fact that Iraq would require a strong Western military-economic presence. In the interwar period it seemed forever politically turbulent, yet socially and economically backward. As detailed in Chapter 5 above, the Rashid Ali pro-Axis coup of 1941 and the subsequent British invasions served to underscore the State Department's established wish to stay physically uninvolved and to let Britain continue its "responsibility" there.[4]

IRAQ DURING THE WAR

Iraq in the early 1940s, as after World War I, seemed to spearhead the Arab world in anti-British fervor. However, that fervor seemed to abate when the Rashid Ali Revolt of April 1941 was crushed during the following month by the British, who in turn restored the Hashemite monarchy and Nuri Said. Though no longer threatened, the British nevertheless wanted to counter Axis blandishments and win the friendship of Iraq and indeed, of the entire Arab world, whose eyes at that time were very much on Iraqi events. Accordingly, Britain made the overt gesture of encouraging pan-Arab union, thoughts on which were then being bruited about in Baghdad, Amman, and Damascus. At the end of May 1941, Foreign Secretary Anthony Eden stated that the British government would "give their full approval to any scheme that commands general approval." Since Iraqi Prime Minister Nuri Said was then the chief spokesman for unity and federation, Eden's words strengthened the candidacy of Iraq in particular, in 1941–42, as leader of pan-Arabism.[5]

However, Nuri's ideas on federation met with wide resistance, notably from Iraq's anti-Hashemite rivals, Egypt, Saudi Arabia, and Syria. In Nuri's scheme, a "Greater Syria," consisting of a close federation of Syria, Lebanon, Palestine, and Transjordan, would be linked to (and under) Iraq, thus forming a political "fertile crescent." The plan also envisioned Palestinian Jews and Lebanese Maronites possessing semiautonomy under great-power guarantee. At a later stage, other Arab states would be invited to join the federation.

Not to be outdone, Egypt came forward with federation plans of its own, plans which would eventually lead to the formation of the Arab League, in 1944–45. Partly because they were broader and looser in their conception of federation and allowed for more "states rights," Cairo's plans would prove to be more attractive than Baghdad's to a diversified Arab world prepossessed with individual goals of national sovereignty.

Egypt's entry as pan-Arab formulator, notably in 1943, was encouraged by the British. The result would be, for Iraq, a downward process by which Baghdad lost its bid for pan-Arab leadership. Why did the Foreign

Office switch from Iraq to Egypt? Because it increasingly felt that Iraq's Hashemite monarchism was a losing horse to bet on for future regional leadership, and because it simply calculated that British wartime investments in Egypt (even apart from the Suez Canal Zone) were much greater than in Iraq. The moment for the British reversal presented itself after the period of strict military and police controls in Egypt, during and following the final battle of El Alamein. Just as Iraq had required an olive branch after the repression of Rashid Ali, so Egypt presumably deserved one now. By early 1943 the Foreign Office expressly favored Cairo over Baghdad as leader of postwar Arab federation. In the British view, Iraq thus returned to the secondary status which had been its norm before 1941.[6]

WARTIME POLICIES PRIOR TO 1945

With the outbreak of World War II, FSOs in Iraq pursued a highly cautious policy, consisting chiefly of periodic reportage of internal events. They watched and waited and, more than anywhere else in the Middle East, acquiesced to British hegemony in Iraq on the military, political, and economic levels. FSOs assisted their British colleagues and the Hashemite ruling family personally, in the troubled first days of Rashid Ali's coup. The 1942 authorization of Lend-Lease to Iraq—requested by Baghdad on the grounds that its rivals Egypt and Turkey were becoming recipients and also recommended by the Foreign Service because of Lend-Lease's "moral effect and prestige value"—was permitted by the Department to be subject to Britain's prior approval and subsequent supervision, via MESC.[7]

Because IPC production was slow and because of the minuscule number of Americans then resident in Iraq (estimated as less than fifty, and connected chiefly with missionary, archeological, commercial, and oil interests), NEA also saw no valid reason to push for the open door or for the rights of American nationals. For example, it could have challenged Iraq's alleged infringements of certain tax rights of resident Americans, when the problem came to its attention, but it chose not to.[8]

Another reason for Departmental noninvolvement related to the increasing messiness of Iraq's politics after May 1941 and the low caliber of its politicians—not that such internal factors ever prevented any external power with a *major* interest from getting involved with a lesser power. Still, it is noteworthy that many Foreign Service estimations, even of politicians like Nuri, were low. Implicit was the warning that Iraq would remain a weak and unstable state, simply not worth becoming too committed to.[9]

It even appeared that Nuri, in 1942 at least, was rather too dependent on British support for FSO tastes, and this, too, prevented a close direct relationship between Washington and Baghdad. When, for example, Iraq levied customs duties on American war materials in transit to and from the country, the Department protested. The Iraqi Foreign Office suggested that if such materials were shipped under British auspices, they could be exempt from customs, given Britain's treaty privileges. Protesting such obvious self-subordination, the Department then asked for a bilateral executive agreement with Iraq. But this was a move which Nuri, doubtlessly under the "guidance" of the powerful British ambassador Sir Kinahan Cornwallis, was not yet ready to take up.[10]

However, if Nuri could not or would not let the United States in by the front door, there was always the back door. In January 1943, Iraq informed the Department that it was imminently going to declare war on the Axis, ostensibly because the Axis was promoting rebellion against the restored Hashemite regime. Unquestionably, there was evidence of Axis subversive activity, among the Kurds especially. But a more important motive was to get Iraq in on the ground floor of the United Nations and thereby strengthen its bid for pan-Arab leadership.

Furthermore, Iraq desired both to reduce British political influence *and* to obtain more British economic assistance by playing Washington against London. It thus used a calculated declaration of war as a tool to become an ally of the United States. The United States, stated Nuri, would henceforth be able "to enjoy without further ado all privileges, immunities, et cetera, to which British forces are entitled under the Anglo-Iraqi Treaty of Alliance."[11]

These ulterior motives were transparently obvious to the Foreign Service, which knew in addition that Nuri had no intention whatever of sending the Iraqi army abroad to fight the Axis or even to order a general mobilization. Nevertheless, Hull expressed "personal gratification" that Iraq had aligned itself on the side of the U.N.[12]

Beyond this minor milestone in American-Iraqi relations, however, the Department hardly energized its Iraqi policy until 1945. Minor consular functions, watchful waiting, consultation with the British on the chances of Arab acceptance of Nuri's fertile crescent scheme, and occasional altercations with Nuri for alleged discriminatory practices against the American companies in IPC typified the relatively high points of diplomacy.[13]

On the planning side of the Department, too, the lack of discussion and of position papers on Iraq was apparent. Because Iraq was of interest primarily to the British and, indirectly, to the American Department of War more than to the Department of State, Iraq never commanded the attention of the planners. It also did not command attention because, after 1941, Iraq posed no threat, present or future, to the Department's general postwar goal of harvesting Arab good will. Also, because it was technically a sovereign state, without problems of border rectification, Iraq did not come under scrutiny as a dependency, mandate, or security problem.

True, planners were concerned that existing Kurdish and Assyrian separatist aspirations, like Zionist aspirations in Palestine, would fragment, destabilize, and irreparably antagonize the Middle East's Sunni Arab majority. For these reasons the planners' opposition to all such balkanization was swift and total. Having laid the Kurdish and Assyrian spectres to rest, however, they had precious little to say about Iraq.[14]

Nonetheless, if one strains one can see some of the tiny exceptions to the rule (any other description would be an exaggeration) which, retrospectively, seem to indicate the start of a larger Departmental interest in Iraq during the last year of the war. Such glimmerings (mainly after D-Day, during the confident second half of 1944) included the Department's intermittent efforts to have Lend-Lease to Iraq made on a more bilateral basis in order to bypass MESC, and the Department's increasingly publicized intention to make the highest American diplomatic rank in Baghdad equal, in terms of protocol and influence, to that of the British ambassador. From Middle East planners Ireland and Yale came recommendations to send American postwar "advisers" to the Arab world, Iraq included. From FSOs came reports of Iraq's tilting away from dependence on Britain and its approaching the American ambassador in November 1944 with the desire for "closer relations" with the United States after the war.[15]

Face to face with members of the British Foreign Office, Department officers also felt freer to assert themselves, instead of merely taking note, with regard to Iraqi affairs. The bedouin tribes and the Kurds, said Wallace Murray to his counterpart Sir Maurice Peterson, ought to be treated in more enlightened fashion. In particular, the low level of Iraqi public affairs would greatly benefit from the assimilation and infusion of "fresh and virile" Kurdish blood. For his part, the new ambassador to Baghdad, Loy Henderson, was busy in 1944 traveling throughout Iraq, filing reports and prognoses, actively conferring with local leaders, establishing rapport, and spreading good will and the image of a powerful, friendly America beyond the seas.[16]

1945

The desire for closer relations with the United States, broached in November 1944, was repeated with greater intensity and regularity through much of 1945. Iraq felt somewhat discarded by (yet still frustratingly dependent on) Britain, which was favoring Egypt as pan-Arab leader and as chief British investment. It also felt rather poor and neglected compared with Saudi Arabia, in terms of oil productivity, foreign capital investment, and royalties. It therefore sensed that the time had come to actively solicit attention. For other reasons, too, Nuri's government felt that the moment was opportune and critical: The end of the war was already foreseeable, large decisions would be made, denouement was shortly expected in the cases of Palestine and Arab federation. Iraq continued to aspire to a conspicuous role in the postwar United Nations Organization.

Accordingly, Iraq sought America's friendly assistance. It wanted the Department to encourage American oil companies to develop the Mosul and the Basra areas (in particular, the latter). It solicited help in arranging for the construction of a large new pipeline, presumably the kind only the United States could build. Other levels of American participation and investment were broached.[17]

It was clearly Nuri's hope that American and British capitalists would scramble for the opportunity to "exploit" Iraq. Regardless of who won, Nuri looked forward to a period of combined Iraqi oil wealth, power, and modernization. With these he would be in a good position to best his rivals Egypt and Syria (together, relatively modern, populous, but with little oil) and Saudi Arabia (oil-rich, but remote and medieval). That kings Farouk and Ibn Saud had given lengthy and luxurious asylum to Nuri's enemy Rashid Ali, who had been condemned by Iraq to death in absentia, gave further point to Nuri's competitiveness.[18]

Nuri's relations also grew warmer with the Soviet Union, increasingly active in the general region (especially Iran) by 1945. Moscow was more and more praised in the Arab press as a powerful friend of the Arabs against Zionism and British imperialism. Soviet diplomatic recognition had already been reextended to Baghdad in August 1944. If he had "flirted" with the anti-British Nazis back in 1940, before the Rashid Ali coup, Nuri was willing in 1945 to befriend the Soviet Union, too.[19]

In effect, Nuri's approach was to play one great power against the other through dexterous use of carrot and stick. For London, Iraqi oil was the main carrot and the probability of a sudden increase in Iraqi friendship for Washington was the stick. For Washington, Iraqi oil was also the carrot and the probability of Iraqi overtures to Moscow was the stick. (However, toward Moscow there were distinct limits in the degree of friendship Nuri, upper-class Westernized nationalist that he was, was willing to offer. Also, there is no indication that he ever offered Moscow the carrot of Iraqi oil.)

Under Roosevelt, the Department seemed almost to miss its cue by not immediately responding to Baghdad's invitations. The President had personally excused himself from meeting the Iraqi regent after the Yalta

Conference of February 1945 on the grounds that his trip from Yalta to the Suez Canal Zone, where he met alternately with King Farouk, Emperor Haile Selassie, and King Ibn Saud, was unplanned and purely ceremonial. These excuses were untrue. As for the real reason, it appears to be simply that Roosevelt, not feeling well to begin with, did not think it important to meet the regent. Instead, he extended the regent an open invitation to visit him in Washington.[20]

However, Nuri's repeated overtures impressed NEA and Undersecretary Joseph Grew, whose influence on Secretary Edward Stettinius, Jr., and on President Truman, particularly in the latter's first months of office, was great. The final result was a number of meetings between Nuri and the Department and between the Iraqi regent and Truman in May–June 1945. The atmosphere was always cordial, and platitudes and pledges of Departmental assistance and private investment were reiterated. But in return, the Department wanted Iraqi to break more boldly from Britain by supporting, for example, American-Iraqi bilateralism in commercial aviation and radio-telephone communications. The Department also wanted support for its principle of equalization of diplomatic rank.[21]

Indeed, by mid-1945, NEA and the Foreign Service were urging not only Iraq but also all other Arab states to renegotiate their treaty relations with Britain in order to cancel Britain's diplomatic precedence. The Department would then elevate its own ministers to the rank of full ambassador. The Department believed that this process of commercial bilateralism and diplomatic elevation would set the stage for a larger American role and for the full implementation of the open door principle. Such steps would also prove to the Arabs that their fears that America was undependable, Zionist-controlled, and likely to retreat into postwar isolationism were unfounded.[22]

Though Nuri promised to fulfill Departmental wishes and gave indications of trying to alter the Anglo-Iraqi Treaty, the results for both Baghdad and Washington were slim. True, direct Lend-Lease was finally authorized in July 1945. Yet with regard to oil, it is noteworthy that American companies did not seem to respond much at all to the opportunity to do business with Iraq. The Department itself seemed to be unable and unwilling, in the hectic months of mid-1945, to respond fully to Nuri's initiatives. Nor can it be said that Nuri, for his part, pushed with vigor to break with London in favor of bilateralism with Washington. Thus the pipeline concession went to a British firm, IPC increased production, and Britain remained economically predominant.[23]

In sum, it can be said that Nuri's strategem partly worked. Overtures to Washington were at least minimally successful. Relations with Moscow continued to be correct and hence continued to force America and Britain to pay attention to Iraq. Iraq under Nuri was still in the competition for pan-Arab leadership. And probably most importantly, London was pushed into appeasing and developing Iraq more seriously than before.

CONCLUSIONS

American private (oil) interests in Iraq before and during the war were vocal in the 1920s and early 1930s, but quiet thereafter, because either satisfied or uninterested. The interests of the Department ran parallel, except that in the 1920s and early 1930s the Department was largely reacting to American companies' charges of British discrimination, while in 1945 it was being asked by Baghdad to initiate interest among private American companies.

From another perspective, Departmental interests flowed parallel to British interests in Iraq, though less deeply. The special relationship between London and Washington, together with the special subsurface rivalry between the two, made each "partner" automatically interested in the bilateral affairs of the other, and not merely those connected with oil and IPC. If Iraq's stance relative to Arab union, Palestine, Germany, and Russia was of interest to the British Foreign Office, it was therefore, if only for that reason, of interest to the Department of State.

As noted, the Department had its own expectations of a large postwar harvest in the Arab world. While Iraq was never a focal point of such plans, the Department certainly did not wish to see British political and economic influence expand there. Ironically, however, Iraq's own wish for America to play a bigger role generated, in effect, a bigger British economic role at the end of the war. Yet America's ultimate postwar influence on Britain and on Arab states outside of Iraq would put Iraq as much in the American sphere (though at one step removed) as it was in the British sphere.

NOTES

1. For citations on Departmental protests on oil and the Agreement of 1931, see notes 4 and 6, Chapter 3.

2. On the negotiation of the commercial treaty, see *FR* 3 (1936): 401. The treaty was finally signed on 3 December 1938. However, ensuing trade was slight. Still, in the Department's perspective, every little bit helped, and it perceived that overall American trade in the region by the mid-1930s was much larger than it had been. The Department had already noted, in 1933, with obvious satisfaction, that "Prior to the [First World] War, American interests in the Near East consisted chiefly in our educational and philanthropic institutions and in a small trade. Since the war our interests have expanded in a striking manner. Not only has our trade expanded in all parts of the Near

Eastern area, but numerous American investments have grown up" [*American Foreign Service Journal* 10 (1933): 17].

3. On early U.S. interests in IPC, see Neil Jacoby, *Multi-National Oil* (New York: Macmillan, 1974), pp. 28–31; *ARAMCO Handbook*, pp. 93 ff.; and Feis, *Diplomacy of the Dollar*, pp. 49 ff.

4. Note the conclusion on U.S. relations with Iraq in DeNovo, *American Interests and Policies*, p. 354.

5. On Iraqi-Axis relations, see Chapter 5. On the Foreign Office's espousal of Arab union, see Louis Frechtling, "Axis Prepares New Thrust in Middle East," *Foreign Policy Bulletin* 20 (6 June 1941): 2–3; and Majid Khadduri, "The Scheme of Fertile Crescent Unity in Inter-Arab Relations," in Frye, ed., *The Near East and the Great Powers*, pp. 139–40. Eden's personal interpretation of his famous Mansion House speech of 29 May 1941 was to note retrospectively that the speech but "dealt with post-war economic affairs, and had significance as the first declaration by a British government to espouse Arab unity" (Eden, *The Reckoning*, p. 301).

6. The literature on Arab unity and Nuri Said is considerable. On the early period, prior to the formation of the Arab League in March 1945, see Khadduri, "Fertile Crescent Scheme," pp. 137–40; Cecil Hourani, "The Arab League in Perspective," *Middle East Journal* 1 (1947): 128–32; Elie Kedourie, "Pan Arabism," pp. 100–111; Kimche, *The Second Arab Awakening*, pp. 140, 146–47; Sachar, *Europe Leaves the Middle East*, pp. 398–406; and Monroe, *Britain's Moment*, pp. 90–93.

On State Department attitudes, see note 16, Chapter 3. On Egypt's emerging role in pan-Arabism, see Chapter 10.

7. Minister Knabenshue (Baghdad) to Hull, 9 January 1942, *FR* 4 (1942): 343.

8. W. Murray, Memorandum, 26 January 1942, 890G.00/613.3; and W. Farrell (Baghdad) to Hull, 28 August 1942, *FR* 4 (1942): 353–54.

9. FSO W. Farrell wrote that Nuri was no great intellect, though "perhaps more straightforward than the general run of men of his type in this part of the world" (Farrell to Hull, 19 September 1942, 890G.00/629).

10. Farrell to Hull, 24 August 1942, p. 350; and Hull to Farrell, 14 September 1942, p. 351, both in *FR* 4 (1942).

11. Nuri Pasha to British embassy in November 1942, quoted by minister T. Wilson (Baghdad) to Hull, 2 January 1943, *FR* 4 (1943): 641.

12. "Iraq has declared war in order to join United Nations to secure its own postwar interests and those of the other Arab states" (FSO T. Wilson to Hull, 20 January 1943, *FR* 4 (1943): 638). Wilson added the point about the Nuri government having no intention of assisting the war's military effort. Also, see Hull to Wilson, 2 February 1943, ibid., p. 639.

13. Welles to Wilson, 11 March 1943, *FR* 4 (1943): 649–50. See correspondence among Hull, Welles, and Wilson in February–March 1943, in *FR* 4 (1943): 648–53.

14. On the planners' decision on the Kurds and Assyrians in Iraq, see note 10, Chapter 3. Further analysis of the Kurdish and Assyrian problems is in Conversations on Iraq (W. Murray and Sir M. Peterson), 18 April 1944, p. 2, Stettinius Papers, Box 251, Folder: "London Mission—Murray"; and FSO W. Birge, Jr. (Baghdad), Report on the Assyrians, 11 April 1945, 890G.00/4–1145.

15. On the issue of elevation of rank, see Conversations on Iraq (W. Murray and Sir M. Peterson), 18 April 1944, p. 2, Stettinius Papers, Box 251, Folder: "London Mission—Murray." Also, see the communications on the issue in the

period July–October 1945 among Henderson, G. Merriam (enthusiasts) and Acheson (nonenthusiast), in *FR* 8 (1945): 19 ff. On advisors to Iraq, see C. P. Grant and W. Yale, Paper on Advisers for Middle East, H-186 Preliminary, 3 August 1944, p. 4, Notter Papers, Box 60, Folder: "H Pol. Sum. 180–89." On Iraq's wish to tilt toward the U.S., see Minister L. Henderson (Baghdad), Memorandum, 25 November 1944, 890G.00/11–2544.

16. See Conversations on Iraq (W. Murray and Sir M. Peterson), 18 April 1944, p. 2; Henderson, Memoranda of 13 March 1944, 890G.00/695, and 3 November 1944, 890G.00/11–344; and note 21, Chapter 4.

17. See J. Grew, Memorandum of Conversation (Nuri Pasha and upper echelons of the Department), 29 May 1945, *FR* 8 (1945): 49–50, also p. 51, n. 10.

18. On the bitterness of the Hashemite monarchy on account of the Saudi asylum for Rashid Ali, see FSO W. Moreland (Baghdad) to Secretary James Byrnes, 4 October 1945, 890G.00/10–445.

19. Veering toward the East was not unique to Nuri; nor was it held by the Department against those who did so. To NEA, unless the U.S. showed interest in the region by elevating its legations, for example, the Arabs were "likely to turn away from the West for aid in their struggle to raise the social and economic levels of the Arab peoples" [Memorandum, G. P. Merriam, 29 October 1945, *FR* 8 (1945): 21].

On Nuri's earlier flirtations, see Chapter 5, note 16.

20. See Roosevelt's communication to the Iraqi regent, 23 February 1945, *FR* 8 (1945): 5. On Iraqi resentment at Roosevelt's (and Churchill's) slight of the regent after Yalta, see *New York Times*, 27 February 1945, p. 4.

21. On the Iraqi visits, see J. Grew, Memoranda, 27 April 1945, vol. 7 (4); 28 May 1945, vol. 7 (19); and 7 June 1945, vol. 7 (26), Grew Papers, MS Am 1687.3. Also, William Phillips, Speech in Honor of the Regent of Iraq, 2 June 1945, *Bulletin* 122 (2 June 1945): 1037; and *FR* editors' synopsis of Regent's visit, *FR* 8 (1945): 586.

At the first state dinner honoring the regent, W. Phillips, then special assistant to the Secretary of State, presided. At this time he gave the first official American approval to the newly organized Arab League. Subsequently, at a luncheon given by Thomas Watson, president of IBM, 125 representatives of business, military, educational, and religious fields attended to honor the regent (*New York Times*, 3 June 1945, p. 15).

22. On diplomatic elevation, see note 15 above.

23. On the pipeline bid, see memorandum from Petroleum Division to NEA, 5 September 1945, *FR* 8 (1945): 56. Another reason for failed bilateralism was Iraq's political and military turbulence, caused by Kurdish uprisings, upon the regent's return from the U.S. Yet some bilateral commercial air rights were concluded. The Department was patient and philosophic. "While this represents something less than our ultimate goal it is considered nevertheless a significant step forward" (W. Moreland, Airgram, 30 September 1945, p. 2, 890G.00/9–3045).

10

Egypt and the Suez Canal Zone

PREWAR POLICIES IN EGYPT

The interests of the State Department in Egypt after World War I were as a rule of a secondary nature, closely mirroring the generally low-level if slowly increasing commerce between the two countries. Departmental passiveness was also due to the facts that oil was hardly a factor in Egypt and that British primacy in Egypt, until the late 1930s, was basically accepted as a constant. That the British were adept (certainly more so than the French in the Levant) in side-stepping and palliating occasional American grumblings over commercial discrimination, and that NEA and the Foreign Service, much like their cousins in the British Foreign Office, were psychologically not especially attracted to the stereotypes of the Egyptian "national character" or to Egypt as a career post, were also factors explaining, on the subjective side, the general lack of Departmental interest.[1]

On one issue, however, Departmental interest was strong and consistent, namely, in the demand that the United States be recognized by the British as a bona fide member of the great-power club "interested" in Egypt, with all the rights, privileges, and status inherent therewith, such as were enjoyed by states like Britain (the club's de facto president), France, Italy, and Belgium. Before the pivotal Montreux Conference of 1937, achieving this demand took the form of firm moralistic-legalistic notes and assertions directed at the British Foreign Office: to wit, that America's rights and immunities under the capitulation system were no less than those of Britain. (When, however, American nationals came into direct legal contests with the Egyptian government and when the protective efforts of FSOs failed to change that government's mind, then the typical Foreign Service attitude toward British power was different. FSOs tended to forego the basic rivalry with the Foreign Office, to become more friendly than usual, and to seek advice and assistance from their more experienced British "colleagues.")[2]

After the Montreux Conference, which abolished foreigners' special immunities and courts, the Department's demands for great-power status took the form of making an impression directly on Egypt. Thus the Department was expansive in its congratulations to Egypt on its finally gained sovereignty. Although the Department continued the traditional close covert consultations with Britain (which indeed had advised the Department to react sympathetically to Egypt's insistence on abolishing capitulations), the Department was also beginning a more overt and unilateral approach.

The Department expressed the view to the Egyptian government that capitulations were not in the spirit of the times and were not really necessary to protect American nationals. Furthermore, as apostle of the open door, America was increasingly presented as preferring wholesale abolitions—not only of the old, pre-British capitulatory system, but of all the more recent, British-inspired forms of privilege and discrimination which still underlay Britain's predominance in Egypt. The message implied was clearer and more stark than it had been, notwithstanding a number of pre-1937 precedents to the same effect: if Britain claimed that it was "sympathetic" toward Egypt's national aspirations, America was *more* sympathetic, and more genuinely so, than Britain and indeed than all the other Western powers, with their grudging concessions, selfish motives, and basically Old World machinations.[3]

A main reason for the Department's one-upsmanship toward London and unilateralism toward Cairo appears to have been that the conciliating efforts made by the British, in connection with the 1936 Treaty and the 1937 Montreux Conference, provided the Department with both dangers to evade and opportunities to exploit. The dangers were in the rapprochement between London and Cairo, which might well keep Washington and an American depression economy seeking markets out in the cold. The opportunities were in the steady growth in Egypt of nationalism and a fixation over sovereignty, developments which in the abstract were historically dear to American hearts and which therefore the Department could espouse with more ardor and seeming conviction than the British. By projecting America as intrinsically the truer, potentially more powerful yet more disinterested friend, the Department thus helped to undermine the alliance which London was seeking with Cairo and fed into Egypt's basic paranoia toward the British.

In sum, 1937 was an approximate marking point after which the Department's approach in Egypt became steadily more competitive with and independent of Britain. The process was subtle and not so subtle. It was not so subtle, if one judges from the way NEA and FSOs tried to leapfrog over the British. They initiated direct relations with Cairo, and, somewhat in the tradition of emissaries to the American Indians, did the most to propagate the image of America as great white father across the sea who wished only to trade and be a good friend. Yet the process was also subtle, if one judges from the fact that rather than seek equality in the sense of *gaining equal privileges* with Britain and other members of the great-power club in Egypt—as the Department did in the early 1930s—the Department in the late 1930s sought equality in the sense of *encouraging the abrogation of any and all privileges* of Britain.

The Department's assumption was that such a democratic and selfless policy line would enhance America's prestige locally and regionally. In a way, it was a tradeoff: petty capitulatory privileges exchanged for the image and "privileged" position of being the friendliest and least imperialistic of all Western powers. Given its faith in the American free enterprise system, the New Deal notwithstanding, it was also the Department's assumption that under conditions of no privileges and no discrimination, Egypt and the entire Arab world would prefer American over British and French imports.

The Department sincerely held to the view that in the long run the wholesale and region-wide abolition of imperialistic privilege would also be for the good of its British and French colleagues. As noted in Chapters 1 and 3 above, this "abolitionism" was based in the 1930s on three articles of faith. The first was the traditional gospel of the open door and laissez-faire. The second was the good neighbor principle, recently exemplified by America's low-tariff policy with Latin America, which was supposedly a proof to obtuse London and Paris that profits need not be based on exclusivist spheres of influence. The third was an abiding feeling that anti-imperialism in the non-European world was the ineluctable wave of the future.[4]

These three axioms thus represented the Department's tacit credo that maximum and region-wide concessions were necessary, now. Generosity would pay. Otherwise, Britain and France—and perhaps the United States too, if it were too closely associated with Britain and France—would be faced later with much cost, pain, and native xenophobia.

EGYPT DURING THE WAR

Anglo-Egyptian relations were severely strained in the period between September 1939 and November 1942. Egyptian parties agitated for British withdrawal, and pro-Axis sentiments, ambivalently coupled with anxieties over the probable effects of Axis victory, were widespread. The times seemed propitious for pressuring London: by September 1940 the British home islands, bereft of allies, were under the Blitz. Moreover, in April 1941 Egypt's historic rival, Iraq, was in rebellion against Britain. Unless Egypt behaved similarly, Iraq would win the competition for symbolic leadership of the Arab world.[5]

However, and as told in Chapter 5, the British maintained themselves in Egypt, twice forcing Axis offensives into retreat. One result was that, just as they had built up their unwanted presence in Egypt during World War I, so did they during World War II. In the process, they also made Egypt the undisputed center of the Arab world. The vital importance of the Mediterranean theatre and the Suez Canal made Egypt the "keystone of the British defense structure." The establishment of MESC's headquarters in Cairo and of new military and air bases elsewhere in the country, the wide police and censorship powers, the creation of a new supreme and regional ambassadorial post ("British Minister of State for the Middle East")—these and other examples represented the enlarged British power and presence.

The British were aware that their increased controls were on a collision course with Egypt's heightened, Wafd-led nationalism. They therefore calculated that the best way to keep the lid on internal eruptions while the Axis still threw its shadow over the region was to return the Wafd to power. It was predicted that corruption and inefficiency would undoubtedly increase, but more importantly, so would collaboration and peaceful relations. To effect Wafdist cooperation, however, the British had to reverse their pro-Palace tradition and use strongarm tactics. That the Palace was increasingly pro-Axis strengthened British resolve. In a famous incident of February 1942, British tanks surrounded the king's Cairo palace, and Ambassador Sir Miles Lampson issued an ultimatum to anti-Wafdist Farouk: his deportation or his consent to allowing the premiership to go to Wafdist leader, Nahas Pasha. Farouk capitulated.[6]

The results, Wafdist corruption and collaboration with the British, were as expected. Profiteering and very uneven income distribution were furthered, too: Egypt would be enjoying a war boom by 1943, derived from MESC-based industries and general allied expenditures.

Finally, as Axis defeat and a postwar United Nations structure both became more probable, the Wafdist government decided to switch sides overtly and to declare war on the Axis. However, until Yalta, British leaders like Churchill felt that Egypt's nominal neutrality, like Turkey's, served British purposes better than would Egypt's nominal belligerency. Egypt did not declare war until February 1945, after the Yalta Conference and after the signing of a separate agreement for direct Lend-Lease from America in January 1945.[7]

On another level, the British as of 1943 began to counterbalance their internal security controls by expressing sympathetic words of encouragement toward Egypt's emergent bid for pan-Arab leadership. Historically a late and never fully persuaded convert to the cause of pan-Arabism, Egypt nonetheless by the middle of the war was already fully immersed in all pan-Arab political issues touching on federation, Zionism, and the spectre of the Hashemite rulers of Iraq and Transjordan gaining more regional power. To win more popularity and to strengthen its own bid for leadership, both against the Palace internally and Iraq externally, the Wafd turned its militant rhetoric toward these issues. To the traditional and strictly local nationalist calls for revising the 1936 Treaty and gaining more Egyptian control over the Canal, the Sudan, and Libyan Cyrenaica were now added vehement pronouncements on Palestine and the Hashemites. Thus, solidarity with the Arab world beyond its borders, hitherto chiefly based on the religious tie of Islam, was increasingly voiced in terms of political, cultural, and racial ties.

Although some Egyptian nationalist groups felt that the old isolationism better served Egypt's interests than the new secular regionalism and that in any case Egypt was not yet strong enough internally to lead pan-Arabism, Egyptian nationalists who believed otherwise won out. In October 1944 the Alexandria Conference was held, representing a major step toward the Arab League and toward Egypt's preeminence therein. The catalyst of the conference was the presumed threat to all Arabs of the growing wedge-like Jewish presence in Palestine.

For their part, the British—given their investment in Egypt and the Canal and given their (mistaken) belief that they could handle the Egyptians and hence deal with any Arab union which Egypt might lead— had by late 1944 already persuaded Iraqi and Syrian leaders to accept Egypt's primacy in any future pan-Arab entity. On the grounds that Egypt was the largest regional state, Britain contended that a union without Egypt would be a nullity. Furthermore, it implicitly endorsed the Egyptian view that Egypt should not join at all unless Egypt would be the leader and unless the union was all-inclusive and loosely structured. It had always been Egypt's belief that the emphasis on centralization in Iraqi and Transjordan proposals of Arab union—and even the anti-Zionist declarations emanating from Baghdad and Amman—were mere covers for Hashemite ambitions of aggrandizement.[8]

Concurrent with the Foreign Office's support of Egyptian-led Arab union, the British stopped backing the Wafd party. As the last vestiges of an Axis threat in the Mediterranean theatre had been removed by the second half of 1944, Britain no longer saw the need, from a military view of local stability, to single out the Wafd for support. Farouk in turn saw his opportunity, and he dismissed his adversary, Nahas Pasha. Power thus returned to the Palace. One effect was to make Egypt's espousal of Arab union more conservative and "moderate." This was reflected in the Arab League Pact of Cairo, March 1945, a document less flamboyant in its regional aspirations than the Wafd-inspired Alexandria protocol of the previous October.

However, the return to power of the Palace by no means made Egyptian internal politics moderate. The Wafd, the Moslem Brotherhood, and a host of other parties, including the Egyptian communist party, stepped up their agitations. The overall result, made more apparent in the years following World War II, was intense nationalism to the point of terrorism and fanaticism and to the point at which Britain was more and more on the defensive from all segments of Egyptian politics, the Palace included.

By the early 1950s, Britain would be in a major retreat, voluntarily and forcibly induced. Its anticipated control over Egypt and hence over Egypt's leadership of the Arab League—the old method of "indirect control" of British imperialism—would prove to be a fiction. Docile Egypt, instead of being Britain's proxy and collaborator, would become a leading antagonist to British influence not only in Egypt, but throughout the region. The United States, as will now be seen, abetted these trends almost from the beginning.

WARTIME POLICIES IN EGYPT

In contrast to their position in Iraq, NEA and the Foreign Service expressed more interest in Egypt in the early rather than in the late war years. Developing the post-Montreux Conference trend of unilateralism, FSOs in Egypt in 1940–1942 began urging a large American military-political-economic buildup in Egypt—at the very time the British were being confronted with Axis thrusts west of Alexandria.

Department officers singled out Egypt in the early 1940s (mainly before the "turning of the tide" at El Alamein, November 1942, which somewhat restored British prestige and power in Egypt) because, much like the British, they saw Egypt as a center of the Arab world and keystone of the Mediterranean theatre. A large American presence was also seen as necessary to coordinate burgeoning economic interests connected to the war—MESC, American military missions in Egypt and the Persian Gulf, and vital resources like Arab oil and Turkish chrome. That the United States Ninth Air Force and great quantities of American Sherman tanks were both located in Egypt gave impetus to the Department's tilt in 1942 toward unilateralism.

In addition, because American prestige was high while Britain's was "at a low ebb," the Department's middle managers deemed it opportune to establish a special political-military representation in Egypt, on the order of Britain's recently established ministry of state in Cairo. In sum, the Department's objectives were first to stop the Axis and impress the Arabs with American power; then to displace British military predominance. A strong American military and political presence would in turn establish the pre-conditions for eventual American economic predominance.[9]

The Foreign Service in Egypt, notably chief of mission Alexander Kirk, became more insistent and impatient for other reasons, too. Kirk felt that the upper echelons at home were not being responsive enough to his calls for action. The European and Far Eastern theatres so commanded the upper echelons' attention, he implied, that they failed to appreciate the Middle East's new significance as a primary foreign policy interest. Moreover, Kirk tried to convince the Department that the Axis would eventually enter the Mediterranean in force, despite the fact that Hitler's invasion of Russia in June 1941 seemed to show that the Eastern Front was temporarily more important in Axis strategy than the Mediterranean.[10]

Finally, FSOs wanted a strong American presence in Egypt because, like the Egyptians, they had increasing contempt for local British officials. The British were viewed as socially supercilious and militarily inept, their "bungling... demonstrated time and again," in Egypt and elsewhere. It is worth noting that American contempt for the British became common throughout the region on the FSO level. Irrespective of the merits of the cases involved, it was a trend which could not help but increase bad faith between Americans and British and was doubtlessly in itself a factor which promoted a competitive, unilateralist "we-can-do-it-better" attitude in the Department.[11]

Most of the arguments of the middle echelons persuaded Hull and Welles, though rarely to the degree of intensity in which they were offered. On occasion, middle management's wishes were directly contravened: for example, when the British openly pressured Farouk in February 1942 to permit the Wafd to govern, NEA Chief Wallace Murray recommended that the Department issue a protest against such imperious behavior. But Welles overruled Murray on the grounds that Egypt's internal affairs were within London's sphere, much as Latin America's were within Washington's. As the Department would certainly resent Britain's meddling in Latin America, so it was only fair to let Britain handle Egypt the way it wished.[12]

Murray did not accept the analogy, but he acquiesced to his superior. However, if NEA was checked in this instance, it is worth recalling that in terms of Departmental tenure Murray outlasted Welles, and Hull, too; as noted in Chapter 4, the longevity and continuity of NEA's managers represented a factor which in itself gave more weight over the long run to NEA's views than those views might otherwise have had.

If in general the upper echelons were somewhat less than fully converted regarding NEA's recommendations on Egypt, the Department of

War was much less persuaded. In essence, it disagreed with and vetoed the State Department's desire for a "large" policy for Egypt because if that policy were implemented, it would make Egypt and the Middle East an American rather than British military responsibility. The British also registered objections to NEA's wishes.[13]

Nonetheless, the State Department, mainly by means of Welles' influence on Roosevelt, succeeded in partially circumventing all extra-Departmental protests. The Department proposed sending a special mission to the Middle East; it would, however, be temporary and not of the highest level. It would be headed by Lt. Col. Harold Hoskins, Roosevelt's and Welles's mutual acquaintance who was then working as a liaison between the Departments of State and War. Admiral William Leahy, who headed the Joint Chiefs of Staff, and British Minister Anthony Eden initially objected even to this proposal, but Roosevelt overrode them.[14]

Ostensibly, the purposes of the Hoskins Mission were to make a regional economic survey and to help in a general way to combat Axis propaganda. The more basic purposes were to make personal contact with influential local leaders and to promote American propaganda via the Office of War Information (OWI), the regional headquarters of which was in Cairo. In all cases, the Mission was to operate "as an independent American organization and not, as might be suspected, as a 'front' for the French and British"—even though it was of course also supposed to work, as formal ally and friend, in "close cooperation" with the British and Free French.[15]

The Hoskins Mission fulfilled all its purposes, overt and covert. It also served as a precedent for later Departmental missions to the region, like the Culbertson Mission of 1944. Because they were temporary and not of the very highest level, such missions, as intended, managed to avoid arousing protests from the War Department.

Finally, the Hoskins Mission gave encouragement to FSOs who had been accustomed to rendering private and sympathetic oral "assurances" to Arab leaders that America's official position, impressions to the contrary notwithstanding, was solidly behind the Arab independence movement. Because Hoskins and the OWI gave such assurances, FSOs felt that their own past, present, and future assurances, even without the explicit consent of the President or the Secretary of State, were justified.

Still, NEA and the Foreign Service had often felt that to give private assurances was to labor under a cloud of legal ambiguity. They had long wanted, and would in the future continue to want, such assurances to be made public in order to set the record straight and prove to one and all that the Department's war aims were unequivocally on the side of Arab national aspirations. NEA and the Foreign Service also felt that to compete more effectively with the Axis in the Arab world they would have to compete more publicly against Axis propaganda. A case in point was the German-Italian joint declaration of July 1942, which had condemned British domination and had called for "Egypt for the Egyptians."

Periodically, Hull seemed agreeable to such middle-echelon wishes. But because of British and Jewish fears and opposition, and because Hull's own fears that such opposition would put the Department and himself in a bad public light, the Secretary abandoned the idea of a ringing pro-Arab declaration. Instead, he preferred the traditional practice of making vague pronouncements, when pronouncements were deemed necessary, while allowing the practice of giving the Arabs private assurances to continue.[16]

Notwithstanding the Department's half-successes, as represented by the Hoskins Mission and by the continuation of back-door practices like giving assurances, the middle echelons were checked in their larger ambition to further American political and military interests in Egypt, and in the Arab world generally. Obstruction was due to the reticence of the Department's upper echelons to get too involved, to the outright objections of the War Department and the British Foreign Office—but most significantly, to the success of the allegedly inept British military, which by the end of 1942 seemed to solidify British military, and hence political, hegemony throughout the region (except Saudi Arabia). The subsequent tendency of NEA and the Foreign Service relative to Egypt was thus to forego political-military competition with Britain and to fall back on the more traditional modes of competition and influence-peddling, namely, promoting favorable public relations and American private economic interests.

In such matters, as in everything concerning America's interests in Egypt, Minister Kirk was a zealous entrepreneur. Throughout 1942, he kept urging the Egyptian government to send a high-level trade delegation to Washington. In his dispatches (chargé Ray Hare was drafting officer) he reported with satisfaction that there already existed in Egypt American military and economic interests (oil, film, insurance, the YMCA, etc.) totaling millions of dollars. Kirk pointed out that the Egyptian press was pro-American and that it wanted America to play a bigger role locally. At one point, when the British allegedly acted the part of obstreperous senior middleman and blocked the purchase of American passenger planes by the three governments of Egypt, Saudi Arabia, and Greece, Hull and Kirk (who was minister to all three) pointedly bypassed the British. Hull made it clear to the three governments that the United States fully supported their wish for unhampered commercial bilateralism.[17]

The American-Egyptian economic tie increased when at the end of 1942 Lend-Lease via Britain was made available and when in the same period the United States Ninth Air Force opened near Cairo one of the largest military airports in the world. Indeed, for the rest of the war, trying to strengthen the economic tie was the overriding interest of the Department in Egypt. Frustration with British interference was inevitably one result, though another was more psychological affinity between Egypt and the Department, based on (if nothing else) the truism of misery loves company. Both, for example, resented Britain's allegedly unilateral expansion of Royal Air Force air fields, and Britain's restrictive controls of the purchasing policy of Egypt's Misr Air Works. To the Department these misdeeds were but one more reason to hasten the dissolution of MESC.[18]

The Department also tried to use Lend-Lease as a lever against the British whenever possible: thus it expressed interest in the postwar title rights of the then recently completed Suez-Cairo oil pipeline, built by the British military and used by the Shell Oil Company. On the grounds that it was built with Lend-Lease materials, the Department argued that it (the Department) should have the final authorization over the pipeline's title. (Actually, the Department was willing to settle for joint Anglo-American control with token Egyptian participation.)[19]

At the same time that it was trying to cozy up to the Egyptians, however, the Department glimpsed a number of instances which showed that to deal directly with the Egyptians would not necessarily be an easy task. Such instances consisted of periodic points of friction in 1944–45 involving the American military: the latter did not apparently show proper respect for Egyptian sovereignty. In other instances, the Department protested Egypt's imposing a 15 percent export tax, on top of a 15 percent royalty charge, on oil exported from Egyptian ports by American oil interests; while Egypt rebuked the United States for allegedly unfair trade practices in the international market which hurt Egyptian cotton.[20]

On the political level, too, the Department was becoming increasingly aware of the quagmire that Egyptian politics represented. In Minister Kirk's own words, such politics were typified by "immaturity," a "sophomoric character," "bankruptcy of leadership," and a "subservient slave complex." The long bout between Egyptian King Farouk and Wafdist Prime Minister Nahas Pasha, particularly in April 1944, elicited exceedingly low opinions of each side from the Foreign Service and induced a greater realization that Egypt's problems were not all of Britain's making.[21]

And yet, the unpleasantness seemed to attract more than repel. To Minister Kirk, Egypt seemed to be looking to America for "a helping hand... not only for direct assistance but for inspiration and guidance in harmonizing the development of Egyptian institutions." An American hands-off policy, predicted Kirk, would allow Egypt's governing classes to repress public opinion, with worse crises then erupting from below. To

James Landis, chief American civilian representative to MESC, consultations with the British on Egypt's internal affairs were clearly necessary. Writing directly to Roosevelt, he added with point that such consultations should be "preliminary to any action that the British Government may take."[22]

Hull, however, nipped in the bud all such advocacy of "we-must-save-the-Egyptians-from-themselves-and-the-British." Egypt, Hull wrote the President in direct rejoinder to Landis, was a British responsibility. Problems there, "at their present stage at least, need not be discussed with the British by this Government... the British should assume the initiative in dealing with the present crisis." Hull had the last word. His hands-off approach, already fully endorsed by the War Department, remained without further internal questioning the Department's norm for the rest of the war, even after his resignation in November 1944.[23]

Overall, then, wartime relations with Egypt, as conducted by NEA and the Foreign Service, were limited and secondary, except for dramatic calls for activism in the first half of 1942 and to a lesser degree in April 1944. Similarly, the long-run interest in Egypt of the Department's postwar planning apparatus was also in the passive category. The Political subcommittee had succinctly summarized, as early as March 1943, what was and what would remain the planners' total political-military policy towards Egypt: "It is not thought advisable for the present to consider any change in the status of Egypt or the Suez Canal." In essence, this meant that the uneasy equilibrium between British hegemony and Egyptian sovereignty should be maintained for the war's duration.[24]

Indeed, upholding the status quo was tinged with some negativism toward Egypt on the part of the planners. When the Italian and German presence was removed from Libya at the end of 1942, and Egypt laid claim to Cyrenaica, that claim came up for discussion. Although the planners felt the possibility of boundary "rectification" in favor of Egypt was a viable alternative, Egypt's territorial claim as a whole was not taken seriously. When in 1943 Egypt also began expressing interest in pan-Arab federation, the planners' reaction was similar. In their discussion of a future federation the previous year, Egypt had not even been considered as a likely member. In 1943, when Egypt was so considered, its potential membership and leadership were still treated rather as anomalies.[25]

Traditionally, if Egypt was ever linked in the eyes of observers to regionalism, such regionalism was westward and southward, not eastward vis à vis the Arab states of Asia. As noted, Egypt's territorial claims, historically, were toward areas held by Libya, the Sudan, and Ethiopia. Among planners, therefore, the 1943 consensus was that Cairo's primary aim must still be to oust the British not only from Egypt proper but also from Britain's hegemony in states that Egyptian irredentists coveted— Libya, the Sudan, Ethiopia. Beating the drums for Arab federation to the east, it seemed, was a decoying tactic toward these ends. By intensifying and leading anti-British Arab nationalism in the east, Egypt would thus be bolstered by a wave of Arab support and would be able to aggrandize itself in the west and south.[26]

But, the planners intimated, if Arab nationalism was led by an Anglophobic Egypt, then even the minimal cooperation with Britain that federation would require would be missing. Moreover, Cairo's bid for pan-Arab leadership might intensify inter-Arab competition for the post, with the possibility of federation being wrecked and the region destabilized.

Still, was not Egypt's espousal of Arab federation more than political maneuvering? Was not Cairo sincere? The planners appeared willing, within limits, to answer yes. What of the rumor that Egypt was trying to revive the caliphate and the spectre of holy war against the Christian West? Hardly, dismissed chief Middle East planner Philip Ireland, not aware of the depths and growth-potential of xenophobia nor aware that a decade thence an anti-Western *jihad* would indeed be waged under the rubric of Nasserism.

In any case, the military power of an Egyptian-led federation, or of a federation led by anyone else, would in the final analysis be weak, said the planners. Not only because of anticipated fissures like Arab rivalry or lethargy, but because even the most united and viable Arab federation imaginable would for the indefinite future lack an indigenous air force— the sine qua non of military potency, according to contemporary strategists.[27]

For all the projected weakness of federation, the planners remained wary of Egypt's regional ambitions. However, beyond this wariness, chiefly in the spring of 1943, there was no further recorded discussion of Egypt or Egyptian-led federation by the planners.[28] With respect to the Suez Canal, limited discussion also typified the Departmental record; yet in a fundamental way the Department's perspective of the Canal was quite different from its perspective of Egypt, as the next sections will make clear.

THE SUEZ CANAL

After World War I, the parties most directly involved in the already old question of how control of the Suez Canal should be exercised were the British government, the Egyptian government, and the Compagnie Universelle du Canal Maritime de Suez. (The Compagnie was the international corporation which operated the Canal; French private interests controlled the majority of the Compagnie's stock.) While treaty conventions had long sought to delineate the scope of each party's powers, the basic problem of who had ultimate sovereignty ever remained: thus, for example, the 1936 Anglo-Egyptian Treaty stated that the Canal was an integral part of Egypt—yet at the same time the Treaty gave Britain nearly exclusive rights to protect the Canal. Thus, too, the Compagnie from the 1920s to the 1950s granted periodic concessions to Egypt for a gradual "Egyptianization" of the Canal's commercial operations and personnel—yet at the same time the Compagnie held to the view that it itself was sui generis. As such, the Compagnie felt that it was inappropriate and illegal that Egypt should seek to Egyptianize it the way Egypt was often seeking to Egyptianize other foreign corporations on its territory.[29]

The problems of sovereignty over military defense and of sovereignty over commercial operations were compounded by the problem of international status. According to international law, the Canal was definitely a neutral international waterway, open to all nations in time of both war and peace. However, neither the British forces in the Canal Zone nor the Egyptian government was consistently neutral in periods of war. (Thus Britain deneutralized the Canal in Britain's own interests in World Wars I and II. Egypt would do the same in 1948 during the Arab-Israeli war of that year and during the subsequent years—including periods of de facto peace, and despite formal armistices terminating belligerency between Egypt and Israel in 1949 and in 1973.)

Historically, the Anglo-Egyptian conflict over the Canal began later than other Anglo-Egyptian conflicts, such as that over the Sudan. Nonetheless, from the early 1930s on, the Wafd party, in the native nationalist vanguard, steadily intensified its demand that the British and the Suez Company be displaced. Through public demonstrations and acts of provocation and violence, through legally renegotiated conventions with London, and through the ready abrogation of such conventions before the ink was even dry, the Wafd kept the pressure on. In the 1940s only two other issues vied with the Canal as Egypt's major imbroglio: the Sudan and the Palestine question.

Meantime, Britain was vastly expanding its troop strength in the Canal Zone, beginning mainly in 1940. When in that same year Paris, and hence the headquarters of the Compagnie, fell to the Germans, the British also took over the commercial operation of the Canal. Initially, Britain's military buildup in the Canal Zone was aimed at Italy, which had already used the Canal to ship its forces to Ethiopia in 1935 and which seemed in 1940 to be embarked on similar actions in the vicinity of the Canal. Italy continued to use the Canal until June 1940, but thereafter, the British disallowed it. In 1941 Italian military and naval forces in the region were defeated by the British Middle East Command, and the Italian threat to the Canal nearly ceased altogether.

While Britain's wartime control of the Canal was never in real jeopardy after 1941, the usefulness of the Canal was somewhat checked by German bombings (from Crete), which intermittently forced its closure to traffic during the war for a total of about seventy days. Another wartime problem was Britain's mounting exhaustion and economic debt, even while Egypt, spared Axis invasions by the British and greatly aided by the war boom and Allied spending, emerged not only as Britain's political harasser but also as an economic creditor.

One result was that in the decade following World War II, Britain would increasingly retreat not only from Egypt proper but also from its erstwhile Gibraltar-like position in the Canal Zone. Under the Labor government of Clement Atlee and Ernest Bevin, Britain would feel that placating Cairo paid. Furthermore, with the empire in the process of disestablishment, notably in India, the significance of the Suez imperial lifeline would supposedly be less than it used to be. The British would also tend to believe, taking their cue from past Nazi air strikes in the Canal Zone, that long-range bombers and nuclear weapons reduced the strategic value of the Canal.

However, a countervailing argument would arise from the realization that the rehabilitation of postwar Europe required friendly, Western control of the Canal so as to ensure easy passage of oil tankers from the Persian Gulf to the Mediterranean Sea. But when Britain would embrace this argument in 1956 and try to undo what its Conservative government finally perceived as a disastrous erosion of power, it would be too late. Britain's Suez "adventure" would fail, largely because Britain by 1956 would simply be too weak and irresolute for a comeback, and its adversaries, the Department of State among them, would be too strong.[30]

While America's role in 1956 as Britain's "rival" in the Middle East would scarcely be new, the role would have its ironic and unprecedented aspect. This was because during the prewar and wartime periods, as will now be seen, the Department—despite desires to supplant British influence in Egypt and elsewhere in the region—never actually sought British abdication in the Canal Zone.

WARTIME POLICIES REGARDING THE SUEZ CANAL

In itself, the Canal was an important American national interest, less immediately so than it was for Britain, but important nonetheless. Yet unlike other mutual interests, the Department did not compete with Britain for this prize. Before, during, and at the end of World War II, the Department accepted without question Britain's permanent military responsibility in the Canal Zone. The legality of Britain's "ultimate sovereignty" was less flatly accepted because of the obvious anti-Egyptian political implications, but in practice sovereignty was accepted as legal.

The British were solidly entrenched in and identified with the Canal Zone. Indeed, from a military and geopolitical perspective, it was quite natural to regard the Canal Zone not as a part of Egypt but as a British Mediterranean fortress in a string of such fortresses, like Gibraltar, Malta, and Cyprus. Moreover, much as the Departments of both War and State preferred that British rather than American troops perform the ungratifying tasks of repressing the Rashid Ali coup in Iraq in 1941, of invading Vichy Syria the same year, and of policing the Jews and Arabs in Palestine, both Departments also preferred that the British handle the Canal and the related Egyptian protests which were potentially violent and messy.

All in all, the Department tended to pigeonhole the Canal as a special case, as if it existed in a territorial vacuum. It accepted the viewpoints not only that the Canal was a unique British military responsibility, but also that the Canal was essentially divorceable first from American relations with the Egyptian government and second from American relations with the British in the rest of Egypt. It thus tended to abstract the Canal and to regard it as one of the safe "constants" in the region.[31]

For these reasons, the Canal did not come up for discussion among policy makers of the middle or upper echelons, neither before the war nor during its entire course. Among wartime planners, research and discussion on the Canal were also scant. Still, the record on the planning side is at least not negligible, and in fact what little there is illuminates why the United States refused to challenge Britain's authority in the Canal Zone.

In early 1943 the Canal indirectly came up for discussion several times. The focus of attention was on the postwar disposition of Libya and of the Turkish Straits. In the process of discussion, and as touched on in Chapters 4 and 5, Philip Ireland took the view that whatever the ultimate solution for Libya, he was concerned about Libya being in the possession of a state capable of massing air power against the nearby Canal Zone. Implied was the thought that Libya should be in the sphere of a friendly Western state, capable of meeting any future Russian threats to Western shipping in the Canal.

Ireland's colleague William Yale took exception to the view that Russia was a potential threat to the Canal. Yale expressed the counterviews that Russia had no ambition of controlling the Mediterranean and that Russia was not even seriously interested in a Mediterranean outlet to the Atlantic and Indian Oceans. As to the related issue of Soviet interest in the Turkish Straits, said Yale, that was perfectly natural, yet it hardly symbolized an encroaching first step southward towards the Suez Canal. Furthermore, if Moscow wanted to convert the Dardanelles into a Soviet naval zone, it was clearly for security purposes alone. By analogy, did not the United States, he asked, have an interest from the point of military security in the Panama Canal? Would the United States give up its right of fortification there?

The implied answers of course were "yes" to the first question and "no" to the second. Clearly implied also, as the discussion did not go any further, was a tacit agreement that Britain should not be expected to give up its rights of controlling the Suez Canal—nor could Russia be expected to give up its ambition to fortify the Dardanelles.[32]

Intermittently thereafter, the question of whether or not the Department should push for postwar internationalization of the Suez Canal was half-raised among wartime planners. Internationalization was obviously a symbolic term with a positive aura and an anti-isolationist connotation. It was consistent with the Atlantic Charter. Implemented in the Suez Canal, internationalization would strike a blow against British imperialism and for American prestige. However, any such heady thoughts never got beyond the asking stage. The reason was simple, involving once more the analogy of the Panama Canal: it was expected that Britain, and probably France, would raise as an embarrassing quid pro quo the proposition of the postwar internationalization of the Panama Canal. The Department, in short, feared being hoist with its own petard.[33]

Another reason the planners did not object to British control of the Suez Canal was due to the Department's negative impressions of Egypt's political maturity. In a study for the Territorial subcommittee on the implications of Egyptian acquisition of the Canal, the author, Halford Hoskins, recommended against such acquisition for two other reasons: that the Canal, historically, had not been a major asset to Egypt; and that Egypt would be under economic and diplomatic pressure to give way, it was implied, to powers like the Soviet Union, which were potentially hostile to Britain and the United States.[34]

Essentially, the planners believed that if immature Egypt did eventually acquire the Canal from Britain and the Suez Company, it would be due to the influence, or the folly, of one or more of the great powers. At the time it was inconceivable that, as would happen approximately a decade thence, Egypt itself would act by fiat to take the Canal as its own. Nor could any in the wartime Department foresee the day when Egypt once having taken the Canal, rather than succumbing to economic and diplomatic pressures from great powers, would in a number of instances exert economic and diplomatic pressures of its own on the so-called great powers. That Egypt, in possession of the Canal and with the weapons of Arab League leadership, pan-Arab radicalism, mass militancy, and oil, would in years to come defy at various times Britain, France, the United States, and the Soviet Union—and successfully get away with it—was during World War II in the realm of the unthinkable.

CONCLUSIONS

The spirit of competition with Britain was the engine behind Departmental policy in Egypt. When the British appeared strong, the Department of State adjusted itself to a secondary role, typified by moderate cooperation on the political and military levels and by moderate competition on the economic and public-relations levels. When the British appeared to be weakening and/or conciliatory, in the period 1937–42, the Department (its middle managers especially) saw large opportunities to exploit and competed, moderately and sometimes almost intensely, and on all levels.

Power, prestige, and markets were the Department's definite, albeit undeclared, goals. To wretchedly poor, haughtily nationalistic Egypt, America's "friendship" was the goal: money from America, the land of the proverbial streets paved with gold, was sought so as to make Egypt strong enough to dispense with its dependence on both British financial ties and British military "protection."

On the planning side, little research and discussion were devoted to Egypt. This was because Egypt was considered a sovereign state, not a dependency, and because British control of the Suez Canal was regarded as a desirable constant, which meant that it was unnecessary to plan for change. Furthermore, most of Egypt's anti-British nationalist aspirations were not judged as obstacles to the Department's own aspirations of de facto regional hegemony. Therefore, it was assumed that any increased momentum toward greater Egyptian sovereignty also made planning unnecessary: such changes as would occur would undoubtedly be popular, pro-American, and not destabilizing. In the few areas where Egypt might become a destabilizing factor and thus blight America's postwar regional harvest, planning discussions were held. Hence some attention, but without any follow-through, was given to the possibilities that Egypt might confound Arab federation and the borders of its immediate neighbors.

With respect to the Suez Canal, the Department did not directly contribute to Britain's postwar ouster from the Canal; and hence America's siding with Egypt in 1956 against Britain on the Canal issue was unprecedented in terms of earlier State Department policies and plans. Yet the Department did contribute indirectly to Britain's ouster from the Canal by having long eroded British hegemony in the "buffer zone" around the Canal Zone (that is, in Egypt proper). However, the Department's overconfidence in its own views and its legalistic-bureaucratic habit of compartmentalizing and abstracting issues had prevented it from seeing that erosion, once begun in one area, tends to spread to another. It was almost as if the wartime Department had never heard of the domino theory.[35]

With the benefit of hindsight, one can say that the State Department, like the British Foreign Office, overestimated its own talents and underestimated Egyptian nationalism. From 1943 on, the Foreign Office had given support to Egypt's bid for pan-Arab leadership on the assumption that Britain could handle the docile Egyptians. Similarly, the Department's middle managers consistently abetted Egypt's desire to oust the British on the assumption that once British obstructionism and discrimination were displaced, American-Egyptian relations would automatically be solid without being entangled and the Suez Canal would stay impervious to all adjacent changes.

Secretary Hull and the upper echelons, though more reticent, essentially agreed with these latter assumptions. It was, after all, a basic wartime Departmental consensus that a big diplomatic push for the economic open door in the Middle East as a whole (1) need not incur expensive or entangling political-military commitments to the Arabs, and (2) was a principled, therefore safe, way of removing British and French influence from the region. Presumably the British and French would not be able to compete with American exports in a free Middle Eastern market, nor could they in good conscience easily complain, as by complaining they would incriminate themselves as defenders of discrimination and imperialism.

In essence, the Department believed it could manage vast transfers of power, chiefly through the force of America's principles, example, and the conveying of a great-power presence. Such optimism, of course, combining naiveté and boldness, was and is a peculiarly American trait. On reflection, however, and in the postwar contexts of Britain's steep decline and of the Pandora's box of Middle Eastern problems, it can hardly be said that this trait has served America usefully or successfully.

NOTES

1. For a full listing of American educational, medical, religious, and charitable institutions in Egypt, as of May 1937, see *FR* 2 (1937): 660–62.

2. On the Department's moralistic-legalistic pressures on London and Cairo for economic and capitulatory rights, together with its selective acquiescence before Britain's leadership, see correspondence in *FR* 2 (1920): 931 ff.; (1930): 142–49; (1930): 145 ff.; (1932): 62–657; (1933): 841 ff.; *FR* 1 (1934): 752; (1935): 566–72. Also, DeNovo, *American Interests and Policies,* pp. 366–83.

3. See Hull to Judge Bert Fish (Cairo), 30 March 1937, *FR* 2 (1937): 634 ff.

4. The motivation behind abolitionism in the 1930s had no connection with

the future realities of the 1940s. The Department had no expectation that Britain and France would become economic allies, and dependents, of America in a second world war. Nor did the Department foresee the day when it would regard British and French concessions to the Arabs as an imperative in order to head off both Axis and Soviet pro-Arab propaganda.

5. On Egypt's geopolitical and military role in the period 1939–42, see cited works like Lenczowski and G. Kirk and note 7, Chapter 5. Also, see communications in FR 3 (1940): 465–86; FR 3 (1941): 264 ff.; and FR 4 (1942): 73–82.

6. See note 12 below.

7. On Egypt and the U.N., see Russell, History of the United Nations Charter, pp. 538, passim. On Lend-Lease, see Hull's missive, 17 April 1945, FR 8 (1945): 88–89.

8. On Egypt's interest in pan-Arabism and federation, see note 16, Chapter 3. See also, Seale, The Struggle for Syria, pp. 16–23; Marlowe, Anglo-Egyptian Relations, Chapter 15; Lenczowski, The Middle East in World Affairs, Chapter 16; Khadduri, "Fertile Crescent Scheme," pp. 140 ff.; and Anwar G. Chejne, "Egyptian Attitudes Towards Pan-Arabism," Middle East Journal 11 (1957): 253–68. On Egyptian internal dissents to pan-Arabism, see New York Times, 6 January 1944, p. 7. Also on federation, see Chapters 3 and 9.

9. "As a result of British military defeats, the prestige of Great Britain in the Near and Middle East has fallen to a low ebb. Our own prestige in the area, however, remains high, since the local inhabitants realize that we have no territorial ambitions or imperial designs" [Paul Alling to Hull, Memorandum, "Need for Over-All American Political Representative in the Near East Assisted by a High-Ranking Army Officer," 8 May 1942, FR 4 (1942): 76].

10. "After all we cannot do everything everywhere but we can do something somewhere and I maintain that even in the scheme of all the operations on the limitless front special emphasis on the Mediterranean area is fully justified. In short we need here American plans under American supervision to fight in the American way, and we need them at once" (Kirk to Hull, 17 April 1942, ibid., p. 75).

11. Quotation is from Kirk to Hull, 16 February 1942, ibid., p. 72.

12. See the exchanges (February 4 and 5, 1942) between Welles and Murray, ibid., pp. 68–71. It is interesting to note Welles' thesis, so contrary to the public image of Wellesian-Hullian anti-spheres-of-influence ideology. Wrote Welles: "Egypt is so clearly within the British sphere of influence that the British Government very naturally would resent a demarche of this kind on our part. I could not agree for one moment to similar interference on the part of the British in domestic affairs of one of the American republics and I would suppose that the British would take that point of view if we attempted this sort of interference in the domestic affairs of Egypt" (ibid., p. 70).

13. In the summer of 1942, a time when the British were losing the first battle of El Alamein (before the famous second battle in October and the turning of the tide under Montgomery), the Department was in a rueful I-told-you-so mood. Until the British October counteroffensive proved it wrong, the Department felt that its foresight was superior to that of the War Department and that the latter had blundered by allowing Egypt to remain a British responsibility. Wrote Welles, on the War Department's opposition to the idea of an overall political representative: "It would seem to me unfortunately that events of the past ten days have shown the wisdom of the suggestion which the Secretary and I and Kirk have been making" (Welles to Acheson, 29 June 1942, ibid., p. 76, n. 18).

Still, the Department of State, as usual, was able to snatch a semi-victory from the jaws of defeat. *Mutatis mutandis,* a regional American representation, *was* established (though strictly speaking, it was more economic than political) when the U.S. joined MESC in June 1942. See note 7, Chapter 8.

14. The Joint Chiefs' view was based on a procedural objection to the Department's apparent unilateral intervention in a military theatre, and on the assumption that as the mission would be under the aegis of State, not War, it would not be very useful. Also, it might, implied Leahy, worsen existing tensions between American and British military staffs [Leahy to Hull, 18 September 1943, *FR* 4 (1943): 33–34].

Eden stressed the complexity of the Middle East, to which the mission and its anti-Axis propaganda lauding freedom would only add. He argued that any American statement on liberty "would infallibly be taken in the countries to which it is intended as containing both an implication that 'liberty' is being withheld and an assumption that it is the intention of the United States Government to hasten its achievement. No implication could be more welcome to Axis propaganda, could be more readily turned against the occupying forces or could be more calculated to increase the tension of the existing situation and to threaten the security of the Allied command" [British Aide-Memoire to the Department, 15 September 1942, *FR* 4 (1942): 32]. A further objection of the British was that the mission would cut across the activities of the MESC. On Hoskins, see Chapter 4.

15. Quotations are from Hull to J. Winant [London, 27 August 1942, *FR* 4 (1942): 28]. Of the mission, Hull added: "American propaganda throughout the Near East will be increased enormously and quickly in both volume and effectiveness over what has been done to date. It has already been discussed with OWI that there should be made available in the shortest possible time an increased amount of American news for Arabic newspapers, an efficient photo newspaper service, pamphlets, gadgets, etc., as are being offered in other parts of the world" (Ibid., pp. 27–28).

16. On Hull's rejection of a public declaration on the Middle East, see his *Memoirs,* vol. 2, p. 1500, cited in *FR* 4 (1942): 33, n. 18. Also, Chapter 14.

17. Kirk to Hull, 10 January 1942, 883.01/1–1042; Kirk to Hull, 21 November 1942, 883.00/1306; Kirk to Hull, 27 November 1942, 883.00/1307; Acheson to Egyptian minister Hassan, 3 December 1942, *FR* 4 (1942): 97.

On the bypassing of Britain, see Hull to Chief of Staff Leahy, 25 May 1943, pp. 1–3, and Hull to Kirk, 7 June 1943, p. 71, both in *FR* 4 (1943). Periodically, the Department and the Foreign Office would seek (not very successfully) to smooth out their differences. On such attempts relative to Egypt's commerce, see Conversations on Egypt (W. Murray to Sir M. Peterson, et al.), 14 April 1944, p. 1–5, Stettinius Papers, Box 251, Folder: "London Mission—Murray."

18. On FSO resntment and desire to enhance America's reputation at British expense, see, e.g., Kirk to Murray (personal), 16 February 1943, *FR* 4 (1943): 67; and Departmental correspondence of June–August 1944, in *FR* 5 (1944): 56–62. On the evolving American animus toward MESC, see Chapter 8.

19. On the pipeline, see Stettinius' correspondence in February 1944, in *FR* 5 (1944): 63 ff.

20. See dispatches of 28 March 1944, ibid., p. 70; and of 10 January 1945, p. 94, and 21 February 1945, p. 96, both in *FR* 8 (1945).

21. Quotations are from Kirk to Hull, 28 April 1944, 883.00/1387, p. 10. Also see Kirk to Hull, 22 April 1944, 883.00/1380, p. 2; and the negative views of Egypt the year previous, in ST Minutes 14, 2 April 1943, Notter

Papers, Box 79, Bound volume: "Minutes on Security Technical Problems (1—."

22. Quotations of Kirk are from Kirk to Hull, 28 April 1944, 883.00/1387, p. 10. Also, see Kirk to Hull, 22 April 1944, 883.00/1380, p. 3. Quotations of Landis are from Landis to Roosevelt, 20 April 1944, 883.00/1378, p. 2.

23. Hull to Roosevelt, 21 April 1944, 883.00/1378.

24. P-214, 12 March 1943, p. 15, Notter Papers, Box 3, Folder: "Documentation: Subcom. on Polit. Probs., Tentative Views of Committees."

25. On the 1942 view of Egyptian irredentism, see P. Ireland, Memorandum on Libya, T-209, 8 January 1943, Notter Papers, Box 32, Folder: "T Docs. 199–209." On the 1943 view of Egyptian pan-Arabism, see ST Minutes 14, 2 April 1943, Notter Papers, Box 79, Bound volume: "Minutes of Security Technical Problems (1—."

26. Ibid., pp. 1–5.

27. Ibid., pp. 5–8.

28. See note 16, Chapter 3.

29. For useful information relative to the sovereignty issue and the international "role" of the Canal, see Lenczowski, *The Middle East in World Affairs*, pp. 487–500; Halford L. Hoskins, *The Middle East: Problem Area in World Politics* (New York: Macmillan, 1954), Chapters 3 and 4; and Hugh J. Schonfield, *The Suez Canal in Peace and War, 1869–1969* (Coral Gables, Fla.: Univ. of Miami Press, 1969, rev. ed.), Chapter 13.

30. The literature on the origins and events of the 1956 Suez invasion is considerable. See, e.g., M. A. Fitzsimmons, "The Suez Crisis and the Containment Policy," *Review of Politics* 19 (1957): 419–55; and Frederick L. Schuman, "Case Study One," in Schuman, *International Politics: Anarchy and Order in the World Society* (New York: McGraw-Hill, 1969), pp. 362–94.

31. Compare the Department's similar "abstraction" of Algeria (which it supported as part of metropolitan France) from French North Africa and the Levant (where it pushed the French out). Compare also the Department's separation of the European Jewish refugee problem (toward which, to a limited degree, the Department was sympathetic) from Palestine as a national Jewish home (to which it was wholly opposed). In all cases, Departmental sympathy and endorsement "on the one hand" toward the British in the Canal Zone, the French in Algeria, and the Jews in Europe, were utterly nullified by Departmental antipathy "on the other hand" toward the British in Egypt, the French in North Africa and the Levant, and the Jews in Palestine.

32. The relevant documentation is in ST Minutes 10, 24 February 1943; ST Minutes 11, 3 March 1943; ST Minutes 12, 10 March 1943; and ST Minutes 13, 17 March 1943, all in Notter Papers, Box 79, Bound volume: "Minutes on Security Technical Problems (1—." Also, see above, note 26, Chapter 4, and note 25, Chapter 5.

Two years later at the Potsdam Conference, the problem of fortified waterways was more fully aired, although it still did not get resolved. In July 1945, Truman and Churchill were agreeable to the idea that the Soviet Union should have untrammeled passage rights in the Turkish Straits for both merchant and naval vessels, but both were covertly opposed to Stalin's desire to build a naval base there. Stalin tried to exert pressure and confound his opponents by asking how demilitarization and internationalization of the Panama and Suez Canals would sit with them. The impasse remained. See Conference Proceedings, 23 July 1945, pp. 303–4; and 24 July 1945, pp. 365–66, 372, both in *FR Conference of Berlin (Potsdam)* 2 (1945).

33. ST Minutes 10, 24 February 1943, and ST Minutes 13, 17 March 1943.

34. Halford L. Hoskins, "The Suez Canal and Egyptian Interests," T-302, 1 April 1943, Notter Papers, Box 34, Folder: "T Docs. 300–309."

35. The Department's box-the-circle belief that it could undermine Britain, yet expect Britain's position in the Canal to remain secure, is seen in the following postwar policy statement: "Our view is that the revision of the [1936] treaty is primarily a question for solution between Great Britain and Egypt. Our main concerns are to see that the solution reached provides for stability and security in the area and that it does not violate United Nations principles. The U.S. considers the security of the entire Middle East to be of fundamental importance to its own security. We have never sought to undermine the special treaty position which Great Britain enjoys in Egypt. Nevertheless, we would regard as outmoded any revision which left Britain in a paramount political position in Egypt. We would not object, however, to an amicable arrangement for continued British military responsibilities in the Canal Zone" (From Department of State, "Egypt: Policy and Information Statement," 1 July 1946, p. 1, James Byrnes Papers).

11

Saudi Arabia:
Oil Industry Interests

PREWAR POLICIES TOWARD OIL AND SAUDI ARABIA

After World War I, oil quickly became of major importance in international diplomacy, though plentiful domestic and Latin American sources militated against America's need either to nationalize its own oil companies or to scramble abroad for new sources. Nonetheless, the State Department both feared and disliked the thought of being closed out of new oil regions by other great powers, notably Britain and France, which were both needier and more imperialist-minded than the United States. The Department felt their scrambling, if unchecked, would reduce America's options, as well as being demeaning and discriminatory. From another angle, oil was important because total American interwar investments in oil were greater than those in any other commodity and because it was an open secret that oil had a larger role in forming Departmental policy than any other single economic factor. Actively helping American nationals retain and obtain exploratory and other "rights," so that foreign oil would be available to America in times of both war and peace, was always treated by the Department as a cardinal function.[1]

Accordingly, and with regard to the Middle East alone, the 1920s and 1930s offer considerable evidence of Departmental protests and veiled threats against French and British discrimination, along with official urgings to allow entry and equal opportunity to American concession-seekers. However, as noted in Chapters 3 and 9, these protests originally focused on Iraq. Saudi Arabia—although it would prove to

204

be *the* great American oil bonanza—was *not* the object of special Departmental attention in the interwar period.[2]

Indeed, the Department did little to push for either great-power status or open door rights in Saudi Arabia, whether in regard to oil or to conventional trade. The United States was one of the last powers to recognize Ibn Saud's kingdom. Although negotiations had begun in 1928, recognition was not extended until 1931; earlier, NEA had felt that there was not a minimally sufficient commercial and political importance in Saudi Arabia to make American recognition "warranted." In this period NEA was more interested in treaties of recognition with neighboring Iraq and Yemen. It was not until mid-1939 that diplomatic representation was established in Jidda. Yet even this was insubstantial: the FSOs involved were not actually stationed in the peninsula, but worked out of the Cairo legation.[3]

In a sense, the Department's passivity toward Saudi Arabia was extraordinary, given the fact that oil diplomacy was so important in the interwar period. But for all the irony, the Department's passive stance does not defy explanation. While the kingdom's remoteness and its surface poverty were factors, Departmental negligence derived chiefly from the fact that the California Arabian Standard Oil Company (CASOC; in 1944 knowns as ARAMCO) was doing satisfactorily on its own. Unlike American companies in Iraq, or Kuwait, which in the period around 1930 needed and received assisting Departmental protests on their behalf, CASOC needed only minimal consular and diplomatic support from the Department.

One reason was that Ibn Saud, relatively, was more independent of direct British influence than the rulers of Iraq and Kuwait and had granted CASOC rights over which the company did not have to compete with British companies. Apart from factors like climate and puritanic codes, therefore, Saudi Arabia was an untroubled place for the company to work in. Furthermore, when in the course of the 1930s CASOC needed consular assistance, it used British facilities in the peninsula and Bahrein. To a degree, Britain was willing to offer its good offices for the larger purpose of Anglo-American amity.[4]

This is not to say that CASOC and its parent companies were averse to an American diplomatic presence in Saudi Arabia. On the contrary, both before and after formal recognition was extended in 1931, these companies repeatedly raised spectres and predictions of the sort that were common during the periodic "oil scares" after World War I. To them official nonrecognition and then perennial nonrepresentation were patent absurdities responsible for a long train of abuses. They alleged that Americans suffered a loss of prestige and lacked protection; that other powers had unchecked designs; that exports of Saudi oil were not boosting America's export sales as much as they could; and finally, that Persian

Gulf and Saudi oil, predicted as vital when domestic and Caribbean supplies would begin to falter, might even be lost to America. FSOs in Cairo and elsewhere, sharing this thinking, also spoke of the need for American representation in Saudi Arabia.

Nonetheless, both Wallace Murray and Paul Alling of NEA moved slowly, in some instances apparently even resisting company importunities as so much special pleading. NEA regarded Saudi Arabia, as late as November 1941, as still basically in the British sphere. Another reason for NEA's slow motion was that oil experts had not reached consensus over questions concerning either the potential of Saudi oil reserves or the likelihood of depletion in the traditional fields of the western hemisphere.[5]

By 1938–39, questions on Saudi oil at last began to be resolved when CASOC started exporting oil and when the vast extent of oil in the ground in Hasa, the kingdom's eastern province, was increasingly ascertained. Yet the technical feasibility of refining Saudi crude oil for the anticipated use by the American Navy, and for the projected use by a future American air force, remained in doubt for approximately another three years.[6] Hence, though its concern and its relations with Ibn Saud steadily increased after 1938, the State Department felt restrained by the Navy's views. It did not establish a full-time diplomatic mission in the kingdom until the spring of 1942. Thereafter, however, the Departments of Navy, War, and Interior rapidly followed the Department of State in viewing Saudi oil as tantamount to a vital wartime national interest.

Despite official tardiness, the lack of overt governmental representation of CASOC actually served that oil consortium well. This was because, unlike the foreign policy of other powers whose Middle Eastern oil companies were government-directed, the official American policy toward Saudi Arabia could be, and was, credibly presented by CASOC (and later NEA) as one of utter political disinterest, free of any ulterior or imperialist motive towards either the kingdom or the company. As such, the independence, trustworthiness, and general virtue of CASOC could be represented to the king as absolutely unique in the annals of the international oil industry.[7]

Besides the paramountcy of oil, there were other reasons for the Department's increasing its relations with Ibn Saud from 1939 on. One was the fear that NEA came to share with CASOC and the Foreign Service with regard to German, Japanese, and British political-economic inroads and blandishments. The crystalizing assumption that Ibn Saud was spokesman for several score millions of Arabs and several hundred millions of Moslems was another. The view that "remote" Arabia, like the Middle East as a whole, was a strategic crossroads and would inevitably become more important, was a third.

A fourth reason was the hope that discreet Departmental and Presidential appeals to Ibn Saud's assumed chivalry—conjoined to a steady flow of American arms and alms (above and beyond British subsidies, oil royalties, and after 1942, Lend-Lease)—might soften the anti-Zionist zeal of the Wahabi king and his millions of admirers. If that were achieved, the Department would presumably be better able, with the British, to work out a compromise with the Jews and Arabs on the Palestine question and thus finally remove that vexation from the path of American policy making.[8]

A fifth reason for the Department's increasing prewar interest in Saudi Arabia was the direct result of CASOC's stepped-up lobbying at the end of the decade for diplomatic and economic aid. Notwithstanding harmonious Saudi-CASOC relations, especially after the big oil discoveries of 1938, the company was becoming anxious, one reason being the desire to safeguard those very discoveries. Unlike its rather independent stance in the early 1930s, it increasingly expressed a need for governmental help. While CASOC, as will be noted below, did not always appeal directly to the Department or receive support on every point when it did, the "case" it presented for regarding its own material interest in Saudi oil as a vital national interest took effect. In the years after Pearl Harbor, the Department would clearly be at CASOC's side when the latter sought diplomatic support.

SAUDI ARABIA DURING THE WAR

Though not a British colony when war began in September 1939, Saudi Arabia was a peripheral part of Britain's military sphere in the Middle East and Persian Gulf, was part of the sterling bloc, and was loosely subject to the political-economic influence of Britain. As in World War I, Ibn Saud seemed "benevolently" neutral in World War II, for which stance he was regularly rewarded by the British. For example, when Dr. Fritz Grobba, German minister to Baghdad, sought permission in 1940 to open a legation in Jidda, Ibn Saud agreed; but then, turning to Britain, he said he would refuse Grobba if Britain guaranteed supplies and a loan of £250,000. Britain accepted, whereupon Ibn Saud told Grobba that he could open a legation "whenever the Germans occupied Suez."[9]

Conversely, Ibn Saud knew that certain actions might well bring on British disfavor. When Rashid Ali made his coup the following year and asked Ibn Saud for support, the request went unfilled. Though happy to see his Hashemite enemies in Iraq discomfited by Rashid Ali (to whom Ibn Saud gave sanctuary after the war), the king replied that he had "faith" in Britain—a vague orientalism in which the British Foreign Office invested, as it would ruefully learn, too much of its own faith.

Meantime, and coincidental to the beginnings of World War II, CASOC's role in the Saudi economy grew. Not only would this role reflect the upcoming contest over whether the kingdom was to be in the economic sphere of the American dollar or the British pound; it would also stimulate a contest over whether the kingdom was to be in the American or British military-political spheres.

Oil was a major cause of such contests, but it is interesting to note that despite the discoveries and high expectations in the late 1930s, Saudi oil as such was actually an insignificant factor during the entire war. Indeed, and in the words of the company handbook, CASOC's wartime operations "gradually came to a halt," in some measure due to the shortage of tankers, inaccessibility of commercial markets, and hazards of shipping. Slight damage was also done to Dhahran by Italian bombers in October 1940.[10]

It is also interesting to note that in terms of world production, Saudi Arabia ranked seventeenth in 1941. Not one gallon of American civilian or military needs was met by Saudi oil. As for Britain and its military, the big producing countries which were leaned on during much of the war were Trinidad, Iraq, Iran, and the Dutch East Indies. In fact, in Iran, the Anglo-Iranian Company, assisted by Lend-Lease, increased both producing and refining facilities precisely as Hasa's facilities were being shut off. Even Egypt produced more oil for war purposes than Saudi Arabia.[11]

During the war, then, CASOC attended to matters other than producing oil. It began to build a new refinery in 1943 with materials specially allocated by the Roosevelt administration. It diversified its goals within Saudi Arabia so as better to entrench itself and to extend the company's infrastructure in preparation for the postwar period. It "kept busy" by undertaking numerous useful projects relative to the kingdom's transportation, food, water, and agriculture. Meager in immediate profit, such projects were excellent in terms of good will and public relations. Moreover, with one eye on British competition for Ibn Saud's favor, and another on projected postwar markets and military needs, CASOC lobbied in Washington and stepped up its dire predictions and golden promises.[12]

But the more Saudi Arabia was projected as a tremendous prize, the more insecure and anxious became the State Department that some administrative act of stinginess or indiscretion might either undermine or antagonize His Majesty, Ibn Saud, and drive him towards the waiting arms of the British or the Axis. Thus was the ardent desire to "hold" Saudi Arabia for the Americans joined to the ardent desire to keep the king personally friendly, and powerful in his realm, at all cost. The result of these converging imperatives was and would be an extraordinary stream of placating tribute, in the form of personal gifts, honorific messages and invitations from Presidents Roosevelt and Truman, and munificent bilateral aid of unprecedented scope, which emanated from nearly every executive department and agency of the federal government. Such aid took the form of special missions of advisers (military, agricultural, mining, transportation, health), Lend-Lease early in 1943 (despite laws which required a recipient to be an active belligerent), and special grants and subsidies of silver from the United States Treasury (delivered directly, with staged pomp, by the American Navy).

It should be noted, however, that much of this wartime flow from America was covert, for at least two reasons: the State Department and the administration generally did not want to be publicly scalded by domestic oil companies, liberals, and pro-Zionists for "selling out" to a bigoted feudal monarch and a privileged corporation; and Ibn Saud, himself public relations-conscious, did not want to be accused more than he already was by his fellow Arabs of being a flunky to Western imperialism.[13]

In terms of his wartime regional foreign policy, Ibn Saud's personal likes and dislikes guided his "foreign ministry." His animosities were directed chiefly toward the French in the Levant, the Jews in general but particularly in Palestine, and the regimes and regional-federation projects of the Hashemites in Iraq and Transjordan. With respect to Egypt and Syria, Saudi relations became closer during the war, ties of Islamic religiosity being a common cement with Egypt, personal and family ties between leadership circles being a common cement with Syria. In addition, as Egypt and Syria began to align themselves against the Hashemite front of Iraq and Transjordan, Saudi Arabia began to join the former two as a third partner.

In March 1945, Saudi Arabia, together with Egypt, Syria, Lebanon, Iraq, Transjordan, and Yemen, became a signatory to the formation of the Arab League. In that same month, Saudi Arabia became a charter member of the United Nations Organization, having declared war on Germany to qualify. Subsequently, the Saudi delegation to the U.N., initially led by Ibn Saud's son and ultimate successor, crown prince Feisal, would take an active role, particularly on the Palestine question.[14]

By the end of the war, Saudi Arabia thus emerged as an important regional factor. It was wealthier, more modernized, and more absolutistic and "sovereign" than in 1939, when it had been in the British sphere. The house of Saud had pulled far ahead of the rival and originally more prestigious Hashemites. Parenthetically, however, Saudi wealth and political power were not all that obvious during the war, even to neighboring states, largely because they grew covertly and were exerted on the region more indirectly than directly. Typically, Ibn Saud would express concern, and restrained wrath, over a regional problem; worried, the State Department in turn would scurry to pressure the Jews, the French, the British, as the case might be.

WARTIME POLICIES RELATIVE TO CASOC–ARAMCO

In the thickening wartime tangle of American-Saudi relations, the specific relations of the State Department and CASOC–ARAMCO were primary. These latter relations can be explained by considering three interrelated topics. In order of their chronological sequence, they were the case of James A. Moffett; the question of whether the American government should buy into the company; and the question of whether the American government should build a pipeline for the company.

In the period April–September 1941, James Moffett, an oilman prominent in Standard Oil of California's holdings in Bahrein (SOCAL was the first, and main, parent company of CASOC), was assigned by CASOC to persuade Hull, Roosevelt, and Federal Loan Administrator Jesse Jones to arrange a loan to Ibn Saud. It was to be a loan of public, not company, money, to total $30 million spread over five years. CASOC had already promised the king the money to make up for expected wartime revenue losses stemming from the decline in the pilgrim trade and the slowdown of oil production. The company saw an opportunity to make good on its promises at no cost to itself when, in March 1941, Congress approved Roosevelt's Lend-Lease Bill.[15]

It was CASOC's fear that if the king did not receive the money quickly, company concessions would be jeopardized, to Britain's advantage. (Of course, in his brief before the President, Moffett did not stress CASOC's vested interests; instead he noted the problems which an impoverished and therefore presumably unstable Saudi Arabia would create for the entire Middle East.) As to why CASOC did not at this time raise the loan from its own capital or from private sources, the causes were two. One fell under the rubric of "financial reasons," that is, company reluctance to advance the king ever larger sums out of its own pocket, even though it was possible. The second, in Moffett's own admission, was that CASOC

feared to become involved in the strife between the Jewish and Arab factions with resulting damage to the domestic business of Aramco and its parent companies, Socal and Texas, by reason of their having financed the Arabian king's army in a war against the Jews.[16]

However, Moffett's lobbying mission was only half successful. On the negative half, there were governmental problems of financial arrangement and legal precedent, stemming from the Roosevelt administration's cautious political-mindedness over any aid program which might run counter to American anti-big-business sentiment or to still powerful pro-isolationist sentiment. In addition, the Departments of Navy and War were not then interested in Saudi oil. Furthermore, neither the upper nor middle echelons of the State Department were much involved in the Moffett case specifically; and Hull in fact was negative toward Moffett's wish for federal intervention.[17]

On the positive half, Moffett generally succeeded in raising the consciousness of all his respondents, inducing them at least to take a more sympathetic view of Saudi oil and CASOC's role and predicament. Moffett also got Jesse Jones, through the intercession of Presidential Adviser Harry Hopkins, to agree to "stipulate" to the British that, in return for American loans to Britain, Britain had to take care of Ibn Saud's financial problems (and thus bail out CASOC). Subsequently, when the British complied, the company told the king that it was only through CASOC's prodding in Washington that London gave him money. (NEA would also express that self-serving view to the Saudis in due course.)[18]

By early 1943, CASOC's cultivation of governmental sympathy began to pay off. Not only did Moffett's efforts help, but so did the fact that CASOC's parent, SOCAL, had some of its own men on the payrolls of the State Department and other federal agencies as petroleum experts and counselors. In January, Assistant Secretary Dean Acheson wrote to then Lend-Lease Administrator Edward Stettinius, Jr., that Saudi Arabia needed and merited Lend-Lease—and in any case, it was in the national interest to render such aid. A month later, Roosevelt signed into law his personal approval of the measure.[19]

Although CASOC missionized successfully in Washington, in itself missionizing did not represent the main cause behind decisions like that of Lend-Lease to Jidda. Rather, in 1943 the main causes included the fully crystalized view of the entire Department—and of all other executive departments—that Saudi oil was an immense and lucky prize that had to be jealously guarded as a vital national interest. In addition, the Department at this stage was animated with the spirit that isolationism and withdrawal were passé. Translated into the Saudi Arabian context, this meant that the British must finally be prevented, in Roosevelt's phrase, from "horning in" on the kingdom and that other departments must be prevented from horning in on the State Department's function of making foreign policy, including foreign oil policy.[20]

In this latter connection, the Department's most acute rival was the Department of the Interior, under Hull's old personal rival for the President's ear, Harold B. Ickes. In December 1942 Ickes had become Petroleum Administrator for War as well. In July 1943 he also headed a new federal agency designed to coordinate foreign oil policy, the Petroleum Reserves Corporation (PRC).

Ickes believed America's domestic reserves were insufficient, and he was persuaded by CASOC, and his own judgments, that Saudi oil was vital to the remaining war effort but was being jeopardized by British intrigues. Strongly backed up by his then undersecretary of the Interior,

Abe Fortas, Ickes took the New Deal-Big Government position that the American government ought to buy into CASOC in order to guarantee the accessibility of Saudi reserves for anticipated wartime needs.[21]

For his part, Hull regarded Ickes as "impetuous" and worse. In general, the State Department criticized Ickes' idea of minority stock acquisition on three counts: first, any degree of acquisition would lead to an outcry among domestic oil producers that the government was going to compete with them in the oil business; second, acquisition would provoke countermeasures, like nationalization of private American oil interests overseas, particularly in Latin America; and third, acquisition would be a unilateralist and protectionist step contrary to the multilateralist, nondiscriminatory philosophy to which the Department of State was ever trying to convert the world.

Hull laid emphasis on this final point, writing to Roosevelt in mid-June 1943 that Ickes' proposal would cause a repetition of the post-World War I scramble for oil, a distasteful time when, wrote Hull, "the atmosphere and smell of oil was almost stifling." In addition, Hull was anxious both about the State Department's leadership role being usurped and about the unpleasant prospect of a public wrangle between Ickes and himself. As for NEA and the Foreign Service, the emphases in these quarters were on sympathy for CASOC's plight and for the case against New Deal federal interventionism, joined to the fear that Ibn Saud would react adversely to any such interventionism in his oil domains.[22]

What course of action, then, was the administration to take? It was Hull's view, based largely on the view of Economic Adviser Herbert Feis, that for the time being, a contractual relationship should be made: that is, "immediate arrangements with U.S. companies to develop their production and refining in Saudi Arabia . . . and agreements setting aside such reserves as the Army and Navy deemed necessary for their requirements."[23]

However, PRC disagreed, contending that stock acquisition in CASOC would be but a short-run emergency measure, that it would be limited and one of a kind, and that the State Department's anxiety over precipitate action and dangerous precedents was a species of scaremongering. As for a contract with CASOC, PRC felt that if anything, a federal contract had the same defects as acquisition—with the added danger that under a contract the company might more easily evade responsibility and might not leave adequate reserves.[24]

PRC's disagreement with Hull was shared by the majority of the Interdepartmental Committee on Petroleum Policy (a high-level interim committee made up of PRC and the economic advisers of the Departments of State, War, and Navy). At the same time, however, the Committee's majority also disagreed with Ickes' proposal of minority stock acquisition on the grounds that the government would be "in the vulnerable position of a co-adventurer or junior business partner with large oil companies . . . which operate under quota and cartel systems."[25]

The upshot was that the Committee's majority concluded that the least disadvantageous position was for the American government to gain *majority* stock acquisition, that is, a *controlling* interest in CASOC and hence the Saudi concessions. This was a tour de force no one had expected. The Committee was persuaded to take this position by the Joint Chiefs of Staff, who singled out as their reason wartime military and civilian needs. Ironically, despite its reservations and its differences of opinion within the Committee with respect to the definition and method of achieving a "controlling interest," even the State Department agreed at the end of June 1943 to cosign with the other Committee members a memorandum to the President recommending 100 percent acquisition of CASOC![26]

Hull's apparent backsliding and acquiescence to the controlling-interest option were kept secret from the Department's middle echelons, but the news was soon leaked from within. Informed by Lt. Harold Hoskins, Minister Kirk in Cairo wrote to Hull, urging the restoration of full governmental support of CASOC *sans* acquisition. Hull was displeased with Hoskins' disclosure, but he did not repudiate the position he had taken in the Interdepartmental Committee.[27]

In any case, dissent such as Kirk's was overridden by the Interdepartmental Committee, whose controlling-interest preference was given a fillip when another body, the Army-Navy Petroleum Board, decided in July 1943 that a refinery ought to be built by the American government, though presumably with company agreement. It was the Board's view that Saudi-Persian Gulf oil would be needed to fuel military operations in the expanding Pacific theatre and that it was better to use and deplete such oil rather than domestic reserves.

Furthermore, in the autumn, another prop of the anti-control argument was kicked away. The long-standing trepidation in the Department that Ibn Saud would be suspicious and wrathful toward any direct involvements by the American government proved unfounded. In fact, the king appeared to express pleasure at the prospect, "and seemed to consider U.S. Government participation as perfectly natural."[28]

At this juncture, however, CASOC itself, seeing that its lobbying for help had given birth to the Frankenstein of "big government," broke off negotiations with PRC—even after Ickes had revised downward the government's total-control percentage from 100 percent to 70 percent to 51 percent to 33⅓ percent. The company's rationalization was that governmental "protection" of CASOC was no longer needed, in view of the fading away of Axis threats to the Middle East by the second half of 1943.[29]

For its part, the Department of State was both relieved and anxious.

It was relieved because the total-control thesis, which it had accepted without enthusiasm, was now dead and because PRC's defeat was reckoned a gain for State. But the Department was anxious lest Ibn Saud interpret the administration's return to noninvolvement as a sign of isolationism and unreliability. If he did, the king might gravitate back to Britain's embrace.

To "take charge" from PRC, save face with Ibn Saud, and also deal conclusively with the British on mutual oil policy, the Department decided to step into the arena of oil policy making in a large way. As will be seen in Chapter 12, it began elaborate plans and procedures for attaining a new Anglo-American oil accord for the postwar period. It also sought to strengthen the American monopoly in Saudi Arabia by supporting proposals that the American government build a pipeline in Saudi Arabia.[30]

THE PIPELINE CONTROVERSY

While the utility of a pipeline from the Hasa fields overland to the Mediterranean had been bruited about in commercial circles long before the war, the idea was first introduced in governmental circles by War Secretary Henry Stimson and Navy Secretary Frank Knox, within PRC proceedings. Hull, however, was the only PRC director who opposed the idea initially; typically, he felt it would be imprudent, also unilateralist and counter productive, for the government to build, own, and operate a pipeline in Saudi Arabia.[31]

In December 1943, CASOC wrote NEA Chief Wallace Murray that the company felt it was necessary to build a large-scale pipeline and that the company wished to build the pipeline itself, but within Departmental guidelines. In view of the prize of Saudi oil, the company stressed its hope for Departmental support and cooperation. On the stated grounds that its plans were still premature, but more for the reason that it feared adverse publicity, the company also informed Murray that no other federal agencies—meaning PRC and the military—were presently being informed. Murray was pleased with the letter.[32]

Ironically, Commodore A. F. Carter, the Navy's petroleum adviser, was concurrently elaborating plans and advising Ickes of his proposition whereby the American government ought to finance, by means of a loan to the company, a pipeline from Saudi Arabia to the Mediterranean. Carter calculated that the pipeline would cost $125 million, to be amortized over twenty-five years, and would be able to carry 300,000 barrels a day. His plan's key proviso was that CASOC would always maintain a reserve of one billion barrels for use by the military.[33]

As a result of these similar proposals circulating almost simultaneously, by the beginning of 1944 there was interdepartmental agreement on the idea of a pipeline—but sharp disagreement over details. The lines of division paralleled those in the stock acquisition issue: thus, Petroleum Administrator Ickes and the Army-Navy Petroleum Board pushed for unilateralism and full, permanent governmental control of the proposed pipeline. The Department of State, ostensibly concerned with long-run precedents and principles, accepted the idea of governmental ownership only if it was for a short initial period.

A compromise was reached when all departments and agencies agreed that governmental ownership would last for the duration of the war, after which the issue of ownership would be reviewed. By February 1944, the Joint Chiefs of Staff and the President had also accepted this compromise, as did the company (now renamed ARAMCO), with the understanding that the company would keep 20 percent of the expected total production as reserves.[34]

Despite these agreements, the State Department was still unhappy over PRC's leadership role in the proceedings. It claimed PRC's overt unilateralism was liable to endanger the Department's plans for reaching an Anglo-American global oil accord, and it tried to persuade the President to suspend PRC operations. However, Roosevelt disagreed. Hull was thus forced to continue to defer to Ickes' "impetuous" leadership of oil policy making.[35]

Apart from that problem, it needs to be said that the Department's relations with other departments and agencies, on oil and other matters, were consistently good, even if the Department had to acquiesce and forfeit a visibly central role more than it liked. For example, in March 1944 the Department, and especially its planning apparatus, was increasingly willing to let the American military have the final word on the pipeline issue and on all questions of implementation. It contended that implementation was an operational and to some extent military-security matter, and as such that it could be separated from the more proper Departmental function of making high policy, like an Anglo-American global oil accord.[36] Thus one motive for its acquiescence to the military was the self-deceptive belief that "mere" operations were beneath the Department's consideration and could be separated from policy making.[37]

The Department also wished to disengage itself from the pipeline issue so as to prepare for scheduled talks with the Foreign Office (the Department's "London Mission," headed by Undersecretary Stettinius). These talks took place in April 1944 and covered a wide range of topics on the Middle East and other regions, although the Department refrained from detailing any information on the proposed pipeline. However, other topics relative to global oil and Saudi Arabia were discussed, chiefly by Wallace Murray and his counterpart, Sir Maurice Peterson.

Murray sought to disabuse the Foreign Office of any fears it might have had of an American oil offensive or of a serious conflict over Saudi Arabia between Washington and London. At his diplomatic best, and ever "British" in his own demeanor, Murray probably inspired more trust than was warranted. For its part, the F.O. "assured" Murray, amid good feeling and wartime camaraderie, that the British "certainly have no intention" of objecting to "American oil interests in Arabia or in interfering with them in any way."[38]

Both sides, of course, were lying through their teeth. Murray, in a conversation a week later with the Saudi minister to Britain, spoke in an entirely opposite vein. Murray claimed an American predominant interest not only in Saudi oil, which the British since about 1942 had reluctantly accepted as a fait accompli, but also in Saudi finance and military security. These were matters in which the British had continued to insist that theirs was the predominant interest. Indeed, in a sort of tradeoff for British recognition of America's oil rights, the Department had previously assented to this British claim—but no longer.[39]

Despite its skills in handling customers—talking one way with the Joint Chiefs, another way with the Foreign Office, a third way with Ibn Saud and ARAMCO—the shadow of the government's pipeline proposal finally fell on the Department. When the proposal became public knowledge, the Department was able neither to escape the public spotlight nor the charge of responsibility. Nor could it persuade Congress to desist from its paralyzing fight over the pros and cons of a government-built pipeline overseas. And in fact, the domestic debate in America was loud and long. Although in a related move the Department did succeed in getting both Houses of Congress to shelve pro-Zionist resolutions then in the offing lest Ibn Saud vent his spleen on ARAMCO, the Department did not succeed in palliating the various Congressional critics of the proposed government pipeline.

In order of influence, the main critics were Congressman from the Southwest, representing domestic oil producers who resented ARAMCO's apparent easy access and privileged relationship with the Departments of State and War. That the government should build a tax-funded pipeline—which would benefit essentially only three companies (Standard of California, Texas, and Gulf)—was thus going too far. In Congress, Senator E. H. Moore of Oklahoma was in the forefront. Senator Owen Brewster of Maine was prominent as well. Also speaking for domestic producers and against the pipeline was the American Petroleum Institute.

Even some usual allies of the Department-ARAMCO entente were opposed to the government's pipeline proposal and the risky American unilateralism and dependence relationship involved. James Moffett, the Council on Foreign Relations, and former Economic Adviser Feis were among the opponents. Other, if less influential, voices were raised, and for other reasons: laissez-fairists disliked the implications of socialism and/or fascism which surrounded the idea that the government again seemed ready to begin a petroleum cartel; Anglophobes had no faith in the pipeline because they felt the Department was incorrigibly "soft" on Britain; and pro-Zionists saw danger in the Department's willingness to appease what they saw as a Judophobic, obscurantist desert despot and a WASPish monopolistic corporation.[40]

The upshot was that by June 1944 the harassed Department suspended its own limited efforts in support of the pipeline pending the relaxation of public tension and the prior signing of an Anglo-American accord on oil. However, the former condition did not materialize; while the accord, as will be seen, would be repeatedly postponed and, though signed by the Department and Foreign Office, would never be ratified by the United States Senate.

By the close of 1944, feeling that the idea of a government pipeline was becoming a lost cause, Hull advised Ambassador William Eddy in Jidda to desist from holding it out as a promise to the king. By the beginning of 1945, the Department learned that ARAMCO, tired of government delay and eager to expand production, was planning to finance, build, and operate the pipeline alone; in July 1945, ARAMCO established a company, Tapline, for this purpose.[41]

Although the pipeline would be out of its hand, as it had always wished, the Department would still know some gratification, even if gratification had to be postponed until Tapline's work was completed some six years later. Saudi oil would then be hugely and profitably increased, the pipeline built, the American monopoly strengthened, the national security supposedly enhanced and reserves set aside—all without the drawbacks of American soldiers' being required to stand guard over the pipeline, or of the Department's being required to stand in the glare of criticism. True, the increased Saudi oil flow would never fuel the war effort, as the Departments of Navy and War, the originators of the government pipeline proposal, had thought. And true, the Department saw its "failure" to win Congressional approval as one more sign that it was unappreciated and without the power it deserved. For all that, nearly all the goals which the proposed pipeline of 1943–44 was supposed to bring about would in fact be realized in due course.

In 1944–45, however, this glad future was yet to be known. Instead, the Department was taking stock of the situation. It concluded that the entangling confrontations with PRC and Congress in 1943–44 must be avoided. Irrespective of the importance of the viewpoints of the Congress, the President, and the relevant departments, foreign oil policy henceforth must be in State Department hands for safekeeping. Moreover, the tried and true approach the State Department had used in 1940–42, before PRC and Congress interfered, had to be revived. An art form, that approach had emphasized (1) maximal direct economic aid to Ibn Saud; (2) close cooperation with, support of, but not interference or acquisition in, ARAMCO; and (3) steady pressures on, and blandishments to, Britain to do two things—stay away from Saudi oil, yet open up its doors outside of Saudi Arabia to American oil interests. How these goals were defined and implemented is the subject of Chapter 12.

NOTES

1. Feis, *Diplomacy of the Dollar*, pp. 48–60; John A. Loftus, "Petroleum in International Relations," *Bulletin* 13 (5 August 1945): 174. Also see Hull's letter to Roosevelt in June 1943, quoted in note 26 below.

2. On American pressures in Iraq and the Persian Gulf, see notes 4 and 6, Chapter 3. On the legalistic guise of the Anglo-American oil rivalry after 1919, see E. L. Golyer, "Some Aspects of Oil in the Middle East," in Frye, ed., *The Near East and the Great Powers*, pp. 128–30.

3. On NEA's reluctance to recognize Saudi Arabian sovereignty and to implement diplomatic relations, see DeNovo, *American Interests and Policies*, pp. 361–63; correspondence in *FR* 2 (1930): 547–54; and the allusion to FSO Leland Morris' negativism in 1936, in Messersmith to Fish (Cairo), 24 May 1939, *FR* 4 (1939): 824–25. The latter is also cited in Williams, ed., *America and the Middle East*, p. 45.

It is interesting to note that when recognition was finally negotiated, the U.S. acquiesced to Saudi wishes and did not claim the right to manumit slaves (presumably, Saudi employees of American staff)—a right which, quite to the contrary, the British consul in Jidda did claim. Such compliance with "local custom" would become a hallmark of American policies in Saudi Arabia. See, on manumission, *FR* 2 (1933): 990.

4. See correspondence in *FR* 1 (1934): 828 ff.

5. See DeNovo, *American Interests and Policies*, pp. 363–65; W. Murray, Memorandum (on the Department's rejection of Ibn Saud's request for a $10 million loan), 25 November 1941, 890F.00/74; and Chapter 12.

6. In 1941 Secretary of the Navy Frank Knox wrote that, after investigation, he found Saudi oil "not suitable for Navy use," and "it could not be used in airplanes." While he "appreciate[d] the gravity of the situation in the Middle East" relative to Saudi Arabia, he did "not believe, however, there is any sound business reason for mixing [financial] help [to Ibn Saud] up with the purchase of the type of oil produced in that field" [Roosevelt, 20 May 1941, *FR* 3 (1941): 636].

7. "[By 1932, prior to being allowed into Saudi Arabia,] the Americans had established a good reputation in Bahrain. They had demonstrated, among other things, that their interests were confined to oil and involved no political entanglements or ambitions" (*ARAMCO Handbook*, p. 108). This is a typical self-description of good behavior and political disinterest—in itself a pro-status quo position with "political implications"—and has run like a red thread in all of ARAMCO's public relations.

8. On the adumbrated tradeoff of American aid for Ibn Saud's benevolence on Palestine, see the correspondence of A. Berle, Jr., and W. Murray, both of whom, at least in the period of May 1941, were inclined to favor arranging

the tradeoff. The idea was that as "protector" of the Jews of Palestine, the king would use his influence "with his co-religionists in Palestine towards preventing any widespread massacres. We would be justified in making such an approach because of the large number of American nationals of the Jewish race actually living in Palestine" (Murray to Berle, 3 May 1941, 867N.01/1778 PS/RT). Also, *FR* 3 (1941): 603–4.

9. de Gaury, *Feisal*, p. 65.

10. *ARAMCO Handbook*, p. 120.

11. Ibid., p. 87; and Louis Frechtling, "Oil and the War," *Foreign Policy Reports* 17 (1941): 70–80.

It is interesting to note that despite this lack of contribution, it has long been widely accepted that Saudi oil was vital to the war effort. See, e.g., the testimony of Defense Secretary James Forrestal before a Congressional Investigating Committee on Relations between the Oil Companies (1948), and the lack of rebuttal of even a perceptive committee chairman like Senator Owen Brewster. Said Forrestal: "But I think that the Government got very substantial benefits. In other words, they got oil which otherwise, if the development of this field had not been pressed with the competence and vigor with which it was pressed, would not have produced at a very decisive time in the war, when oil was needed; (Williams, ed., *America and the Middle East*, p. 48).

12. On the company's wartime activities in the kingdom, see *ARAMCO Handbook*, pp. 120–26.

13. On the details of aid, see Lenczowski, *The Middle East in World Affairs*, pp. 439–43; Fisher, *The Middle East*, pp. 554–55; Mosely, *Power Play*, p. 156–58; and the rest of Chapters 11 and 12 herein. On Arab animosity to Ibn Saud as flunky, see Graves, ed., *Memoirs of King Abdullah*, pp. 259, 267.

14. Actually, the British Foreign Office pumped for Saudi Arabia's admission to the U.N. more than the Department of State. Britain's motive was transparent, namely, to counterbalance the friendly gesture of Roosevelt's meeting with Ibn Saud at Great Bitter Lake with a gesture of its own. Or, as Eden piquantly said to Molotov of the inclusions in the Crimean Conference communiqué being drafted, "[It is] good to have a Moslem or two. Ibn Saud is having [a] cup of coffee with [the] President" (Foreign Ministers meeting, 11 February 1945, p. 9 of Alger Hiss's typed handwritten notes, Notter Papers, Box 285, Folder: "Hiss Notes"). Also, on the early Saudi relations to the U.N., see Russell, *History of the U.N. Charter*, p. 508, passim; and de Gaury, *Feisal*, pp. 73–74.

15. There are a number of reports on the Moffett case, e.g., Mosely, *Power Play*, pp. 145–48; and Shwadran, *The Middle East, Oil and the Great Powers*, pp. 304–6. A key primary source is R. S. Jr. (?), Memorandum, 23 June 1948, "Arabian American Oil Co., James A. Moffett Suit," pp. 1–17, James M. Landis Papers, Box 31, Folder: "1947–49 Arabian Am. Oil Co. Case." (In a complicated postwar litigation, Moffett sued ARAMCO and won damages for $1.15 million, although the court did not accept Moffett's charge that, as a result of his efforts, the Roosevelt administration in 1941 had conditioned a loan of $425 million to Britain on Britain's assumption of Ibn Saud's budget requirements.)

16. Ibid., p. 1. In testimony before the Brewster Committee, cited in note 11 above, Moffett expressed the same thought, though with a few interesting variations: "[CASOC] felt, in view of the general situation, and in particular the racial situation existing between the Arabs and the Jews, that from the standpoint of their stockholders in the United States they could not afford to place themselves in the position of financing the King's army against the Jews,

which they had been doing through the previous advances [of capital]..."
(Williams, ed., *America and the Middle East*, p. 46).

17. Memorandum, 23 June 1948, pp. 8, 10, cited in note 15 above.

18. On the once famous question whether Jones "stipulated" or merely
"suggested" to the British, see ibid., pp. 13, 16–17. For an illustration of the
Department's belittling the motives behind British loans to Jidda, see note 39
below.

19. Acheson to Stettinius, 9 January 1943, *FR* 4 (1943): 855. When Roosevelt signed the executive order for Lend-Lease to Jidda on 18 February 1943,
it had the exceptional clause that Saudi Arabia, unlike other receiving countries in the region, would not have to pay cash for civilian supplies (ibid.,
p. 855).

For references to Departmental oil advisors coming from the executive ranks
of SOCAL, see Hull, Memoirs, vol. 2, p. 1517; Acheson, *Present at the Creation*, pp. 98–99; and H. Feis, *Three International Episodes Seen From E.A.*
(New York: Norton, 1966, first published 1946), p. 120.

20. Thus, FSO Kirk's caveat that by having channeled aid to Jidda through
the British, "we have thereby lost considerable prestige in the eyes of Saudi
Arabians who have been given increasingly to feel that the British were their
only friends in need" [Kirk to Hull, 18 January 1943, *FR* 4 (1943): 857].

21. On Ickes and the PRC, see Feis, *Three Episodes*, pp. 120–22; Shwadran, *The Middle East, Oil and the Great Powers*, pp. 308–12; and Gardner,
Economic Aspects, pp. 234–36. Also, telephone interview with Abe Fortas,
3 August 1972, Washington, D.C.

22. The quotations of Hull are from Hull, *Memoirs*, vol. 2, p. 1520; and
Hull to Roosevelt, 14 June 1943, pp. 4–5, Hull Papers, Box 82, Folder: "C. H.,
Petroleum—U.S. Policy 1943."

23. Ibid., p. 10. Also, see Feis, *Three Episodes*, pp. 113–16.

24. For PRC's arguments, see Memorandum for War Mobilization Committee (James Byrnes, chairman), Subject: Saudi Arabia Oil Reserves, 1943,
James Byrnes Papers, (Box 168 ?) File: "Production 4." Also, Interdepartmental
Committee, Memorandum to the President, 26 June 1943, *FR* 4 (1943):
929–30.

25. Ibid., p. 930.

26. Ibid. On the Joint Chiefs' view, see Leahy to Roosevelt, 8 June 1943,
FR 4 (1943): 921. Also, note Hull to FDR, 14 June 1943, ibid., pp. 922–24.

Before signing the Interdepartmental Committee's memorandum of 26 June
1943, Hull had sought to define "control" as minimally as possible—and simultaneously, had felt it incumbent to try to persuade the President that the
Department should not have its authority over oil matters reduced.

In an interesting passage from his 14 June 1943 letter [a passage deleted,
for imminently obvious reasons, from the version in *FR* 4 (1943): 922–24],
Hull tried to show that on oil matters the historical record testified to the vigor
and reliability of the State Department. "It was with this determined purpose
that the State Department employed its diplomatic establishment and influence to assist American interests to acquire the large concessions now held in
Latin America and in several points in the Middle and Far East; such assistance, for example, was essential to the acquisition in 1929 of the concession at
Bahrein and opened the way for the concession at Kuwait and also that now
possessed in Saudi Arabia" (Hull to Roosevelt, 14 June 1943, p. 1, Hull Papers,
Box 82, Folder: "C. H., Petroleum—U.S. Policy 1943").

Regardless of whether Hull was overstating the Department's historic role
or accurately depicting it, and regardless of whether that role was "right" or

not, Hull in defending the Department's record was obviously putting his foot in his mouth inasmuch as the memo could have leaked—that is, insofar as critics of the Department and "American imperialism" were, and are, concerned.

27. Kirk to Hull, 27 July 1943, p. 937, and Hull to Kirk, 5 August 1943, p. 937, both in *FR* 4 (1943). Another example of Hull's effort to keep things secret from Kirk was when he (Hull) requested oil company information, in confidential code, from Jidda (Hull to James Moose, 23 July 1943, ibid., pp. 932–33). On the Army-Navy Petroleum Board, see Feis, Memoranda, 26 July 1943, pp. 933–34, and 3 September 1943, pp. 937–38.

28. Moose to Hull, 3 November 1943, p. 941, *FR* 4 (1943).

29. Shwadran, *The Middle East, Oil, and the Great Powers,* pp. 314–15; and Feis, *Three Episodes,* pp. 129–33.

30. On the intensive correspondence at this stage relative to State-PRC relations, see Hull to Ickes, 13 November 1943, pp. 942–43; W. Murray (advisor on political relations) to Hull and Stettinius (undersecretary), 24 November 1943, p. 945; Murray to Hull and Stettinius, 14 December 1943, p. 949; and Stettinius to Winant (London), 11 January 1944, p. 947, n. 45, all in *FR* 4 (1943). Also, Hull to Ickes, 5 January 1944, pp. 10–12; Ickes to Hull, 7 January 1944, pp. 13–15; and Hull to Roosevelt, 8 January 1944, p. 16, all in *FR* 5 (1944).

31. Charles Rayner, Policy Committee Minutes, 23rd Meeting, 10 March 1944, p. 2, Notter Papers, Box 15, Folder: "Pol. Com. Minutes 10 March–24 May 1944."

32. CASOC to Murray, 27 December 1943, p. 9, and Murray's reply, pp. 12–13, both in *FR* 5 (1944).

33. See, e.g., A. F. Carter, Memorandum, 17 January 1944, *FR* (1944): 17–20; Leahy to Hull, 26 January 1944, ibid., pp. 20–21; and Stettinius to Kirk, 3 March 1944, ibid., pp. 24–25.

34. This 20 percent, however, would not be given gratis but would be sold to the military at a 25 percent discount. (After all, to the company, business was business, and oil was not to be given freely to anyone, regardless of all the talk of wartime emergency and the need to sacrifice, or of the fact that the government was going to build the pipeline for ARAMCO.) See Shwadran, *The Middle East, Oil, and the Great Powers,* p. 321; PRC release, 3 March 1944, *FR* 5 (1944): 24–25; and other documentation in period January–March 1944, ibid., pp. 20–27.

35. Roosevelt to Hull, 10 January 1944, ibid., pp. 16–17.

36. View of Policy Committee, ECA-5, 10 March 1944, pp. 1–2, Notter Papers, Box 14, Folder: "Pol. Com. Docs.—ECA."

37. The Department was also willing to acquiesce because it doubtlessly sensed that the liberal press and anti-Departmental Congressman would automatically think the worst if they learned that the Department was an active supporter of a government-built pipeline for ARAMCO in Saudi Arabia. Surely, the ensuing public exposure and hearings would kill the proposal and quadruple the Department's ulcer problems. Finally, it seems that the Department wished to leave the pipeline to the military in order to curry the Joint Chiefs' favor. The Chiefs were clearly all-powerful in the making of much foreign policy, but they did not often look upon the Department with great regard. The Department knew these unpleasant facts of life; as well as letting the Chiefs handle the pipeline question, at various times in their shared committee work it made a point of showing them that it was just as "tough" and anti-British as they.

38. Murray "endeavored to dispel any misapprehensions which may have arisen in the minds of the British authorities by the unrelated coincidence of the issuance of the Truman [Senatorial] report on oil and of the pipeline announcement [of Ickes] with the invitation extended to the British for oil discussions in Washington" (Foy Kohler, Memorandum of Conversation, "Discussion of Saudi Arabia," 12 April 1944, p. 7). Other quotations, p. 2, Stettinius Papers, Box 251, Folder: "London Mission—Murray." Also, see Kohler, Memorandum of Conversation, "Discussion of Saudi Arabia," 26 April 1944, Stettinius Papers, Box 251, Folder: "London Mission—Murray"; and "Agreed Minute: Anglo-American discussions regarding the Near and Middle East," 28 April 1944, pp. 2–3, Stettinius Papers, Box 251, Folder: "London Mission—Murray."

39. W. Murray, "Saudi Arabian Minister and Mr. Wallace Murray," 19 April 1944, pp. 1–4, Stettinius Papers, Box 251, Folder: "London Mission—Murray."

40. Shwadran, *The Middle East, Oil and the Great Powers*, pp. 322–25; Feis, *Three Episodes*, pp. 146–55; Feis, *Petroleum and American Foreign Policy* (Palo Alto, Calif.: Stanford Univ. Press, 1944); and H. F. Sheets, "The Oil Situation in the Middle East," 25 March 1944, no. A-B103, in *Studies of American Interests in the War and the Peace* (New York: Council on Foreign Relations, 1942—).

An example of the anti-pipeline feelings, and fears, of domestic producers was J. H. Pew, President of Sun Oil Co., who spoke before the Petroleum Industry War Council: "To make a petroleum cartel effective in this country it must necessarily be implemented by the lash of governmental authority so that every unit in the industry, every independent producer, every small refiner, as well as large companies, must conform to the cartel restrictions" (*New York Times*, 26 October 1944, p. 26).

41. Hull to Eddy, 16 October 1944, *FR* 4 (1944): 34; Shwadran, *The Middle East, Oil and the Great Powers*, pp. 331–32; and *ARAMCO Handbook*, pp. 148 ff.

12

Saudi Arabia:
Arab and British Interests

If one goal of Departmental wartime efforts was to increase the accessibility of Saudi-ARAMCO oil, another was to keep the British from "horning in." Though entwined with the former, this latter goal was also related to the Department's general desire to reduce British hegemony regionwide. That is, oil was the main prize and catalyst for Anglo-American competition in the peninsula, but even if oil had not existed, the general competition for influence would have remained. The fact is, however, that the bids for Saudi oil and regional influence often converged, *making the wartime rivalry of the two major allies more keen in Saudi Arabia than anywhere else in the Middle East,* if not in the world.

Furthermore, it should be understood that this rivalry was not simply a struggle of an old imperialist Britain trying to conserve its status against the dollars and power of a more youthful American interloper. While there is much truth in this conceptualization, it is also true that to a considerable degree, America—that is, ARAMCO—was the older power; and Britain, with "large" plans of its own, such as a postwar MESC, was the newcomer that wished to unseat America.

Overall, the Department followed several strategies in Saudi Arabia. From the strictly petroleum point of view, it emphasized a defensive approach, "holding actions" so as to maintain the status quo of the American oil monopoly against British designs. However, from the general economic point of view, because the kingdom was traditionally a part of the sterling bloc and retained British advisers, the Department by 1943 pursued a more offensive approach against *that* status quo.

When, in that year, it successfully began to wean Jidda away from the sterling bloc, the Department extended its ambition and protective embrace. Supported by the Departments of War and Navy (but only partially so, as shall be seen), the State Department sought to take Saudi Arabia out of Britain's political and military spheres, too, basically on the grounds that it appeared increasingly illogical and unseemly—in short, "contrary to" to the national interest and national security—to allow a valuable state in the American petroleum and economic spheres to remain in another's political and military spheres. By the close of 1944 the Department had succeeded in these latter spheres, with the result that British influence was almost entirely displaced.

Outside of the already cited supportive efforts on behalf of CASOC–ARAMCO and outside of largesse for Ibn Saud, like Lend-Lease, what was the content of the Department's strategies? First and foremost was the calculated, friendly Departmental and Presidential cultivation of the king's personal good will—a cultivation that was distinct from but parallel to ARAMCO's like efforts. The other side of this psychological front was the economic and military fronts, namely, the Department's ongoing efforts to generate more and more largesse and protection so as to promote the kingdom's "stability." Next in importance was the Department's effort to set up, in conjunction with Departmental planners and economists, and with counterparts from other departments, a detailed structure to plan on a global scale for America's long-run oil needs. A corollary to this organization of an oil planning apparatus was the Department's effort to gain British compliance, as quickly as possible, to American plans for Saudi Arabia in particular and oil in general. It was held that compliance should be formalized in a new Anglo-American oil accord, and toward that particular goal the Department worked assiduously.

The order of priorities notwithstanding, it is best first to examine these Departmental long-run planning efforts and the topic of the Anglo-American accord. These set the stage for a better understanding of the specific psychological, economic, and military efforts the Department pursued bilaterally with Saudi Arabia.

GLOBAL LONG-RUN PLANNING FOR OIL NEEDS

In the first half of 1943, the Department began to set up a more detailed and centralized planning structure than existed before. The purpose was to intensify the Department's traditional search for oil accessibility. There were other reasons, too: the need to head off the competition posed by other departments' oil planners, the need to coordinate the academic research on oil and the diplomatic tactics required towards the

British, and the need to achieve some consensus interdepartmentally and intra-Departmentally on certain fundamental questions. For example, *was* there an imminent or foreseeable oil shortage for the United States? (NEA said yes and discounted optimistic reports that the future was bright because of America's domestic reserves and the promise of technological breakthroughs. The Economic subcommittee of the postwar planning apparatus disagreed with NEA's affirmation, but nonetheless felt it was worthwhile to build up, as NEA wanted, a future supply position in the Middle East, even if it meant erring on the side of safety.)[1]

Another basic question was: Should the development of Saudi oil precede a comprehensive and global oil study? (Navy planners said yes; Economic Adviser Herbert Feis, who was also chairman of the Department's Petroleum committee, said that the two objectives should be pursued at the same time.) Also, should the Department try to negotiate with the British about opening up Middle Eastern oil regions to American companies before or after the Department firmed up to the point of invulnerability its relations with Ibn Saud? (The Navy and the Department of the Interior's Petroleum Reserves Corporation said after. Feis' committee said before, out of fear of the ill effects which excessive American unilateralism in Saudi Arabia would allegedly have on postwar economic internationalism in general and on relations with Britain in particular. Even so, Feis' committee recommended that Lend-Lease be used, in carrot-and-stick fashion and as had been suggested in earlier instances by James Moffett and CASOC, to pressure London to accede to American oil policy.)[2]

Administratively, the Department's handling of oil matters underwent the following mutations: a Special Committee on Petroleum had been established in June 1943 under Feis; and concurrently, under the impetus of Max Thornburg, Departmental consultant on petroleum matters, a number of active programs were put into motion, including the assignment of petroleum attachés to legations in Latin America and the Middle East. Thornburg resigned that same summer, over his reported conflict of interests (he was a SOCAL executive); and Feis resigned from the Department in November, presumably out of fatigue and frustration. In any case, by December 1943 an Interdivisional Petroleum Committee was set up in the Department, parallel to an interdepartmental group of oil technicians.

In February 1944 a Cabinet Committee on Anglo-American Petroleum Conversations was established, with Hull as chairman and Ickes as vice chairman. This committee in turn set up an Interdepartmental Petroleum Committee in April. Heading it was Charles Rayner, who was also acting chief of the Department's Petroleum Division. This division was new, too, and was created in March along with other additions in the Department's economic-oriented offices. (The same week that the Petroleum Division was set up in the Office of Economic Affairs, the Aviation Division was set up in the Office of Transportation and Communications.) Also under the Hull-Ickes committee was a technical group, again headed by Rayner. Its purpose was to prepare for the exploratory conversations on oil in mid-April, within the framework of Undersecretary Stettinius' scheduled talks in London with the Foreign Office.[3]

In overview, the winter–spring of 1944 represented the high point of administrative reorganization relative to oil. For the duration of the war and into the postwar period, these new staffs worked efficiently with all related Departmental divisions. In addition, the Department decisively replaced Ickes' Department of Interior as the main force in the making of the administration's foreign oil policy. Within the State Department, standing geographic divisions like NEA and standing planning committees like the Post-War Programs Committee and the Economic subcommittee continued to be directly involved in helping to formulate oil policy. Similarly with American legations abroad, particularly as there were periodic increases in the number of petroleum and economic attachés assigned to Foreign Service posts and in the number of countries which the attachés covered.

Yet it seemed that the more the Department expanded its oil staff inside, the more intense and confusing became the great oil debate outside. Pressures to be more unilateralist and less appeasing toward the British increased, as did counterpressures. The Joint Chiefs wanted oil refineries above and beyond those planned the previous year for Saudi Arabia by the PRC. From the Senate, the Truman Committee attacked the Department for not pursuing a vigorous enough oil policy abroad. Opposing views, chiefly from domestic oil producers, were also pressed to the fore.[4]

For all that, the Department exerted pressure of its own on Congress, notably in executive session with the Senate Foreign Relations Committee, chaired by Senator Tom Connally, and with the House Foreign Affairs Committee, chaired by Representative Sol Bloom. Each committee was cultivated and persuaded to accept most Departmental oil and Middle Eastern (including Palestine) policies. For example, Assistant Secretary Breckinridge Long has graphically recorded how senatorial sympathy for the then pending bipartisan Wright-Compton and Taft-Wagner Congressional Resolutions—both of which solidly endorsed open Jewish immigration into Palestine and, for the first time, an American commitment thereto—was quite literally dissolved in Saudi oil.[5]

Because of divided public opinion on oil, the Department also made some gestures to survey public attitudes in detail. At bottom, however, it tended to ignore the pressures and din outside, including its own surveys. To make foreign policy according to the percentage figures of uninformed public opinion or the dictates of a pettifogging Congress simply was too much to stomach.[6]

Public controversy notwithstanding, the Department saw fit to forge ahead in its plans for Saudi Arabia and for formalizing an Anglo-American accord. In addition, there were four new policy thrusts in 1944, initiated chiefly by NEA and the two most high-level Departmental planning committees, the Post-War Committee and the Policy Committee. One was that henceforth the Department ought to avoid to the maximum the hamstringing effects of Congressional scrutiny of oil policy. The point was urged—indeed, *with* the explicit approval of Congressional leaders consulted, particularly from the Foreign Relations and Foreign Affairs Committees—that the Department make its oil accord with Britain an executive agreement rather than a treaty requiring a two-thirds majority in the Senate.[7]

Second, on contentious questions whereon executive agreement was not thought politically practicable—as on the questions then before Congress and the public of how much control the federal government should or should not exert over ARAMCO and Saudi oil—the Policy Committee concluded, and the Department agreed, that the argument of "military security" should here be used. The Department should give out the view that such questions did not belong in the public domain at all because of security considerations. Because this issue of governmental "controls" was so troublesome, the Department also felt it should take the position that the issue constituted a "technical" rather than a "policy" problem and hence belonged to the military. As noted in Chapter 11 on the pipeline controversy, the Department found a ready refuge under the "security" and "technicality" blankets of the Joint Chiefs of Staff, who were of course unaccountable to the public.[8]

Third, the Department began actively to encourage and even prod American oil companies to participate more in the expected global scramble to obtain oil rights. The flag, as it were, was used here to push, not just follow, trade. Latin America and the Middle East were singled out; the traditional anxiety was expressed that if American companies did not move quickly, British and other companies would.[9]

Fourth, with regard to concessions already won in Latin America and the Middle East by both the United States and Britain, the Department wished to take further steps to legally guarantee their status. Since, however, the United States in 1944 had more concessions in Latin America than in the Middle East, the ulterior motive behind this policy thrust was to put Latin America more securely in a closed door American sphere. This motive was fully revealed in an increasing number of Departmental position papers and conversations, which saw as fundamental to postwar America (1) a general increase in Middle Eastern oil production, and (2) a general decrease in Latin American oil production.[10]

The reason for this regional division of labor was twofold. The Department in 1944 wanted to have more American firms commercially develop, market, and profit from the postwar sale of Middle Eastern oil, to Western Europe chiefly. It also wanted to keep Latin American oil out of British producers' hands and out of European, and Soviet, markets. The essential idea was to retain Latin American oil mainly for the postwar American domestic market—and also as reserves for the American military, the contingency plans of which appear to have required Western hemisphere oil for postwar Western hemisphere defense.[11]

Restriction of Latin American production, however, would create a postwar consumer dependence on oil from the Eastern hemisphere, chiefly the Middle East. Curtailment would thus cause a mad scramble for Middle Eastern oil by all of Europe and by the Soviet Union, too. The Department felt that Britain should therefore be interested all the more in a joint accord which could help prevent such a scramble. It was the Department's logic that, in the projected global context, rather than in the short-run Middle Eastern context alone, it was in Britain's interest to actually welcome American "participation" in Middle Eastern oil development.

Britain, as it were, was thus to be given the choice of either holding out in the Middle East against the desires of America and all of Europe, including Russia, for access to oil—or stepping down, giving in to the United States and becoming its junior partner, so as to better keep Russia and all other encroachers away from Middle Eastern oil fields. To the British, this was a dilemma and a subtle diktat—even if it was clear from the start which way Britain of necessity would turn.

For its part, the Department viewed its Latin American-Middle Eastern strategy as the quintessence of moderation and enlightened self-interest: relative to Middle Eastern oil, it seemed to the Department that its oil strategy demoted, yet protected, British interests; furthered the road to American regional hegemony, but not aggressively or unilaterally; and opened the oil doors to the winds of free trade, but not the extent of allowing an anarchic scramble which the Soviet Union could join. Furthermore, the Department believed that its oil strategy would best assure, for consumers and producing states alike, the "orderly development" of the region's oil reserves.[12]

THE ANGLO-AMERICAN OIL ACCORD

In 1943, while the Department, like a millipede, was with one set of arms and legs trying to organize an oil planning apparatus and trying to thrash through domestic pressures and counterpressures, with another set of arms and legs it was already starting to negotiate with the Foreign Office a new accord. The immediate object was to abrogate the prewar restrictions which bound the international oil cartel and which were hitherto consented to by the British and American governments.

By the end of 1943 Hull and Murray were anxious for fuller talks with the F.O. Pending these, they wanted all current oil negotiations between the administration and private oil companies suspended. Moreover, they wanted the talks toward an accord to take place in Washington, not London, to be held quickly, and to concentrate on the Middle Eastern regional oil scene.[13]

When, as noted, the Department's long-run oil strategy crystallized in the first half of 1944, an accord was viewed as all the more important to help implement that strategy. The result was that, after several compromises, such as having the bulk of the talks in London within the framework of Stettinius's Mission in April, and after much lower-level pushing and pulling with the Foreign Office, the latter signed in Washington in August 1944 a Departmentally initiated Anglo-American Petroleum Agreement.[14]

However, the Senate, especially its Special Committee Investigating Petroleum Resources (in contrast to the Foreign Relations Committee), insisted that the accord be subject to the procedures of treaty ratification. On the defensive, and with the pipeline furor fresh in mind, the Department was divided: Acheson opposed compliance, Long and Hull favored it, on the theory that appeasing Congress was the best way to get support. The latter view carried; but it backfired when Congressional proceedings dragged on and on. Roosevelt's special message to Congress urging quick ratification did not help. This, despite the lure that in asking the Senate for support, "the Administration has set a pattern which, if followed, could broaden rather than restrict Senate influence in the field of international affairs."[15]

Though disheartened, the Department managed with Roosevelt's help and through its own manipulativeness to extract the accord from the slow jaws of the Senate. Thereafter, it worked to revise the accord to meet the chief objections of Congress and of the administration's powerful Industrial Advisory Panel, the orientation of which favored maximum freedom from federal regulation for domestic oil producers.

The Department's problem was largely one of public relations. Being saddled with the stereotype as the habitat for un-American appeasers sympathetic with everything from monarchism to communism, the Department often had to prove its Americanism. In the case at hand, its main task was to persuade the accord's domestic critics that the Department was not giving in to the British, which in reality it was hardly

doing. Nor was it advocating foreign or socialistic price controls and regulation of the American oil industry, as some had construed from the fact
that the August draft favored the creation of a regulatory-advisory
International Petroleum Commission.

Rewritten, the new draft sought to avoid any offensive intimations of
postwar entangling relations with the British, while it made explicit that
the commission-to-be would have advisory powers only. More diluted,
too, was the Departmental commitment to support the legality of existing
British concession rights, notably in the Middle East. The purpose of this
particular revision was to leave more legal maneuverability for American
concession-seekers to challenge the so-called "privileged" and "discriminatory" regulations which were basic to existing British oil concessions.[16]

In reformulating the accord, the Department also decided to drop all
references to its Latin American-Middle Eastern oil strategy, a strategy
which had raised too many questions from both the Foreign Office and
domestic producers. Needless to say, dropping the references in no way
meant that the Department was actually dropping the strategy.

The Department was hopeful, at the end of 1944 and in 1945, that it
could push over the top, as it were, an incontrovertible and successful
accord. Dean Acheson was charged with the responsibility for the revised
draft, in consultation with Ickes and Senator Connally of the Foreign
Relations Committee. Talks were resumed with the Foreign Office in
September 1944. The aid of the Anti-Trust Division of the Justice Department was solicited. Postwar planners participated, too.[17]

From the Policy Committee, for example, came the familiar recommendation that Hull avoid the treaty route requiring a two-thirds Senate
majority—though the Committee added some interesting embellishments.
It asked Hull to tell the Senate that the Department had a change of
mind and indeed no longer favored a joint Anglo-American oil commission. The Department could state that it preferred instead merely an
informal agreement with Britain, on broad principles, acknowledged by a
simple exchange of notes. Simultaneously, the Department might organize
an informal group of both consuming and producing states, with the
"official" purpose being to convene a multilateral oil conference. This
action would serve, suggested the Policy Committee, to convince Congress
that the Department was shifting from a disadvantaging bilateralism
with Britain toward an international situation wherein America's leadership would be more certain.[18]

For all its manipulativeness and pertinacity—two qualities which under
most circumstances brought success and which were probably more than
any other two qualities the Department's internal "secret weapon" in
besting the opposition—the Department again failed either to bypass
Congress or to win its ratification. Despite revisions and dilutions, the

Senate remained suspicious. Even despite the fact that the Foreign Office reluctantly signed the Department's second accord, in September 1945, Senatorial opposition and delays, intentional and otherwise, caused the accord to shrivel on the vine.[19]

Withal, this rare failure of the Department to get its way was ultimately of small consequence. In fact, the generalization can be made that, like the Department's "failure" to get a government-built pipeline for ARAMCO, the Department lost the battle for a formal Anglo-American accord, but it still won the oil war. Certainly, the Department's failure was hardly a victory for the Foreign Office—even though the endless Senatorial delays probably allowed the British to continue their own Fabian tactics against American oil companies somewhat longer than a formal accord on the Middle East would have permitted.

First, formal accord or not, the traditional push for the open door *and* the relatively new Latin American-Middle Eastern strategy were the Department's fundamental oil policies from 1944 on. Second, the Department steadily intensified during and beyond 1944–45 its economic unilateralism and quest for hegemony, chiefly in Saudi Arabia, though elsewhere, too. As demonstrated in all previous chapters on the Middle Eastern countries in the British sphere, a major Departmental goal was to establish a de facto Anglo-American understanding according to which British power and pretenses on all matters, not only oil, would be reduced once and for all—yet Britain would be "retained" as junior partner and traditional ally against any third power.

As for the effect on American-Saudi relations of the Department's failure to get a formal Anglo-American oil accord, Saudi Arabia was as a consequence considered—by the White House, by all executive departments, *and* by Congress—as all the more necessary to hold. Within the Department it was a common feeling that because the accord had failed—and allegedly with it, the principle of "multilateralism"—it was necessary to switch to the more practical principle of "unilateralism."

There were other reasons for the rising importance of Saudi Arabia in the second half of the war. In light of the uncertain length of the war and hence of oil needs in 1943, and in light of the emerging shift of war in late 1944–early 1945 to the Pacific, the logistical importance of Saudi Arabia, in a global not just regional perspective, took on more immediacy. As will be noted, to the Departments of State, War, and Navy, military-strategic reasons thus appeared, on several occasions, to be as important as oil reasons for a large American stake in the peninsula. (Accordingly, while the State Department habit of wrapping Saudi Arabia in the cloak of "military security" was usually a disingenuous way of evading Congressional scrutiny of oil policies, it was not always or completely so.)[20]

THE CULTIVATION OF SAUDI GOOD WILL

An ongoing process that would develop into a high art and which would involve nearly all executive departments of the federal government, cultivation of Ibn Saud's friendship by the Department of State began in earnest in early 1942. At that time an agricultural mission was set up, headed by Karl Twitchell of concession-hunting fame and, since the early 1930s, a personal friend and informal agent of Ibn Saud with respect to economic and mining projects. While Roosevelt's letter to the king singled out as the innocuous reasons for Twitchell's mission the wartime economic needs of Saudi Arabia and the desirability of increasing its agricultural production, Assistant Secretary Berle's letter to Twitchell spelled out the mission's essential function, that of furnishing "friendly council [sic]."[21]

Almost simultaneously, a permanent legation was established in Jidda under FSO James Moose, Jr., posted from Teheran.[22] Soon, too, the practice began whereby letters drafted by NEA to be signed by Roosevelt and sent to Ibn Saud invariably began with the salutation "Great and Good Friend" instead of the earlier "Your Majesty" or "Your Excellency."

By early 1943 Moose's rank was elevated to minister resident. By the summer Roosevelt invited Ibn Saud to visit him in Washington and also began a precedent of transmitting written assurances to the king with respect to the Palestine problem. According to the Department's 1943 draft to Ibn Saud, which Roosevelt accepted, the United States was committed to the principle that no decision "altering the basic consideration of Palestine should be considered until after the conclusion of the war." Furthermore, no decision would be considered until after the king had been "fully consulted and his agreement sought." In the autumn, Crown Prince and Foreign Minister Feisal, in place of his father, paid an official visit. (Hosted by an attentive Department, he directed his most lengthy and angry remarks at Hashemite ambitions, particularly at Nuri Said's Greater Syria Plan which, said Feisal, his father saw as an effort "to surround Saudi Arabia and strangle it.")[23]

Concurrently, FSOs were also busy weaving Saudi-American bonds of trust and friendship, usually by trying to discredit British motives and influence before their Saudi hearers. Moose and his British counterpart in Jidda (Philip Jordan) were at daggers drawn for much of 1944 in a remarkable case of national rivalry and foreign service gamesmanship becoming unusually personalized. Alexander Kirk also stoked the fires of Anglo-American tension. Kirk, ever given to the grand phrase, wrote that the Arabian peninsula was "becoming an active battleground in the implementation of two systems of foreign policy." Presumably, the global fate of free enterprise and etatism would be shaped there. Future FSOs responsible for Saudi Arabia, like Colonel William Eddy and after the war NEA veteran J. Rives Childs, were of the same bent as Kirk.[24]

Probably the two most symbolic highpoints in the Department's efforts to create good will occurred in August 1944 and February 1945. The first date represented the establishment of an official consulate at Dhahran in the Hasa region, a region increasingly important not only for oil but, it will be seen, for American military and aviation purposes. The second date represented the famous face-to-face post-Yalta encounter between Roosevelt and Ibn Saud aboard the *U.S.S. Quincy* on Great Bitter Lake in the Suez Canal, 14–15 February. There are many references in various memoirs to this encounter, and to Roosevelt's oft-cited remark afterwards that he learned more about the problems of Palestine and the Middle East in five minutes of talking with Ibn Saud than from all previous sources. Yet the meanings of the meeting and the later comment have long remained differently interpreted, even among persons intimate with the President.

In view of the fact that Roosevelt died within two months of the meeting, it is perhaps moot whether his positive impressions of Ibn Saud reflected the President's sincerity, flattery, or senility. Suffice to say that the encounter was hardly a last-minute improvised affair, even though this was how it was presented, in understatement, at Yalta to Eden, Churchill, and Stalin. Rather, the encounter, like the entire preceding range of official acts and expressions of friendship, was carefully staged and precision-engineered in advance by the Department of State.[25]

More significant, despite Roosevelt's death and despite subsequent Arab regrets over his death and their disappointment in Harry Truman, the February 1945 summit did not give way to any diminution in Saudi-American relations. To the contrary, cultivation of good will and psychological ties intensified, with the illustrations for 1945 far outnumbering those of earlier years. A symbolic example was Feisal's second visit to Washington in July–August 1945. The Department's reception, as usual, was decorous, high-toned, and exuded the "sincerity" and "candor" of a very special friendship. Summing up, Undersecretary Joseph Grew said, "The United States wished to strengthen Saudi Arabia and to help Saudi Arabia strengthen itself."[26]

The question arises, how real were all these benevolent gestures of good will? Were they but diplomatic toasts, or more? They were more. The Department literally worked itself up into a froth of passionate belief in the total beneficence and indispensability of a Saudi-American entente. Although the Department, as indicated, was highly calculating with respect to Saudi Arabia, it is important to recognize that typically the Department was neither cynical nor opportunistic. Perhaps it was baldly opportunistic in the first half of 1942; yet by 1945 all of its own gift-offerings, ritualized messages, and well-staged meetings had succeeded in making the Department, led by NEA and the Foreign Service, something of a true believer in the Saudi Arabian mystique. Habitual auto-suggestion—combined with the older Departmental desires for oil and infatuations with Arabia Deserta—thus created a special faith.

Hence, the Department tended to overreact to the widespread charge in the American media that Saudi-American relations were based strictly on selfish monetary or anti-British considerations. It protested these base thoughts and tried to convince others, and itself, that "in fact" genuinely friendly and selfless reasons were at the bottom of Saudi-American relations. In the same vein, the Department was acutely sensitive to the likes and dislikes of Ibn Saud. This led to the continual and sincere, albeit debasing, desire to placate his every wish.

Indeed, it is important to recognize that the anxiousness to allay any hint of the king's displeasure became, by 1942, probably *the* major reason for the Department of State's "instinctive" opposition to Jewish immigration and to a Jewish state in Palestine—and *also* to a Hashemite-conceived Arab federation in the Middle East. With respect to the Department's opposition to the French in the Levant and to the British in the region generally, the wish to placate the king was again an important motive, though less singularly so. After all, the British and French presence—unlike that of a Jewish state or Arab federation—represented established facts, and the king could be expected to be realist enough to see that the United States could not magically and quickly erase these facts. Therefore, Ibn Saud's displeasure with the British and French caused Departmental "concern," but no anxiety attacks.

In sum, the Department was a hypersensitive believer in Saudi Arabia. Dissent within the Department was very minor. Sumner Welles considered Ibn Saud a backward despot; Herbert Feis felt too much American unilateralism would contradict the Atlantic Charter's call for multilateral cooperation and might lead to entangling commitments to the king. However, they seriously registered their views only after leaving the Department.[27]

ECONOMIC AND MILITARY INSTRUMENTS

If after World War II, the Department was able to lobby efficiently for, and then implement, various large-scale foreign-aid programs, it was to a considerable degree because of the experience which the Department had gained during the war from developing such programs for Saudi Arabia. Indeed, massive wartime aid to Saudi Arabia was, because of the kingdom's location, essentially "postwar" or peacetime aid. Inevitably, therefore, aid programs for Saudi Arabia would serve as a key precedent for the Point Four Program of 1949 and more.

In 1943, besides inspiring the authorization of Lend-Lease to Jidda, the Department persuaded the Department of the Treasury to release a large shipment of silver bullion for the king. Such "direct lendleasing," unprecedented and not brought before Congress, was made at least superficially legal as a result of the elasticity of the Lend-Lease law and as a result of efforts by Treasury Undersecretary Harry Dexter White and his staff.

Treasury had accepted Wallace Murray's argument that Saudi Arabia required the bullion to stabilize its economy, that it was a good credit risk, and that the exportation was altogether in the American national interest. Less said but equally meant were (1) State's eagerness (in March 1943) to exploit the fact that Britain had no silver of its own to export, and (2) State's nervousness (in July 1943) that the British might recoup by setting up, as rumored, a branch of Barclay's Bank in Jidda and a Saudi-British currency board in London.

By the fall, however, the Department tasted victory. Both by sending the silver and by insisting that the British accept American participation on questions relating to Saudi Arabia's currency system, the Department built up, on top of ARAMCO's influence, the federal government's economic influence. As such, Saudi Arabia began to be weaned away from the sterling bloc and toward the dollar bloc.[28]

In 1944 the process of building up and weaning away advanced. Despite the general reduction of Lend-Lease grants globally, Lend-Lease was reextended to Jidda. To cut the economic cords further between Jidda and London, the Department also tried to pressure Britain to cancel Ibn Saud's debt to Britain of $50 million. Implicit, as in all such pressures and protests, was of course an anterior threat, in this case that if Britain did not cancel the king's debt, the United States might not cancel London's own Lend-Lease debts to Washington.[29]

The Department also opposed Britain's granting of private loans to Saudi merchants, on the grounds that industries in Britain and India would benefit, while in Saudi Arabia inflation would result. The Department believed any British loans should be (uncapitalistic) government-to-government loans. Furthermore, the Department locked horns with the Foreign Office as to whether Ibn Saud's economic adviser should be an American or British subject. The Department felt that since Saudi Arabia was increasingly in the American economic orbit, it would be appropriate that the king's adviser be an American. The British disagreed with this version of the "new realities"—much as they disagreed that Ibn Saud was in such dire need of money as he always said he was, and as American FSOs were so quick to accept as true.[30]

In February 1945 Karl Twitchell acted as the king's liaison with the Departmentally influenced Export-Import Bank. In May, Joseph Grew and Dean Acheson persuaded President Truman and the Departments of

War and Navy to override the views of Harold Ickes; Acheson's colleague, Will Clayton; and Leo Crowley, head of the Foreign Economic Administration. (Each of these three had intermittently expressed his lack of faith in the efficacy of America's commitment to Jidda.)

The result of these moves would be a trend toward more money for Ibn Saud, with less Congressional debate and legislation. In September (and again in 1946) Lend-Lease to Saudi Arabia would once more be authorized as an exception to the rule. Under its terms, the War Department, without Congressional scrutiny, would continue to administer Lend-Lease and supply the kingdom with both civilian and military supplies.[31]

Despite all the above, FSOs involved in Saudi Arabia like Kirk, Eddy, and William Sands were never satisfied at what they felt were these insufficient and delayed offerings. Because of aid that was too little and too late and because of America's stained reputation for pro-Zionism, they ever warned that the king might still "go British." To such caveats, Grew and Acheson replied by counseling patience and by urging FSOs to realize that relations with Saudi Arabia were more complex than they, in their narrow field, realized. Furthermore, Grew and Acheson contended that the Department had to move slowly so as to build better for the sake of the Department's long-run objectives in Saudi Arabia. By December 1945, such objectives included a comprehensive bilateral commercial treaty; an elaborate five-year assistance program; and a twenty-year Export-Import Bank loan.[32]

It is significant to note that such objectives had long been on the drawing boards, and when actualized, they represented, in part, the fruit of the Department's postwar planning apparatus' earlier deliberations and drafts in the period July–November 1944. At that time, planners like Christina Grant, Philip Ireland, and particularly William Yale had urged that Saudi Arabia be the recipient of long-run financial aid, an American "advisory" system, an economic development plan which would set up an Arabian Development Corporation, and aid from the Export-Import Bank.[33]

The American military was also very interested in the economic development and bilateral agreements regarding Saudi Arabia. Saudi oil and presumed geopolitical centrality were the chief reasons. The military supported the State Department's insistent quarrels with the Foreign Office, especially on two demands in the period 1944–45: for American military air rights; and for an air base at Dhahran, to be built and controlled by the War Department. The rationale, which the British did not accept, was that both would be crucial for transmitting manpower and oil to the expanding war theatre in the Pacific.

It must be pointed out, however, that the Department of State exploited the "military security" argument for its own long-run objectives in Saudi Arabia. It did this particularly in the early and the late stages of the war. In the spring of 1942, when Rommel was still a threat to the region, the Department had wanted the American military to take over from the British the military responsibility for Saudi Arabia. The Department of War had refused, not wishing to assume any new burdens. The following year, however, the Department of War was persuaded that Saudi oil was of vital importance for the war effort, the end of which was not yet in sight. Like the Petroleum Reserves Corporation under Harold Ickes, the military urged direct official intervention and acquisition with respect to ARAMCO operations and a Saudi pipeline. As noted, these were courses of action which, in the State Department's view, overshot the mark.

Beginning in late 1944, when the war's end was foreseeable, and definitely by mid-1945, the Department of War, again like the PRC, lost interest in Saudi Arabia—thus undershooting the mark, in the opinion of the State Department. Accordingly, the latter tried to offset the military's "error in judgment" by framing security policies in Saudi Arabia by itself. It did this by stressing the term "national interest," not "military security." National interest of course presupposes a military-security interest, but deliberately avoiding the latter term allowed the State Department to avoid the accusation that it was usurping the role of the War Department.[34]

What all this meant, broadly speaking, was that if Saudi Arabia's geo-political value to the United States rose toward the conclusion of the war, it was due more to the assertions, half-sincere, half-deceptive, of the Department of State than to those of the Department of War. It was the diplomats considerably more than the generals who pushed for the continuation of American military missions and the building of Dhahran air base—even after the military, in several dissenting reappraisals, had concluded that none of these was any longer justified in terms of the war effort.

Such dissents—the most notable being that of War Secretary Stimson in May 1945 that there was no justification to make the airfield a major military base—put only a temporary crimp in the State Department's plans. In June Acting Secretary Joseph Grew wrote a detailed brief to Truman affirming the necessity of the base's construction, on grounds that American prestige and Ibn Saud's faith in America would otherwise falter. In July Acheson received the President's approval that the base would be built with existing War Department funds, thus avoiding Congressional hearings. On 8 August 1945, at the very close of the war, the Department's manipulativeness and pertinacity met their usual ultimate success when Ibn Saud signed an agreement allowing the United States to build a military airfield.[35]

There were other instances of assertiveness by diplomats, not generals, in the realm of "military security." In the spring of 1945 the Department had willfully and deceptively stretched the security argument in seeking to get British compliance to an expansion of American air rights, both military and civil, in and across Saudi Arabia. Toward this end it also repeatedly invoked the "Fifth Freedom," or "open skies," principle.

The Department also pushed for direct telegraph-radio communications between the United States and Saudi Arabia. In this matter, it succeeded both in encouraging Ibn Saud to request that Britain revoke its exclusive communications rights and in pressuring Britain directly to give in to the Department's demand. The rationale for direct communications was the usual blur of open door principle, military security, and the alleged sore need of Americans, civilian and military—even though existing British facilities in adjacent Bahrein were known to be capable, with slight modification, of handling all American communication needs in Saudi Arabia.[36]

CONCLUSIONS

By 1945, after Ibn Saud had long and skillfully played the great powers against each other, the games of cunning, chiefly among Washington, London, and Jidda, were resolved. American primacy in the kingdom on all levels had become so strong that in December 1945 "imperialist" Britain, ironically, was urging Saudi Arabia to assert itself against American control and to push for Saudi self-determination and decolonization! But it was to no avail. The mutual benefits accruing both to Jidda and Washington were and would be too considerable. Both affection and profit underlay the Saudi-American marriage, and it was thus highly, or doubly, successful.

Besides pursuing Saudi oil in a manner conspicuously friendly both to ARAMCO and the king, the Department of State pursued its "British must go" policy on several fronts and with various and intercalculated strategies. With patience it built up the king's good will and personal friendship. It managed to keep the Palestine and Arab federation problems at bay. It exploited British economic weakness and pushed through a flow of unprecedented aid programs and bilateral agreements with Jidda under cover of the open door and military security.

When, toward the end of the war, the military reduced its stake in the peninsula, and when rivals for the President's ear—like Ickes, Crowley, and even Department Assistant Secretary Clayton—felt that the Department was going "overboard" on Saudi Arabia, the Department pushed all the more for a strong American military and economic presence. Due to Roosevelt's positive feelings towards Ibn Saud and due to Truman's faith in Grew and Acheson, the Department's commitment invariably won Presidential support.

NOTES

1. Memorandum regarding proposed Anglo-American Oil Conversations, E 253, 15 January 1943, pp. 1–2, Notter Papers, Box 91, Folder: "E Docs 236–61."

2. Petroleum M-1, 15 June 1943; Summary of Petrol. M-2, 27 July 1943, p. 1; and Petrol. M-2, 27 July 1943, all in Notter Papers, Box 106, Folder: "Petroleum Minutes 1–2."

3. On the evolution of the Department's oil apparatus, see, e.g., G. M. R. Dougall, Memorandum on History of Petroleum Division, October 1944; and Summaries, both in Notter Papers, Box 106, Folder: "Petroleum—General." Also, see Release, 1 April 1944, *Bulletin* 10 (1944): 303–4; and H. Ickes and J. Byrnes (exchange of letters), "Formulation and Implementation of Foreign Oil Policies," 2 December 1945, *Bulletin* 13 (1945): 894–95. On the resignations of Thornburg and Feis, note Roosevelt to Welles, 30 June 1943, Roosevelt Papers, PSF, Box 88, File: "State Dept. 12 June 1943."

4. Leahy to Hull, 26 January 1944, *FR* 5 (1944): 20–21; Policy Committee, Minutes of 10th meeting, 10 February 1944, Notter Papers, Box 15, Folder: "Pol. Com. Minutes 1–22;" and note 40, Chapter 11.

5. After stating that the U.S. had no special commitments regarding Palestine and the "so-called" 'Balfour Declaration,'" Long wrote that he then read figures "to indicate the enormous quantity of oil" in Arabia, compared with the original underestimations. "At this point there were expressions of amazement and concern on the part of each of the Senators present." They expressed their "entire approval" as to governmental participation and oil negotiations, each expressing "grave concern over the effect the passage of the [Taft-Wagner] resolution might have upon the continuance of the concession under which the U.S. operated." "They each placed emphasis upon the military aspects of the possession by the U.S. of such oil [for present and future needs]." "Each of the Senators was so positive in his statements and so confident in the expression of his belief that the oil there was of paramount necessity that my memory does not separate the remarks one made from the remarks made by another. They were each outspoken and positive . . . that nothing should be allowed to interfere with the continuing acquisition of the oil" [B. Long, Memorandum of Conversation (Senators Connally, Barkley, George, Vanderberg, La Follette, and Assistant Secretary Long) regarding Arabian Oil and Palestine, 5 February 1944, pp. 1–3, Long Papers, Box 201, Folder: "Petroleum 1944"].

6. Seeking enlightenment and, hopefully, endorsement of its pro-pipeline thesis, the Department paused from time to time to listen to vox populi. It concluded a survey in March 1944, the response to which singled out the following as the public's main opinions: concern for the possibility of an oil shortage, yet doubt and suspicion if there really was or would be one; fear of the socialistic-sounding precedent of the government's building and owning the Saudi pipeline; fear of military involvement and great-power rivalry among allies; concern that an American monopoly in Saudi Arabia would be a violation of the Atlantic Charter's principles; approval of the military defense of American overseas interests; approval of an international oil agreement; and

a questioning if direct government involvement in Saudi Arabia would conflict with the government's backing (as presumed by the American public) of the Jewish national home in Palestine. Source: Report No. 15, U.S. Arabian Oil Policy, 18 March 1944, Div. of Public Liaison, Off. of Public Information, Stettinius Papers, Box 389, Folder: "S. D. Miscell.," File, Public Attitudes on Foreign Policy September 1943–May 1944.

7. PWC Committee, Minutes of 6th meeting, 3 March 1944, and of 18th meeting, 10 April 1944, Notter Papers, Box 21, Folder: "PWC Committee." The consent of domestic producers and their Congressmen was, to some degree, gained as a result of the potential escape clauses in the Agreement's draft: that is, the emphasis in the draft was on wartime, not postwar, Anglo-American cooperation.

8. See note 37, Chapter 11.

9. "The Department is informing them [American oil companies] that this Government, because of the wartime and long-range importance of oil, favors the development of foreign oil resources and welcomes the participation of American companies in that development. This Government takes the clear position that, if any country grants to foreigners rights concerning the exploration for or development of petroleum resources, the nationals of the United States should be accorded equal opportunity with the nationals of any other country to obtain such rights" [Stettinius airgram to FSOs in Colombia, Venezuela, Ecuador, Paraguay, 17 February 1944, *FR* 5 (1944): 23].

10. The key paper—until 1947 "the only official statement of foreign petroleum policy"—was "Foreign Petroleum Policy of the United States," 11 April 1944, *FR* 5 (1944): 27–29. (The quotation is from the *FR* editors, p. 28, n. 32.)

11. Ibid., p. 29. The paper also noted that despite Rumania's being Russia's traditional source, "Russian oil production, unless the [internal] tempo of exploitation is greatly accelerated, will probably continue to be barely adequate for Russia's expanding industrial requirements" (ibid., p. 29). Beyond this, the Soviet Union was not, in any explicit sense, an important factor in the "foreground" of the Department's formulation of oil plans. Rather, it was always an important "background" factor.

There were other matters not seriously considered: e.g., the postwar position and oil needs of the Axis powers and the problem of getting American cash on the Saudi barrel—that is, the problem of marketing the oil in countries with traditionally nonconvertible currencies. [Later, however, the Department, despite such uncertainties, would grow confident that America's power and open door gospel would succeed in breaking down nonconvertible currencies. See *FR* 8 (1945): 918, 961–62.]

It is also noteworthy to contrast the Department's April 1944 global policy position with an earlier one of the non-Departmental War Mobilization Committee, whose position was close to that of the PRC. In August 1943, this committee (under James Byrnes) had concluded that Latin American oil was to be developed for *both* American and British *postwar* domestic needs, while Middle Eastern oil (Iran, Iraq, Saudi Arabia) was to be developed to the fullest and quickest degree in order to fuel the *present* war effort (Memorandum for Meeting of War Mobilization Committee, 18 August 1943, Byrnes Papers, Box 620).

Finally, it is interesting to note the sharp contrast between the Department's oil strategy and that of the Foreign Office. According to Sir Norman Duke, Secretary of the Petroleum Division of the Ministry of Fuel and Power: "1. Britain in future cannot depend upon Middle Eastern oil for strategic purposes, and 2. Britain's interest is increased, therefore, in Latin American oil resources" [Duke's words, as reported by ambassador Winant (London) to Secretary Byrnes, 19 November 1945, *FR* 8 (1945): 58].

12. "Foreign Petroleum Policy of the United States," 11 April 1944, *FR* 5 (1944): 29–30.

13. The Foreign Office responded by saying in essence, yes, it favored an accord, but it wanted the talks on its terms, that is, in London and not to be confined to Middle Eastern oil. See correspondence December 1943–January 1944, *FR* 4 (1943): 944, n. 41, and 947–52.

The restrictions referred to included the Red Line Agreement of 1927, which forbade any participant in IPC from exploiting, independently of the others, any concession in the eastern half of the Middle East (that is, the area approximating the former Ottoman empire). Another restriction limited refinery building and concessions in Transjordan, Palestine, Syria, parts of Iran, and Afghanistan. See notes 41 and 42 in *FR* 4 (1943): 944; and note 1 above.

14. The details of the negotiating and redrafting activity can be found in Policy Committee, Minutes of 38th meeting, 1 May 1944, pp. 1–2, Notter Papers, Box 15, Folder: "Pol. Com. Minutes"; G. M. R. Dougall, Memorandum on History of Petroleum Division, October 1944, p. 29, Notter Papers, Box 106, Folder: "Petroleum—General"; PWC 171–4, 19–22 May 1944, Notter Papers, Box 18, Folder: "PWC Docs. Nos. 156–83"; Yale and Ireland to Philip Mosely, Memorandum, 24 May 1944, Yale Papers, Box 3, Folder: "#6, SA"; and Draft of 22 February 1944, CD I–C, pp. 4–5, 811.6363/4–1144.

15. Quotation is from *New York Times,* 25 August 1944, p. 5. Also, see G. M. R. Dougall, Memorandum on Petroleum Division History, p. 39.

16. Ibid., pp. 21–22, 34, 39.

17. The Anti-Trust Division advised that if the Agreement became law by first having become a treaty, it could be voided by an anti-trust suit; whereas if it became law because it was an executive agreement, it could not be challenged in the courts, as "it would be clear that no existing statute would be overridden in the absence of further action by the Congress" [E. Levi (Anti-Trust Division of Justice Department) and C. Rayner, Memorandum, 27 October 1944, Long Papers, Box 201, Folder: "Petroleum 1944" (Levi would be U.S. Attorney General, 1975–1976)].

18. Policy Committee, Oil Recommendations, ECA-11, 13 November 1944, p. 1, Notter Papers, Box 14, Folder: "Pol. Com. Docs. ECA"; and Policy Committee, Minutes of 91st (final) meeting, 29 November 1944, p. 4, Notter Papers, Box 15, Folder: "Pol. Com. Minutes 81–91 (25 October–29 November 1944)." Also, see John Loftus (Petroleum Division), Memorandum, 31 May 1945, pp. 51–54, and 1 June 1945, p. 55, both in *FR* 8 (1945). The formal drafts of the accord (8 August 1944 and 30 September 1945) are in *Bulletin* 11 (1944): 153–56, and *Bulletin* 13 (1945): 481–83.

19. After September 1945, the agreement again went to the Senate. Hearings scheduled for 20 January 1946 did not begin until June 1947. Despite opposition, the pro-Department Foreign Relations Committee approved the agreement on 1 July 1947. But when it was sent back to the Senate for ratification, the matter was allowed to lapse once more! In the words of Benjamin Shwadran, "this was the end of the effort to get some commitment from Great Britain for the development of American oil reserves in the Middle East"—and, he could have added, the end of what was in any case the limited faith the Department had had in Congressional cooperation on foreign oil affairs (Shwadran, *The Middle East, Oil and the Great Powers,* pp. 330–31).

20. On unilateralist plans for Saudi Arabia, see below, notes 31 and 32. On the growing (yet sharply waning) military interest, see note 33.

21. Roosevelt to ("Your Majesty") Ibn Saud, 13 February 1942, p. 563; and Berle to Twitchell, 19 March 1942, pp. 565–66, both in *FR* 4 (1942). Wrote Berle: "The Department is convinced that the personal relationships which the Mission's personnel establishes with Saudi Arabian officials and individuals in civil life can play an important part in the success which the Department sincerely trusts will attend the Mission's work, and believes that these relationships should be carefully cultivated" (ibid., p. 566).

22. Moose would be chargé at Jidda; while Alexander Kirk, though stationed in Cairo, would continue until 1943 as the accredited minister to both Egypt and Saudi Arabia.

23. On the importance attributed to elevated diplomatic rank, see Hull to Roosevelt, 30 March 1943, *FR* 4 (1943): 830.

On Roosevelt's 14 May 1943 "Great and Good Friend" letter, drafted by Murray and Lt. Harold Hoskins, Sumner Welles wrote to Hull, quoting the draft: "Do we wish to commit ourselves at this moment so definitely to the principle that no decision 'altering the basic consideration of Palestine should be considered until after the conclusion of the war'; and should we now make the commitment that we will not take part in any settlement of the Palestine problem until after King Ibn Saud has been 'fully consulted and his agreement sought'? For obvious reasons it would seem to me more expedient for the President to be far less specific in his reply" (Welles to Hull, 15 May 1943, 890F.00/5–1443).

Roosevelt overruled Welles, though he emended the Murray-Hoskins draft somewhat. A key line would finally read as follows: "I assure Your Majesty that it is the view of the Government of the United States that no decision altering the basic situation of Palestine should be reached without full consultation with both Arabs and Jews" (Roosevelt to Ibn Saud, in Hull to Kirk, 26 May 1943, *FR* 4 (1943): 787).

On Feisal's visit, see Paul Alling, Memorandum of Conversation, 1 November 1943, pp. 845–47; and Stettinius to Kirk, 26 October 1943, pp. 853–54, both in *FR* 4 (1943).

24. On Moose's local war, see *FR* 5 (1944): 673, passim. On Kirk's view, see Kirk to Hull, 25 April 1944, ibid., pp. 690–91. Also, see note 11, Chapter 4.

25. On the establishment (August 1943–November 1943) of a consulate in Dhahran (despite some initial Saudi objections that if Jidda permitted a consulate for the U.S., it would have to do the same for Iraq, Iran, and Britain), see *FR* 4 (1943): 833–34, 840.

References to the Roosevelt-Ibn Saud meeting are numerous, though all are inconclusive. Relevant is the following bibliography, chiefly of autobiographies of historical witnesses and near-witnesses: Memorandum of Conversation (Roosevelt, Ibn Saud), 14 February 1945, *FR* 8 (1945): 2–3, and other documentation, pp. 4–10; Eddy, *FDR Meets Saud*, pp. 34 ff.; Charles E. Bohlen, *Witness to History 1929–1973* (New York: Norton, 1973), pp. 203–4; Leahy, *I Was There*, pp. 326–27; Winston Churchill, *Triumph and Tragedy* (Boston: Houghton Mifflin, 1953), pp. 397–98; Sherwood, *Roosevelt and Hopkins*, pp. 871–72; Welles, *Where Are We Heading?*, pp. 264–66; Edward Stettinius, Jr., *Roosevelt and the Russians* (Garden City, N.Y.: Doubleday, 1949), pp. 278, 289–90; de Gaury, *Feisal*, p. 73.

26. Quotation is from *FR* 8 (1945): 1004. For other details of the Department's role as host, see pp. 1000–1007.

27. To Welles, Ibn Saud was "an absolute dictator. There is probably no potentate of the modern world who possesses more complete authority within

his realm" (Welles, *Where Are We Heading?*, p. 261). On Feis, see note 40, Chapter 11.

28. The relevant documentation on silver currency and Saudi finances is in *FR* 4 (1943): 869–91; also, H. D. White and W. Murray exchange, 15 July 1943, 8111.5151/282 PS/MJN.

29. On the reextension of Lend-Lease, see *FR* 5 (1944): 670 ff.; and *FR* 8 (1945): 951 ff.

30. On the opposition to British loans to Saudi merchants, see *FR* 5 (1944): 739, 747; on the economic advisor question, see ibid., pp. 696, 699, 713, passim; on the debate over Ibn Saud's indigency, see ibid., pp. 724–28. (In October 1944 Ibn Saud finally chose a British Indian Moslem as his official financial advisor.)

In overview, it should be noted that traditionally the British were interested in Saudi Arabia essentially for political, not economic, reasons. The interest in Saudi Arabia as a friendly power in the British sphere had preceded, chronologically and otherwise, the interest in Saudi Arabia as a potential oil reserve, even though the second interest buttressed the first. With the Americans the interest in oil had and would come first, the interest in geopolitics second, and of course each would reinforce the other.

31. On Twitchell, see *FR* 8 (1945): 851; on the Grew-Acheson vs. Ickes-Clayton-Crowley competition, see ibid., pp. 850, 870–71, 880 (note 84); 896, 900–903, 952–57.

32. On the FSOs' demand and on the upper echelons' counseling patience, see *FR* 8 (1945): 879, 893, 908–10, 813, 915, 918, 955–56, 967, 975, 980, 987–88, 995–96, 1010. On the projected aid package, see Memorandum of Conversation (G. P. Merriam, British embassy officials), 30 November 1945, ibid., pp. 973–74; and Acheson to Eddy, 20 December 1945, ibid., p. 982.

33. See W. Yale, Memorandum, CAC-303 Prelim., 6 October 1944, p. 7, Yale Papers, Box 3, Folder: "SA, #4." Yale's model for joint development in Arabia was Chile's (1939) Coporacion de Fomento de la Produccion, while the best precedent he saw for the proposal of an Ex-Im Bank mission to Jidda was the 1942 Bohan economic mission to Bolivia [W. Yale, Memorandum, 28 March 1944, Yale Papers, Box 1, Folder: "7, file xxiv"; and Memorandum (n. d.), Box 3, Folder: "SA, #4." Also, W. Yale, "Certain New Instrumentalities for Economic Development in the South American Republics," 12 November 1944, *Bulletin* 11 (1944): 571–676].

Other planning documents on Saudi Arabia include W. Yale, "Part V: Saudi Arabian Political Relations With Adjoining Areas as They Affect Security Interests of American Interests" (first four parts missing; n. d., probably autumn, 1944), Yale Papers, Box 3, Folder: "SA, #4"; W. Yale, "Proposed Plan for Safeguarding American Interests in Saudi Arabia" (presented 18 October 1944 by Murray and Alling to Departments of War and Navy), Yale Papers, Box 3, Folder 2: "Saudi Arabia"; and W. Yale, "Preliminary Steps in the Initiation of a Long-Term Economic Development Plan for Saudi Arabia," CAC-323 Prelim., draft of 7 November 1944, Yale Papers, Box 3, Folder: "#6, SA."

34. For the military's fluctuating interest in Saudi Arabia, see *FR* 3 (1941): 636; *FR* 4 (1942): 567, 569, 584; *FR* 5 (1944): 17–20, 661–69. In the summer of 1945, Grew wrote a highly confidential and illustrative memo to Eddy in Jidda that as the War Department intended to redeploy troops to the Far East via the U.S. rather than via Saudi Arabia, there was diminishing necessity of Dhahran for military use, and that War Department funds for building

the airbase might even be of doubtful legality. However, though it was no longer militarily justified, the base was still felt by "interested departments" to be in the national interest, and they "recommended that the matter be presented to President on national interest basis" [Grew to Eddy, 25 June 1945, *FR* 8 (1945): 915].

35. This is not to say that Truman was deceived by the State Department. When Acheson wrote him the following month that since the Dhahran airbase had doubtful World War II use, Acheson noted that construction had to be founded on "broader considerations involving the national interest" [Acheson to Truman, 22 September 1945, *FR* 8 (1945): 957–58]. On Stimson's view, as sent to Jidda, see ibid., p. 893. On Grew's brief, see Grew to Truman, 26 June 1945, ibid., pp. 916–17. On the final signing, see ibid., p. 958.

36. On air rights, see *FR* 8 (1945): 886, 932–33, 966–71, 979–80, 987–90. On communication rights, see ibid., pp. 1018–31.

13

Palestine Through 1942

PREWAR POLICIES TOWARD AMERICAN JEWS AND ZIONISTS AND TOWARD PALESTINE

Regarding "the Jews," the Department of State reflected a good measure of the late nineteenth-century's ambivalence: fascination-repulsion, admiration-envy, pity-contempt, respect-fear. In the American context of mass immigration from southern and eastern Europe and the nativist debate as to their assimilability, ambivalence to the Jews also meant the question of whether or not foreign types like the Russian Jew could ever become loyal American citizens. In the context of the Department's wish to have good relations with the Turkish-Moslem overlords of the Middle East, later with the Arab-Moslem majority of the Middle East, there was a counterpart question, namely, could those same East European Jews become nondisruptive, assimilated, and loyal to the Turkish-Arab Moslem world? In short, would they, not having fit in anywhere, ever fit in, in the United States or in the Middle East?

These questions were not formally asked; but had they been, there is little question how the Department would have replied. Unsympathetic to begin with, and less accountable to the public than most other parts of the federal government, it would have answered no. The Department would have held that "realistically," the Jews would not fit in either place, and that therefore America should hold itself aloof from any misguided humanitarianism which might seriously alter the admittedly unfortunate Jewish status quo in the East European Pale of Settlement (the Jewishly populated area extending from the Baltic Sea to the Black Sea).

245

True, there were before World War I individual expressions and acts of benevolence toward the Jews within the Department: for example, those of Warder Cresson in the 1840s and General Lew Wallace in the 1880s relative to Palestine, and of Andrew White relative to Czarist Russia. But these were not taken seriously by the Department's majority. Far more typical was the attitude, expressed in 1912 by Alvey A. Adee, the indefatigable and ageless Assistant Secretary of State who, since 1886, had been the chief formulator of Departmental policy: "For thirty years and I know not how much longer, Turkey has writhed under the dread of a restoration of the Judean monarchy.... The [Zionist] project is chimerical."[1]

When war began in 1914, the United States was a neutral until April 1917; in that interval, the Department became the representative of all allied interests in Ottoman Palestine. The Department also became a secondary party to relief and evacuation efforts on behalf of Palestinian Jews of American and allied nationality. While thus becoming more involved and intimate with Palestine, the Department nonetheless went strictly "by the book" in its attitudes, which differed in no wise from the properly legalistic attitudes taken in other wartime situations where the rights of American nationals were in jeopardy. That it still opposed Zionism as "chimerical" would soon be evident, too.[2]

Thus, toward the Morgenthau Peace Mission of July 1917, the Department was somewhat hopeful of inducing Turkey to withdraw from the war. However, the Mission (in part set up by Colonel Edward House and headed by Henry Morgenthau, Sr., ex-ambassador to Turkey) was not accomplished. The Department would come to believe that Zionist dissuasions of Morgenthau, ordinarily a staunch anti-Zionist, were responsible.[3]

Toward the Balfour Declaration of November 1917, the Department was not only ideologically opposed but also subjectively resentful, as that policy position in its numerous drafts was largely the result of Jewish private diplomacy (to the Department, an arch-heresy) involving Chaim Weizmann, Nahum Sokolow, Louis Brandeis, Woodrow Wilson, Colonel Edward House, and of course, Lloyd George, Arthur Balfour, and others of the Foreign Office. Secretary of State Robert Lansing had been pointedly excluded.[4]

Furthermore, on the Jewish New Year of 1918 Wilson began what would become a Presidential custom of issuing a statement broadly sympathetic with the Balfour Declaration. While not in the category of a Presidential address, it was nonetheless the kind of statement which, by virtue of dealing with foreign affairs, normally would be cleared with the Department. However, the Department was not consulted by Wilson. It would therefore riposte in the future that, officially speaking, the United States (that is, the Department) had never approved the Balfour Declaration.[5]

Toward the Zionist delegation at the 1919 Paris Peace Conference, the Department worked as counterweight and, in an uncommon display of cooperation, worked together with the experts of Colonel House's former "Inquiry" who were, in Paris, part of the American delegation's Intelligence Section. Thus both the Department and the Western Asia Division (headed by Cornell Professor William Westermann) of the Intelligence Section sought to minimize the role of the Balfour Declaration. In this endeavor, the Department was assisted by other anti-Zionist forces: the Arab delegation, the British Colonial Office, Jewish anti-Zionists, and Protestant missionaries. Indeed, the missionaries, along with Westermann, were particularly instrumental in persuading Wilson in March 1919 that a scientific inquiry based on the principle of self-determination and the wishes of the population of what was then known as Syria was necessary prior to any American commitments on Palestine. But the instrument of this inquiry, the King-Crane Commission, fell into disuse, and with it its anti-Zionist conclusions of August 1919. Anglo-French indifference, Zionist counterpressure, Wilson's physical collapse, and the growing mood of American political isolationism were the main determinants.[6]

Despite these setbacks and the fact that in July 1922 Britain became the mandatory power in Palestine, with "responsibilities" to the Balfour Declaration, the Department never accepted the Declaration as a fait accompli, let alone as official American policy. Thus in June 1922 the reaction of Secretary of State Charles Evans Hughes and of NEA chief Allan W. Dulles was negative to a Congressional Joint Resolution on Palestine. Sponsored by Senator Henry Cabot Lodge and Representative Hamilton Fish and signed by President Warren G. Harding, the resolution gave, albeit without commitment, a clear moral endorsement of the Balfour Declaration.[7]

Moreover, in December 1924, after two years of negotiation and redrafting with the Foreign Office, the Department advantaged itself in a compromise accord which became the Anglo-American Convention on Palestine (ratified by Congress, December 1925). True, on the strength of the 1922 Congressional Resolution, the Foreign Office was able to embarrass a grudging Department into accepting the Balfour Declaration's explicit inclusion in the 1922 Mandate's preamble. On the other hand, the Department was able to keep any mention of the Jewish national home out of the body of the articles of the Convention (more important than the preamble). Also, the British failed to win their point that Departmental insistence on the open door was inappropriate and usurping, given the special needs and international significance of Palestine. The Department did not accept the special-case thesis, and it succeeded in extracting reassurances that as in other mandates the British in Palestine would not discriminate against (presumably, Christian) American economic, educational, and missionary interests.[8]

American Zionists considered the Department's signature to the Anglo-American Convention an appropriate legal protection of American Jewish nationals and property in Palestine. Moreover, American Zionists now believed that if Britain should wish to alter the Palestine Mandate by minimizing the Balfour Declaration, they would have recourse to the Convention's clause which required British consultation with the Department prior to the implementation of any serious change in the mandate. This clause (which was found in all bilateral conventions relating to British and French mandates) was seen as confirmation of the older American Zionist belief that, in the event of any British tampering with the mandate, the Department would hasten to consult with the American group most interested in Palestine, the American Zionists. In fact, the latter sometimes tended to think that they had an ultimate veto over State Department and Foreign Office decisions in Palestine.[9]

The Department, of course, had absolutely no intention of seriously consulting with Zionists or of interfering with whatever Britain did or did not do to the Declaration. The Zionists did not grasp this. Nor did they understand that after the Department had failed within the American delegation at the Paris Peace Conference to override the Declaration, it had resolutely set its face against any American interference on behalf of Jewish interests relating to Palestine.

In the duel between the State Department and American Zionists, the latter were increasingly the losers from the mid-1920s on—despite pro-Zionist endorsements and testimonials to the contrary on the Congressional and state legislature levels, despite seasonal White House proclamations of cordiality, and despite all the appearances of political-ethnic "clout." A replica of the highly organized but also competitively and poorly organized American Jewish community, American Zionism was frequently weak, from the standpoints of funds, leadership, membership, American-Jewish immigration to Palestine, internal democracy, spirit, and public relations. And if, in general, American Jews and Zionists looked to European Jewry for initiatives and leadership, the darkening fate of Jewish communities in Central and Eastern Europe after 1933 cast a shadow and brought out the internal weaknesses of American Jewry even more. Materialistic assimilation and, at the opposite pole, leftist radicalism attenuated American Jewish ranks; while native and imported anti-Semitism, concurrent with economic anxieties induced by the Great Depression, inhibited American Jews' willingness to stand up, as Jews, and be different.

As a result, Jews did not speak out or campaign vigorously against the official hands-off attitude toward the emerging and mingled problems of European Jews' need to emigrate from Europe, their wish to immigrate to the United States and/or to Palestine, and the Yishuv's wish to get more settlement rights in Palestine so as to accommodate immigration.

This hands-off theme was regularly sounded by the Department, each occasion reinforcing the next. For example, at the time of the 1929 Arab riots at the Western Wall, G. Howland Shaw, then NEA chief and later an assistant secretary, expressed the Departmental view thus:

It was suggested to Rabbi [Stephen] Wise [American Zionist leader] that to argue that because eight American [Jewish] citizens had been killed in Palestine therefore the American Government was under some sort of obligation to assist in presenting the Zionist side before the Commission of Investigation was clearly fallacious reasoning. Why should the American Government assist in presenting either the Jewish or Arab side?[10]

Seven years later, the same note was sounded. The Department did not wish to become entangled in the British-Jewish problem over immigrant quotas. Britain, it said, was the mandatory power with sole legal responsibility; the United States was not, and furthermore, given its own strict immigration laws, was in no position to tell Britain to liberalize the immigration laws relative to Palestine.[11]

In 1938, at the time of the Arab Revolt under the Mufti, the Jews of Palestine and their brethren abroad were again regarded by the Department as a bothersome group, one which had long outworn its sufferance, was too large for Christian and Moslem sensibilities, yet was still too small to represent power. To senior FSO Knabenshue, then minister in Iraq, it was particularly the uneducated East European Jew who stubbornly opposed partition and minority status who was most at fault that troubled year. George Wadsworth, then consul general in Jerusalem, wrote that he was impressed with what he saw as the anarchical, Bolshevik-sounding proclamations of the Revisionist Zionists. The latter, in employing direct action and counter-terror, had spoken in terms of blood, iron, and vengeance. The prior use by the Arabs of direct action and terror drew no such caveats, for to Wadsworth the side of light was clearly that of the Arabs. Indeed, to the entire Foreign Service (as to Marxist observers, too), Arab riots were objectively progressive—that is, the climax of a classic nationalist uprising with popular and moral roots against the spectres of Jewish domination and of reactionary British imperialism.[12]

The wish to stay aloof from the Palestine mess also led to a Departmental loss of interest in an economic open door there. True, immediately after World War I, the Department, as in Iraq and the Persian Gulf, formally opposed alleged acts of British discrimination against American oil exploratory rights in the Negev and against American rights to bid on construction projects in Haifa harbor. The Anglo-American Convention of 1924, as noted, also emphasized the salience of American economic rights. By the late 1920s, however, it seemed that mainly trouble, not oil or trade, came out of Palestine. (That actually much trade and an extraordinary amount of capital exchange were involved between the United States and Palestine was, as will be noted, ignored, on the premise that such transactions were Jewish and were part of the artificial, hence discountable, economy of the Yishuv.)[13]

Furthermore, the overall mood of neutralism and isolationism of the 1930s made the Department, already "turned off" by Zionism, even more sensitive than before toward becoming in any way whatever drawn into Palestinian affairs. Too much economic contact with Palestine would also have negative repercussions on American prestige in Arab countries.

On another level, a reluctance to embarrass Britain developed after September 1939, a time when Britain was in economic straits, even as its special relationship was being converted into a de facto alliance with the United States. Therefore, the Department acceded for the short run (pending Lend-Lease, enacted March 1941) to the British thesis. This argued that for Britain to allow American imports and to terminate its protectionist policies would lead to the export from Palestine of an already short supply of dollars. As a result, Britain's own economic and defensive situation, as well as its ability to carry the mandate, would be undermined.[14]

Finally, the root cause of Departmental aloofness—namely, anti-Zionism—became more intense in the late 1930s. Parallel to the views of the British Foreign Office and Colonial Office, the Department's traditional view had been that Zionism was a chronic nuisance and chimerical hope. Now, in light of Axis propaganda, the atmosphere of impending war, Palestinian Arab riots and pan-Arab militancy, and the revival in the face of Hitlerism of Revisionist Zionism and its "Jewish State" thesis, Zionism seemed a danger to the "peace."

Accordingly, one sees two variants emerging within the Department's aloofness policy: one, a pro forma habit of informing the Foreign Office, "for the record," that American Jews were keenly interested in Palestine; two, a tendency to criticize Britain for being insufficiently in control of the Palestine problem. The Department increasingly wished to encourage the Foreign Office to clamp down on political Zionism and to take its cue from "spiritual" Zionists opposed to political Zionism, like Judah Magnes.[15]

By the late 1930s, the Department thus was less economically but more politically interested in Palestine than previously. Moreover, as in the Levant, its political interest and particularly its prompting of Britain to be more decisive increased, even while it took pains to stay offstage and avoid involving the United States. Caution and a regard for its public appearance were its implied watchwords. For example, relative to the 1937 Peel Commission's report, the Department was hardly eager to take a public stand on the report's novel recommendations of partition and the creation of a small Zionist state. On one hand, it wanted to avoid Zionist hostility; on the other, it did not want to acquiesce to the idea of partition. It thus resorted to subterfuge. It publicly protested, not against the Peel report, but against the publication of the report, on the principle that it had the right to be consulted over any basic changes in the mandate. But this protest was strictly pro forma *and* was understood as such by the Eastern Department of the Foreign Office. Moreover, the Department willingly desisted from pursuing its protest, once made. It accepted the British view, as expressed by Foreign Secretary Anthony Eden, that American assent was only applicable when modifications of the mandate affected the rights of American nationals—by which were implied essentially the business rights of non-Jewish nationals.[16]

The following year, with the reversal of the Peel report, the Department again maneuvered amidst the shoals. Deluged with pro-Zionist telegrams from a reactivated American Jewish community, it took matters in stride, replied courteously that it was giving the delicate Palestine problem its serious consideration; and in October, the month before elections, when nods to Zionist aspirations had become a political ritual, Secretary Hull likewise expressed his sympathies and admiration—but added that the United States was not empowered to prevent mandate modifications.[17]

The Department's verbal talents were soon tested anew, as the Palestine problem reached a feverish pitch in the period surrounding May 1939, when the MacDonald White Paper was issued. Arab pressures mounted. Ibn Saud wrote of his hostility to Zionism to Roosevelt. The latter allayed the king's fears by the usual Departmentally drafted reply that officially, the United States was not a party to the Balfour Declaration. Various other Arab leaders and conferences also bitterly demanded that America be "impartial"—by being partial to the Arab side, the side of justice. FSOs took due note and conveyed to the Department the need to be sensitive to Arab sensibilities.[18]

The Department's reaction to Zionist pressure, as always, was different from its reaction to Arab pressure, though on the surface equally correct. Subjectively, reaction was of the order of "here we go again with the Jews." When Wallace Murray warned Hull in early March that Jewish pressure would soon restart and would stress the (presumed fraudulent) moral-humanitarian aspects of Zionism, he was hardly conveying the need to be sensitive to Jewish sensibilities. It is worth noting that Murray's warning came considerably before the May 1939 White Paper was issued in London, but after the Department had already been consulted, *and* its non-objection to the White Paper received, by the Foreign Office.[19]

It is also worth noting that NEA was anxious lest Hull show weakness or play politics before Zionist remonstrances. In this frame of mind, old Middle East hand J. Rives Childs prepared an elaborate clarification of the Department's Palestine position. After reiterating the view that the

American connection to Palestine was minimal, Childs entered a new argument. He contended that American Jews erred if they thought their capital investments in Palestine, allegedly made out of faith in an American commitment to the preamble of the 1924 Convention (the Balfour Declaration), could "induce this Government to withhold its assent to any change in the mandate which may impair the obligations assumed by Great Britain under the Balfour Declaration." Not only, therefore, was the "American Government" (meaning, Childs) averse to interfering with British "modifications" of the mandate; it was averse to the reprehensible Zionist intimation that the American flag should follow Jewish capital to Palestine (notwithstanding the fact that NEA was hardly averse anywhere else in the Middle East to using the flag to protect American capital). Indeed, Childs endorsed the curious view that it was basically wrong (for American Jews vis à vis Palestine, that is) to export American capital abroad, much as if such activity depleted the national wealth.[20]

For his part, Hull supposedly felt a personal objection to the 1939 White Paper. (Childs would feel Hull was a principle-breaking "politician.") In his memoirs, Hull would note that Roosevelt originally shared his opposition and that both believed the White Paper was something the United States could not give approval to. Yet it was Roosevelt, Hull would write defensively, who vetoed Hull's alleged suggestion that the Department send a criticizing note to the Foreign Office. Instead, the Department "agreed" to the President's approach, which was that the Department "limited" itself to a cable to Ambassador Joseph Kennedy in London, instructing him to mention "informally and orally" to Foreign Secretary Halifax that opinion in America, especially in Zionist circles, was disappointed in British policy.

It is interesting, however, that some five years later (March 1944) Hull would not be displeased that the Department had been so vague on the MacDonald White Paper's issuance. In 1944, as will be noted, the Department would feel pressed to counter a Zionist announcement, authorized by the President, that the American government never approved the White Paper. Hull was accordingly able to instruct FSOs to tell the Arabs that the American government, while never approving the White Paper, also "had never taken a position relative to it," that is, had never disapproved of it, either.[21]

In 1939 pro-Zionist pressures against the White Paper, while longer and more "impressive" than previous ones, were ineffective. In Washington, Welles and Roosevelt easily fobbed off the request of Justice Brandeis and Chaim Weizmann to help delay Britain's announcement of the White Paper. Statements by Congressmen and by pro-Zionist lobbies like the Pro-Palestine Federation of the American Federation of Labor were by turns courteously received or scornfully dismissed as high-pressure tactics, but in either case, they were rejected. Within Jewry, there were the usual numerous factions and crosscurrents which always made it easy for the Department to contend that Zionists, when they spoke in the name of Jewry, actually spoke "merely" for themselves.[22]

True, there was near unanimity among Jews against the immigration clauses of the White Paper; but Jewish dissents and acts of sabotage against the Zionists' growing counterdemand for a Jewish state did much to weaken the impact on the Department of that unanimity. For example, the non-Zionist American Jewish Committee had already threatened, after the Peel recommendation of a Jewish state, to end its affiliation with the Yishuv's government-in-preparation, the Jewish Agency; while a former pro-Zionist and now rabid anti-Zionist, Reform Rabbi Morris Lazaron, tried (unsuccessfully) to get his acquaintances in the Department, like George Messersmith and Sumner Welles, to have the British ambassador intervene in the spring of 1939 against Chaim Weizmann's visiting the United States.[23]

On another level, however, the mood of pro-Zionism was growing in America, among Jews and non-Jews. But unlike the political-nationalist, or "Herzlian," variety of Zionism which typified the Yishuv, the American variety by and large was a nonpolitical, humanitarian Zionism, that is, refugeeism. True, American Zionist leaders, notably Rabbi Abba Hillel Silver, were often Herzlian; but it is doubtful if their following, in 1939 certainly, was as politicized. Put otherwise, Jewish national and political consciousness was emerging in America, but was still feeble or abstract; while Jewish insecurities and apathy were still substantial. There were a number of indices. In 1938 25 percent of American Jews opposed a greater admission of persecuted Jews to the United States. In 1940 many Jews would be unenthusiastic about the possibilities of a separate Jewish army.[24]

Similarly, Jewish protests against the White Paper and against the State Department's acquiescence were limited. There were no large-scale boycotts of British goods, no violent disrespectful demonstrations in front of the White House or State Department. Typically, the Jews relied on the law for redress. The American Jewish Committee did not demonstrate, it "argued" that the White Paper prevented American citizens from entering Palestine or purchasing land and was therefore discriminatory against American citizens of Jewish origin. The Department argued otherwise and claimed that, in any event, the difficult international situation precluded travel to Palestine. The Department could also have said that, arguments aside, not many American Jews were apparently ready to emigrate to Palestine to settle and thus to "test" the White Paper's alleged discriminatory features; nor was any important American Jewish organization apparently ready to mobilize its legal talents and force a testing of the White Paper in the courts. (Indeed, despite occasional proposals toward these ends, apparently nothing of the sort was ever done between March 1939 and March 1944.)[25]

In the months preceding the beginning of World War II, therefore, American Jews agitated, but "legally" and ineffectively. Moreover, they had no basic leverage, as during World War I, and they were beholden to the Foreign Office and the State Department as the lesser of the world's anti-Jewish evils. The Department, for its part, had the excuses of the White Paper and numerous international exigencies to hide behind in order to ignore Jewish "special pleadings." Though there were some 9,100 American nationals, chiefly Jewish, in Palestine in 1939, and though they represented 78 percent of all American nationals in the *entire* Middle East, these facts did not make the Department look upon the Jewish case with greater consideration. Nor did the fact that, of the total American dollar investment in Palestine in 1939 ($49 million), $41 million was from American Jews *and* was a sum larger than that invested in all the Arab countries combined (excluding Saudi Arabia). It was, after all, tacitly assumed that American Jews were not really Americans (especially naturalized Americans resident in Palestine) and that the dollar figures did not really represent solid economic investments but rather, as J. Rives Childs noted, wasteful contributions to the Yishuv's economy. Though admirable and pioneering in some respects, that economy was perceived in the main as artificial, parasitic, in short, "chimerical."[26]

PALESTINE DURING WORLD WAR II

The Jewish Agency reacted to the May 1939 White Paper by calling it "a breach of faith and a surrender to Arab terrorism," in this, "the darkest hour of Jewish history." If Whitehall felt only the Arabs would use force, but never the Jews, it was mistaken. "Repressing a Jewish rebellion against British policy would be as unpleasant a task as the repression of the Arab rebellion had been."[27]

Still, shock and verbal defiance were the typical Jewish replies. Mass reactions and Jewish violence were yet to come. Meanwhile, Britain stuck to the letter of the law and put into effect strict land and immigration regulations, including complete suspension of immigration from October 1939 to June 1940.

Land restrictions were soon defied by the unannounced setting up of Jewish farm settlements and by using loopholes in the land law found by the Agency's purchase office, the Keren Kayemet. Immigration restrictions, however, were much more difficult to fight. Failure often marked the efforts of various Zionist groups, efforts which in fact long preceded the White Paper, to bring in "illegal" Jewish immigrants. The Jews' flight from the Nazis toward the Balkans in 1939 was checkmated by the British blockades of the only land route (Turkey was pressed to keep its borders closed) and then of the direct Mediterranean shipping route. The results were incredible tragedies for a number of floating-coffin refugee ships, like the *Patria* (1940) and *Struma* (1942), and were a source of bitter anti-British frustration among Jews.[28]

Fear of provoking Arab anger by "giving in" to the Jews was the root reason for Britain's decision to maintain the White Paper. Even when the White Paper was sharply questioned by pro-Zionists in the Conservative, Liberal, and Labor parties, these, too, were usually persuaded that the Arab spectre, *inter alia*, required that Palestine be shelved until the war's end. There were other fears, half-believed, half-manufactured, which made up the British justification of the White Paper: for example, the fear that Gestapo spies and fifth-column elements were planted amongst the Jewish illegals; and the old fear, constantly disproven but never shed, that Palestine could not feed or absorb new immigrants.[29]

As for the fact that the Permanent Mandate Commission of the League of Nations, in June 1939, unanimously found the White Paper to conflict with the accepted interpretation of the Mandate, the British reply was that the League Council, scheduled to meet in September, had not met because of the war and had not ratified the Commission's findings. Hence those findings were not binding. In any case, the Foreign Office held that League interference was inappropriate, since the White Paper supposedly did not involve the kind of modifications in the Mandate which called for League action.[30]

As for Winston Churchill's contention that the White Paper alienated America and American Jewry, the Foreign Office parried that the Jews could do no harm to Britain, for however they felt toward Palestine, "the cause of their co-religionists in Europe required them to help the Allies to victory." Furthermore, said the F.O., "the loss of Jewish support [for Britain]

might not affect American opinion as a whole; it was indeed possible that a too conspicuously pro-Allied attitude on the part of the American Jews might defeat its object by suggesting that the Jews were trying to drag the United States into the war.[31]

Meantime, Jewish resistance in Palestine increased, albeit in uncoordinated fashion and with ambivalence towards the British. David Ben Gurion's famous declaration that the Yishuv would fight with the British against the Nazis as if there was no White Paper, and against the British White Paper as if there was no war, illustrated this ambivalence—though at the time such a balancing act seemed not only necessary but plausible. It was assumed that England would both need and be grateful for Jewish manpower assistance, all the more notable when compared to the apathy-hostility of the Arabs' war effort. Added to the pressure from the refugees, the United States, and pro-Zionist British politicians, such Jewish cooperativeness in Palestine would presumably wean Britain away from the White Paper—much as Jewish cooperativeness during the first phase of the Arab Revolt in 1936 seemed to have won Britain over to the favorable Peel Report the following year.[32]

Thus, despite the fact, as will be detailed, that efforts to raise a full-scale Jewish army (like that of the Polish government-in-exile) would fail because of British hostility, more than 30,000 Palestinian Jews were volunteers in the British Eighth Army; and additional numbers made up three local companies on garrison duty. Concurrently, the Haganah, the military wing of the Jewish Agency, was reorganized, resulting in the creation of special squads and strike forces, the beginnings of intelligence, arms manufacture, and procurement branches, and the preparation of various contingency plans. These included actions against specified British military units, Arab terrorists, and Jewish informers, as well as plans in case of a future war against a revived and expanded Arab revolt, or a war against the British, or a war with the British against a German invasion. [The Haganah's leftist composition was challenged by the military arm of the rightist Revisionist Zionists, the Irgun, or Etzel (begun in 1937, revived in 1941), and a smaller, classically terrorist-separatist faction, Lehi, or the Stern Gang (1943). These in turn had their own cadres, plans, etc.; and like the Haganah, despite a common ideological base, they were often at internal cross-purposes.] Yet for all its attributes as an independent underground, the Haganah regularly cooperated with the British during the war; and it represented, with the Jews in the Eighth Army, a pro-British military front in the Middle East.[33]

On the economic front, the Yishuv was also important to the British Middle East Command. If before the war Palestine was the region's main entrepot and importer of Arab exports, after 1939 and especially after 1943 those roles expanded. The Yishuv became a major supplier not only of citrus and foodstuffs but also of chemicals and metals. Within the framework of the Middle East Supply Center (MESC), Palestine thus became an industrial center, rivaled only by Egypt.[34]

On the diplomatic front, Zionist efforts were initially devoted to trying to drum up support in Britain in order to negate the White Paper. Beyond that, the long-run object was to gain British recognition of a Jewish commonwealth in western Palestine or in a part of it, under British sponsorship, and associated with a regional pro-British federation of Arab states. Basically, such efforts and ideas were only variations on the old theme of holding Britain accountable to the Balfour Declaration. Nonetheless, they were "packaged" differently, and by 1942 they increasingly crystallized in a new-style movement for an independent Jewish nation-state. (On the other hand, one may also say that this movement merely represented the polarization of mainstream Labor Zionism toward Revisionist Zionism and back towards the legacy of state-minded Zionist founders like Theodore Herzl and Max Nordau.) In any case, Ben Gurion and Rabbi Abba Hillel Silver of the Zionist Organization of America (ZOA) became the movement's catalyzers, realpolitikers, and prophets, in tension with the similarly determined but more evolutionary and seemingly more acquiescent approaches of their rivals, the traditional Zionist leaders Chaim Weizmann and Rabbi Stephen Wise.

To Ben Gurion and Silver the times called for new responses, for a way to cut the strings and Gordian knot of Jewish dependence on Britain, the reluctant stepmother. They came to believe that Britain would not be weaned from the White Paper; that Arab and Nazi pressures would grow; and that significant portents were implicit in the recent entrance into the war by America, a presumably friendly military giant, and in the entrance onto the stage of world Jewish affairs by American Jews. In spreading these beliefs throughout mainstream Zionism, Ben Gurion and Silver helped create a new emotional climate. One result was the Biltmore Conference in New York, May 1942. There the Zionist program came out clearly and firmly in favor of "unalterable rejection of the White Paper... a Jewish military force fighting under its own flag... and [all of western] Palestine [to] be established as a Jewish Commonwealth integrated in the structure of the new democratic world."[35]

However, there was an immediate, if distinctly peripheral, dissent from antinationalists within American Jewry. These included segments of the Orthodox Aguda, the upper-class Reform Jews of the American Jewish Committee and the newly formed American Council for Judaism, and the Bundist-Yiddishist Jewish Labor Committee (though not the Jewish Buro of the American Communist Party). In Palestine, the New Immigration Party (German and Austrian Jews), the binationalist and pacifist Ihud group centered around Hebrew University president Judah Magnes, and segments of the leftist Hashomer Hatsair dissented. Also opposed were the ultra-nationalist Stern Gang and, in America, Peter Bergson's (Revisionist) Committee for a Jewish Army (in 1943 renamed the Hebrew Committee of National Liberation). Still, the Biltmore Program thenceforward became Jewish, not just Zionist, majority opinion.[36]

British policy toward the Jewish state movement evolved essentially independent of the Biltmore Program. For the better part of 1942, the British in the Middle East were preoccupied with the Axis campaign in western Egypt and Libya. In Palestine, though the administration, now under Sir Harold MacMichael, still acted vindictively toward the Yishuv in countless small ways, the administration cooperated with the Haganah for security purposes, as it had in 1936. When the German threat receded in 1943, however, the policy of cooperation seemed no longer necessary and was replaced by one of suppression of the Haganah. The Biltmore Program, accordingly, told the Palestine administration nothing new and apparently had no direct impact.

On higher levels, the British government grew more determined to hold onto the Middle East, including Palestine. As the war developed, the spectre of Nazi victory was increasingly being replaced by the less dark, but still grim, spectre of a postwar allied victory which, inter alia, meant that the Soviet Union and the United States would emerge as major global powers and would compete for influence in the Middle East. If Britain let go of empire, the Conservatives, at any rate, felt Britain would cast itself into the category of loser. The central question was how to entrench the postwar British position in the Middle East. The Foreign Office's answer was old and obvious: forge friendly relations with the region's leadership and majority population. Its concomitant was: keep the Jews from obstructing those relations, in short, ignore the Biltmore Program and also the occasional revival of partition proposals, maintain the White Paper or at least the existing population ratios, and do nothing to encourage Zionist plans for a pro-Allies independent Jewish army that would only provoke the Arabs and later threaten the mandatory government.[37]

However, the British position was not monolithic, and indeed leaders like Churchill still believed that Jewish and Arab aspirations were reconcilable and/or that partition was possible. A number of acts of British friendship and promise seemed to coexist with the cited examples of administrative anti-Zionism. In May 1944 the unmet five-year quota of the 1939 White Paper was extended. That same month the Labor Party's platform endorsed both the Balfour Declaration's primacy *and* the proposition that in the postwar period a population transfer should be implemented, with refugee Jews to go to Palestine and Palestinian Arabs to go to underpopulated Iraq. In September 1944 an attenuated Jewish army in the form of a Jewish Brigade attached to the British Eighth Army was finally established. In October the unpopular MacMichael was replaced as high commissioner for Palestine by the more statesmanlike Lord Gort.

While such positive illustrations suggested that the situation was still fluid and that Britain was not fixed on an anti-Zionist course, in overview they were but minor crosscurrents. British "mainstream" policy, largely set by the Foreign Office, was on an anti-Zionist course. The Jews, ever hopeful, tried persuasion on the Foreign Office: the Yishuv was dynamic, they said, while Arab society, though much larger, was static and therefore less valuable militarily and economically to the British. The Arabs were basically realists who respected power: they would accommodate themselves to a Jewish state, if only the Allies would put their collective foot down and insist on it. The Jews were basically pro-British and wanted the British to stay in the Middle East if the latter supported the Balfour Declaration; the Arabs, said the Zionists, did not want the British to stay, no matter what Britain did or did not do for them. Indeed, for Britain to foster pan-Arab unity, *vide* Arab-Moslem imperialism, was to feed a viper.[38]

Other Jews tried terror, either in order to influence British policy to desist from anti-Zionism (the Revisionists) or in order to force the British to abdicate and withdraw from Palestine (the Sternists). However, although persuasion and terror each won adherents, neither was particularly successful in altering Britain's basically minimalist attitude toward the Balfour Declaration. The spirit, and much of the letter, of the 1939 White Paper remained, even though the expiration date of March 1944 was extended, thus allowing a continuous trickle of Jewish immigrants.

Arab anti-Zionism of course continued, too, but it was not yet politically or militarily effective. Renewed efforts of conciliation (for example, by Jewish Ihudists like Martin Buber, who favored a binational state, and by Chaim Kalvarisky's League for Arab-Jewish Rapprochement) diminished Arab anti-Zionism only slightly, as did Britain's exiling of the Mufti of Jerusalem. But the larger reason the (Palestinian) Arabs were ineffective, and therefore less important to the Jews as adversaries than the British, was the apathy, disorganization, and frozen leadership endemic in the Arab community. Furthermore, the Palestinians' hostility to Abdullah of Transjordan was sometimes as intense as it was towards Zionism, which detracted from their concentration on the Jews.[39]

It is worth noting that Britain was aware of such weaknesses among the Palestinian Arabs. Indeed the Foreign and Colonial Offices habitually perceived the Arabs as downtrodden natives, underdogs who deserved more help than the presumably well-backed, politically sophisticated Zionists.

Withal, by 1945 Jewish despair over the bared details and results of the Holocaust was channeled into a new level of defiance and solidarity. Jewish frustration was no longer impeded by forced delays due to wartime necessity or to Zionist leader Chaim Weizmann's stake in British friendship. Efforts to persuade Britain and to make peace with the Arabs had failed and seemed fated to continue to fail, irrespective of whatever missed opportunities and Zionist inadequacies may have existed. The dominant Jewish spirit was thus a determination to fight it out, with the support of a military and economic infrastructure established mainly during the war years, and with the political-financial support of American Jews. Concurrently, Zionist factional strife (between the World Zionist Organization-Jewish Agency and the Revisionists, and between the Haganah, the Irgun, and the Sternists) was papered over, so as at least to prevent civil war. V–E Day in Europe in effect meant D–Day in Palestine.

POLICIES TOWARD AMERICAN JEWS AND ZIONISTS AND TOWARD PALESTINE, THROUGH 1942

In November 1940, a refugee ship, the *Patria*, after being refused landing rights by the British, was supposed to be immobilized by Haganah explosives in Haifa harbor. Due to miscalculation, however, the explosives caused the ship to sink. Of the some 1,770 illegals on board, about 250 perished. In London, to offset public outcries, the decision was made to let the survivors enter Palestine, but with the condition that subsequent quota figures were to be reduced on a matching basis. What were the reactions to the British decision? In each case, true to form (yet from an overview, bizarre): the Jews saw the decision as merciful and hoped it would become a precedent; the Arabs saw it as another nefarious instance of Jewish influence and power; and the mandatory government in Palestine was disgusted and "let down" by London's extralegal concession.[40]

These reactions, as recorded and interpreted by the American consul general in Jerusalem, George Wadsworth, testified to the extreme polarities in the perceptions of the Palestine problem. Worth noting, too, is that not only did Britain maintain the White Paper in order to placate Arab opinion (though Britain might have to bend on occasion, as in the *Patria* case, to pro-Zionist public opinion). More, Britain believed that strict quota regulation and the detention or expulsion of illegals were necessary in order to "discourage" the Nazis from their "tactic" of trying to disrupt British-Arab relations with illegal Jewish traffic. To the British, Jewish immigrants were thus part Nazi weapon, part Zionist extortion—and part curse, since the Arabs often interpreted Jewish immigration, in 1940 as in the years before, as a tool of British imperialism. As for the State Department, it basically shared, and certainly did not object to, the mandatory government's perception of the *Patria* case and the general British belief that Jewish immigration was dangerous and to a degree Nazi-inspired.[41]

The Department was fully familiar with all aspects associated with the Jewish immigration problem, particularly in connection with Palestine and American immigration laws. Indeed, often the general Departmental antipathy to Jewish immigration was a homegrown rather than imported attitude. Thus, Hull did not need any British urging to swear that he would not violate his oath of office by giving Jewish refugees illegal asylum in the United States. Hull felt, on moral grounds quite unconnected to the Middle East or Britain, that no country should be asked or expected to change its laws to receive refugees—lest dictatorships be encouraged to expel unwanted minorities onto the Western hemisphere and create instability. Dictatorships, as it were, must be forced to keep these minorities and behave in a civilized manner.

As for the idea that the problem of Jews and Jewish immigration deserved special consideration in view of Hitler's special war on them, Hull again put his foot down on the side of civilization. He felt that to single out Jews would be a form of discrimination. It was his view, which he doubtless thought was friendly toward Jews, that no distinction or preference should be made among refugees on the basis of race or religion. He failed to realize, however, that *not* to set up a special rescue to counteract Hitler's special hunt for Jews—that is, not to "discriminate" *for* the Jews, at least a little—was a certain way of guaranteeing success to Hitler's hunt. Breckinridge Long, and even strong anti-Nazi Department officers like George Messersmith and William Dodd, were also unsympathetic to any "special" efforts on behalf of Jewish refugees. (Later, by 1944, when the Nazis' genocide of Jews was more well-known, there was as a result more pressure and public uproar over bureaucracy in the Department's Visa Division. Hull and Long then defended their record as a matter of course and in addition would take to blaming their subordinates "down the line" for the Department's inadequacies.)[42]

With respect to Palestine, FSO Wadsworth was typical of the Foreign Service in implying that the Jews were trying to make pro-Zionist capital out of refugee persecutions—even while the Jewish Agency, he said, tacitly admitted it was having difficulties absorbing refugees—though it never did this openly, lest Zionism lose public support. In a like spirit of self-righteousness, the Department successfully protested the sending of aid to refugees in Palestine from the American Red Cross (pledged at the urging of Rabbi Silver). In the Departmental view, the pledge was unfair because other relief needs in the region were not covered (and it might appear in Arab eyes that the United States was letting the Jews get special treatment). As was its habit, however, the Department hid behind the British: in opposing Red Cross relief to Palestine, it was, said the Department, simply backing the British view in the common war effort, and the British view was not to incite the Arabs.[43]

Despite its dislike of the refugee problem and, by extension, of the refugees, the Department concurrently admonished the Jews not to resist British policy in Palestine, on the thesis that if Britain was weakened and lost the Mediterranean, "the extermination of the Zionists in Palestine is only a question of time." The Department also turned to flattery: the Jews, given their brains and reasonableness, should take the initiative in compromising with the Arabs and British.[44]

The responses of Zionists, though varied, emphasized to the Department the following themes: Britain and America should favor their "friends," the Jews, over the Arabs for the reason that the Jews' loyalty in the war effort was certain and the Arabs' was not. (This view wrongly assumed that Britain and America regarded the Jews as friends worth having. In any case, if Jewish loyalty was so unconditional, why reward it?) The Zionists also contended that they, unlike the Arabs, were not demanding that Britain or the United States choose between the Arabs and the Jews. Zionists were not opposed to Arab nationalism or aid to the Arabs anywhere—so long as Palestine, a fractional part of the Middle East, was reserved for the Jews.

Zionists argued that Arab-Jewish differences were not inevitable. Indeed, Arab hostility, presumed by many Zionists to be founded on the natural antagonism of a traditional society to a modern one, would supposedly dissipate the more the Arab world was developed under Anglo-American tutelage. Zionists added that they were always willing to negotiate political issues like Jewish sovereignty and partition, so long as their bottom-line position in favor of unrestricted Jewish immigration was accepted as non-negotiable—and even that position, before Nazi expansion in the late 1930s, was negotiable. However, even assuming that Britain would not interfere in direct Arab-Jewish negotiations, where, asked the Zionists, was the Arab leadership to deal with?[45]

In this context, the name of Ibn Saud was bruited about. At various times since 1939, sometimes Saudi adviser H. St. John Philby, also Chaim Weizmann, Moshe Shertok, Churchill, Eden, Roosevelt, and in the Department Lt. Harold Hoskins, Adolph Berle, Jr., and Wallace Murray gave separate and occasionally coordinated thought to the proposition of a British-Jewish-Arab deal. The object was to gain Saudi neutrality and presumably, therefore, pan-Moslem neutrality towards the existence of an autonomous Jewish entity in Palestine. As has been and will be noted, however, the idea came to nought, though it is interesting that through 1941 at least Berle and Murray were willing to give it a try.[46]

For his part, Undersecretary Welles was not optimistic that Arab-Jewish reconciliation was possible, particularly since the Arabs felt that, as the entire region would be theirs anyway, there was no reason to compromise on Palestine. Welles also expressed disagreement with NEA Chief Murray and Minister in Cairo Alexander Kirk with respect to the Department's handling of Zionist leaders. Kirk regularly condemned Zionism as a misconception flying in the face of history and geography, and Murray regularly relayed such missiles from the field to Hull and Roosevelt. Implicit was the view that the less the Department had to do with Zionist leaders, the better.

To their annoyance, Welles felt otherwise, not because he was as sympathetic to Zionism, and least of all Herzlian Zionism, as Jews mistakenly believed; but because keeping leaders like Wise and Weizmann "informed" and appeasing their eagerness for easy access and consultation with the Department seemed like good public relations and low-cost diplomacy. To Welles, such an approach prevented or at least delayed Jewish groups from hurting the British war effort or adding to anti-British feelings in America.[47]

Between Kirk and Murray, however, there was scant difference on Zionism, except that their focuses were different. Like other FSOs, Kirk's ire was directed chiefly towards the Yishuv and the Jewish Agency; Murray, like others manning the Department's ramparts in Washington, was upset chiefly by American Jews who called themselves Zionists.

A propos, it is important to note that, to the Department as a whole, the ideal American Jew was a refined American of Mosaic persuasion, a patriotic Reform Jew (like Rabbi Morris Lazaron and others like him who, in 1943, would found the American Council for Judaism). An American Zionist was therefore the antithesis, and dangerously so, since such a person was guilty of dual loyalty, which in turn provoked presumably justifiable, if regrettable, anti-Semitic reactions on the part of other Americans.[48]

As for European Jews, these, to Murray at any rate, were apparently a different type. Representing the core of the "Jewish problem," they required a permanent solution, though not by means of wholesale postwar repatriation, or assimilation, as in the case of America's Jewry. Preferable would be a Zionist-type territorial solution—but not in Palestine. Murray, caught up in the various refugee schemes dating back chiefly to the Evian Conference of 1938, felt—in 1940 at least—that "the Benguila Plateau in Angola offers by all odds the most suitable and promising place of settlement."[49]

In January 1942, a somewhat new note was sounded from Jerusalem. Consul General L. Pinkerton expressed pique and impatience with Britain. Britain did not seem to be fully or consistently clamping down on the Yishuv; it seemed unduly concerned about alienating the so-called pro-Jewish position of America. Indeed, and this was the crux, it was blaming the United States by in effect telling the Arabs that, were it not for Washington, London's policy would be more pro-Arab.[50]

Partly as a result, NEA sought to determine how strong Zionism actually was in America. It concluded that there was no reason to fear alienating pro-Zionist feelings, since American Zionists were statistically unrepresentative of America's Jews who, in turn, were an atypical minority. Ideologically, too, the Zionists supposedly did not represent the American Jewish majority, which was conservative, and which favored the passive and compromising approaches of Rabbi Magnes. Unfortunately, said Murray, that Jewish majority was "unorganized and comparatively inarticulate in its opposition to political Zionism."[51]

Still, the Department partly belied its conclusions above by virtue of the fact that it felt it necessary to be eternally vigilant toward Zionism. In a way it had to be alert if only because of the sometimes staggering volume of pro-Zionist mail, Congressional statements, and media features. Considerably more significant to the Department, however, was the lesser volume of anti-Zionist warnings and expressions from pro-Arab circles and Foreign Service posts in Moslem countries.

Even so, the Department tried to show that it was not insensitive to

Jewish persecution or mindless of the fact that to Jews, persecution proved the need of a political-geographic solution to the Jewish Problem. In 1941–42, several committee meetings of the newborn postwar planning apparatus were devoted to what was considered the latest and best interim solution both for saving refugees and for dissipating political pressures to open the gates of Palestine—namely, refugee absorption in Latin America, particularly Brazil and Colombia.[52]

Meantime, among American Jews, a new activism emerged in early 1942. Activism took two main forms—promotion of the Jewish Army idea; and stepped-up conversion of American opinion, Jewish and non-Jewish, to a belief in the Jewish State idea.

The idea of a Jewish army fighting alongside other Allied armies went through several permutations both on the Jewish Agency side and the Revisionist side. In 1939–1940 the idea had been presented by Vladimir Jabotinsky, leader of the large breakaway wing of militant Zionist Revisionists, as an expansion-restoration of the Jewish Legion idea of World War I. Jewish volunteers who were stateless or from neutral countries like the United States were to constitute the troops. By 1942, even as Revisionists continued to lobby (in America, under Peter Bergson), another Jewish army plan had developed. This began under mainstream Zionist auspices, represented by the Jewish Agency for Palestine, and as a result of contacts with the Churchill government. This second plan, which was to be based mainly on Jewish volunteers from the Yishuv, became both a Jewish Agency and American Zionist proposal, and a plank of the Biltmore program in May.[53]

Concurrently, the traditional leadership of the Yishuv and American Zionism, as noted, was being challenged in 1942 by men like Ben-Gurion and Rabbi Silver. Indeed, the surge to Jewish militance was becoming among Jews a worldwide phenomenon, born of the personal desperation of those Jews caught in the wheels of war, and of the frustration of those other Jews who, though safe, read the newspapers and felt compelled to do something: thus, the stepped-up Jewish partisan and ghetto resistance; the pronounced Jewish participation, out of proportion to their numbers, in the Red Army; the new post-Biltmore Zionist leadership in America; and in Palestine the growth of several paramilitary groups, of resistance to the 1939 White Paper, and, when the British permitted it, of undercover sabotage efforts against German forces in North Africa and Eastern Europe.

The new Zionist leadership was nonetheless aware that, as the State Department had concluded recently, American Jews were still not truly in the Zionist camp. Indeed, many Jews and Zionists were even more fully aware than the Department was to what extent American Jewry, despite its high proportion of formal education, represented a huge semi-literate provincial wasteland, from a Jewish-consciousness point of view. Yet this was the Jewry which because of its size, because world power was passing to the United States, and because traditional Jewish centers were exterminated or immobilized, seemed fated to be at the center of Jewish affairs.

To fulfill this sense of destiny, American Zionists, after much internal wrestling and external prodding from both Weizmann and Ben-Gurion, prepared. First, they had to put their organizational houses in order and build up their stagnant membership figures and finances. Second, they had to convert the Jewish public and to neutralize, at least, the traditional anti-Zionist and non-Zionist leadership of Jewish establishment organizations. Third, they had to organize, crusade, peddle, lobby, push, beg, and "sell" the Zionist thesis among all segments and levels of the general non-Jewish public, whether via the rough-and-tumble of New York election politics or the preachments of rural Bible-oriented Christian ministers. Thus would the public and Congress, already receptive and moved by the refugee problem, put cumulative pressure on the White House and the Department of State. The chief instrument for achieving these efforts on the part of the various Zionist groups in America was the American Zionist Emergency Council (AZEC), founded in 1939, but effective only by late 1943, under the leadership of Rabbi Silver.[54]

Needless to say, the Zionists were not working in a vacuum. Anti-Zionist pressures from the Department's Arab "constituencies" abroad, from the Foreign Office, from the increasingly oil-conscious Departments of Interior and War, and a wide variety of other sources unfriendly to Zionist "obstructionism" and "ethnic politics" were also at work. Given the Department's receptivity, one might say that the anti-Zionists had the inside track, and indeed, did not have to run as hard to lobby for their cause as the "aggressive, pushy" Jews did. Nonetheless, the Department still had to contend with the Jews; by the summer of 1942 it was preparing some preventive actions.

In June NEA and, for the sake of reinforcement, several upper echelon cohorts like Legal Adviser Green Hackworth and Adviser on Political Relations James Dunn drafted a letter to Hull, for Roosevelt's approval, stressing in absolute terms the alarming effects in the Middle East caused by the agitation for a Jewish army in Palestine. The letter contained the caveat that it would be impossible to use the Middle East as an operational base against the Axis "if in addition to combatting the Axis forces, we [Britain and America] have to defend ourselves against the local populations."[55]

NEA also urged the President to issue a Middle East policy statement singling out the Atlantic Charter principle that majority self-determination would resolve postwar territorial questions. The statement would also recommend enforced parity between Jewish and Arab volunteer units in the military service of the mandatory government. Otherwise, it was felt, the Jews would monopolize such service, to the alarm of the British and Arabs. Finally, NEA deplored the fact that officials of the Roosevelt administration had been silent, despite all previous alarms from the Department. Such silence, it said, "appear[s] to support the objectives of political Zionism."[56]

However, Roosevelt disappointed NEA and did not enact its call for a policy statement. It was his thesis that any statement, no matter what it did or did not say, would be counterproductive. Partly as a result of the President's silence, however, pressure for a Jewish army continued unimpeded. By the end of August, Berle was informing Welles that the Committee for a Jewish Army was "besieging" the White House, and Welles was informing Berle that the British ambassador was "very much exercised" over the matter. Left to its own devices, the Department tried to take the wind out of the sails of the Jewish army drive: Welles urged the British embassy to fight Jewish "propaganda" with its own accurate "information" from the British Office of War Information. Berle recommended a policy of cooperation with the Jews, but with the aim of stalling them.[57]

In Britain, meantime, Parliamentary debates, interspersed between June–August 1942, delayed resolution of the Jewish army proposals. On the one side were ranged men like Churchill who felt and always would that a large Jewish force helping to fight the Axis had an aspect of cosmic justice to it. Moreover, it would relieve British garrisons in Palestine for European duty; would be well received in the United States; and would thus help to firm up the Anglo-American coalition. On the other side were those like Colonial Secretaries Lord Lloyd and Lord Moyne who stressed the provocation-to-the-Arabs thesis, which seemed to be more accepted in the British Cabinet as a whole after the anxiety-causing Rashid Ali coup in Iraq the previous year.[58]

In any event, the debate was largely suspended by October 1942, when the critical atmosphere surrounding both Rommel's advances and the call for a Jewish army diminished in Britain and America. The general causes were the successful counteroffensive at El Alamein and the British feeling that more attention must now be restored to the long-range goal of retrenchment in the Arab world. Indeed, the opportunity seemed ripe, as the Arabs, now sensing that the Axis might lose the war, showed themselves more pro-Allies than heretofore. On the Jews' part, one must note that the incredible reports of late 1942 that filtered out of Eastern Europe and described the Nazi mass extermination programs were often a bewildering and demoralizing factor. Although they kept the Jews' sense of crisis acute, such reports hardly helped them concentrate on implementing a specifically Jewish army.

For its part, towards the autumn of 1942 the Department, like the

Foreign Office, was also giving thought to long-range policy in Palestine. It had already in August and early September gone through lengthy discussions of the possibilities of a sovereign Jewish Palestine on the Herzlian model, including the reemigration of Palestinian Arabs to Iraq and the purchase of land in Transjordan by Jews. At intervals in 1942, it had and would give brief consideration to the future of possible Maronite, Kurdish, and Assyrian small states.[59]

But these were strictly theoretical exercises, done "for the record." They only confirmed the Departmental doxology, as long articulated by NEA and now the planners' Territorial and Political subcommittees, that small states in general ("balkanization") and political Zionism in particular were impossibilities. The essence of the Department's argument was that that Arabs would accept the postwar offerings of independence, aid, etc., as their *rights,* but they would not, in return, recognize the Jews' rights, or claims, even for Jewish "home rule" in Palestine, let alone Jewish statehood. (The idea of withholding aid and recognition of Arab states' independence until the Arabs consented to Jewish rights in Palestine was never raised.) Therefore, the Department's argument ran, force would have to be imposed on the Arabs to secure a Jewish state. But if the British proved unwilling, the United States, in contravention to the Atlantic Charter principle of majority self-determination, might become entangled and responsible—if it allowed itself in the first place to be manipulated into the position of endorser of a Jewish state.[60]

Ideologically refortified, as it were, the Department pushed anew for a Presidential public statement. It tried to reconvince Roosevelt that his silence allowed vocal pro-Zionist Congressmen to speak for his administration. When the President remained unresponsive, the Department sought to meet the Congressional threat more directly. Indeed, it embarked at this stage on a long duel with Congress; the more the latter became Zionized, the more the Department pushed in the other direction.

This see-saw relationship was almost amusingly illustrated when in November 1942 the Department deleted, for the first time, any and all mention of Palestine in its annual pro forma statement commemorating the issuance of the Balfour Declaration—while Congress, when it issued in December its Balfour Day Declaration, added more signatures and degree of endorsement than ever before. Thus, Hull, in the Department's typically elusive, say-nothing style, said: "The Jews have long sought a refuge. I believe that we must have an even wider objective; we must have a world in which Jews, like every other race, are free to abide in peace and in honor." Whereas Congress noted that

[Since 1922 it has become] the declared and traditional policy of the United States to favor the restoration of the Jewish National Home.... In fact, the case for a Jewish Homeland is overwhelmingly stronger and the need more urgent now than ever before.... We declare that, when the war is over, it shall be the common purpose of civilized mankind... above all, to enable large numbers of the survivors to reconstruct their lives in Palestine.[61]

Still feeling that the commander-in-chief was sitting on his hands, NEA's officers continued to seek their own ways of fighting Zionism. William Yale, though he was not yet hired by the Department to head the planning desk on Palestine, suggested in correspondence with the Department that it take the initiative by contacting non- and anti-Zionist Jews among Jewish capitalists, socialists, Orthodox, et al, in America and England. However, such counterinsurgency was apparently too activist and risky for the Department's publicity-conscious upper echelons to enter into. From NEA's standpoint the ideal solution would have been for just such an indigenous American Jewish "popular front" to rise up and deZionize American Jewry.[62]

The Department's silent wish for such a development seemed perhaps to be answered when, in November 1942, one of its friendly Jewish "contacts," Rabbi Morris Lazaron, wrote a personal "dear Sumner" letter to Welles. Lazaron said that the American Council for Judaism had recently been established to fight Zionism (chiefly in reaction to the Biltmore Program of May), and he proposed that Welles write a public letter addressed to Lazaron in the informal style of Lord Balfour's letter to Lord Rothschild. It would not be a formal declaration of policy and therefore such charges could be easily denied; nonetheless, it would presumably have the same profound effect as its prototype. The letter, suggested Lazaron, should express the typical expressions of sympathy for Jewish suffering and appreciation for Jewry's contribution to the war effort but would make no explicit pledges and would refer to Palestine only in the context of its being a symbolic center for three, not two, faiths.

Asked for comments, Murray wrote Welles that he fully endorsed such a clear policy pronouncement, especially Lazaron's emphasis on Christian participation. The latter would move the conflict from the dead center of Jew versus Moslem, would "vastly" enhance American prestige and power, and would, as Lazaron phrased his ultimate motive, "stop this reckless Zionist agitation."[63]

However, neither the popular front idea nor Lazaron's informal declaration idea materialized—even though the Christian-Moslem-Jewish thesis (actually, an idea at least as old as the mandate) would appeal later, as shall be noted, to Roosevelt and, to a lesser extent, to NEA, too. In any event, several other trends materialized at the end of 1942 which probably did more to alter America's Palestine policy than anything before.

Despite strong earlier crosswinds like the Rashid Ali coup, Pearl

Harbor, the Biltmore Program, news of the Nazi Final Solution, and the El Alamein victory, the Department had tended to pace itself, without discontinuity of speed or direction, behind the British "frontrunning" position on Palestine. The first discontinuity, however, appeared in December 1942. This occurred when the Department sensed that despite El Alamein, Britain's prestige regionwide seemed to be waning and that, as a result of Operation TORCH being added to the "reservoirs of good will" built up by American missionaries and businessmen over the decades, America's prestige seemed to be waxing. The second discontinuity appeared almost concurrently as a result of the crystallized consensus throughout the federal government that, though it had traditionally been in the British sphere, Saudi Arabia ought henceforth to be considered a "vital interest" to the United States. The following chapter examines the meaning of these discontinuities, along with other significant trends in the remaining war years.

NOTES

1. Quotation is cited in Manuel, *American-Palestine Relations*, p. 114. For benevolent expressions, see ibid., pp. 10–11, 50–54; and C. Adler and A. Margalith, *With Firmness in the Right: American Diplomatic Action Affecting Jews 1840–1945* (New York: American Jewish Committee, 1946), pp. 42 ff.; and Appendix. Documentation of anti-Jewish bias on the everyday, consular level is in Z. Szajkowski, "The Consul and the Immigrant: A Case of Bureaucratic Bias," *Jewish Social Studies* 36 (1974): 3–18; as well as in these notes and in those of Chapter 14, passim.

2. On the Department during World War I, see Manuel, *American-Palestine Relations*, Chapter 4; Adler and Margalith, *With Firmness in the Right*, p. 63; and J. C. Hurewitz, "United States Policies on Palestine (1830–1950)," *American Jewish Historical Quarterly* 40 (1950): 112–14.

3. On the Morgenthau Mission, William Yale would write extensively: e.g., Yale to Berle, 12 March 1942 and 23 March 1942, 867N01/1800. (Morgenthau was also 1916 Democratic Financial Committee chairman, and as such was a direct counterwieght to the Zionist influence on Wilson of Louis Brandeis.) See, too, Manuel, *American-Palestine Relations*, pp. 155–95.

4. On the Balfour Declaration, Departmental policy was epitomized in the words of S. Edelman, a *Jewish* FSO who was the American consul in Jerusalem in 1917: "'A Jewish State should not be tolerated'" (Manuel, *American-Palestine Relations*, p. 171). On Secretary Lansing's nonrole, see ibid., pp. 167, 177, passim; also, Lansing to Wilson, 13 December 1917 and 28 February 1918, *FR* (*The Lansing Papers, 1914–1920*), vol. 2, pp. 71, 107–8.

5. On Wilson's general ignoring of the Secretary and the Department, see D. Smith, "Robert Lansing," in Graebner, ed., *An Uncertain Tradition*, pp. 114–25. Also, see R. Silverberg, *If I Forget Thee O Jerusalem: American Jews and the State of Israel* (New York: W. Morrow, 1970), Chapter 3.

6. On the Peace Conference, see Manuel, *American-Palestine Relations*, pp. 220 ff. The Zionist proposals are documented in S. Katz, *Battleground: Fact and Fantasy in Palestine* (New York: Bantam, 1973), Appendix B. A tentative

proposal (January 1919) of the Intelligence Section of the American Delegation, markedly pro-Zionist, and short-lived, is documented in Appendix D.

On the King-Crane Commission and missionary influence, see Manuel, *American-Palestine Relations*, pp. 215, 236–54; Grabill, *Protestant Diplomacy*, pp. 156, 163, passim; Antonius, *The Arab Awakening*, Chapter 14 and Appendix H; and H. Howard, *An American Inquiry into the Middle East: The King-Crane Commission* (Beirut: Khayat's, 1963).

7. The 1922 Joint Resolution said that the U.S. "favors the establishment in Palestine of a national home for the Jewish people." The first draft had read "pledges to support," but Secretary Charles Evans Hughes had changed the verb and diluted the commitment. Even so, as Manuel has noted, the resolution troubled the Department, as a joint resolution signed by the President was regarded by some in NEA as having the effect of law, which in this case suggested that, if Britain defaulted, America would have responsibility for the Balfour Declaration. In due course, however, the Department overcame its anxiety; and its typical response to all Congressional resolutions favoring Zionism would be that they were empty electioneering gestures, without any legal basis. See Manuel, *American-Palestine Relations*, pp. 277 ff., especially p. 283; and *FR* 3 (1936): 451.

8. On the 1924 Convention, see J. C. Hurewitz, *The Struggle for Palestine*, pp. 114–15; Manuel, *American-Palestine Relations*, pp. 284–90; Adler and Margalith, *With Firmness in the Right*, pp. 81–82; and Department of State (NEA), *Mandate for Palestine* (Washington, D.C.: GPO, 1927), pp. 75 ff.

9. R. Fink, ed., *America and Palestine: The Attitude of Official America and of the American People Toward the Rebuilding of Palestine as a Free and Democratic Jewish Commonwealth* (New York: American Zionist Emergency Council, 1944), p. 51.

10. Memorandum by G. Howland Shaw, 23 September 1929, *FR* 3 (1929): 59. Indeed, the Department felt the Jews were clearly at fault. Wrote Paul Knabenshue, then consul in Jerusalem, "It is my opinion that the Moslem attacks were precipitated by provocative acts of the Jews." "It would appear inadvisable of the U.S. to make such official representations in this matter to the British government, for such action would undoubtedly create resentment against us here and in other Moslem countries" (Knabenshue to H. Stimson, 24 August 1929 and 19 September 1929, ibid., pp. 48, 58).

11. P. Alling to Assistant Secretary R. W. Moore, 6 November 1936, *FR* 3 (1936): 454. [Secretary Hughes' negative attitude on the immigration question a decade earlier served as a precedent, as noted in W. Murray to Moore, 10 May 1937, *FR* 2 (1937): 883.]

12. Knabenshue to Murray ("Dear Wallace" letter), 31 March 1938, *FR* 3 (1938): 916; Wadsworth to Hull, 10 July 1938 and 6 September 1938, ibid., pp. 933, 944.

13. On the Department's post-World War I interest in Palestine's economic possibilitiees, see correspondence in *FR* 2 (1919): 258–59; and *FR* 2 (1921): 102–3, passim.

14. See correspondence with the Foreign Office in *FR* 3 (1940); 857–64.

15. Hull to Ambassador Bingham (London), 27 April 1937, *FR* 3 (1937): 881–82; Knabenshue to Murray, 3 March 1938, *FR* 2 (1938): 909; Wadsworth to Hull, ibid., p. 930; and Murray, Memorandum (on Magnes), 29 November 1938, ibid., 989.

16. See Memorandum of Conversation (Murray, Alling, and Foreign Office), 1 June 1937, *FR* 2 (1937): 885–86. For the bases of "assent," see ibid., pp. 900–904; and Manuel, *American-Palestine Relations*, pp. 305–7.

17. Department release, 14 November 1938, *FR* 2 (1938): 953–55. Also, see Adler and Margalith, *With Firmness in the Right,* p. 93.

Hull's articulations were based on clarifications he had earlier sought from his experts in NEA. As could be expected, NEA brushed aside the 1922 Resolution as insignificant. NEA also stated that the 1924 Convention, despite its allusions to the Mandate and Balfour Declaration, differed in no material way from the eight other conventions on mandated territories signed after World War I. The purpose of all the conventions, said NEA, was but "to gain for American nationals the same rights and privileges which nationals of states members of the League of Nations enjoyed" [Alling to Hull, 20 October 1938, *FR* 2 (1938): 962].

18. Ibn Saud, Memorandum, 29 November 1938, *FR* 2 (1938): 996; Welles to Roosevelt, 9 January 1939, *FR* 4 (1939): 694; and, e.g., Wadsworth to Hull, 25 October 1938, *FR* 2 (1938): 966.

19. Murray to Hull, 4 March 1939, *FR* 4 (1939): 723–25. For the British aide-memoire relative to the forthcoming White Paper, see ibid., p. 751. The course of Foreign Office—Department of State consultations is detailed in W. L. Krieg, "Official American Interest in the British White Paper on Palestine," (covering period March–August 1939), 25 April 1944, 867N.01/2325 PS/BGG.

20. In the indignant words of the assistant legal advisor consulted by Childs: "It requires little discussion to establish that it is not a proper or sensible function of a government to enter into treaties for the purpose of encouraging its nationals to deplete the national wealth by contribution of funds or investment of funds in foreign countries and it is incredible that anyone could seriously believe that the Government of the United States has adopted by treaty or otherwise the policy of encouraging its nationals to establish domiciles in foreign countries with consequent risk—in the case of naturalized citizens—of becoming subject to the presumption of expatriation and denial of American protection" [J. Rives Childs, Memorandum, 8 March 1939, *FR* 4 (1939): 729]. Other references, pp. 725–26. See, also, Childs, *Foreign Service Farewell,* pp. 102–19.

21. Quotations from Hull's *Memoirs,* vol. 2, pp. 1529–31, 1536. Also, Hull to Kennedy, 23 May 1939, *FR* 4 (1939): 765.

22. See Manuel, *American-Palestine Relations,* p. 308; and correspondence in *FR* 2 (1938): 928; and *FR* 4 (1939): 749–50, 768.

23. S. Halperin, *The Political World of American Zionism* (Detroit: Wayne State Univ. Press, 1961), pp. 119 ff.; and Messersmith's memorandum on Lazaron, *FR* 4 (1939): 810.

24. See Silverberg, *If I Forget Thee,* pp. 141, 182–83; and Adler and Margalith, *With Firmness In the Right,* p. 393.

25. Ibid., p. 395; and J. B. Schechtman, *The United States and the Jewish State Movement: The Crucial Decade, 1939–1949* (New York: Herzl Press and T. Yoseloff, 1966), p. 20. Note communications between J. Slawson (American Jewish Committee) and G. P. Merriam (NEA), 10 April 1944 and 28 April 1944, 867N.01/2328; and P. Ireland to Merriam, 8 July 1944, 867N.01/6–3044.

26. Figures are from DeNovo, *American Interests and Policies,* pp. 345–46. Note, too, Table B, "Comparative Data on Middle Eastern Countries," in Janowsky, *Foundations of Israel,* p. 149; and Appendix 4, "American Jewry's Financial Contributions to Palestine," in Halperin, *Political World of American Zionism,* pp. 325–26. Also, see note 34 below.

27. Laqueur, ed., *The Israel-Arab Reader,* document 18.

It is to be noted that this section (Palestine During World War II) will examine only the main developments during the war years, internally and with respect to the Arabs and British. The Yishuv's relations with the White House, the State Department, America in general, and with American Jews and Zionists will be treated in subsequent sections of this and the next chapter. The Holocaust and Rescue attempts, and the connections thereof with American Jews, Palestine, and State Department refugee policies, are essential parts of the topics under analysis, but they will not receive in this work the detailed examination they deserve. This is regrettable, as "only against the background of the concentration camps and the crematoria is it possible to understand the frantic, the obsessive, indeed, the irresistible determination of the surviving members of European Jewry to find a home of their own at last" [H. M. Sachar, *The Course of Modern Jewish History* (New York: Delta, 1958), p. 459].

28. On land restrictions, see Bauer, *From Diplomacy to Resistance*, pp. 69–71; and Sykes, *Crossroads to Israel*, pp. 258–59, n. 1. On immigration restrictions, see Bauer, pp. 53, passim; Parkes, *Whose Land?*, pp. 284 ff.; and Koestler, *Promise and Fulfillment*, p. 56. For wartime population figures, note the following:

Table 1: Annual Population, Palestine

Year	Moslems	Jews	Christians
1938	900,250	411,222	111,974
1939	927,133	455,457	116,958
1940	947,846	463,535	120,587
1941	973,104	474,102	125,413
1942	955,292	484,408	127,184
1943	1,028,715	502,912	131,281
1944	1,061,277	528,702	135,547

From Lenczowski, *The Middle East in World Affairs*, Appendix 6, p. 547.

Table 2: "Legal" Jewish Immigration to Palestine

Year	Jews
1939	27,561
1940	8,398
1941	5,886
1942	3,733
1943	8,507
1944	14,464
1945	13,121

(Between 1919–1948, some 31,000 additional "illegal Jewish immigrants" entered Palestine.) From Janowsky, *Foundations of Israel*, document 8, p. 145.

29. Koestler, *Promise and Fulfillment*, pp. 57 ff.; Sykes, *Crossroads to Israel*, p. 266.

30. Koestler, *Promise and Fulfillment*, pp. 55 ff.; and Woodward, *British Foreign Policy*, p. 556.

31. Woodward, *British Foreign Policy*, p. 556. On the other hand, the Foreign Office "would not like to feel that Jewish support was being given to [the Allies] for any other reason than that the Jews shared the ideals for which the

Allies were fighting and realized that an Allied victory was in Jewish interests.... There must be no misunderstanding as to the possibility of rewards,
whether in the form of further immigration into Palestine or otherwise" (pp.
555–56).

32. Sykes, *Crossroads to Israel*, Chapter 10; and Bauer, *From Diplomacy to
Resistance*, pp. 352–53, passim.

33. See Bauer, *From Diplomacy to Resistance*, pp. 47 ff., and Allon, *Shield
of David*, pp. 140 ff.

34. See, e.g., A. Dorra, "Palestine and Economic Development," pp. 101–2.

35. Quotation from Laqueur, ed., *The Israel-Arab Reader*, document 19. See
also, relative to the Biltmore Program, cited works by Bauer (Chapter 6);
Sykes (pp. 281 ff.); Halperin (Chapter 9); and Schechtman (pp. 59–62.)

36. On the dissenters, see cited works by Sykes (pp. 285–87); Esco, *Palestine* (vol. 2, pp. 1098–106); Halperin (Chapter 5, p. 172). On binationalism,
see the formulations in M. Buber, J. L. Magnes, E. Simon, eds., *Towards Union
in Palestine: Essays on Zionism and Jewish-Arab Cooperation* (Westport,
Conn.: Greenwood Press, 1972; originally, Jerusalem: Ihud Association, 1947).

37. On British great-power strategy, see Hurewitz, *The Struggle for Palestine*, Chapter 13.

High-policy coolness toward Zionism fed into the often automatic anti-
Zionism on the Mandate level. The result was remarkable instances of the
currying of Arab favor. E.g., British radio propaganda, obviously fearing Arab
fondness for Hitler and trying to decondition the Arabs, implied that Hitler,
unfortunately, as it were, was not really the foe of the Jews, or the perpetrator
of mass killings. And when Abdullah and the anti-Husseini faction in Palestine
denounced the Mufti as a collaborator with Hitler, this was censored, presumably lest the information only make the Arabs more supportive of the
Mufti. See Koestler, *Promise and Fulfillment*, pp. 79, 84.

38. On the Jewish thesis, see D. Horowitz, *State in the Making* (New York:
Knopf, 1953), p. 12, passim; Ben-Horin, *The Middle East*, Chapter 9; and
numerous contemporary speeches, etc., a good example of which is D. Ben
Gurion, "Test of Fulfillment," 12 May 1942, in *Jewish Frontier Anthology*
(New York: Jewish Frontier Association, 1945), pp. 100–120.

39. Put otherwise, the Arabs knew absolutely what and whom they were
against, but not what they were for. In view of the variety of their ethnic and
class differences, etc., as noted in Chapter 2, the comparative lack of an Arab
national consciousness in western Palestine is hardly surprising. See Y. Shimoni,
"The Arabs and the Approaching War with Israel," *Hamizrah HeHadash*
(Jerusalem, 1962), vol. 12, English summary, pp. 1–9; Sykes, *Crossroads to
Israel*, p. 316; and Khadduri, "Fertile Crescent Scheme," passim, in R. Frye,
ed., regarding Abdullah.

40. Wadsworth to Hull, 2 December 1940, *FR* 3 (1940): 853.

41. Schechtman, *The U.S. and the Jewish State Movement*, p. 34; J. Rives
Childs, Memorandum of Conversation (British Consul), 22 November 1940,
FR 3 (1940): 850; and Department to British Embassy, ibid., 23 November
1940, p. 852.

42. For Hull's approach to the refugee problem, see his *Memoirs*, vol. 2, pp.
1537 ff.; N. Goldmann, *The Autobiography of Nahum Goldmann: Sixty Years
of Jewish Life* (New York: Holt, Rinehart, 1969), pp. 201–2; and Adler and
Margalith, *With Firmness in the Right*, pp. 438–39. On the views of others in
the Department, see J. M. Blum, ed., *From the Morgenthau Diaries* (Boston:
Houghton Mifflin, 1972), pp. 520–33; and S. Shafir, "George S. Messersmith,"
Jewish Social Studies 35 (1973): 32–41; and note 12, Chapter 3.

Useful sources on the Jewish refugee problem and its political entanglements include H. Feingold, *The Politics of Rescue* (New Brunswick, N.J.: Rutgers Univ. Press, 1970); A. Morse, *While Six Million Died: A Chronicle of American Apathy* (New York: Random House, 1967); S. Spear, "The United States and the Persecution of the Jews in Germany 1933–1939," *Jewish Social Studies* 30 (1968): 215–42; D. Brody, "American Jewry, the Refugees and Immigration Restriction 1932–1942," in A. Karp, ed., *The Jewish Experience in America*, vol. 5 (New York: Ktav, 1969); S. Friedman, *No Haven for the Oppressed: United States Policy Toward Jewish Refugees 1938–1945* (Detroit: Wayne State Univ. Press, 1973); and J. Stein, *Britain and the Jews of Europe, 1933–1939* (Ph.D. diss., St. Louis Univ., 1972).

43. See communications in *FR* 3 (1940): 836, 846, 868–74. Elsewhere, too, the Department was on its guard lest the pushy Jews appear in Arab eyes, or its own, as favorably "chosen." Thus in the contemporary instance of discrimination and humiliation for many Jews in Morocco, before and after Vichy rule, the Department refused to "interfere." See correspondence between M. Waldman (American Jewish Committee) and A. Berle, Jr., *FR* 3 (1941): 592–95; Adler and Margalith, *With Firmness in the Right*, pp. 407–14; and Murphy, *Diplomat Among Warriors*, pp. 147–48, 161–62.

44. The quotation is from Berle to Murray and Welles, 14 April 1941, *FR* 3 (1941): 598. Also, see Schectman, *The U.S. and the Jewish State Movement*, pp. 52–55. For "flattery," see Murray, Memorandum of Conversation, (NEA, C. Weizmann), 6 Feburary 1940, *FR* 3 (1940): 838–39.

45. On Jewish loyalty to the allies, see J. Rives Childs, Memorandum of Conversation (Murray, American Jewish delegation), 8 October 1940, *FR* 3 (1940): 873. On Zionist views of Arab nationalism, see Memorandum of Conversation (Murray, Weizmann, et al.), 6 February 1940, *FR* 3 (1940): 837–38; also, the representative views of M. Sharett, "Israel and the Middle East," 10 April 1953 (New York: Israel Office of Information, n. d.); and M. Keren, "Israel and the United States," in R. Frye, ed., *The Near East and the Great Powers*, pp. 106–13. Also, see note 38.

46. See on Hoskins, note 12, Chapter 3 above; on Berle and Murray, note 8, Chapter 11; and notes 2, 3, and 4, Chapter 14.

47. On the Welles-Kirk-Murray disagreements, see *FR* 3 (1941): 599–600; 611, 622–23. Also Schectman, *The U.S. and the Jewish State Movement*, pp. 58–59.

48. On American Jews, note Murray to Berle, Long, and Hull (regarding M. Lazaron), 7 March 1940, 867N.01/1699. Also, see material on Murray in Chapter 4.

49. Murray to Berle, 13 September 1940, 867.01/1718 1/2 PS/MFM.

50. "Britain is not [justified] in placing responsibility upon our shoulders when doing so weakens our own standing in Arab communities without strengthening the standing of the British.... Nazi propaganda among the Arabs that we are going to force England to give Palestine to the Jews is bad enough without having our friends the British back then up" (Pinkerton to Murray, 5 January 1942, p. 2, 768N.01/1788).

51. Murray to Berle, 11 February 1942, 867N.01/1797 PS/ET.

52. E.g., report on Intergovernmental Committee on Refugees, 3 January 1941, *Bulletin* 4 (1941): 15–16; Minutes of ER-4, 17 April 1942, Notter Papers, Box 91, Folder: "E Minutes J & EP & ER;" and note 28, Chapter 1.

53. On Jewish-army proposals, see Silverberg, *If I Forget Thee*, pp. 182–83; and Schectman, *The U.S. and the Jewish State Movement*, pp. 43–49.

54. On the AZEC, see Doreen Bierbrier, "The American Zionist Emergency

Council: An Analysis of a Pressure Group," *American Jewish Historical Quarterly* 60 (1970): 85–105; Halperin, *Political World of American Zionism,* Appendix 5 (membership figures), and passim; and the section on the AZEC and ZOA in Chapter 14.

55. Murray to Hull and Roosevelt, 2 June 1942, *FR* 4 (1942): 539.

56. Ibid., p. 540.

57. See communications of Welles and Berle, *FR* 4 (1942): 544–46.

58. See Churchill, *Triumph and Tragedy,* Book 1, Appendix C, and passim; Kirk, *The Middle East in the War,* pp. 237–38, 335; and Esco, *Palestine,* vol. 2, pp. 1029 ff.

59. See B. V. Cohen, "A Plan for the Accelerated Development of Jewish Settlement in Palestine and the Speedy Recognition of Palestine as an Independent State Either Within or Without a Middle Eastern Federation," and "Accompaniment," 4 September 1942, P Document 66, Notter Papers, Box 63, Folder: "P Docs. 66–100." Also, note 10, Chapter 3.

60. Territorial Minutes, T-19, 4 September 1942, Yale Papers, Box 1, Folder 7; P Minutes 25, 5 September 1942, MacLeish Papers, Box 41, Folder: "Political Subcommittee."

61. On the Department's wish for a Presidential statement, see Hull to Roosevelt, n. d., 867N.01/1812 PS/LBC. Quotation from Hull is from Department release, 30 October 1942, *FR* 4 (1942): 548. Quotation from Congress is from statement signed by 63 Senators and 182 representatives, in ibid., 4 December 1942, pp. 549–50.

62. W. Yale, Memorandum, 22 September 1942, 867N.01/1812; and note 31, Chapter 4.

63. Lazaron to Welles, 23 November 1942, 867N.01/11–2342; and Murray to Welles, 27 November 1942, 867N.01/11–2342.

14

Palestine, 1943–45

The organization of this chapter is in four thematic parts, each embracing the period of late 1942 to mid-1945 as one continuum. This is an artificial time line, though not totally so. As will be seen, TORCH in North Africa and oil in Saudi Arabia marked late 1942 as something of a new point in American power and self-awareness in the Middle East. The summer–fall of 1945, however, which is where we conclude our analyses, is admittedly less satisfactory as an end point. The fact that it marked the war's end, also the full disclosure of the Holocaust, and the beginnings of the Arab League, the Cold War, and the U.N. Organization, was of minor impact so far as the Department's policy toward Palestine was concerned. Only toward the end of 1945, because the pace of events within Palestine intensified and because President Truman increasingly took charge of Palestine policy, can one speak, albeit with qualifications, of any changes of pace and direction in Departmental policy. These will be noted in due course.

The first part of this chapter covers the Department's reactions, positions, nonpositions, and methods of "handling" the Arabs and the Jews outside the United States relative to Palestine. Included will be the Department's evolving positions on bringing Ibn Saud into the Palestine picture as a decision maker and the Department's refugee solutions. The second part covers the Department's reactions to domestic lobbying, chiefly Jewish, though by no means totally pro-Zionist. The third part covers the Department's main responses to the Executive Branch (specifically, Roosevelt, Truman, and the Department of War) and the Legislative Branch (Congress). And the fourth covers the Department's "great-power" diplomatic relations with Britain. Included here will be the highlights of the Department's own postwar plans for Palestine.

POLICY TOWARD ARABS AND NON-AMERICAN JEWS, AFTER EL ALAMEIN AND OPERATION TORCH

Foreign Service and other agency reports on America's new power and prestige, on top of the old "reservoirs of good will," reached a high point in the second half of 1942 after El Alamein, TORCH, and the crystallized administrative consensus approving Saudi Arabia as a vital national interest. Such reports were invariably interwoven with alarms lest Zionism, or European imperialism, or administrative ineptitude in Washington, upset the applecart.[1]

With these reports and alarms in mind, the Department chose to dissociate itself gradually from British policy on Palestine. The proximate cause was an apparent renewal in December 1942 of Zionist and British interest in arranging a deal with Ibn Saud. The idea behind the deal was that Britain would make him "boss of bosses" of the Arab world if he would accept Jewish funds to help him pay off his debts (chiefly to Britain) and if he would be willing to work out with Dr. Weizmann a compromise solution to the Palestine problem.

Wallace Murray's reaction to the proposed deal was much more negative than it had been in the spring of 1941. He now posited the following: Ibn Saud's relations with the British were not good; the Arab world would not accept the "boss" idea; Ibn Saud was a zealous Moslem and anti-Zionist; Weizmann would not compromise. However, if Weizmann were persuaded to offer a Magnes-type plan which would limit Jewish immigration and guarantee that "the Arabs will always be in the majority," then, wrote Murray, he believed a modus vivendi could be worked out. Under an Arab majority, there could presumably be established between Jews and Arabs "full confidence and a mutual give-and-take." However, give-and-take would not be possible, implied Murray, under a Jewish majority ("Jewish ascendancy"), even if maintained by foreign bayonets or agreed to by Ibn Saud himself.

On the British, Ibn Saud distrusted them, Murray elaborated, and did not wish to extend his dependence on them. Growing American air and oil interests were also factors suggesting that it would not be in American interests to strengthen British-Saudi ties, ties which would be automatically increased should America encourage a Weizmann-Ibn Saud deal on the Palestine mandate. Particularly, such endorsement would be unwise as "there are clear indications that Ibn Saud would welcome a far greater American participation in his country than exists at the present time."

The best approach to the Palestine problem, Murray concluded, would be a joint Anglo-American one—but a collaboration that would be divorced from the possibility of a collaboration involving Ibn Saud as an active third party. The advantage for America lay in the fact that the British had lost their credibility with the Arabs, while the American star was still rising.[2]

The implications were clear: Murray wished to twist the Churchill-Weizmann initiative all the way around. Rather than countenance Britain's effort, as in 1941, to get American diplomatic support for a softening of Ibn Saud's position, Murray essentially counterproposed that Britain moderate Weizmann's position. Implied, too, was that the Department could take credit for the new initiative and the possibly moderated Jewish position when it would have future audiences with the king. Furthermore, because Murray's proposal never gave up the Department's traditional insistence that Palestine was solely Britain's responsibility, his ideas had a fail-safe gyroscope built into them. If Britain succeeded in implementing his proposal of softening Weizmann's position, there would certainly be no loss to American prestige in the Arab world, and any Jewish expressions of outrage and betrayal would be deflected onto the Foreign Office, not the Department. But if the British failed to bring his proposal off, they, not the Americans, would draw the lightning of Jewish resentment—after all, Palestine was a British responsibility.

By early 1943, Murray became even more antipathetic to the possibility, remote as it was, of a tradeoff between Weizmann and Ibn Saud. Periodically reinforced by the dire views of FSOs in Cairo and Jidda, Murray, in memoranda to Welles, tried to dissociate the Department from Weizmann's thesis that a deal was possible only if openly backed by both London and Washington. Moreover, he viewed Weizmann's suggestion of a $80 million Jewish loan to Ibn Saud for development purposes as a way the "Zionists could extend their influence and activities outside Palestine" which "appears to have the character of economic imperialism backed by international sanction."[3]

Indeed, fearing that even the slightest encouragement by the Department would jeopardize American oil interests, Murray went beyond his December 1942 approach, and advocated discouraging *any* American association with a Jewish-Arab deal. In the event that the king consented to see Weizmann, he wrote, it should be made "perfectly clear to the king that the discussions are entirely bilateral, *and that neither we nor the British are urging any particular solution.*" (Emphasis added).[4]

Welles, however, disagreed. Welles believed generally that the United States should not sit out and wait until the end of the war before commiting itself to postwar solutions; and in the case of Palestine, he shared Weizmann's belief in the present need and efficacy of great-power influence. And, while aware of the Arab-Jewish impasse, he was also historically aware that an Arab-Jewish summit meeting was not unprecedented, given the Weizmann-Feisal meetings after World War I. Roosevelt approved of Welles' attitude. Welles' friend, Arabic-speaking Colonel Harold Hoskins, was chosen as the emissary to broach the idea to Ibn Saud of a direct meeting with Weizmann. Although he was somewhat less averse to political Zionism than others in the middle echelons, Hoskins was not approved of by Zionists. Their criticism was mute, however. In any event, Hull, Churchill, the Foreign Office, the Jewish Agency's Political Department all had foreknowledge of Hoskins' mission. Noone was optimistic.[5]

Fears came true. Indeed, the final report from Hoskins was so negative as to discredit henceforth the views of Welles and Weizmann in the eyes of the White House and the Department. For its part, the reaction of Hull and NEA to the mission's failure was one of I-told-you-so relief and angry embarrassment that such a predictable blunder had been set in motion in the first place. That the failure was a factor in Welles' resignation shortly thereafter, albeit a minor factor, is also plausible.[6]

Compensating for its error, Departmental policy toward Jidda became one of greater apology and munificence than before. Sensitivity to Ibn Saud's reactions to, for example, pro-Zionist Congressional speeches in the electoral campaign of 1944 reached a new acuteness. Then, on the very eve of the Yalta Conference (4–12 February 1945), Ibn Saud delivered a well-cued speech, one of his most violent, on the cursed Jews. Palestine will be a land drenched in blood, he said; the United States, in whom Arabs have always had great hopes, must choose for or against Arab friendship.[7]

In the context of both Palestine and oil, therefore, it was logical that the Department should try to cement relations on the highest levels. It did so when the Department secretly arranged a meeting between Roosevelt and Ibn Saud immediately after Roosevelt had deliberately shortened the prior Yalta Conference. Even so, as will be noted, that cement became somewhat weakened beginning in September 1945, when President Truman overrode the Department and favored admission of 100,000 Jewish Displaced Persons into Palestine.

Arab pressure other than Ibn Saud's was steadily increasing in the period 1942–45. There were the usual constants: anxiously reported alarms by FSOs and occasionally by agents of OWI and OSS. As with Ibn Saud's anti-Zionism, the Department assumed that there were, no doubt, some layers of artificial political gamesmanship and British orchestration behind Arab protests, but that at the core, Arab anti-Zionism—

and highly potential anti-Americanism—was sincere and wrathful, not to be taken lightly. It is worth noting that Iraq, partly because of its unique pro-Axis and anti-Jewish background and partly because of all the Arab states, it had the oldest ministerial credentials in Washington, was probably the most vocally anti-Zionist state. It often served as unofficial wartime spokesman for the Arab world and led the pack when some Congressman precipitated a "crisis" by speaking favorably of Zionism.

When the Arab League was formed in March 1945, a new factor emerged. Similarly, in the same period ministerial representatives in Washington and at the U.N. Organization increased from the other Arab states. Ethnic Arab-American lobbying also became more of a factor than hitherto. Non-Arab Christian groups, both domestic and foreign, added to the total thrust: representatives of the Y.M.C.A. and Presbyterian missionary board, editorials in the prestigious *Christian Century*, and probably most significantly, anti-Zionist warnings from the Vatican, were among them. Finally, periodic dispatches from military attachés added the notes of a *basso profundo* to the anti-Zionist chorus by reporting that, as a result of the British and Americans' "selling out" of the Arabs to the Zionists, the Arabs were looking to none other than the Russians.[8]

The Department's reactions were of course sympathetic; beyond that, it habitually importuned for a public Presidential and/or joint Anglo-American statement against political Zionism. Barring that, it lobbied for a statement in favor of majority self-determination in Palestine. Barring that, it sought a statement asserting that the Palestine situation was to be frozen until the end of the war. And barring that, it sought to give private assurances, sometimes over the President's signature and sometimes without authority, except its own. Not only to Ibn Saud, but also to all other Arab heads of state, the Department regularly pledged that no act hostile to the Arabs nor any decision on Palestine without full prior consultations would be made.

Of all instrumentalities, the last named—private assurances—was the major one used and the only one normally possible, because of pro-Zionist counterpressures. In these private assurances the Department habitually explained away any public Presidential or Congressional endorsement of Zionism as merely expressing a vague approval of a Jewish national home, not the advocacy of a concrete commonwealth in Palestine. When Roosevelt was put on record in 1944 as not "approving" the 1939 White Paper, Hull, as noted earlier, immediately told the FSOs to tell the Arabs that while Washington did not give its approval to the White Paper, it did not give its disapproval, either. Finally, to allay Arab anxieties over pro-Zionist party platforms and the like, the Department tended to deprecate such as rather wild, basically meaningless idiosyncrasies of "politicians."[9]

Conversely, toward pro-Zionist pressures, the Department stressed three lines of counteraction. It worked in executive session with key Congressmen in order to kill or at least postpone pro-Zionist Congressional resolutions, on the thesis that the latter would threaten military security and oil accessibility in the Middle East. It neutralized by all manner of diplomatic finesse and word manipulation (it did not "approve" the White Paper) Zionist lobbyists. And third, the Department formulated within the bowels of the postwar planning apparatus new "preferred solutions" for postwar Palestine and for the Jewish refugee problem.

On the thesis that the outcry for and against Zionism and the British White Paper policy would subside if there were no immigration pressures on the gates of Palestine, the Department spent considerable, though irregularly applied, time on working up paper schemes to solve the Jewish refugee problem. Reference has already been made to such plans in 1941–42. More were composed in 1943, but by 1944 most of them had been written off as impracticable. Then, too, even though no one guessed at the enormity of the Nazi Final Solution, the fact that Jewish numbers were being methodically reduced by the Nazis was known. Put crudely, this fact eliminated the need to ponder the refugee question overmuch. Still, the character of the Department's refugee solutions is important to touch on, if only because it sheds further light on the Department's mindset on Jews and Zionists.

Actually, only a minority within the Department seriously thought that a territorial solution was the answer to the Jewish Question, especially when earlier Latin American schemes petered out. While many plans and ideas came across their desks, Murray continued to favor Angola. ("[There] we should relieve the pressure upon the Jews in Europe and at the same time relieve the pressure of the Jews upon the Arabs in the Near East.") Planner Isaiah Bowman and Lieutenant Hoskins opted for Cyrenaica in Libya. However, Welles thought repatriation in a rehabilitated Europe free of anti-Semitism was the answer, though at one point he recorded his friendliness to the Egyptian minister's "bright thought... to send a batch of them to each of the [29] United Nations."[10]

Like Welles, the majority of NEA and the upper echelons, and also the Foreign Office, felt that repatriation and reintegration were the answers. Within the planning apparatus on the highest levels, Myron Taylor was the chief advocate of this point of view. Not only was integration presumably in accord with American idealism, not to mention the American way of handling its own Jewish population; it was also recommended because the option of large-scale immigration schemes seemed either anachronistic or radical, in either case contrary to the spirit of the Atlantic Charter.

In a sense, the Department shared the Zionist thesis that mass migration and territorial dispersion "will in the end serve merely to transfer the problem [Jews confronting indigenous populations] from one country to another." However, the Zionists drew the conclusion that Jews should therefore go to an already one-third Jewish Palestine where the "problem," as it were, was already known and familiar and, they felt, susceptible to accommodation and solution once and for all. Not so the Department; it drew the opposite conclusion, based on the bad experiences in Palestine, that there should be no more host territories, no more Palestines, Palestine included.[11]

One might note that this conclusion was based on the larger premise that the more the Jewish problem was atomized, the better. The more Palestine was separated from the Jewish refugee problem, the more the Jewish refugee problem was intermixed with the general refugee problem, the more American Jews were separated from Zionism, the more Jewish war service was assimilated into allied armies rather than in a Jewish army, the more Jewish issues within the Department were treated by separate offices and divisions rather than a single Office of Jewish Affairs, the better. Both the ogre of Jewish nationalism and the ogre of anti-Semitism, of which Jewish nationalism was believed to be a chief cause, would disappear.

Meanwhile, because the goal of repatriation and reintegration would have to wait until the war's end, and then some, what to do with existing refugees outside Axis reach and with the American Jewish clamor on their behalf? The Department's basic retort was a paraphrase of Hull's Balfour Day statement of 1942, that in the total destruction of Hitlerism was the Jews' salvation. The Jews, it was implied, must not clamor or push for special treatment, but must wait their turn, lest the Hitlerite claim that the war was a Jew war be vindicated. For its part, the Department said, it would continue to give the refugee problem its sympathetic consideration and would endorse forums like the Bermuda Conference of April 1943 (successor to the Evian Conference of 1938). That both were futile assemblies, and that travesty was committed when the topic of Palestine was expressly excluded from the Bermuda agenda, did not deter the Department from believing that it was actually an unsung champion of the refugees.[12]

There came a point, however, when Departmental weapons (namely, words) failed to keep the Jews at bay. Pressure on the White House, particularly by Treasury Secretary Henry Morgenthau, Jr., finally forced Roosevelt to press the Department and also to create a new agency, the War Refugee Board (June 1944). The latter tried to expedite rescue and asylum operations, although usually they were in the category of too little, too late.

As for immigration to Palestine and the question of the 1939 White Paper, which was set to expire March 31, 1944, Hull pressed, albeit mildly, British ambassador Lord Halifax to extend the deadline. His reason was

America's "international interest in the Jewish situation, based primarily on the residence and citizenship of some 5 million Jews in this country." The middle echelons in NEA, the Foreign Service, and the planning apparatus were disappointed in Hull's initiative, so apparently motivated by domestic politics.

However, Assistant Secretary Breckinridge Long supported Hull's "appeasement" of the Jews. Both Hull and Long were personally quite anxious about pressures from Jews and liberals, before whom they felt they in particular were Roosevelt's scapegoats. They thus believed that keeping the immigration tap in Palestine open to a trickle (the quotas assigned had not been used up as of March 1944) was better than shutting it off (as NEA wanted), doing nothing—and waiting for a new burst of ulcer-giving Jewish acrimony against the Department. Another, though minor, reason for mollifying the Jews by extending the quotas was the Department's realization that the underground military strength of the Yishuv was stronger than that of the Palestinian Arabs. Though this awareness hardly persuaded the Department to be pro-Zionist, it did persuade the Department, in an indirect way, of the folly of being in favor of a strictly Palestinian Arab state.[13]

Without American and Palestinian Jewish militance, it is clear that the Department would not have had any serious reason to be concerned about even slightly relieving the Jewish refugee problem. What the situation showed was that the nonmilitant Prophet Isaiah approach of "let us reason together," which was the approach of Zionist envoys like Weizmann, Nahum Goldmann, and on the American side, Stephen Wise, failed resoundingly. They did not realize the *depths* of the Department's antipathies, and in fact they had never fully grasped this fact, as noted in the previous chapter's discussion of Departmental Zionophobia going back even before the Balfour Declaration. Hence Weizmann's philosophic argumentation that there was less injustice to the Arabs in awarding Palestine to the Jews than there would be injustice to the Jews in not allowing them to have Palestine sounded to the Department like a broken record of Zionist propaganda. When he eloquently expressed the view that given all that the Arabs would get out of the war and all that the Jews lost in the war, equity would be rendered if Palestine, a fraction of the Middle East, were assigned to the Jews, the Department, and the White House, too, were unmoved and cynically "realistic."[14]

The Department and the President were, to be sure, moralistic as well as realistic in their approach to foreign policy. As frequently noted, the Atlantic Charter was their neo-Wilsonian credo, and in consequence they were often sympathetic to the causes of underdogs and anti-imperialist states. In the case of Weizmann, moreover, officialdom respected him very highly. Such respect was given, however, to Weizmann the person, the elder statesman, not to Weizmann the political Zionist. And that was because political Zionism, in the Department's perception, was a moral-idealistic species apart, a chimerical theory which did not and had never fit into the Wilsonian doctrines of majority rule and local self-determination.[15]

DOMESTIC JEWISH LOBBIES

While the Department was trying to keep Palestine quarantined from Ibn Saud, from Jewish refugees, and from Congressional interest, and while it was pushing for Presidential statements or making private assurances, it was still faced with a domestic rear-guard war against what sometimes seemed like daily onslaughts of Jewish delegations and mail. On the basis of the quantity of documents and the time spent, the Department basically had to contend with three Jewish groupings, most frequently with Zionists, mainly of the American Zionist Emergency Council (AZEC), and usually in tandem with representatives of the Zionist Organization of America (ZOA), the World Zionist Organization, and the Jewish Agency. The Department had to contend next most frequently with Jewish anti-Zionists, mainly representatives of the American Jewish Committee and American Council for Judaism. In third place were representatives of the Revisionist New Zionist Organization and (indirectly, not face-to-face) the Peter Bergson group.

The remonstrances of the second grouping, the Jewish anti-Zionists, bore significance for several reasons. First, rather like the conversion of a Jew to Christianity, Jewish anti-Zionism to the non-Jew was a significant phenomenon in itself. Second, the Department could not help feeling that such anti-Zionism, irrespective of its factional and sometimes crackpot character, legitimized its own hostilities and its view that the Zionists were not representative of either the will or votes of the Jews. Third, because the bitter and defamatory quality of Jewish anti-Zionist expressions often *exceeded*, by far, that of the Department's own anti-Zionist expressions, the Department was relieved of any inhibition about its own condemnations as possibly being unfair or touched with Anti-Semitism.[16] And fourth, as noted in the previous chapter, the anti-statist, pro-assimilationist views of the American Jewish Committee and the American Council for Judaism, together with the solid impression, organizational skill, and "elite" membership of both, were fondly seen by the Department as representing a viable alternative to Zionism. Indeed, the Department saw these two organizations as a "rallying ground" for the presumably inchoate American Jewish masses in the grip of the Zionist chimera. Although ideas bruited about in the Department in 1942, like promoting an anti-Zionist popular front among Jews or using Rabbi Morris Lazaron as a conduit were dropped as too risky, the Department came to develop a special liaison with the Committee and the Council.[17]

Morris Waldman, New York Judge Joseph M. Proskauer, and Lessing Rosenwald were these two organizations' main contacts with the State Department. In the aftermath of the newly formed American Jewish Conference (first session, August–September 1943) and the secession therefrom by the American Jewish Committee when that Conference backed the Biltmore Program of May 1942, Waldman was a regular visitor, and "informant," to NEA and Breckinridge Long. Thus in January 1944 he spoke ominously of the Committee's fears of a "greatly increased" postwar anti-Semitic movement, of its ardent wish to put a "stop" to Zionist "agitations," and of its decision to start "a publicity campaign in opposition to the pro-Zionist cause." Moreover, he disclosed all sorts of interesting tidbits, such as the Committee's effort to gain control over the Zionized Jewish Telegraphic Agency, his resentment towards Nahum Goldmann ("an alien"), and his rather ridiculous chauvinism towards the first secretary of the British embassy (Isaiah Berlin) whom he called "an English Jew of eastern European origin... not regarded as a representative of the best elements among Jewry," and on and on.[18]

Proskauer and Rosenwald tried from time to time to operate at higher levels. On at least one occasion, Proskauer wrote a "dear Ed" letter to Undersecretary Stettinius, who had earlier "expressed bafflement at the disagreements in ideology between Dr. Wise and myself [Proskauer]." Rosenwald was also in communication with Stettinius, typically to protest Stephen Wise's alleged Zionist manipulations. Reciprocally, the Department on occasion looked to the Committee and the Council as Jewish lobbies to neutralize the pro-Zionist lobby in Congress.[19]

All in all, however, the value to the Department of Jewish anti-Zionists was as symbol of what American Jews might be and should be, and not (as the Committee and the Council imagined) as working allies of the Department, counterthrusting against the Zionists. The fact is that the Department, although feeling periodically "besieged" by Zionists and conveying that impression to gain sympathy, did not really need the aid and information of the Committee and the Council.

Still, one cannot overlook the fact that such Jewish anti-Zionists performed yeoman service, as it were, in battling Zionist views and in undermining public pro-Zionist sympathies. Thus they were warmly received by the Department, and indeed, there is evidence that the Department sought to use them, for example, to have the American Jewish Committee "walk out of the [American Jewish] Conference" in order to disrupt it. At the same time, the Committee and the Council represented American Zionists' major domestic threat of a nongovernmental, non-Arab nature. Injuring the Zionist cause at every opportunity, and thus in effect hurting the Jewish refugees, the two groups proved that Jewish unity was a myth. Their efforts highlighted the fact that the Arabs, who had no counterpart groups like the American Jewish Committee and the American Council for Judaism, were absolutely united on the Palestine question, notwithstanding their reputation for being utterly divided.[20]

Toward the Revisionists and their goal of a Jewish State on both sides of the Jordan, the contrast in the Department's attitude was considerable, although it should be noted that that attitude was not uniformly hostile. True, the Bergson group was consistently scorned as on the "lunatic fringe" by one and all in the Department. (It was also scorned by the militants in the ZOA and Jewish Agency as an ideologically unsound rival which sabotaged Zionist efforts to achieve Jewish solidarity.)[21] However, the older Revisionist group, the New Zionist Organization (NZO), was frequently treated by NEA and the Foreign Service legation in Cairo (where Agency and Revisionist Zionists often presented their policy positions) with the formal courtesy and surface interest accorded to any legitimate lobby. Its frequent representative in Washington, Benjamin Azkin, seemed also to have built up a certain rapport with officers like Loy Henderson, perhaps out of their strong mutual anticommunism.[22]

Moreover, NZO representatives were apparently "interesting," if only to converse with, because of their no-nonsense realpolitik which scorned the lofty moralism associated with Weizmann and Wise (moralism which Welles, for one, appreciated and which made Welles therefore probably the most hostile member of the Department toward the Revisionists). The Revisionists appealed straight out to national self-interest and presented themselves as outright allies and admirers of Western imperialism, including American oil interests. Once they had preferred the British, but by the middle of the war, it was the Americans—although Revisionists in Britain still hoped for dominion status for a Jewish Palestine within the empire. Jewish and American national interests in the region were thus presented as harmonious, with the Jews serving as an outpost of Western influence. As for Arab opposition, Revisionists held that the Arabs ought to be persuaded to accept a Jewish state or be suppressed immediately, while the Allies had large military forces in the region.[23]

However, by late 1945 general Jewish frustration and militant resistance were increasing in America and Palestine as a result of the hard-line anti-Zionism of the Bevin-Atlee Labour government. The Revisionists changed their position, too, and no longer saw salvation in a benign Western imperialism. If Britain did not relent, they threatened, the Jews would start major violence which the world would rue. As for NEA's pro-Arab line and its tendency to shunt off the Palestine problem to the new U.N. General Assembly, the New Zionist Organization expressed disappointment. Its representative, Azkin, sought to circumvent NEA by presenting Revisionism's theses to the Department's Europeanists, presumably more sensitive to great-power realpolitik and the refugee problem.[24]

From start to finish, however, these persuasions and threats were of no avail. The realpolitik of Revisionists, interesting as it was, particularly as counterpoint to the moralistic stance of mainstream Zionism, was seen by the Department as incongruous when juxtaposed with the Department's own realpolitik and aspirations in the Middle East.[25]

Toward the American Zionist Emergency Council, one of the major domestic bêtes noires of the Department during the war years, Departmental in-house reactions were hostile, though nuanced by shifting moods ranging from rage to boredom. Lest Arab good will and oil be endangered, the Department was indefatigable in seeking to blunt the influence of the AZEC and the principal membership group behind it, the ZOA.[26]

Thus the Department waged a long counteroffensive against the Wright-Compton and Taft-Wagner Resolutions. Largely the product of AZEC and ZOA initiative, and drafted in January 1944, these resolutions endorsed a Jewish commonwealth and open immigration and were timed to coincide with the White Paper's expiration in March 1944. The Department was similarly moved to object to and to dilute pro-Zionist party planks inspired by the AZEC and ZOA in the summer and fall of 1944, not to mention numerous other public occasions when, for example, a Jewish convention would seek a Presidential statement of greetings and endorsement of Jewish efforts in Palestine.[27]

In one sense, these frequent clashes between the Department and the AZEC had a fascinating quality of a game of wits, the central question being who could outfox whom. Each side knew that the other cultivated the ears and sought the blessings of Roosevelt and Truman, as well as of pivotal leaders in Congress, the media, and the British Cabinet. On lower and less prominent administrative levels, too, the struggle was constant and important. Several examples from all levels will make the point.

Beginning in 1942, the AZEC sought to publicize and politically capitalize on Walter C. Lowdermilk's recently finished book, *Palestine Report*. Lowdermilk, a distinguished conservationist with the Department of the Interior, had in effect endorsed the Jewish agricultural effort in Palestine as a model to the Arabs. In contrast, associates of NEA assiduously sought to suppress and discredit Lowdermilk's judgment as Zionist propaganda.[28]

In August 1943 New York Congressman Emmanuel Celler tore into the Department's complicity with Britain's "betrayal" of Palestine. He singled out Wallace Murray and Lt. Col. Harold Hoskins by name. "On the contrary," lied NEA in its draft response to Hull, the Department did not wish to silence Jewish agitation. "It had no such object. Its purpose was merely to invite cessation of public political discussion of a nature harmful to the war effort."[29]

In February 1944 Rabbi Silver cast doubt on the military-security thesis which, in various notes that month, the War Department's Henry Stimson, John McCloy, and General George Marshall had transmitted to the State Department as justification for a moratorium of decisions on Palestine. The State Department had used this "evidence" to induce Congress to table its pro-Zionist resolutions. Silver seemed to feel that if it had not been for State Department suasions, Stimson et al, would not have come forward with the military-security argument. This was an exaggeration. But the State Department exaggerated in the other direction, indeed, lied, claiming that the decision on the resolutions was a military one, pure and simple. Wrote Breckinridge Long, "I took it upon [myself] to deny that the Secretary of State had conferred with the Secretary of War prior to the issue by the Secretary of War of the letter he had sent to the Senate Committee in response to their communication."[30]

The following month, March 1944, Rabbis Silver and Wise appeared to outflank the Department by extracting from Roosevelt, for public pronouncement, the view that the United States had never given approval to the 1939 White Paper. The Department, with the President's assent, immediately sought to outflank the AZEC by giving the Arabs, as noted in the previous chapter, private assurances to the contrary.[31]

Moreover, each side, while circumventing and parrying, tried (unsuccessfully) to undermine the other's organizational structure. The Department kept close watch on the composition, finances, public relations, and all legal aspects of the AZEC and ZOA and their affiliates, like the American Palestine Committee, a pro-Zionist Christian group. Its hope was to find evidence requiring the AZEC to register as a foreign agent, with all the restraints against lobbying which that status implied. Concurrently, the AZEC was desirous of pressuring the Secretary of State to get rid of ancient obstacles like Wallace Murray and to centralize affairs relative to Jews and Palestine in an Office or Division outside the Arabist NEA.[32]

By and large, the Department bested the AZEC in close combat, at least up to 1945. Quite apart from the fact that it had the Arab world and the Department of War on its side, in terms of the game of wits the Department was superior to the AZEC. As elsewhere noted, the Department's "weapons" against competing federal departments, Congress, and the British were its pertinacity and manipulativeness. As such, it was expert at hedging, delaying, mollifying, promising, deceiving the Zionists with one hand while pressing and converting the White House and Congress away from the Zionist "fantasy" with the other.

True, the AZEC *seemed* to be increasingly militant and a "champion" against Departmental pettyfoggers, in the context of New York City newspaper headlines. But in direct confrontations with the Department, behind closed doors, it *always* lost the argument, it always had the starch taken out of it; yet it frequently went away optimistically, thinking it had won points. Furthermore, Zionist delegations were often incredibly naive, open, garrulous, gossipy about their quarrels with rivals within and without the AZEC and Jewish Agency. There was little internal discipline, not to say common sense. The Waldmans of the American Jewish Committee and the Rosenwalds of the American Council for Judaism were thus not the only ones, although they were the most defamatory, to talk of other Zionists behind their backs.

The Department, it is a certainty, learned far more about Zionist strategy, lack of strategy, and general backroom information than the Zionists learned about the Department. The Zionists, unlike the Department, naively used words to disclose, not hide, their thinking; and often they replied like eager schoolboys when, after having traveled to London, etc., they were asked by NEA to discuss their travels, whom they saw, and so forth. No Zionist leader was free of these oral compulsions, neither the European-bred sophisticates like Weizmann nor the American-bred militants like Silver—though spokesmen like Rabbi Wise and Nahum Goldmann were more frequently pried open or duped than Silver, the Political Department of the Agency, or (probably least of all), Emmanuel Neumann.[33]

Apart from such personal failings, there was another reason why Zionist leaders were put off their guard. Easy access to the Department, conversational tones, the drawing-room manner, the veneer of respectability and amicable differences of viewpoint deconditioned them from plumbing the depths of the Department's unalterable hostility to their position. They felt themselves to be among adversaries, not enemies, when meetings were held with the Department. They behaved therefore much as if they were a legitimate government-in-exile engaged in diplomatic intercourse, trading views, and so forth. After all, Zionist leaders generally regarded themselves as "establishment" types, functioning both as a provisional government and as a centrist, moderate Zionist grouping, statistically and spiritually representative of mainstream Jewry.

The Department *never* saw things that way. Going back to the pre-World War I period, its view, as noted repeatedly, was that political Zionism was and remained an extremism, a chimera. Therefore its espousers were extremists—hard extremists or soft extremists, but extremists nonetheless, including men like Weizmann, Wise, and Goldmann.

True, these latter were gentlemen easier to talk with, from the Department's view, than rude types like Silver, Neumann, and Ben-Gurion. True, Hull, Welles, and Berle did not actually label Weizmann and Wise as extremists. True, too, "moderates" like Weizmann and Goldmann made the point to their critics, then and subsequently, that their old-school approach was less alienating and more productive than the confrontation approach of the militants. As such, they, and presumably not the militants, were able to extract from the Department and/or the Foreign Office a concession here for a Jewish refugee ship, an extension there of White Paper quotas.[34]

Nonetheless, the moderates' advantage was in overview outweighed by the disadvantage they set themselves up for, namely, a continuous squirrel cage of diplomatic consultations and conversations with the Department, the only purpose of which, from the Department's view, was to delay and fend off, in short to freeze the 1939 White Paper policy as the indefinite policy for Palestine. Second, in terms of the mindset of NEA and the Department generally (despite Hull, Welles, and Berle), the gentlemanly qualities of Weizmann et al, did not change their spots, that is, their identity as political extremists. Third, the negativeness of that identity was always reinforced in the eyes of the Department because of the sordid associations of the AZEC with "dual loyalty" and "ethnic politics." In sum, to the Department the basic difference between Wise and Weizmann on one side, and Silver and Ben-Gurion on the other, was tactical: the former were believed willing to proceed step by step toward a Jewish commonwealth or state, the latter openly declared for it now.

In 1945, however, the Zionists became a little less divided and, in consequence, smarter. In the United States and Palestine the tendency towards Revisionist thinking brought the Revisionists back into the World Zionist Organization. In Washington this meant that representatives of the NZO and ZOA met jointly with the Department of State.

This new solidarity was put to use even by Zionists who emotionally were very anti-Revisionist. Thus Nahum Goldmann employed a stalking-horse tactic—which had been begging to be used before but rarely had been. Instead of trying to curry favor, as in the past, by defaming opponents, particularly Revisionists, Goldmann now said that if the Department was not more forthcoming to moderates like himself, then it would soon have to deal with a new, more hard-line Zionist leadership as represented by Rabbi Silver.[35]

The ultimatum implicit in a stalking-horse tactic was made more explicit under the AZEC leadership of Silver and Emmanuel Neumann. A somewhat dramatic instance was Neumann's threat to Acting Secretary Acheson in September 1945 that American Jewish resentment against British policy in Palestine might well translate itself into opposition to American financial assistance to Britain. ("The five million Jews of America, of whom 95% are warm supporters of our cause, are not going to stand for it.")

How did the Department react? According to Rabbi Silver's version, Acheson was "visibly irritated"; and the new director of the Office of Eastern and African Affairs, Loy Henderson, went out of his way later to smooth down the Zionists' ruffled feathers. According to Henderson's version of the same conversation among Acheson, Neumann, Silver, and himself, there is no mention of Acheson's irritation, except that Acheson was said to have implicitly counterthreatened that Zionist interference relative to Britain would generate dual loyalty charges ("interference... would be unfair to the millions of loyal, patriotic Jews in the United States"). Clearly by this date, the perennial AZEC-Department struggle was escalating, with the Zionists showing themselves less "innocent," though not necessarily more able, than previously.[36]

Withal, the Department continued in 1945 to view the AZEC basically as a roaring mouse. True, the Department took note of the AZEC's increasing membership base and militancy and of the fact that since the American Jewish Conference of 1943, American Jewish organizations had swung over to support the Biltmore Program. On a more personal level, it was true, too, that the Zionists "succeeded" in giving the Department an inordinate share of gray hairs and ulcers. For all that, NEA always took comfort in belittling the AZEC and ZOA as unrepresentative of Jewry, and their growth as artificially achieved. Like Stalin and his putative question, "How many divisions has the Pope?" the Department was always size-conscious. On that basis, the Yishuv relative to the Arab world, and the AZEC and ZOA relative to American Jewry, were distinct minorities; therefore, their bark was inherently bigger than their bite.[37]

This was an interpretive error, sincerely and obstinately held by the Department. The error suggests one reason why the Zionists competed more successfully with the Department in 1945, and thereafter, in the game of influence-peddling than they had previously. For in treating American Zionist pronouncements as "so much propaganda," the Department underestimated the real gains, quantitative and qualitative, and particularly the rapidly intensified mood of previously apathetic American Jews. This perceptual lag, or "cognitive dysfunction," was also transmitted to the British Foreign Office by the Department. However, the British were poorly served thereby. If the British had been more realistically apprized, possibly they would have appeased, or repressed, the Jews more than they did.

As for the efficacy of Zionist ultimata, there is no hard wartime evidence that these were either productive or counterproductive. The Department's actual (as opposed to verbal) reaction could not be tested, since, for example, Zionists did not go through with their intimation that they might spearhead an effort to block loans to Britain. This intimation had been an offshoot of the Revisionist tendency within the AZEC; but that tendency never became a majority tendency, and it is probable, too, that Acheson's veiled warning of anti-Semitic backlash weakened that Revisionist tendency further. Also, Jews generally did not want to wage war against Britain: they only wanted to make it relent in Palestine. Trying to block loans would have been in the category of economic warfare. In any case, what can be said is that the earlier old-school approach of Weizmann and Wise definitely did not earn political Zionism more Departmental prestige or broad achievement, even if that approach was less personally antagonistic than the confrontationist approach which prevailed by the autumn of 1945.

DEPARTMENTAL RELATIONS WITH THE DEPARTMENT OF WAR, THE WHITE HOUSE, AND CONGRESS

In July 1943 the Department finally seemed on the verge of arranging a joint Anglo-American statement that no decision on Palestine would be made until the end of the war. Welles had felt the statement's implication of wait-and-see was unsound in principle, but Roosevelt, Hull, and Eden thought otherwise. Yet although the path was clear for issuing the statement, Hull, ever prudent and anxious over possible personal attacks, wanted the full weight of the War Department on his side. He therefore sought its explicit approval of the thesis that the military security of the Middle East was the primary reason for the proposed statement.[38]

The Department of War was for the most part agreeable. But at the last minute Secretary of War Henry Stimson, hitherto uninvolved, returned to Washington and after studying the issue, disagreed. While an Anglo-American statement might have political justification, he said, it did not, given the relatively stable situation in the Middle East, have a military justification. Feeling undermined, Hull in early August voided the proposed statement, to the equal disappointment of Eden. Though requested by both Hull and Eden to reassess his view, Stimson in September reaffirmed his August decision.[39]

However, in the period February–March 1944, Stimson's view changed. A deterioration of the war offensive in Italy, delicate negotiations for a Saudi pipeline, and the anxious wish of the military that there be no disturbing distractions during the final preparations for the Normandy invasion persuaded him to regard the military security of the Middle East as vulnerable. This view, in the form of several letters, was specifically directed this time not toward any Anglo-American statement, but against the then pending Wright-Compton, Taft-Wagner Resolutions, which had been put before the House and Senate between January 28 and February 2. As noted, besides protesting the 1939 White Paper, the spirit and letter of these resolutions went further than any prior Congressional statement toward an American pro-Zionist commitment. As such, they drew the full fire of Arab hostility and FSO alarm and hence were perceived by the Executive Branch as a threat to the regional peace.[40]

Indeed, it should be recalled that the War Department, as shown in

Chapter 12 above, was at this time more activist in the Middle East than before or after, the object being to secure Saudi oil and air rights for the war effort. In fact, the War Department pressed the State Department to be more active in impeding the resolutions. Assistant Secretary of War John McCloy argued that even without military considerations, political considerations alone warranted the State Department's taking a position against the resolutions.[41]

The State Department, not used to being considered a laggard in such matters and still miffed over Stimson's undercutting the proposed joint statement of the previous August, expressed resentment. Murray noted that since military, not political, considerations were supposed to be the really crucial factor, then the administration's wish to squash the Congressional resolutions simply ought to be presented on that basis.[42]

The question remained, however, as to method. Roosevelt and the Department of State wanted to make public Stimson's letter of 17 February 1944, to Senator Tom Connally, chairman of the Senate Foreign Relations Committee. General Marshall of the Joint Chiefs of Staff preferred to see if the administration could not first kill the resolutions in executive session with Connally's committee and Sol Bloom's counterpart committee, the House Foreign Affairs Committee. Stimson seemed open to either tactic. Clearly, all sides were trying to pass the buck of responsibility, in anticipation of Congressional and Zionist protest. In any case, Marshall's suggestion was tried, and worked, thanks chiefly to Breckinridge Long's able, low-key presentations of how Congressional pro-Zionism jeopardized America's prize of Saudi oil.[43]

As the resolutions were dying in committee, the Department of State, riding the new momentum, also tried to reinterest the President in issuing the July 1943 Anglo-American joint statement. That effort failed, however. Roosevelt "did not wish this matter raised at this time. He reiterated his position that he considers the problem now as entirely a military one."[44]

It is worth noting at this point that the Departments of State and War did not have to work hard to get Congress on their side. In general, the wartime Congress was ignorant of the fine points of foreign affairs and was still content to be led to the trough by the Executive Branch—though by 1945 bottled up frustrations would begin leaking out. In the case of the Middle East and Palestine, Congress's pro-Zionism was often easily scaled down by fears fanned by the State Department that not only might oil and prestige be lost, but unwanted military responsibilities might be gained. Thus Sol Bloom, *before* Stimson's first "veto" of 5 August 1943, was "in full accord with the proposed Anglo-American statement and even suggested that it should be strengthened." Tom Connally did not require any arm-twisting either.[45]

In October 1944, Stimson once more rocked the boat. As presumably the military-security status of the Middle East no longer warranted continued opposition to the Congressional resolutions, Stimson withdrew his ban. Coming at the time of an election campaign and the ZOA's 47th annual convention (garnished with the necessary Senatorial and Presidential salutations), his repeal resulted in new waves of Arab protest and Departmental worry, the latter especially in connection with possible reprisals by Ibn Saud.[46]

Congress for its part seemed more ardently pro-Zionist than ever. While election politics certainly were a factor, a widespread and genuine, if often unsophisticated, Congressional belief in the essential rightness of the Zionist thesis was an at least equally important factor. Many Congressmen, moreover, represented states with no "Jewish vote" to speak of. Furthermore, each one who identified as a friend of Zionism often had a different set of personal reasons. While this is not the place for detail, it is worth noting the reasoning of notable Congressmen. William Borah leaned toward pro-Zionism because he was anti-British and did not want Jewish refugees immigrating to America; Hamilton Fish, because he hated appeasement and was an admirer of Churchill, the pro-Zionist and British imperialist; Robert Taft, because he was anti-British, anti-Roosevelt, and a friend of fellow Ohioian Rabbi Silver; Henry Wallace, because he was an agrarian populist who admired the Yishuv's kibbutzim; and Robert Wagner because he saw in Zionism a reflection of his own liberalism and internationalism.[47]

In November 1944 the Wright-Compton Resolution was reintroduced in the House by Bloom (Representative from New York City), who was under much constituency pressure; it passed. However, the State Department managed to get Connally's committee to table in the Senate the Taft-Wagner Resolution, while Roosevelt persuaded Senator Wagner to go along with deferral. The Department's argument consisted of its previous caveats, with newly added references to rising Soviet interests in the Middle East. Roosevelt spoke of his fear of an Arab "massacre" of the Jews, although another reason he wanted the resolutions tabled was that he felt their passage might restrict him at the upcoming Yalta Conference.[48]

It is noteworthy, too, that the Zionists were divided over the wisdom of pushing the resolutions. Moderates like Wise and Goldmann were opposed in part because of what they considered the poor timing and poor formulation of the resolutions. However, Silver was in favor. Knowing of this split beforehand, as a result of anti-Silver communications and remarks by Wise and Goldmann, the President and the Department were inspired to press their opposition all the more. In any case, the final results seemed desirable to the Department on all counts: the resolutions were cancelled; Silver, who had disregarded an AZEC decision to defer the struggle for passage, resigned his leadership in the ZOA and AZEC;

and there was very little outcry against the Department from the Zionist camp.[49]

Even so, when Roosevelt readied himself for Yalta, both the Zionists and the Department moved forward to get the President's ear. It seemed the last cards were being played, and the multi-hued context of events had true drama: the end of the terrible war was in sight; Europe's Jews were still being daily cremated en masse; Arab and Jewish pressures were mounting ever higher; and the aged American leader was leaving for a final wartime summit conference with Churchill, pro-Zionist but the head of a weakened empire, and the inscrutable Stalin, anti-Semitic and anti-Western by reputation, yet sometimes affectionately known among his summit confrères as Uncle Joe.[50]

Relative to Palestine, the results at Yalta were inconclusive, given the President's scattered and informal discussions on the matter. This was less the case following his talks with Ibn Saud. Conjecture was hence rife as to the impact of the Saudi monarch's view, and in March–April 1945, literally up to 12 April, the day Roosevelt died, old pressures from the Department, the Arabs, the AZEC, and Congress swirled about, seeking the President's yea or nay on the conjecture. The President reacted by speaking with a forked tongue. In a talk with Colonel Hoskins on 5 March, Roosevelt expressed full agreement with the view that, Zionist denials notwithstanding, given the numbers in the Arab world and the limited capacity of Palestine's land, Palestine as a Jewish state "could be installed and maintained only by force." He also still seemed interested in the idea of Palestine as a special international trusteeship of the U.N. and of Christianity, Islam, and Judaism. Yet on 16 March, in conversation with Stephen Wise, Roosevelt reendorsed unrestricted immigration to Palestine and a future Zionist state.[51]

Gnashing its teeth, the Department in turn reacted as usual by sending out statements to FSOs, minimizing the endorsement and expressing reassurances. More than this, the Department now redoubled its efforts to extract once and for all from the President a stronger commitment to the Arabs. It ardently wished to cease, in a phrase of the period, carrying water on two shoulders, with one Palestine policy for the Jews, another for the Arabs.[52]

Indeed, it definitely seems that the Department took advantage of Roosevelt's state of illness to push its point. On 5 April, the most assuring of all "Great and Good Friend" letters was sent to Ibn Saud over Roosevelt's signature, and similar communications were transmitted directly to all other Arab heads of state. Meantime, Assistant Secretary James Dunn worked on a draft of the *first* public declaration-to-be of such assurances. An affirmation that American policy on Palestine was strictly based on full consultation with both Arabs and Jews was to be made part of a Presidential speech on the occasion of the Iraqi Regent's upcoming visit to Washington. However, the President's death intervened before Dunn's proposals reached the White House.[53]

Nonetheless, the Department continued filling the vacuum of Presidential initiative, a vacuum which in overview would extend roughly from February to October 1945, coterminous with Roosevelt's increasingly ill state of health and the conclusion of Truman's novitiate as President. April was the high point of Departmental initiative; and much as it had pressed Roosevelt in the days before his death, so the Department that month made sure to get Truman's ear immediately after he took office. The object was to head off the Zionists and maintain the pro-Arab momentum since the Roosevelt-Ibn Saud meeting in February.

Thus, Acting Secretary Joseph Grew persuaded the new President, to the latter's later embarrassment, to sign and authorize the sending of letters "from the late President Roosevelt" to Arab heads of state, re-affirming the full consultation thesis. Similarly, and as described in Chapter 9 above, when the Iraqi Regent and Nuri Said finally made their deferred Washington visit in May–June 1945, the Department continued the momentum. Though the idea of a Presidential public statement on Palestine was put aside, from the character of the proceedings it seemed perfectly clear to the participants that the administration would not make any move on Palestine without first consulting its Iraqi friends. This assumption inhered in the fact that during the visit, the Department and Truman focused on increasing bilateral relations (diplomatic, commercial, and oil) and on endorsing the newly formed Arab League. (From Truman's point of view, all this camaraderie with the Iraqis was also meant to serve as a signal to the Soviet Union not to encroach on Iraq.)[54]

Still, as postwar events would show in larger relief, Truman did not completely accept the Department's Palestine position. While a detailed examination of the nexus between and among Truman, the Departments of State and War, and Congress is outside this chapter's province, it should be noted that with respect to the Jewish state idea, Truman, in 1945 and subsequently, tilted back, as it were, to Roosevelt's earlier position of one Palestine policy for the Jews, another for the Arabs. However, on the specific topic of immigration to Palestine, Truman was from the start more positive than Roosevelt. Not that Roosevelt was less sensitive to the Jewish refugee problem as such, or that Truman ever favored unrestricted immigration to Palestine—but Truman did feel that Palestine was the first, not last, logical refuge for at least a quantum of the refugees.

It may be said that his "refugee Zionism" was partly the result of his "role" as Congressman and sympathetic average American citizen, while his nonendorsement of political Zionism was partly the product of his newer "role" as Commander-in-Chief and Chief Executive (who, it ought to be added, deferred to State Department policy positions far more than his predecessor—despite occasional remarks about the Department's "striped-pants boys"). In any event, Truman's effort to steer the proverbial even-handed middle course between pro- and anti-Zionist pressures differed in both method and result from Roosevelt's like effort. An analysis of how Truman handled the postwar Jewish Displaced Person problem in the second half of 1945 will illustrate the point.

On the strength of reports on that problem (chiefly the Earl Harrison Report of September) and despite *total* Departmental disapproval on all levels, including several resignations, Truman was convinced that 100,000 refugees should be admitted forthwith to Palestine on a humanitarian basis. He saw the refugees principally as suffering people who deserved and wanted to go to a new homeland, rather than, as in the Department's view, as mere numbers whose addition to the Yishuv would but enhance Zionism's overweening political ambitions. When the Department in reproof showed him Roosevelt's, and his own, pledges to Ibn Saud, et al., to have consultations on Palestine, Truman proved as slippery as the Department. He had his first appointed Secretary of State, James Byrnes, reply that there had been plenty of consultations, and in any case, having consultations with the Arabs did not necessarily mean reaching agreement with them.

Furthermore, in Truman's retrospective words, "to assure the Arabs that they would be consulted was by no means inconsistent with my generally sympathetic attitude towards Jewish aspirations." He also insisted that his stand on the refugees was neither discontinuous with Roosevelt's nor hostile to the Arabs. As for the charge of both the Department and the Foreign Office that it was "irresponsible" of him to call for immigration while insisting that the United States abstain from military commitments, Truman felt this was a distorted charge, especially since the U.N. Organization would probably be the ultimate arbiter and enforcer of a Palestine settlement.[55]

Still, all the counterpressures from the Department, the British, and the Arabs added up. Although they did not make him repudiate his refugee Zionism, they did force him to "beware" of political Zionism more than he was accustomed to. For example, in November 1945 he opposed Congress's third (and finally successful) effort to pass the 1944 Wright-Compton, Taft-Wagner Resolutions (as a concurrent, not joint, resolution, therefore not requiring the President's signature). Conversely, however, it is significant to note that as a result of Truman's basic lack of enthusiasm for the Arab position on Palestine, the Department and its FSOs were "cued" more so than under Roosevelt to restrain themselves in extending personal assurances and interpretations of Congressional pro-Zionism.[56]

Yet for all these nuances, it was probably Truman's great-power considerations, as will be noted below, which governed his restraint toward political Zionism. Probably most important was his Cold War anxiety that communist Russia would exploit anti-Zionist and potentially anti-American Arab nationalism—even as in Roosevelt's case, the governing factor in overview was probably the fear of alienating Ibn Saud, his oil, and more generally, the good will of the Moslem world.

DEPARTMENTAL VIEWS OF BRITISH POLICIES ON PALESTINE AND POSTWAR PLANS

As noted, the impacts of TORCH and of Saudi oil had by the end of 1942 convinced the Department of what it already knew intellectually— that it had a grand future in the Middle East, and that it was neither wise nor necessary to hinge too closely American policy to British policy—not only in areas like Egypt or Saudi Arabia, where the Department wanted "in," but even in Palestine, where it most definitely did not want in. In Palestine, the Department wanted the British to deal with the Jews more rigorously and vigorously, so that Palestine would not mar America's future in the Arab world. It thus became restive because of Britain's continued vagueness on the degree of its commitment to the 1939 White Paper. Britain was even more vague on its long-run plans for Palestine. The Department, as noted, was also becoming hostile to the British idea of bringing Ibn Saud in as an arbiter of the Jewish-Arab problem.

In 1942 and in the remaining war years, divergencies beneath the Anglo-American alliance were further widened by periodic reports from FSOs that British personnel, usually of the lower echelons, were exaggerating America's pro-Zionism to the Arabs and indeed goading the Arabs into anti-American pronouncements. In other ways, too, the Foreign Service added to the acrimony, if only by reporting that the British were inept and hated in Egypt, were trying to make deals with France in the Levant, and were trying to pull the wool over American eyes via MESC. Finally, at the extremities, as it were, of the Department's mind set were two large thoughts which added to the Department's eagerness and anxiousness over Palestine: one, that the United States after TORCH had become, willed or not, a "great Moslem power"; and two, that if it were not heedful, the United States might unleash a massive Islamic "holy war" over Palestine.[57]

However, there was one centripetal force which outweighed all these centrifugal factors and which brought the Department and the Foreign Office to a new shared position by mid-1943. That was the Zionist pressure on both of them (stepped up as a result of reports on the Final Solution). That pressure persuaded each that unless the common Zionist menace was voided, *neither* Britain's postwar ambitions of retrenchment in the region *nor* America's competitive bid, would be achieved.

Unlike Saudi Arabia, where one power's loss was the other's gain, Palestine increasingly seemed to present a no-win proposition. True, in December 1942, in connection to a proposed British-Saudi-Zionist deal, NEA's Murray, as noted, had felt that Britain's failure in repressing political Zionism would hurt British, but not American, prestige in the Arab world. But by 1943 this thesis no longer seemed valid to NEA. The Department as a whole now believed that in Arab eyes British softness on Zionism was and would be blamed on America's softness toward American Zionist agitation. Yet to reverse this trend and become hard on Zionism, the Department had to be discreet, since British severity toward Zionism would draw the thunder of the AZEC and Congress not only down on Britain but also down on the Department for "appeasing" Britain.

Out of this common cold war against Zionism, the Department and the Foreign Office pressed (unsuccessfully), as seen in the previous section, President Roosevelt and War Secretary Stimson for approval of a joint Anglo-American statement. As also seen, Hull, to sweeten the pill and cover his flanks from the Zionists, asked the Foreign Office in December 1943 to extend the quota provisions of the White Paper, since wartime conditions had prevented the filling of the allowed quotas. (The F.O. had essentially already decided to keep open after 31 March 1944, the some 20,000 available admission spaces.) When in April 1944 the London (Stettinius) Mission began and a delegation from the Department and NEA convened with counterparts of the Foreign Office and its Eastern Department, it was logical, all things considered, to make Palestine the first and (with Saudi Arabia) the most extensively discussed item on their Middle East agenda.

The London Mission was probably the high point of Departmental-Foreign Office harmony of view on Palestine, especially since the F.O. finally seemed to cut through its habitual vagueness on policy and planning, which pleased the Department. The Foreign Office noted that beyond its intention to continue the White Paper restrictions, it saw a long-run solution for Palestine in the form of a binational state, with the Jews a permanent minority. Although it would have certain "autonomous canton" features, the state would not be sovereign, would be under a continued British mandate, and would also have future economic (not political) ties with an Arab regional federation. Partition, though popular in some British quarters, the Foreign Office considered undesirable.[58]

As for the Department's proposal that they should now revive their 1943 joint statement draft (that no decision would be made on Palestine until the end of the war), the Foreign Office felt that, unlike the previous year, there was no longer an urgency for it. The British felt that an explosion in Palestine affecting military security or deflecting troops was unlikely—so long as there were no American Jewish agitations to get Congress, and the Arabs, embroiled. The F.O. stated that it, and the Colonial Office and British military authorities, too, preferred that the Department hold the draft in abeyance, albeit in a state of readiness.[59]

In related matters, the Foreign Office denied that it had in any fashion goaded the Arabs into anti-Americanism, and indeed, in subsequent months the F.O. seemed on occasion to go out of its way to prove its cooperativeness on that count. For its part, the Department desired to stitch together its own postwar plans on Palestine with those of the Foreign Office. After the Mission was concluded, planners William Yale and Philip Ireland were especially keen on that idea, hoping that their elaborations would guide the British on the right path. The sooner policy integration was done, the better, they argued, as the Zionists could be expected to recommence their pressures when they sensed the moment in the war's final course most propitious to their cause. Murray and key planner Isaiah Bowman agreed. However, others disagreed; NEA's George Merriam expressed the fear that likely leaks to the Zionists, plus British indifference to any plans on a technical, nonpolicy level, would militate against the utility of transmitting them to the Foreign Office. Withal, over the ensuing months the traditional informal exchanges of views would bring the substance of the Department's plans to the Foreign Office's attention.[60]

In view of these considerations, it is appropriate at this juncture to take note of what these Departmental postwar plans for Palestine were. At intervals from September 1942 to June 1943, the Political, Territorial, and Security Technical subcommittees of the postwar planning apparatus held both separate and overlapping formal discussions on Palestine. The Security Technical subcommittee contended that the mandate system was obsolescent in the light of Atlantic Charter principles. Yet it was aware that termination of the system would do harm to America's British ally. The subcommittee thus proposed the compromise of putting Palestine under an international administration. This presumably would both safeguard British security interests while relieving Britain of the burden of the mandate. British troops would be specially contained, on the model of the Canal Zone enclave. The Territorial subcommittee proposed a binational state, while the Political subcommittee suggested that Palestine be an independent state under a special if temporary U.N. trusteeship, unaffiliated with an Arab union. The United States, Britain, Turkey, and several other regional states would constitute the trusteeship council. All previous pledges (Balfour Declaration, etc.) were to be superseded by this arrangement.[61]

While the proposed American commitment to council membership was, in a sense, a "first" for post-isolationist America and denoted a heightened

sense of responsibility to postwar collective security, it also meant that
the planners increasingly felt that only direct American intervention
would thwart political Zionism. Force, it was intimated, might be necessary to use against the Jews, not only to placate the Arabs, but also to
prevent the repugnant possibility that American and British troops would
become committed to defending the Jews and to fighting the Arabs, if a
Jewish state were allowed in the first place.[62]

After this round of discussions in the spring of 1943, William Yale, of
the planners' Palestine desk, made a number of studies relative to immigration, economic absorption, industry, agriculture, and alternate political settlements. As noted in Chapter 4 above, his statistics were usually
based on royal commission reports of the 1930s, his analysis was semi-
Marxist and populist, his tone was ever Catonian. Hypersensitive to
Zionist "propaganda," Yale had long before conditioned himself to react
completely in the opposite direction. If the Zionists spoke of light, Yale
only saw shadow. The problem was that in supposedly redressing the
balance, he had developed an extraordinary tunnel vision that prevented
him from seeing things *except* in shadow. To Yale, Zionist attempts to
modernize and industrialize Palestine produced only negative results:
"Jewish discrimination against Arab workers . . . [and] the lowering of
wages following large-scale Jewish immigration." Periods of prosperity
have been "of an ephemeral nature"; moreover, Egypt and Syria "must
be considered industrial competitors of Palestine." Or,

the state of New Hampshire, with all its water power, had in 1939 only some
50,000 wage earners, with some 235,000 kilowatts of hydro-electric capacity,
while Palestine did not have, though it would soon get, some 120,000 kilowatts,
and yet the Zionists were talking of a minimum of 150,000 workers.

As for other interpreters, like the soil conservationist Lowdermilk, "He
deals with the problem of Palestine ideologically, not scientifically. He is
a protagonist of Zionism, not an impartial student of a complex political
and social problem."[63]

Similarly, Yale reduced all of Palestine's social and political dimensions
to his narrow, putatively scientific prism. Immigration and a Jewish army,
no matter how modest a particular proposal was, were all disguises, "since
the aims of the official Zionists closely resemble those of the Revisionists."
As for the demands of Palestinian Arabs, it was as if Yale had never
heard of the fanatical Grand Mufti of Jerusalem and his influence. The
Arabs, he noted, were less demanding and easier to deal with because
they were but concerned with moral not political issues, namely, the
stoppage of Jewish immigration and unjust takeover. "It may be anticipated that the Arabs will be reconciled with any settlement which assures
them of protection against the political aims of the Zionists."[64]

Yale's "preferred solution" was to make Palestine an international territory, with communal autonomy and limited Jewish immigration, contingent on the prior needs and capacity of both Jewish and Arab communities. The U.N. should administer Palestine as a trusteeship and should handle immigration and foreign affairs. A binational state should be the long-term goal—though unlike the Magnes-Ihudist plan, binationalism should come after, not before, full communal social-economic reconciliation.

As for other possible solutions, they were all deemed counterproductive. Partition to Yale was even more impractical than it had been to the Woodhead Commission in 1938. It would only make matters worse, he said, and if the British were reviving it, it was for "political expediency" alone. Exclusive statehood, whether Arab or Jewish, was also folly. Palestine's special status made it ineligible for becoming an independent Arab state or an integral part of an Arab federation; whereas the perniciousness of Zionist ideology, in addition to Jewish military defenselessness and the general spectre of violence, spoke against the Jewish state idea.[65]

By August–September 1943, all such alternative solutions, research studies, and subcommittee discussions were synthesized into a series of "H–Policy Summaries" which in turn were subject to new discussions, in the period January–April 1944, by the Inter-Divisional Area Committee on Arab Countries (chiefly officers from NEA and the planning Division of Territorial Studies). For the most part, the Area Committee affirmed or extended the planners' lines of direction.

In the economic sphere, the Area Committee added a preference for large-scale projects, under U.N. control, to benefit both communities in Palestine: to wit, a possible Tennessee Valley Authority (TVA) scheme for the Jordan River valley—a scheme that had been often proposed by public figures, particularly Yale's "adversary," the conservationist Lowdermilk. On immigration, the Committee opted for limited immigration, the presumed golden mean between cessation of immigration, maintenance of the White Paper, and unlimited immigration. However, limited immigration would be contingent, inter alia, on the prior cessation of all illegal Jewish immigration and on prior assurances to the Arabs. The Committee opted for a similar intermediate position with regard to future land transfers.[66]

In one important respect, the Area Committee was discontinuous with earlier planning. In its political "preferred solution," it opted not for Yale's two-phased trusteeship-binational-state, but for solution "B": Palestine as "An International Territory With a Board of Overseers Representing the Three World Religions With Interests in Palestine and With Arab and Jewish National Communal Governments Under a Trusteeship." Though Yale and Wallace Murray were not in favor, it appears that

NEA's Merriam and the rest of the Area Committee were. The main reason for the majority view seems to have been that the Committee took its cue from the fact that both Undersecretary Stettinius and President Roosevelt liked the aura, the symbolism, and the presumed utility of having representatives of the Moslem, Jewish, and Christian faiths oversee Palestine. Significant, too, as an influence was the current, and strong, Vatican objections to Zionism.[67]

It is noteworthy that for "eastern Palestine," that is, Transjordan, the Department also made plans in the period March–June 1944, though much less so than for western Palestine. One reason for the new attention was the surmise that the status quo of Amman would change after the war, given the fact that during 1943–1944 the British had implicitly promised to grant Transjordan postwar independence. In turn, that change would allow the Hashemite Emir Abdullah to rule as king and become a more powerful regional figure than he had been. Another reason for attention was the assumed strategic importance of the country to Britain and the United States, notably its air and motor routes, and the potential base of Aqaba. Aqaba would also be a matter of concern "in case of attacks on Transjordan from Arabia." Third, the interest of adjacent states, the planners assumed, would require Washington to take a position on Transjordan, even though such a position was actually contingent on American positions taken previously toward the adjacent states.[68]

Initially, Yale and the Division of Territorial Studies viewed as the most desirable solution alternate "A": Transjordan as an "Independent Territory Under a Security Arrangement with the [U.N.] International Organization." Subsequently, however, a more conservative note was sounded. "A" was deemed too risky; it would probably incite Ibn Saud's anti-Hashemite wrath and might prove detrimental to British strategic and American oil-pipeline interests. A new solution, "C," was presented: Transjordan as a "Modified Form of the Status Quo." According to its terms, London would continue as trustee, and, the planners' general condemnation of the mandate system notwithstanding, the British mandatory administration would continue. While not formally endorsed, the reception to "C" was positive, and it remained uncontested in the Department for the remainder of the war.[69]

These, then, were the Department's more or less completed long-run preferences on Palestine and Transjordan at the time the Department met with the Foreign Office in London, April 1944. Except for the Department's desire to use the term "trusteeship" instead of "mandate," and except for its Overseers-of-three-religions thesis, the Department had largely the same type of plans for Palestine as did the Foreign Office. In Bowman's phrase, between the two sides was "remarkable parallelism of thought." (The parallelism increased when by year's end the Overseers thesis was dropped by the Department in favor of the thesis of international trusteeship and binational state.)[70]

When NEA delegates returned to Washington in May 1944, however, their belief that Palestine was under control was strained by some three trends, already cited: one, increased Jewish activism and terrorism in Palestine; another, increased tension in America, catalyzed by the 1944 election campaign's pro-Zionist pledges and by Stimson's surprise withdrawal in October of his earlier "veto" over the Wright-Compton, Taft-Wagner Resolutions; and another, increased Soviet interests in and diplomatic demarches to all the countries in the eastern Mediterranean.

Blocking the resolutions was the Department's immediate duty. Toward this end Stettinius, after having been tutored by Murray, parleyed in executive session with Congress. There he traded off the lost card of Stimson's veto, which had been based on arguments of "military security" and the "war effort," for the new card of potential Soviet "encroachment." Congress, duly impressed, shelved the resolutions a second time.[71]

A second duty was to persuade the President at the forthcoming Yalta Conference to adopt, in Murray's phrase, a "more positive policy" on Palestine than the "preventive policy" thusfar used. Translated, this meant that the Department wanted Roosevelt to take a more definite position against political Zionism and to push Britain to follow suit. As noted in Chapter 4 above, it also meant the Department wanted to "use" the facts of Soviet interest in the Middle East and of Stalin's anti-Zionism. The Department did not wish to alarm Britain with the facts of Soviet interest (as Murray and Stettinius *did* wish, in the case of Congress and the resolutions); but on the contrary, the Department wished to persuade Britain of the wisdom of *co-opting* Moscow into an Anglo-American-Soviet diplomatic "front" opposed to political Zionism. All in all, Roosevelt seemed vaguely agreeable. However, his superficiality on Palestine at Yalta militated against the Department's initiative. Furthermore, the British were against any plan which would ease Moscow's entrance into the region. Indeed, the F.O. (not Churchill) wanted then and in the future to persuade the Department of the wisdom of the opposite approach, namely, the formation of an Arab *cordon sanitaire* to include a predominantly Arab Palestine against the Soviet Union's projected expansionism.[72]

The reluctance of both the Foreign Office (anti-Soviet) and of Churchill (anti-Soviet, pro-Zionist) to follow the Department's direction proved annoying; and indeed, after Yalta, the Department came to feel, as it had in 1942, that the British government was waffling again on Palestine, both to its own detriment and America's. The Department recognized that that government was split into pro- and anti-Zionist factions, was increasingly burdened financially, and was under unwritten obligation to defer final decisions on Palestine to the post-election government. Still, the Department believed that the British practice of delay, muddle, and short-run reaction to immigration pressures simply had to cease—particularly since the White Paper quotas were expected to be finally used up by the autumn of 1945.[73]

NEA and the planners tried to move the upper echelons toward a position whereby the United States would take more overt responsibility. Article 79, Chapter 12, of the U.N. Charter, which justified action by states "directly concerned" in trusteeships, was invoked in this context. The studies of Yale on immigration and trusteeship were funneled to Loy Henderson, and with Henderson's commentary, thence to Secretary James Byrnes on the eve of the London Council of Foreign Ministers (September–October 1945). With Churchill defeated, with the Labor Party in power and hardening its views of political Zionism, the Department in mid-1945 had reason to believe it was finally getting a handle on the Palestine problem.[74]

Truman's positions, however, posed a major problem. As noted, his approach to immigration went beyond either the State Department's or Foreign Office's acceptance of limited immigration. On the other hand, Truman, like the Department and F.O., was acutely sensitive to Russia's shadow in the Middle East. "The danger that the Arabs, antagonized by Western action in Palestine, would make common cause with Russia" was a concern he "had not lost sight of at any time." However, Truman bore such antagonism towards the Atlee-Bevin government that, relative to Palestine 1945, at any rate, it overrode their mutual fears of Russia and prevented cooperation. Truman's antagonism, inter alia, was based on the Labor government's wish to continue along the lines of the White Paper. But despite his realization that repudiation of the White Paper would lead to Arab armed hostility, Truman ardently opposed to any American military commitment to Palestine.[75]

As a result of this apparent knot of Presidential contradiction, which seemed willy-nilly not only to baffle the Department but also to stymie its initiatives, NEA finally resigned itself, to a degree, to a continuation of a no-win situation in Palestine. Its postwar plans unheeded, its wish for a clear and publicly announced policy statement on Palestine unmet, its briefing papers for the Potsdam Conference in July largely ignored, it on occasion took the frustrated view that it could only sit back and wait until the Palestine problem was once more dumped in its lap. In such self-pitying moods, the Department was even moved to express admiration for the Soviet position, which brooked no internal opposition or contradiction and which made no commitments, but by wise silence was presumably building up Arab good will.[76]

Resignations also increased. By the end of 1945, many if not most of the wartime officers in NEA, the Foreign Service, and the by then reorganized postwar planning divisions had resigned or been rotated. As such, a remarkable longevity and sameness of Departmental personnel dating back to the 1920s drew to a close. The reasons for the departures, clearly, were not confined solely to old age and normal postwar employment shifts.

It is essential, however, to recall that the Department was analogous to a corporate millipede. If one set of hands was relatively tired by the autumn of 1945, another was as resolved and diligent as ever. Murray's successor, Henderson, also Eddy, Wadsworth, Acheson and a proverbial host of lesser lights showed no signs of battle fatigue.

Still, with Truman more sure of himself as President and foreign policy maker by autumn 1945, the Department by and large henceforth carried out, rather than initiated, the administration's foreign policy in Palestine. Henderson's own strict sense of the Foreign Service's hierarchy and discipline indirectly supported this trend, as did Byrnes' general willingness to compromise and the fact that he was less interested in Palestine than was Truman. As a result, the last instance in 1945 of an Anglo-American instrumentality taking shape for achieving a joint accord on Palestine— the Anglo-American Committee of Inquiry Regarding the Problems of European Jewry and Palestine—did not derive from Departmental initiative.

True, the Department did conduct some mediation between Foreign Secretary Bevin and Truman on the numerous and time-consuming drafts of the terms of reference for the Committee-to-be. And true, FSOs continued to issue dire forecasts, notably of Ibn Saud's alleged tilting back toward the British; and in consequence the Department did rush to the breach as in months of old to reassure the Arabs. In a similar initiative, it tried to influence the selection and viewpoints of the Americans picked for the Committee of Inquiry. Overall, however, the Department's role in these matters was distinctly peripheral.[77]

CONCLUSIONS

In overview, it is an irony that under Roosevelt, the Department had considerable say on what American policy should be in Palestine, though it had less than it liked on most other wartime issues. Under Truman, however, the Department regained its general preeminence in policy making, for which it was grateful to Truman—except that in the case of Palestine, it lost influence, for which the Arabist segment of the Department was resentful. (It is furthermore ironic, and the several years after 1945 would show this more clearly, that with respect to the custom of full "consultations" with the Arabs prior to any decisions on Palestine, Roosevelt's literal, or maximal, interpretation of that custom was carried on not by his Presidential successor, but by Bevin; while Churchill's more figurative, or minimal, interpretation was carried on by Truman.)

Finally, it is worth noting that the Department of State in this last half of 1945 raised the spectre of communist Russia far *less* than it did at the end of 1944, relative to Palestine—this, despite the fact that in Europe the Cold War largely began in mid-1945, despite the fears of Russian encroachment elsewhere in the Mediterranean, and despite the fact that men at the helm like Henderson, Acheson, and Truman were each highly sensitive to all things Soviet. Once more, it is as if Palestine proved to be sui generis, the case which did not fit the rule. But secondary concern over the U.S.S.R. also highlights another fundamental, namely, that the Jews, more than the Russians or the Germans or anyone else, were the Department's main Middle Eastern preoccupation and problem, and on the day-by-day level, a major cause of gnashing of teeth. As such, while not in any official sense the enemy, the Jews in effect were regarded as Unofficial Adversary Number One in the Middle East, obstructing America's natural inheritance of hegemony. On the personal level, they appeared to be the proximate cause of more Departmental ulcers, frustrations, and resignations than the whole war effort against the Axis powers.

NOTES

1. Thus the chief regional office of OWI (Cairo) spoke of golden opportunities, given the fact that the Arabs were sick of the British and French, yet were aware they would need help from "a disinterested power without imperialistic ambitions,... [and] desire that the United States should remain as a powerful influence in the Near East after the war" [NEA Memorandum of Conversation with P. West, et al. (OWI, Cairo), 22 December 1942, *FR* 4 (1942): 557].

2. Quotations are from Murray to Welles, 17 December 1942, *FR* 4 (1942): 556. On Murray and Berle's more benevolent view in 1941 of a Jewish-Saudi deal, see note 8, Chapter 11. For bibliography on the proposed deal see note 15, Chapter 4.

3. Murray to Welles, 4 Feburary 1943, 867N.01/1–2643. Also, see Kirk's report, 17 April 1943, *FR* 4 (1943): 769. Presumably, American loans to Ibn Saud and other regimes were and would be different, free of the taint of economic imperialism.

4. Murray to Welles, 4 February 1943, 867N.01/1–2643, p. 2.

5. On Welles' role, see Memorandum of Conversation (Welles, Weizmann), 26 January 1943, 867N.01/1–2643; Welles to Hull, 17 May 1943, 867N.01/ 1857 1/2; C. Weizmann, Memorandum for British Foreign Office (on conversations with Roosevelt and Welles), 12 June 1943, *FR* 4 (1943): 792–94; and Bauer, *From Diplomacy to Resistance,* p. 251.

In addition to Welles, it is interesting to note that Max Thornberg of Standard Oil of California (SOCAL), and the then Departmental petroleum consultant, implied that the risk of a Weizmann-Ibn Saud meeting was worth taking. It was his thesis that reports of the king's Judophobia were exaggerated and that the British were actually behind the king's anti-Semitic expressions.

"I have a feeling that Ibn Saud would not make [a public anti-Jewish statement] without knowing precisely how it would be received in high British quarters.... I would suspect that it has been inspired [and] could be used by others as a means of furthering a policy, without subjecting themselves to the imputation of racial prejudice" (Thornberg to Murray and Alling, 19 May 1943, 867N.01/1967 PS/DAB, pp. 1–2).

NEA in part accepted Thornberg's view and even Weizmann's view that Ibn Saud's interest in Palestine was somewhat artificial, since it was known that no Arab leader could afford to speak less loudly on Zionism than another. But NEA still believed that the overriding fact was that Ibn Saud was also sincerely opposed to Zionism. See J. H. Shullaw (Jidda) to Hull, 7 May 1943, *FR* 4 (1943): 781.

6. According to Hoskins, the king expressed "personal hatred of Dr. Weizmann." Apparently perceiving himself as the noble patriarch and Weizmann as a Shylock offering demeaning *baksheesh*, Ibn Saud alleged that in 1939–1940 Weizmann "had impugned [the king's] character and motives by an attempted bribe of £20 million sterling. Furthermore, the promise of payment... would be guaranteed by President Roosevelt. His Majesty said he had been so incensed at the offer and equally at the inclusion of the President in such a shameful matter that he had never mentioned it again" [Hoskins, Memorandum (Cairo), 31 August 1943, *FR* 4 (1943): 809]. Also, see note 12, Chapter 3.

On NEA's relief, see Murray to Hull, 8 September 1943, 867N.01/9–843; on the equal relief of the Foreign Office and Colonial Office, see Hoskins, "Report on Trip to England," 13 December 1943, p. 1, Breckinridge Long Papers, Box 199, Folder: "ME Affairs 1942–4." On Roosevelt's "surprise and irritation" over Weizmann's alleged inculpation, see ibid. It is interesting that neither the President nor the Department investigated Ibn Saud's charges with an eye toward disabusing him of his interpretation or toward exonerating Welles and Weizmann. For Welles' subsequent hostility to Ibn Saud, see note 26, Chapter 12.

7. On the Department's munificence, see Chapter 12. On the electoral campaign, see Murray to Hull and Stettinius, 23 October 1944, *FR* 5 (1944): 619. Ibn Saud's speech of 1 February 1945 is noted in *FR* 8 (1945): 687. It is worth noting that the Jewish Agency's response to Ibn Saud's vitriol was disdainful and uninformed. It contended that the king's anti-Zionism "was not a serious obstacle in the long run since the country was certain to break up on the king's death"—not recognizing, obviously, *that to prevent such a breakup was an absolutely major goal of the Department of State.*

Conversely, most Arabs were disdainful and uninformed about the Yishuv, contending that it was an artificial entity, that after the war few Jews would want to go there, while most of those already there would want to emigrate back whence they came. See E. Wilson, Memorandum of Conversation (R. Zaslani of the Jewish Agency, G. P. Merriam, et al.), 1 February 1945, 867N.01/2–145, p. 2. Also, L. Henderson (Baghdad) to Stettinius, 2 February 1945, 867N.01/2–245, p. 2.

8. Examples of Arab protests and Foreign Service reports thereof are beyond count; the briefest perusal of the *FR* volumes for 1944 and 1945, under Palestine, will supply more than enough evidence. On Arab-American lobbying, note Fred Khouri, *The Arab-Israeli Dilemma* (Syracuse: Syracuse Univ. Press, 1968), p. 32. On liberal Protestants' anti-Zionism, see H. Fishman, *American Protestantism and a Jewish State* (Detroit: Wayne State Univ. Press, 1973), passim. On the predominant anti-Zionism of the Roman Church, see

Esther Feldblum, "On the Eve of a Jewish State: American Catholic Responses," *American Jewish Historical Quarterly* 64 (1974): 99–119.

On the Vatican's wartime position, note Berle to Stettinius, 15 October 1943, 867N.01/2068 PS/KN, which contains the following warning passages from a letter from the Apostolic Delegate (Washington) to Myron C. Taylor (America's representative to the Vatican), 22 June 1943: "If the greater part of Palestine is given to the Jewish People, this would be a severe blow to the religious attachment of Catholics to this land. To have the Jewish People in the majority would be to interfere with the peaceful exercise of these rights in the Holy Land already vested in Catholics [sic].... If a 'Hebrew Home' is desired, it would not be too difficult to find a more fitting territory than Palestine. With an increase in the Jewish population there, grave, new, international problems would arise. Catholics the world over would be aroused. The Holy See would be saddened, and justly so, by such a move [Catholic arousal?], for it would not be in keeping with the charitable assistance non-arians [sic] have received and will continue to receive at the hands of the Vatican."

On Russia, see, e.g., the report of American and British military attachés, 30 September 1944, *FR* 5 (1944): 615; also, the second half of Chapter 5.

Finally, it should be remarked that the oil interests were conspicuous by their absence from documentation relating to anti-Zionist domestic lobbying. The exact meaning of this phenomenon is hard to establish, as there are fragments which show that ARAMCO, for one, was hardly pleased with the Jewish-Arab strife over Palestine, while there are other fragments which suggest that ARAMCO was not all that worried about a Jewish state's negative effects. Thus, see note 16, Chapter 11, and passim; but cf. note 5 above (on Thornberg) and the research in the Zionist Archives of Bierbrier, "AZEC" ("The American oil interests did not feel unduly threatened by Zionism"). In any case, definitive research on this topic is still to be done.

9. There were many expressions of reassurance over the war years. See Roosevelt's letters to Ibn Saud in Welles to Hull, 15 May 1943, 890F.00/5–1443; note 22, Chapter 12; and Roosevelt to Ibn Saud, 5 April 1945, *FR* 8 (1945): 698. On drafted letters with Roosevelt's signature, to the Iraqi regent and the Syrian president, see (despite the fact that Roosevelt died 12 April 1945) 867N.01/4–1345 (13 April 1945) and 867N.01/4–1245 (20 April 1945). For Truman's expressions, see letters to heads of state of Transjordan, Syria, Lebanon, and Egypt, 19 November 1945, cited in *FR* 8 (1945): 826, 830, 833.

On the White Paper, see Hull's instructions to FSOs (with Roosevelt's approval), 15 March 1944, *FR* 5 (1944): 590–91; and note 21, Chapter 13. Typical of the Department's deprecation of Congressional pro-Zionism was Secretary James Byrnes' remark to Eddy (Jidda) relative to the final passage of the Wright-Compton, Taft-Wagner-Resolutions: "It is merely an expression of the two houses of Congress but in no wise binds the Executive" (5 January 1946, *FR* 8 (1945): 844, n. 67).

10. Quotation of Murray is from Murray to Hull, 7 January 1943, 867N.01/1840 PS/LBC. On Bowman, see Murray to Welles, 18 January 1943, FW 867N.01/1837 PS/LF. On Hoskins, see note 16, Chapter 4; also Weizmann, *Trial and Error*, p. 432. Quotation of Welles is from Memorandum of Conversation (Welles, Egyptian minister Hassan), 30 March 1943, *FR* 4 (1943): 767. On Welles' postwar change of heart on the wisdom of repatriation, see, e.g., his *Where Are We Heaading?*, p. 275.

11. Quotation is from C. Weizmann to W. Murray, "Memorandum on Post-War Emigration of European Jewry and Resettlement Possibilities in Pales-

tine," 3 February 1943, in 867N.01/1836-PS/MEL, p. 2. It is interesting that Murray (until he dropped interest later in 1943) saw his Angola scheme as essentially a third option, between unrealistic Zionism and unrealistic repatriation. See Murray to Welles, 18 January 1943, 867N.01/1837 PS/LF, p. 2. Also, for further citation of Departmental refugee schemes, see note 28, Chapter 1.

12. On the Bermuda Conference (19–28 April 1943), see *FR 1* (1943): 134–249. For all its alleged championing, the Department preferred to put the refugee problem under U.N. auspices. After all, if the Department did as Roosevelt requested (e.g., establish refugee offices in Algiers, Naples, Portugal, Madrid and Ankara, and a second camp in North Africa) "only the United States would become interested and would be paying the bills" (Stettinius to B. Long, quoting FSO Ray Atherton, 11 November 1943, 867N.01/2042).

13. Quotation of Hull is from Memorandum of Conversation (Hull, Lord Halifax), 13 December 1943, *FR 4* (1943): 823–24. Also, see Murray to Hull, 11 December 1943, 867N.00/686; and B. Long to Murray, 19 November 1943, B. Long Papers, Box 199, Folder: "Near East Affairs 1942–4."

On the Department's awareness of Jewish military preparations, see, e.g., Lt. Harold Hoskins, Report, "The Present Situation in the Near East," 20 April 1943, F.W. 867N.01/1857 1/2, p. 5 [summarized in *FR 4* (1943): 782–85]: "It is common knowledge," he noted, that the Haganah was stocking guns and making plans, that the Jews felt they could hold their own in Palestine, although they admitted they probably did not have the power to overcome outside Arab forces without the external aid of either Britain or America.

14. See W. L. Parker, Memorandum of Conversation (Weizmann, members of NEA), 13 March 1943, *FR 4* (1943): 760 ff.

15. On another level, the Department was unreceptive to Zionism because in its perception, the Jews did not have effective power, while the Arabs did. Thus the Jewish refugee problem invited some sympathy, but little more. For all the differences in cause and context, the later Palestine-Arab refugee problem has also invited Departmental sympathy, but little more—while presumably the reality of Israeli power has invited serious respect. See Sarah Botsai, *The United States and the Palestine Refugees* (Ph.D. diss., American Univ., 1972).

16. Among letter writers, individuals identifiable as recent German-Jewish immigrants, Yiddish Bundists, and Orthodox Agudists were the most vituperative. Such letters are thinly scattered through the Departmental files, e.g., 867N.01/1891 PS/LF (10 March 1943); 867N.01/1929 PS/MB (9 August 1943).

17. The term "rallying ground" is from P. Alling to Murray and Stettinius, "Palestine Question," 27 October 1943, 867N.01 2017 1/2, p. 13. For expressions of high satisfaction that the Council's analysis of Zionism exactly dovetailed with that of the Department, see Ireland and Yale to Murray and Alling, 10 February 1945, 867N.01/2–1045; and Murray to Dunn and Grew, 15 February 1945, FW 867N.01/12–1045. On the "popular front" idea, see note 62, Chapter 13.

18. Memorandum of Conversation (Waldman, Murray, et al.), 10 January 1944, B. Long Papers, Box 200, Folder: "Palestine 1944." (Copies of this and other such memoranda were immediately forwarded to the upper echelons, the London embassy, and all Middle Eastern posts. Waldman, executive director of the American Jewish Committee, later shifted to the American Council for Judaism after the former moved from anti-Zionism back to a centrist non-Zionism in the American Jewish ideological spectrum. It is worth noting,

albeit briefly, that between the American Jewish Committee and American Council for Judaism there were some differences: e.g., Waldman, who was anti-Zionist but also anti-White Paper, opposed M. Lazaron, who wanted the American Jewish Committee to support the White Paper (H. Parzan, "American Zionism and the Quest for a Jewish State 1939–42," *Herzl Yearbook* 4 (1961–62): 351).

On the phenomenon of American anti-Semitism, which crested near D-Day (6 June 1944), the Committee and Council seem to have crucially misread some of the main causes. What galled many Americans about American Jews was *not* the "image" of the Jew as Zionist, calling for a Jewish Army to fight, as it were, "its own battles" against the Germans. Rather, the inciting factor was the opposite "image" of the American Jew as assimilated "fat cat." (Whether the image was accurate as a general description is not the point here, though it may be remarked that it was quite accurate in describing the average member of the American Jewish Committee and American Council for Judaism.)

For other factors, and speculations, relative to American anti-Semitism, see C. McWilliams, *A Mask for Privilege: Anti-Semitism in America* (Boston: Little, Brown, 1948); D. S. Strong, *Organized Anti-Semitism in America: The Rise of Group Prejudice During the Decade 1930–1940* (Washington: D.C.: American Council of Public Affairs, 1941); and C. H. Stember et al., *Jews in the Mind of America* (New York: Basic Books, 1966). Also, cf. the later image of the "fighting Israeli," which purportedly has done much to diminish anti-Semitism, at least in Western countries.

19. Proskauer to Stettinius, 18 February 1944, 867N.01/2279; Rosenwald to Stettinius, 7 February 1945, 867N.01/2–745; W. Yale to G. P. Merriam, 30 July 1945, 867N.01/7–3045. For more examples of Jewish anti-Zionist influence-peddling, see Halperin, *Political World of American Zionism*, pp. 352, n. 76, 360, n. 27, and passim.

20. "With regard to the surviving Jews in Europe it would be [soon] evident both that very few remained and that only a small portion really wanted to go to Palestine. He [Sidney Wallach] declared that reports coming out of Europe to the effect that the liberated Jews were almost unanimously in favor of going to Palestine should be heavily discounted as coming from Zionist sources" [E. Wilson, Memorandum of Conversation (S. Wallach of American Council for Judaism, Merriam), 23 August 1945, 867N.01/8–2345, p. 2]. That very same week in August 1945, the Foreign Service was informing the Department that in Iraq, as elsewhere in the Arab world, anti-Zionists included all party leaders and ruling classes and were not an issue of local partisan politics [J. Moose to Byrnes, 20 August 1945, *FR* 8 (1945): 725].

Thus spake Jewish "unity" and Arab "disunity."

On the Department's desire to have the American Jewish Committee disrupt the American Jewish Conference, see Parzan, "American Zionism," pp. 358–59, which cites M. Waldman's memoir, *Not by Power* (New York: International Universities Press, 1953), as source.

21. In essence, the Bergsonites spoke of a Hebrew, not Jewish, nation, consisting of Palestinian and stateless Jews and without "national" links with Diaspora Jews. This view in effect excluded American Jews on the grounds that, as American nationals, they could not concurrently be nationals of a Hebrew state.

22. The phrase "lunatic fringe" is from Henderson to Grew, 12 May 1945, 867N.01/5–1245. To the Jewish Agency, Bergson's organizations were "freak bodies assuming high sounding titles and enunciating policies for which none

but their unrepresentative authors are responsible" (Agency telegram, forwarded by Silver to Berle, 5 June 1944, 867N.01/6–544).

23. "Elements opposing Jewish National Home are the same as those objecting to legitimate extension of American influence in Middle East as indicated by coincidence of [Egypt's] agitation regarding Congressional resolution and oil development" [Extract from NZO memorandum, Kirk (Cairo) to Hull, 4 March 1944, 867N.01/2246 PS/CF]. Also, NZO extract, Kirk to Hull, 4 April 1944, 867N.01/2318, p. 3. An earlier NZO memorandum put the case for a large American presence thus: "America's acceptance of the Mandate over the Holy Land would add to her prestige and strength in the world. The Jews would greet such acceptance as the beginning of a new era for their stricken and homeless people. Europe would welcome this as an assurance that the chronic and irritating Jewish problem would finally be solved. The Arabs, too, would realize that the game of political extortion is at an end, and that their opposition to Zionism can no longer be profitable.

Nor should we overlook the fact that American rule in Palestine would bring substantial material benefits to the United States. Palestine is not only one of the focal points of world strategy; it is also the key to the still dormant and undeveloped, yet vast and rich regions of the Middle East. Under American guardianship, Jewish Palestine would become an outpost of American products and ideals. It would bring to America new markets, wealth and influence in a region which will occupy a central position in the post-war world" [Col. M. J. Mendelsohn (President, NZO) to Hull, 11 August 1943, 867N.01/1907 PS/DAB].

24. The Jews "will be compelled against their own will to become an explosive and dynamic element with repercussions which the civilized should seek to avert for the sake of the world as well as for the sake of the Jewish people" [Ray Hare (London) to Byrnes, quoting Dr. Leib Altman, director of the NZO Political Bureau, 18 July 1945, 867N.01/7–1845]. On Azkin, see Memorandum of Conversation (B. Azkin and Division of Dependent Area (DA) Affairs), 7 November 1945, 867N.01, 11–745.

25. For instances of NEA and FSO hostility to Revisionists' realpolitik, relative to their military buildup in Palestine and to their "insulting" manner toward Roosevelt's "if elected" pledges, see Pinkerton (Jerusalem) to Merriam, 12 October 1944, 867N.00/1244 EG; and Murray to Stettinius, 9 November 1944, FW 867N.01/11–244.

That the Revisionists were perceived by many Jews and Zionists in the Yishuv and America to be "fascists" did not add to the Department's estimation, either. Revisionist influence on the Jewish Agency was profoundly opposed by Weizmann and Magnes, as noted in Pinkerton's report, 10 March 1945, 867N.01/3–1045.

26. On the evolution, structure, and lobbying of the AZEC and ZOA there is a considerable literature, quite apart from in-house, archival, and biographical material. Useful in this section were Parzan, "American Zionism"; Bierbrier, "AZEC"; Halperin, *Political World of American Zionism;* Y. Eventov and C. Rotem, "Zionism in the United States," in *Encyl. Jud.* Extracts, *Zionism;* and Schechtman, *The U.S. and the Jewish State Movement.* A number of other studies, largely secondary in both sources and quality, have recently appeared. They are as a rule subjectively grounded on the premise that the AZEC was a super-phenomenal lobby or a nefarious spider web. E.g., R. P. Stevens, *American Zionism and United States Foreign Policy;* Snetsinger, *Truman and the Creation of Israel* (Ph.D. diss., Stanford Univ., 1970); and E. D. Huff, "A Study of a Successful Interest Group: The American Zionist Movement," *Western Political Quarterly* 25 (1972): 109–24.

27. On the 1944 Congressional resolutions, references are numerous. See *FR* 5 (1944): 561 ff.; *FR* 8 (1945): 843–44; and note 40.

28. On the Lowdermilk affair, see note 31, Chapter 4. Also, Departmental communications of 10 November 1944, 867N.01/11–1044; 23 December 1944, 867N.00/1–245; and 6 February 1945, 867N.00/2–645.

29. Letters of Merriam and H. Villard to Hull, 25 August 1945, FW 867N.01/1984 PS/LC; 25 August 1943, FW 967N.01/1985 PS/LC; and 20 September 1943, 867N.01/1985 PS/LC. Also, Celler to Roosevelt, 18 August 1943, 867N.01/1918 PS/RN.

30. B. Long, Memorandum of Conversation (Long, Silver), 24 February 1944, 867N.01/2248, p. 2. For other false denials of other such charges, note A. MacLeish to Rabbi Wise, 14 February 1945, FW 967N.01/2–1745; and Grew to Wise, 11 June 1945, 867N.01/6–745. On the Department of War's statements, see note 41.

31. See *FR* 5 (1944): 588 ff.; and note 9 above. An almost identical case of a pro-Zionist White House statement colliding with a White House authorized, anti-Zionist private assurance occurred a year hence. See Moreland (Baghdad) to Grew, 18 March 1945, *FR* 8 (1945): 693, and n. 43 and n. 44; and pp. 696 ff. for Department reassurances to the Arabs.

32. See NEA's communications with L. Nemzer, Foreign Agents Registration Section, Department of Justice, 17 February 1944, 867N.01/2204, and 2 August 1945, 867N.01/8–245. Also, Grew, Memorandum of Conversation (Grew, Wise, Goldmann) 1 February 1945, *FR* 8 (1945): 688–89; and H. Gullion, Memorandum of Conversation (J. Dunn, ZOA delegation), 16 February 1945, 867N.01/2–1645.

33. For a lengthy example of Zionist loquacity, see E. Wilson, Memorandum of Conversation (N. Goldmann representing the World Jewish Congress, and NEA), 13 September 1944, 867N.01/9–1344. Also, note Pinkerton to Murray, 4 December 1944, 867N.01/10–444.

It can probably be said that Goldmann was the most active, even gossipy, informant of all Zionists with regard to Zionist plans. As a rule, he visited Foreign Service posts and NEA headquarters alone, a practice which, while not exceptional, was not the norm for Zionist appointments with the Department. While not altogether naive regarding the Department's hostility, he believed, rather like Roosevelt about Stalin, that his own candid and "personal" approach could soften the Department and win him points among other Zionists as one who could successfully negotiate with State. For his approach, note the following: "From the start Dr. Goldmann had feared that [the] introduction [of the pro-Zionist Congressional resolutions] at this time would be a mistake and would result in their being defeated, as actually turned out to be the case. Dr. Goldmann said he had tried to explain to Dr. Silver the inadvisability at this time of such action.... Dr. Goldmann also said he realized that the plan of trying to make out a case that the United States had, on the basis of the 1924 United States-British Convention, assumed responsibility for the carrying out of the mandate in Palestine, is unsound. He said that a number of years ago in Geneva he had looked into this and had found that this was not a correct interpretation of the convention. At the moment, he said, the Zionists were not planning to press for any congressional resolutions" (From H. B. Hoskins, Memorandum of Conversation: H. Hoskins and N. Goldmann, 20 April 1944, 867N.01/2337A, pp. 2–3).

34. Thus, Goldmann has written, "Anyone who has not had years of practical political experience usually fails to realize what a difference the personal attitude of an official in a foreign ministry can make" (Goldmann, *Autobiography*, p. 207). This appears true enough in theory, except that Goldmann in

practice was at times the victim of his own overestimation of the "personal attitude." Particularly, he deceived himself repeatedly in believing that Undersecretary Stettinius' well-known extroverted nature was tantamount to a friendly endorsement of Zionism, despite attempts (by Murray) to disabuse him of that interpretation. Murray to Stettinius, 26 May 1944, 867N.01/2351; and Murray to Pinkerton, 12 December 1944, 867N.01/12–1244.

35. On Goldmann's tack, see E. Wilson, Memorandum of Conversation (Goldmann, Henderson, NEA), 20 June 1945, *FR* 8 (1945): 710–12. Cf. his earlier defamations in 867N.01/2347 (19 May 1944) and in his 13 September 1944 conversation, cited in note 33 above.

36. Quotations are from (n. a., probably A. H. Silver), "Account of the Visit to the Department of State on September 20, 1945," A. H. Silver Papers; and L. Henderson, Memorandum of Conversation, 20 September 1945, 867N.01/9–2045. On the AZBC's ability and the question of Silver's effectiveness (though dealing with a slightly later period, see Zvi Ganin, "The Limits of American Jewish Political Power: America's Retreat From Partition November 1947–March 1949," *Jewish Social Studies* 39 [1977], pp. 1–36).

37. On NEA's mindset toward the ZOA, see E. M. Wilson, "American Jewish Organizations and Attitude of American Jews Toward Palestine," 10 August 1944, 867N.01/8–1044. ("Highly vocal tactics and their elaborate publicity campaigns have been successful in creating the impression both in this country and abroad that their power is far stronger than it actually is numerically.") Also, Murray to Grew, 16 February 1945, FW 867N.01/8–1044. Similarly, a Princeton Office of Public Opinion poll, which showed that 59 percent of the total American population who had heard of the Jewish state idea approved of it, had no apparent effect on the Department. See H. Schuyler Foster to L. Henderson, 5 May 1945, 867N.01/51745.

38. Welles to Hull, 17 May 1943, 867N.01/1857 1/2; Hull to Winant (London), 9 June 1943, *FR* 4 (1943): 790–92; Hull to Roosevelt, 19 July 1943, ibid., pp. 798–800; Hull, Memorandum, 6 August 1943, ibid., p. 802; Hull to Foreign Office, 6 August 1943, 867N.01/1885A PS/DAB; and Hull-Murray-Eden Communications, 12 August 1943 and 21 August 1943, *FR* (*Conferences at Washington and Quebec*) 8 (1943): 674–78, 1116.

39. Stimson to Hull, 10 September 1943, *FR* 4 (1943): 811; Hull's *Memoirs*, vol. 2, pp. 1533 ff.; and, important for all the nuances, Murray, Memorandum for Files, 17 August 1943, 867N.01/1908 1/2.

Also, using British sources, Michael J. Cohen, "American Influence on British Policy in the Middle East during World War II: First Attempts at Coordinating Allied Policy on Palestine," *American Jewish Historical Quarterly* 67 (1977): 61–66.

Although Zionists knew of the proposed joint statement, they were ignorant of the backroom negotiations and the Department's initiatives. Expressing his own surprise that the Zionists were not more upset at the near-materialization of the joint statement, Murray wrote, "The Zionists would, of course, feel themselves much more on the defensive in this matter if they were aware of the [proposed] statement [at the Quebec Conference]" (Murray to Berle and Hull, 27 August 1943, 867N.01/2016).

40. Stimson to Senator T. Connally, 7 February 1944, *FR* 5 (1944): 563; Schechtman, *The U.S. and the Jewish State Movement*, pp. 74–75; Feis, *Birth of Israel*, p. 15. Probably another reason for the administration's opposition to the resolutions was its "fear that appeasement of one minority group might increase the pressure from all other national-minorities, especially in an election year" [Lord Halifax, "Political Review for 1st Quarter, 1944," in

T. E. Hachey, ed., *Confidential Dispatches: Analyses of America by the British Ambassador, 1939–1945* (Evanston, Ill.: New University Press, 1975), p. 174].

41. McCloy to General Marshall, 26 February 1944, *FR* 5 (1944): 576; and Murray to Stettinius, 2 March 1944, ibid., p. 581.

42. Ibid.

43. On method, see ibid.; Stettinius to Long et al., 19 February 1944, 867N.01/2282 and 2280; and note 5, Chapter 12 above.

44. Stettinius to Hull, 11 February 1944, Stettinius Papers, Box 218, Folder: "S-Sec of State (January–February 1944)." Still, the Department never gave up. See Murray to Stettinius, 9 March 1944, 867N.01/3–944. As such, Roosevelt did approve the Department's wish to initiate and achieve a joint statement at the London (Stettinius) Mission in April 1944. E. M. Wilson, "Palestine: Topics for Discussion with the British," 17 March 1944, p. 2, Stettinius Papers, Box 249, Folder: "London Mission—Background Material."

45. On Congress' wartime lag in foreign affairs, see R. Young, *Congressional Politics in the Second World War* (New York: Columbia Univ. Press, 1956); A. C. F. Westphal, *The House Committee on Foreign Affairs* (New York: Columbia Univ. Press, 1942); and Eleanor Dennison, *The Senate Foreign Relations Committee* (Standford, Calif.: Stanford Univ. Press, 1942).

Quotation on Bloom is from Murray, Memorandum for Files, 17 August 1943, 867N.01/1908 1/2, p. 4. Also, see Berle to Hull, 28 January 1944, *FR* 5 (1944): 561. On Bloom, a rather shallow character, see *The Autobiography of Sol Bloom* (New York: Putman's, 1948); and Stevens, *American Zionism,* p. 41, passim.

46. See communications in *FR* 5 (1944): 615–19; also, Manuel, *American-Palestine Relations,* pp. 312–14.

47. Outside of biographies of the Congressmen cited, see Fink, ed., *America and Palestine,* pp. 90 ff. For statistics of Congressional support and the parties' platforms, see Silverberg, *If I Forget Thee,* pp. 249–50; *Near East Report* (Washington, D.C.), special issue of October 1968 on political party attitudes 1944–1968; and Westerfield, *Foreign Policy and Party Politics,* Chapter 11.

It may be noted that Senator Harry Truman was one of the few reluctant endorsers of the Taft-Wagner resolution, chiefly out of his concern for the expenses of the war and expected British-Russian conflict. Truman, senator since 1934 and chairman of the Senate Committee to Investigate the National Defense Program, was no expert in foreign affairs, but not exactly a novice, either (Fink, ed., *America and Palestine,* p. 153).

48. On the Department's brief, see Murray to Stettinius, 24 November 1944, *FR* 5 (1944): 641; and Murray to Stettinius, and Stettinius to Roosevelt, 12 December 1944, 867N.01/12–1244. On FDR's brief, see Roosevelt to Senator Wagner and Hull, 3 December 1944. The Jews want to go to Palestine, said the President, but "on the other side of the picture there are approximately seventy million Mohammedans who want to cut their throats the day they land. The one thing I want to avoid is a massacre or a situation which cannot be resolved by talking things over" (FDR to R. Wagner, 3 December 1944, Roosevelt Papers, Box 93, File: "PSF State Dept., E. R. Stettinius, Jr., December 1944"). Also, Alling to Dunn, 6 January 1945, *FR* 5 (1944): 701.

49. Murray regarded the third result especially as "highly significant." Murray to Stettinius, 19 December 1944, 867N.01/12–1944. Also, Silverberg, *If I Forget Thee, p.* 256; and Schectman, *The U.S. and the Jewish State Movement,* pp. 86–87.

50. Wise addressed himself thus to his "Chief" before Yalta: "A small delegation of us [AZEC] who, it is needless to say, stand gratefully and loyally at

your side, ought to have some time in which to present the case of Palestine" (Quoted in Silverberg, *If I Forget Thee*, p. 257). On the Department's Yalta Briefing Book see note 33, Chapter 5.

51. On the talks at Yalta and Great Bitter Lake, see note 34, Chapter 5, and note 24, Chapter 12. On the President's talk with Hoskins, see Hoskins to Alling, 5 March 1945, 867N.01/3–545, p. 3. (Hoskins' letter is abridged in *FR* 8 (1945): 690–91.) On the three-religions thesis, see G. P. Merriam's formulations and the reactions of Stettinius (positive) and Hull (negative) in November 1943 [*FR* 4 (1943): 816–22]; also note 67. On the President's talk with Wise, see Murray to Grew, 20 March 1945, *FR* 8 (1945); 694 ff.

52. Ibid.

53. With reference to the letter to Ibn Saud, and the Department's pressure on Roosevelt one week before his death, James Byrnes subsequently noted: "I know that he was in no condition at all to be transacting business" [Byrnes-Halifax communications, 19 October 1945, *FR* 8 (1945): 779]. For citations, see note 9 above.

The public statement that the Department had prepared for Roosevelt's meeting with the regent was to have read as follows: "In discussing this [Palestine] question the President took the opportunity to express his deep and abiding concern in an equitable solution of the Palestine problem. He assured the Regent, in this connection, that in the view of this Government there should be no decision affecting the basic solution in Palestine without full consultation with both Arabs and Jews" [Alling to Dunn (Evan Wilson, drafting officer), 12 April 1945 (postdated for regent's scheduled visit, 20 April 1945), 867N.01/4–1245]. Also, see correspondence between Alling and Dunn, *FR* 8 (1945): 702; and note 68.

54. On the influencing of Truman, see Alling to Stettinius, 13 April 1945, 867N.01/4–1345: "I believe we should put President Truman on notice as soon as possible that the Zionists will undoubtedly seize the first available opportunity to elicit from him a commitment on Palestine." Also, note the communications among Grew, Stettinius, and Truman in April, in *FR* 8 (1945): 704–8. On Truman's letters to Arab leaders and his later embarrassment, see note 9 above; and, again, Byrnes-Halifax communications, 19 October 1945, *FR* 8 (1945): 779. On the regent's visit, see note 21, Chapter 9.

The Department's endorsement of the Arab League during the regent's visit, and on subsequent occasions, led to ZOA concern, given the fact that the League's constitution viewed Palestine as an autonomous Arab state. The Department parried by saying that its endorsement was in general, and not in particulars. See Wise-Grew correspondence, 7 June 1945 and 11 June 1945, 867N.01/6–745.

55. Quotation from Truman's *Memoirs*, vol. 2, p. 135. On the background to his reinterpretation of "consultation" and his permission to let Byrnes publicly release Roosevelt's 5 April 1945 letter to Ibn Saud, see ibid., p. 140; release of 21 October 1945, *Bulletin* 13 (1945): 623; Acheson, *Present at the Creation*, pp. 233–34; Schechtman, *The U.S. and the Jewish State Movement*, pp. 120–23, passim; Evan Wilson, "The Palestine Papers 1943–49," *Journal of Palestine Studies* (Beirut) 2 (1973): 38, 48; and H. Parzen, "President Truman and the Palestine Quandary: Initial Experience, April–December 1945," *Jewish Social Studies* 35 (1973): 42 ff.

The Harrison Report is printed in *Bulletin* 13 (1945): 456–63. The extensive arguments of the Department and the British government against accepting the Report are in *FR* 8 (1945): 738–65, 771–79. Truman's own reassurances of his continuity of policy were again relayed to Arab lands (November

1945), not to mention subsequent affirmations after 1945. See, ibid., pp. 826, 830, 833.

On the topic of Truman's "irresponsibility," cf. Truman, *Memoirs,* pp. 136–40; Welles,*Where Are We Heading?,* p. 266; Acheson, *Present at the Creation,* p. 233; and F. Williams, *Twilight of Empire, Memoirs of Prime Minister Clement Atlee* (New York: A. S. Barnes, 1962), pp. 181–200.

56. An example of the new cues and restraints on the Department was the following: when Truman, after the Potsdam Conference, made the statement that he favored refugee immigration to Palestine, but also a peaceful settlement with Britain and the Arabs, and without the use of American troops, Byrnes wrote (18 August 1945) to all Foreign Service posts in the Middle East: "You should not (repeat not) unless otherwise instructed attempt to comment on these remarks or interpret them in any way" (867N.01/8–1845). This warning has been omitted from the version in *FR* 8 (1945): 722, apparently because it reveals too much of the Foreign Service's previous license in matters of interpretation.

57. All previous chapters are replete with examples of Anglo-American competition. On British vagueness on Palestine, note Col. H. Hoskins, "Report on Trip to England," 13 December 1943, Long Papers, Box 199, Folder: "ME Affairs, 1942–44." On British "provocation," note D. Gaudin, Jr., (Baghdad) to Hull, 25 September 1943, 867N.01/1994; L. Pinkerton to Hull, 31 October 1944, 867N.01/10–3144; also, interview with Ray Hare, 4 August 1972.

The notion of America as "great Moslem power" was apparently first phrased as such by the ZOA's Emmanuel Neumann, with reference to the North African occupation and to his Revisionist-like hope that America would force the Moslems to accept an American-Zionist solution in Palestine. However, the phrase, representing, "a new and startling thought," had, if anything, a contrary consciousness-raising effect (Murray to Hull, Welles and Berle, 16 February 1943, 867N.01/2–1643). The term "holy war" was used intermittently, e.g., concerning North Africa by Gen. G. V. Strong, U.S. Army—who, however, was called an "alarmist" by Stimson (Strong to NEA, 13 March 1943, 867N.01/3–1343; Murray, Memorandum for Files, 17 August 1943, 867N.01/1908 1/2, p. 4).

58. See F. Kohler, "Palestine" (conversations on), 11 April 1944, pp. 1–3, Stettinius Papers, Box 251, Folder: "London Mission—Conversations (Murray)," and Isaiah Bowman, "Palestine" (conversations on), 11 April 1944, Stettinius Papers, Box 240, Folder: "Bowman Conversation." ["The meeting was cordial throughout, with remarkable parallelism of thought both during the conference and with respect to the studies that have been made on both sides" (Ibid., p. 1)]. Cf. the fraudulent harmony of view on Saudi Arabia, note 47, Chapter 11.

59. The Foreign Office "felt that issuance now might well irritate rather than calm the Zionists in the United States and this was their principal worry. They do not expect any trouble, either from the Arabs or from the Jews in Palestine, which they will be unable to handle, despite the current activities of the Jewish extremists. If only the United States Zionists can be kept quiet the situation will remain under firm control" [F. Kohler, quoting Sir Maurice Peterson, British Undersecretary of State, "Palestine," 19 April 1944, p. 1, Stettinius Papers, Box 251, Folder: "London Mission—Conversations (Murray)"]. Also, "Agreed Minute: Anglo-American discussions regarding the Near and Middle East," 28 April 1944, p. 2, Stettinius Papers, Box 251, Folder: "London Mission—Conversations (Murray)."

60. On sharing plans with the Foreign Office, note Yale to Ireland, 31 May 1944, 867N.00/689; Murray to Stettinius, 2 June 1944, 867N.01/6–244; Ire-

land to Murray, 29 June 1944, 867N.01/6–2944; and Merriam, Memorandum, 6 July 1944, 867N.01/7–644. On Britain's new cooperation in the field, note Henderson (Baghdad) to Hull, 5 September 1944, *FR 5* (1944): 613.

61. ST Minutes 12, 10 March 1943, Notter Papers, Box 79, Bound Volume: "Minutes on Security Technical Problems (1—." Also, Views of the Territorial Subcommittee, P-214-C, 10 March 1943, and Tentative Views of the Subcommittee on Political Problems, P-214, 12 March 1943, both in Notter Papers, Box 3, Folder: "Doc.: Subcom. on Polit. Probs. Views of Coms." (On the postwar planning apparatus' structure and methods, see Chapter 2; on the role of William Yale and Philip Ireland, sse Chapter 4. For a more detailed and nuanced treatment of the planning apparatus' plans for Palestine, see this author's unpublished manuscript on the subject.)

62. Agenda and Summary of Views to Date, P-215, 19 March 1943, Appendix, Notter Papers, Box 63, Folder: "P Docs. 201–25."

63. In sequence, these typical quotations are from the following T studies authored by Yale: "Palestine-Industrial Labor," T-281, 22 March 1943, p. 9; "Palestine-Industry," T-282, 22 March 1943, p. 11; "Palestine: Industrial Potentialities and Limitations," T-279, 25 March 1943, p. 5, all in Notter Papers, Box 33, Folder: "T Docs. 270–79," and Box 33, "T Docs. 280–89." Also, Memorandum, "Comments on *Palestine: Its Decay and Restoration* (W. C. Lowdermilk)," 15 Feburary 1943, p. 2, Yale Papers, Box 2, Folder 8/H.

64. Yale, "Basic Factors in the Palestine Problem," T-309, 20 April 1943, pp. 11, 13. Notter Papers, Box 34, Folder: "T Docs. 290–309." That such "moral concerns" had political implications—namely, that the end of immigration would not only prevent a Jewish state but would inevitably lead to an Arab anti-Zionist state—never found much place in his analysis.

65. Ibid., pp. 18–26; and Yale, "Palestine: Proposed and Possible Settlements," T-313, 23 April 1943, pp. 7–16, Notter Papers, Box 34, Folder: "T Docs. 310–19."

66. On economic development, note Yale, "Palestine: Economic Development," H-154 Prelim., 11 March 1944; H-154 Prelim. A, 27 March 1944; H-154 Prelim. B, 8 April 1944; and H-154 Supplement b, all in Notter Papers, Box 59, Folder: "H. Pol. Sum. 150–65." On immigration and land transfer, note Yale, "Palestine: Immigration," H-37a, 1 February 1944; and H-37b Supplement, 1 March 1944, both in Notter Papers, Box 57, H. Pol. Sum. 26–39; and Yale, "Palestine: Land Transfer," H-148 Prelim., 29 February 1944, Notter Papers, Box 59, Folder: "H. Pol. Sum. 126–49."

67. Yale, "Palestine: Form of Government," H-47b Prelim., 4 January 1944; H-47c, 26 January 1944; and H-47c Supplement, 27 January 1944, all in Notter Papers, Box 58, Folder: "H. Pol. Sum. 40–55." Also, on the three-religions thesis, see note 51 above.

It is worth noting at this point Yale's retrospective, and revealing, views: "The Office of Postwar Planning in the D of S in 1942–1945 was actually engaged in attempting to formulate policy. *Objective analysis becomes replaced by conclusions as to what should be done.* Those concerned in the process of Postwar Planning begin to think of their work and think themselves as policy makers and then proceeded to convince others of what should be the policy. Certainly I did this, Philip Ireland went along with it, then the Office of Near and Middle Eastern and African affairs until eventually the plan reached the desk of S. Byrnes in August 1945. After August 1945 the British were given an inkling of it. This was after I resigned, someone was sent to London with it. In a modified form it [Yale's binational plan] was embodied in the Morrison-

Grady plan, the British changed it reintroducing the early British proposal of cantonment along the lines of Switzerland" [From Yale's marginalia, 30 September 1965, in preface to his copy of Sykes, *Crossroads to Israel* (in Boston Univ. Mugar Collections). Emphasis added.]. It is questionable whether and to what degree Yale's plan was in fact used and embodied in the Morrison-Grady plan, which was a modified partition plan. The M-G plan is set out in *FR* 7 (1946): 652–67.

68. Quotation is from Yale, "Transjordan: Future Political Status and What Should United States' Position Be?" H-116 a Prelim., 2 March 1944, p. 2, Notter Papers, Box 59, Folder: "H. Pol. Sum. 116–25."

69. Ibid., pp. 3–10; and Department of State, "Jordan: Policy and Information Statement," 9 October 1946, p. 3, Byrnes Papers.

70. See note 58.

71. See Murray to Stettinius, 24 November 1944, *FR* 5 (1944): 641; and 1 December 1944, 867N.01/12–144 (Anglo-American alienation of the Arabs ran the risk of "throwing the whole Arab world into the arms of Soviet Russia," p. 12). Also, see note 41; and note 30, Chapter 4.

72. On Murray's views, and the projected "use" of Soviet interest in the Middle East, and on the President's diplomacy, see notes 33 and 34, Chapter 5.

73. On the British, see Winant (London) to Byrnes, 14 July 1945, 867N.01/ 7–1445; and Kirk (Rome) to Byrnes, 3 August 1945, *FR* 8 (1945): 719. It is worth noting that the Department correctly foresaw that the new Labor government would not implement its pro-Zionist pledges and would but modify the White Paper with respect to immigration. Yale to Henderson and Grew, 30 July 1945, 867N.01/7–3045.

74. See communications among Yale, Merriam, and Henderson, 25 July 1945, *FR* 8 (1945): 717–18; Merriam to Henderson, 30 August 1945, 867N.01/8–3045; and Henderson to Byrnes, 24 August 1945 and 31 August 1945, *FR* 8 (1945): 728–35.

75. Truman, *Memoirs*, vol. 2, p. 149. The kind of "contradiction" which tied the Department and the Foreign Office in knots was illustrated in his first post-Potsdam conference: "The American view on Palestine is that we want to let as many of the Jews into Palestine as it is possible to let into that country. Then the matter will have to be worked out diplomatically with the British and the Arabs, so that if a state can be set up there they may be able to set it up on a peaceful basis. I have no desire to send 500,000 American soldiers there to make peace in Palestine" (Ibid., p. 136). Also, see note 55.

76. For an admiring glance toward the Soviet dictatorship's alleged unity of view, see Moose to Byrnes, 20 August 1945, *FR* 8 (1945): 725. On other laments, note comments of Merriam and P. Allen, 26 September 1945, *FR* 8 (1945): 745–46, and n. 42.

77. On the lengthy negotiations involving chiefly Truman and Ernest Bevin, Atlee, Byrnes, and Lord Halifax, see *FR* 8 (1945): 771–82, 786–89, 795–801, 810–14, 819–23, 827–39; and also, *FR* 7 (1946): 585, passim. On Ibn Saud's alleged "tiltings," see communications from W. Sands and Eddy (Jidda) in October–November, *FR* 8 (1945): 790–91, 802, 824, and 829.

On the Department's effort to influence the composition of the Inquiry committee (e.g., seeking to have a former president of the American University of Beirut, who was an overt anti-Zionist, appointed), see Memorandum no. 1, 29 January 1946, pp. 1 ff., James McDonald Papers, Folder: "Anglo-American Committee Diary;" also, Bartley C. Crum, *Behind the Silken Curtain: A Personal Account of Anglo-American Diplomacy in Palestine and the Middle East* (New York: Simon and Schuster, 1947), passim.

15

The Bottom Line: Conclusions

SUMMARY

The upper and middle echelons of the Department of State in the period between 1919 and 1945 constituted a largely elitist, continuous, and homogeneous group. They strove for prestige and power overseas for the American government, and for profitable business opportunities for American private interests. They also strove for prestige and power for the Department itself, relative to other executive departments which intruded on foreign policy making.

The Department favored, a priori, a "Progressive" reformist approach abroad, a "golden mean" between Soviet-style revolution and British-style reaction. It assumed that the economic open door policy in particular would promote both stability and necessary change within the Middle East. Outside of such Cobdenism, however, the Department in practice maintained a hands-off attitude toward Arab internal politics, and indeed, it got on well with the typically authoritarian leadership associated therewith.

The Department also favored a policy of full national independence for the Arab countries. It believed nationalism and the sovereignty principle would promote the dissolution of the spheres of influence of its economic competitors, albeit wartime allies, Britain and France. In the process, dissolution would increase Arab bilateral relations with the United States.

The Department saw no asymmetry between working to implement

320

the open door, working to maintain the region's internal status quo even while professing a philosophy of reformism, and working for rapid implementation of full national sovereignty. It was indifferent, too, to the historical truism that any struggle for home rule brings in its train other struggles over who shall rule at home.

Among the middle echelons, a core of "middle managers" from NEA, the Foreign Service, and the postwar planning apparatus largely made policy for the Middle East. Despite the tendency it shared with the rest of the Department towards self-pity, this core was successful in the vast majority of cases in gaining the support of the upper echelons, other executive departments, the President and Congress, and thus having in its views implemented as official government policy. Pertinacity, manipulativeness, and a large body of intelligence experts were the Department's comparative advantages. The few cases where positions initiated by NEA, et al, failed to win over the President or Congress were the proposed pipeline for Saudi Arabia, the Anglo-American oil accord, and immigration into Pallestine.

During the war the Department felt that the United States' good-neighbor approach to Latin America was appropriate for all postwar regions, especially the Arab countries. It also felt that the United States' immediate function was to make sure the Axis was defeated, then to make sure the French were removed from the region, the Soviets contained, and the British generally reduced to junior partnership with the United States, the senior partner-to-be.

Especially after the success in North Africa of Operation TORCH (November 1942), the Department's consciousness rose and it came to perceive America as a "great Moslem power." From the Arab view, conversely, America's prestige rose considerably. The Department tried to exploit these opportunities and to extend American economic and diplomatic influence, at the expense of other powers. Overall, however, the Departmental drive for a status of primus inter pares was carried out in a low-key way and did not seriously alienate the Jews, the British, or the Russians; in contrast, the French and the Axis were alienated, which in part helps explain the periodic spates of Franco-American tension in the Middle East after 1945.

The Department sometimes joined with the British Foreign Office to close the regional door to the Soviet Union. However, research based on Departmental documents and confined to the Middle Eastern countries surveyed shows that the positioning of Washington and London opposite Moscow was *not* a major source or cause of future Cold War tension.

The Department's wartime regional relations with the Soviets were limited. Within those limits, Departmental cooperation with the Soviets was comparatively greatest regarding Syria, Lebanon and Palestine, and least regarding Saudi Arabia, oil, and the Suez Canal. With the British,

Departmental relations were far more extensive. Overall, Departmental cooperation was greatest regarding Palestine, Transjordan, Iraq and the Suez Canal; somewhat less regarding Syria and Lebanon; and least regarding Saudi Arabia, Egypt, and oil. American-British and American-Russian cooperation over Palestine was mutually exclusive; thus, the Foreign Office did not cooperate with the Department precisely when the Department sought cooperation with the Soviets.

American military campaigns during the war and the Department's plans to establish a potent postwar United Nations Organization showed that the United States had moved away from the old view that it could be economically involved abroad without any political-military involvement. However, though largely caught up in this anti-isolationist mood, the wartime Department, under the cautious Cordell Hull, continued to apply the old view in parts of the Middle East. Chiefly in Egypt and the Levant, it tended to believe that it could be economically influential without political-military involvement. It believed that if any such "involvement" was necessary, it could be limited to (1) encouraging the British to repress the French (Levant), the Jews (Palestine), or pro-Axis trends (Iraq, Vichy Syria); or (2) encouraging the Arabs to pressure the British to get out (Egypt, Saudi Arabia, DeGaulle's Syria).

The State Department felt that there existed in the Middle East a remarkable set of preconditions for an easy, almost automatic, American harvest of influence in the immediate postwar period. These were: the weakness, unpopularity, or preoccupation elsewhere of other great powers; the accumulated Arab good will toward the United States, stemming from century-old private American missionary and philanthropic efforts; the impact of American military might, particularly TORCH; the preference Ibn Saud had for an American connection; and the accumulated contacts, easy familiarity, and good will built up in the region by FSOs and Departmental Arabists.

The Department enshrined as its credo the neo-Wilsonian Atlantic Charter and the principles of native self-determination and majority rule. This faith helped to lead the Department to the conclusion that the native majoritarian nationalisms of the Sunni Arabs were necessarily benevolent and progressive, not to say overdue, from World War I; while the political Zionism represented chiefly by the Jewish minority in Palestine and in the United States was retrograde, a chimera in the "Arab world," and, in the context of pro-Zionist American politics, an albatross around the Department's neck.

The wartime Middle East increased in geopolitical and economic importance; but relative to other regions, it remained, in the Department's basically Eurocentric perspective, a secondary region. The exception was Saudi Arabia, because of its oil. Palestine was also "important," though for the negative reason of its "obstructionism" to regional "stability" and

Arab-American entente. The fact that for decades there were more American civilian nationals and more American private capital in Palestine than in all other Middle Eastern countries combined (excluding ARAMCO's investments in Saudi Arabia) did not make Palestine important to the Department. The statistics made no impression whatever, apparently because the nationals and capital were Jewish and because the Yishuv's economy was deemed artificial.

The Department's two biggest specific wartime fears in the region did not concern either Axis fascist or Soviet communist influence. They concerned the passage of Congressional pro-Zionist resolutions and, as a consequence, the possibility of Ibn Saud's acting out his displeasure by turning against ARAMCO and towards British oil interests. The Department's biggest "nonspecific" anxiety in the region was that general American "pro-Zionism" might "turn" the disappointed Arabs toward the Russians. By and large, the Department was much more eager for the United States to assume wartime and postwar military responsibility in Saudi Arabia, for reasons of alleged "military security," than the Department of War.

The Department of State failed to recognize that a large measure of the anger and disappointment of the Arabs was its own fault. The Department had over the years "assured" and thus conditioned the Arabs to believe that America was not seriously pro-Zionist. Hence, when Congress or the President did act in a distinctly pro-Zionist manner, that reality sometimes shocked the Arabs more than it should have, had the Department been less deceptive and appeasing toward them.

Furthermore, the Department did not wish to consider the fact that, given American military power and prestige in the region, and given the desire of the Arabs for good relations with America, it had an excellent opportunity to use power and apply leverage—not only on Arab leaders, but on the British and possibly the Russians, too. In carrot and stick fashion the Department could have offered more American assistance in exchange for terms such as their recognition of the right of Jewish immigration into Palestine.

The Department was not enthusiastic about wartime proposals for a political Arab federation. While it preferred federation in principle over "balkanization" and while it would approve the founding of the Arab League in 1945, the idea of Arab unification did not recommend itself. Among the reasons were that federation represented an unknown variable, a *tertium quid*; also, it might become a British tool, or a force led by the unstable leadership of wartime Egypt, or worse, one led by the Hashemites of Transjordan or Iraq, the hated enemies of Ibn Saud.

After World War I, Iraq was the Arab country in which the Department was most interested, if measured by recorded hopes, protests, and demands. Syria and Lebanon were second, the Arabian peninsula was probably last. By 1945, Saudi Arabia was first, Iraq was last, and Syria and Lebanon were still second. The Levant states were the continuous locus of the Department's pro-Arab independence diplomatic thrust.

The Department wanted the British out of Egypt and abetted Egyptian nationalism in this direction. The Department did not want the British out of the Suez Canal Zone. It saw no conflict between the two goals, no awareness that once begun, there was no reason for the erosion of British power to halt at the boundary of the Canal Zone.

THE "IMPORTANCE" OF THE WARTIME DEPARTMENT

To what extent was the wartime Department of State simply riding an historical current which inevitably led to the decreased influence of other great powers and to the increased influence of America? Put another way, if America had entered the war and launched the military operations which it did, including TORCH, *but* if in its size, organization, philosophy, ranking with other departments, and available funds and expertise, the Department had remained in 1945 exactly as it had been in 1939, what would have been the effect on American influence in the Middle East?

As with any counterfactual hypothesis, one can only speculate; nonetheless, it is plausible that, whatever the Department's weight and size, most of the conflicts in the region would have continued along the same trajectories. American prestige would have continued to be high, too, especially after TORCH and the erosion of Axis influence in the Mediterranean.

However, a stagnant Department would probably have led to the belief among all parties in the Middle East that America, as after 1918, preferred isolationism. And, as in the post-1918 period, Britain and France therefore would have sought to entrench themselves and continue their mandates, over the objections of the Arabs. With the United States aloof and with the Soviet Union preoccupied in its own territorial reoccupation until July 1944, chances are that the Arabs would have been forced to make concessions—even though they were in a stronger position in 1945 than in 1919 and the position of the British and French was weaker in 1945 than in 1919.

It is plausible that if the State Department were stagnant, two possibilities would have existed for Saudi Arabia—either it would have stayed in the British sphere; or the American Departments of Interior, War, and Navy would have acted out their wartime wishes, preempted ARAMCO, and built a pipeline, and perhaps then have created a special enclave at Dhahran. In either case, Ibn Saud would have been reduced to the level of a wealthy local sheik, since in the first contingency he would have been unable to play Britain against America, and in the second contingency, he would have been intimidated and restrained by America's military presence.

The British MESC would have continued, although it would have been ineffective for lack of American support and funds. A British-sponsored and Egyptian-led Arab federation would have been established, over French objection, with links to the British Commonwealth of Nations. Bad feeling would have continued between Churchill and DeGaulle over the Levant, but it is likely that each side, as after 1918, would have come to terms with the other's mandates and spheres.

In Palestine, the problem over whether or not to maintain the 1939 White Paper would have persisted; although if America and Russia were only small clouds on the horizon and the British felt retrenched, chances are that Churchill would have modified the Paper and tried to force an accommodation on the Arabs before the end of the war. In exchange for concessions and greater regional roles, Egypt under Farouk and Iraq under Nuri Said would most likely have consented. It is plausible that under these circumstances the Atlee-Bevin successor government, though anti-Zionist, would not have tried to reaffirm the 1939 White Paper.

After 1944, Soviet probes in Palestine, the Levant, and Egypt would have been larger than they were, since despite British entrenchment, the Department's stagnancy would have created a vacuum of sorts. Soviet propaganda would thus have been greater, but Arab urban demonstrations against the British and French would probably have been smaller than they were, since without the wartime urban-industrial developments precipitated by American funds and promises, the region would have been less modernized and urbanized in 1945 than it was.

It is plausible to conclude from this scenario, the theme of which is British entrenchment, that since British control of the region, in actuality, was weak by the war's end, the reason for the weakness lies in the fact that the State Department was actually more active in 1945 than in 1939. The Department "made the difference." But what specifically was it in the Department which made the difference—the enlarged number of Foreign Service posts and personnel in the Middle East, the advanced state of postwar planning, the almost annual efficiency reorganizations, the ardor of NEA? All these were significant, but I would suggest that the crucial factor was simply the Department's repeated "message" to all parties concerned that America did not intend to withdraw into postwar isolationism. As a result of the "accident of war," the presence in the area of American troops—chiefly in North Africa, and therefore far enough to be unentangled but close enough to be "felt"—probably did the most to reinforce that message.

In consequence of this "forewarning," Britain was ever anxious about alienating America. Tired, deep in debt, ambivalent about empire to begin with, it was thus all the more hesitant about pressing the Arabs and making the kind of quids pro quo with the French and with the Soviets that it would otherwise have been willing to make. In contrast, the Arabs and Jews were each emboldened to think the future would be theirs, with the foreknowledge, and "assurances" from friends in America, that America would play a positive role in the region.

THE QUESTION OF AMERICAN POSTWAR REGIONAL INFLUENCE

If the Department of State was successful in intimidating the British and, generally, in setting up the preconditions for an American regional harvest, what happened to that projected postwar harvest? Some say it has already been reaped, in Saudi Arabia; others, that American public support for Israel ruined the harvest; others still, that the expectation of a harvest was to begin with a snare and delusion, given post-1945 trends in Arab states towards radical nationalism, nationalization of the economy, militarization, and given Soviet determination to play a great-power role in the region. One could of course try to answer this question by chronicling events year by year and country by country since 1945; and by constantly taking the pulse of the State Department and of each country, one could determine at any given point in time whether the Department's interest in country X was keen, whether American prestige and influence were high, in short, whether there was any American harvest. And if there was, then one could presumably make a judgment that the Department's wartime efforts proved to be wise and successful.

The problem, however, is that such an approach is too time-bound and simplistic. Harvests and friendship today can go to dust and ashes tomorrow, and vice versa. Therefore, because the post-1945 record is not and cannot be a finished chapter, it is impossible to analyze and judge what was the full, final impact of decisions on the Middle East which the wartime Department made. The difficulty is compounded when one notes that America's record in the Middle East, unfinished though it be, is very spotty, ranging as of the mid-1970s from American "successes" (Saudi Arabia, in general) to "failures" (Iraq and Syria, in general). Finally, it is unrealistic to think that like a puppet on a string, such American successes or failures as *can* be identified have necessarily been the results of American decisions and planning, or of the defects thereof. To think so would assume either American omnipotence, or the insignificance of indigenous trends and other external, but non-American, influences.

"NATIONAL INTEREST" AND MOTES IN THE DEPARTMENTAL EYE

When one speaks of an American success or failure in the Middle East, or of the success or failure of a Departmental policy, "success" is assumed to imply that the national interest was served, and "failure" is assumed to imply otherwise. But this begs the eternal question—what *is* "the national interest"? To be sure, beginning with Chapter 1, this work has presented the Department of State's "desiderata" since the Wilson period, also the Department's outlook and mindset, all of which by definition have made up its perception of national interest. Still, the phrase needs to be focused on.

It is commonly accepted that national interest refers not only to the "general good," but also refers to the most axiomatic values of this nation's past, present, and future majority will, imprecise but irreducible values like national survival, liberty, and economic well-being. With such fundamentals one can hardly wish to argue. However, with their corollaries, which the Department has applied as first principles to the Middle East, one can argue, less perhaps with the well-phrased purposes of these corollaries than with their effects and motives.

Thus in the period 1919–45 the open door principle sometimes became a rationalization for pushy concession-hunting motives (post-World War I Iraq). The good neighbor principle similarly became a catch-phrase, behind which could be hidden tendencies towards American appeasement (Saudi Arabia). Orwellian newspeak entered the picture. The principles of native independence and majority rule were passed off as synonyms of democracy by both the Department and the Arabs. During and after World War II, both downplayed the tawdry concomitants and effects of these principles, viz., the revolutionary tyrannies, intolerant monarchies, and street-mob violence and repression that became typical in the Arab states. In short, the Department, phrasing and constantly repeating, as in a Hindu *mantra,* its sacred principles, often became caught up in words and rhetoric and was not honest with itself or with the American public on the question of actual content.

There were at least three other defects in the wartime Department's understanding of national interest. One was that, as noted in Chapters 1 and 3, ethnic and national "pluralism" in the Departmental perspective represented a hydra-headed monstrosity. In the context of America's domestic politics, the Department rued the fact that there were so many "hyphenated" Americans, and it abhorred phenomena like "the ethnic vote" for a variety of reasons, including the legitimate fear of national disunity in wartime. In the context of the Middle East, it opposed the political-territorial aspirations of Jews, Maronite Christians, Kurds, and

Assyrians for fears of "balkanizing," creating power vacuums, and alienating the Sunni Arabs, the putative majority. It thus preferred to conceive of the Middle East as a monolithic "Arab Moslem world," realities to the contrary notwithstanding.

An additional reason for this preference was the Department's assumption that endorsing pluralism was a practice of bad imperialists who wished to divide and rule, and of course the United States was anti-imperialistic. In sum, the Department reacted to the reality of deep-rooted minorities and communal differences in the Middle East (and also to the reality of the traditional schisms within the Moslem Arab majority) by minimizing that reality. It trusted that minorities would, and should, be simply absorbed by the "native majority," as new immigrant minorities were, or were supposed to be, in the United States.

Another defect was that Palestine was classified and "defined" by the Department strictly as part of the "Arab world." This of course meant that that which was non-Arab in Palestine was regarded as inherently foreign; and that the more Palestine became non-Arab, the more foreign Palestine thus became. Rather than accept such a trend as a new reality, as it did so many other new trends in the name of realpolitik, the Department opposed it all the more; for obviously, such a trend violated the basic definition of Palestine.

If, for example, the Union of South Africa had been regarded in the period through 1945 as strictly part of the "African world," or had Algeria been regarded as strictly part of the "North African world," it is clear how such categorization, in itself, would have disposed the Department to treat the European element in South Africa and Algeria as foreign. The fact is, as noted in Chapter 4, South Africa and Algeria were not so "defined," and they were not handled by NEA or EA & A. Consequently, the Department did not push to Africanize either, the way it wished, if not exactly to Arabize Palestine, certainly to deZionize it.

True, NEA covered non-Arab Greece and Turkey, too, not only Palestine and the "Arab world"; and true, NEA did recognize the reality of the minority Jewish Yishuv in Palestine, and of course Palestine's dimension as *Terra Santa* to people outside the Middle East. But these non-Arab factors were incidentals, hardly enough to change the Department's view that Palestine was, and must remain, a primarily Arab area.

A final defect was the Department's confusion and righteousness over terms like spheres of influence, imperialism, and balance of power. As copiously indicated, these were regarded as unAmerican. This is ironic. Latin America was surely in the American "sphere of influence." It was America's assistance to Britain, France, and Russia which placed the necessary "balance of power" on the anti-Axis side, thus allowing victory. When FSOs called for a "large" postwar Middle Eastern policy, denials notwithstanding, they were calling in effect for American *imperium* (albeit with an open door and without annexation) in the region. Even the prudent Hull and other "minimalists" had looked forward, since the mid- to late 1930s, to America's eventual and natural hegemony in the Middle East.

Why did the Department deny the obvious? Self-righteousness, the pain of recognition, and a sense of sin were probable factors. A definite factor was awareness that the Department had no argument against British and French spheres if it dared to admit that America wanted spheres, too, and therefore was not all that holier-than-thou. Finally, there was the *mantra* effect alluded to, namely, self-indoctrination within the Department, induced by constant repetition of first principles, in a spirit of religious concentration and anxious planning for the future.

The results were that the Department viewed "imperialism" and like terminology as ipso facto undesirable, and "nationalism" (of majorities, not minorities) and like terminology as ipso facto desirable. The thought that some forms of imperialism might serve the general good effectively and humanely, and some forms of nationalism might not, found no lodging among Departmental officers, certainly not those responsible for the "Arab world." It was too "foreign" to think that, in the French expression, *entre le fort et le faible, c'est la liberté qui opprime et la loi qui affranchit.*

Index of Names

Abdullah, 40, 48 n.36, 56, 106, 259, 273 n.37, 303
Acheson, Dean, 7, 8, 13, 22 n.20, 59, 65 n.19, 145, 148, 162, 164, 165, 181 n.15, 211, 235, 236, 237, 239, 244 n.35, 306, 307
Adee, Alvey A., 246
Ali, Rashid, 101, 102, 106, 108, 116 n.3, 177, 207. *See also* Rashid Ali coup
Allen, George V., 89 n.5
Alling, Paul, 68, 69, 72, 82, 96 n.33, 146, 200 n.9, 206, 271 n.17, 310 n.17, 316 n.53 and n.54
Altman, Leib, 312 n.24
Atherton, Ray, 310 n.12
Atlee, Clement, 195
Azkin, Benjamin, 286

Balfour, Arthur, 246. *See also* Balfour Declaration
Ben-Gurion, David, 41, 264, 265, 289, 290
Bergson, Peter, 257, 264, 284, 311 n.21 and n.22
Berle, Adolph, Jr., 8, 13, 65 n.23, 84, 161, 162, 218–19 n.8, 242 n.21, 262, 266, 289
Berlin, Isaiah, 284
Bevin, Ernest, 195, 306
Bidault, Georges, 145
Bierbrier, Doreen, 309 n.8
Bloom, Sol, 226, 293
Borah, William, 294

Bowman, Isaiah, 11, 82, 281, 300, 303, 317 n.58
Brandeis, Louis, 246
Brewster, Owen, 216
Buber, Martin, 259
Byrnes, James, 76, 240 n.11, 297, 305, 306, 309 n.9, 316 n.53, 317 n.56

Caffery, Jefferson, 145
Catroux, Gen. Raoul, 131, 135 n.13
Carter, A. F., 214
Celler, Emmanuel, 287
Chamberlain, Neville, 42
Childs, J. Rives, 76, 96 n.32 and n.33, 233, 251–52, 254, 271 n.20
Churchill, Sir Winston, 16, 57, 64 n.18, 91 n.15, 107, 114, 127, 128, 141, 144, 185, 202 n.32, 233, 255, 258, 262, 266, 277, 278, 294, 295, 304, 305, 306, 325
Clayton, Will, 236, 238
Connally, Tom, 226, 230, 293
Cornwallis, Sir Kinahan, 175
Crane, Charles R., 34–35, 44 n.15
Cresson, Warder, 246
Crowley, Leo, 236, 238
Culbertson, William, 165. *See also* Culbertson Report

DeGaulle, Gen. Charles, 74, 111, 114, 126, 127, 128, 130, 131, 133, 134 n.6, 141, 143, 145, 147, 322, 325
Dentz, Gen. Henri, 101–2

331

Index of Place Names

Africa, 100
Afghanistan, 101
Algeria, 17, 150 n.12, 202 n.31, 328
America. *See* United States *in Subject Index*
Angola, 263, 281
Aqaba, 303
Armenia, 107

Bahrein, 205, 210, 218 n.7, 220 n.26, 238
Balkans, 102, 116 n.5, 255
Belgium, 182
Brazil, 264

Canal Zone. *See* Suez Canal
Caribbean, 3
Colombia, 264
Crete, 195
Cyrenaica. *See* Libya

Dardenelles, 111, 115
Dhahran, 208, 233, 236, 242 n.25, 243 n.34, 324

Egypt, 29–33, 102, 159, 173, 174, 176, 177, 182 passim (chapt. 10), 209, 256, 257, 298, 322, 323, 324, 325; external trade of, 33, 191; roles of British imperialism in, 32, 186
El Alamein, 54, 100, 103, 173, 187, 200 n.13, 266, 269, 277
Ethiopia, 102, 192, 194

France (*and* French), 100, 123 passim (chapts. 5 and 6), 182, 209, 307 n.1, 320, 321, 322, 324, 328, 329; influence of in Middle East, 50, 51, 107, 234; interest of in Soviet assistance, 120 n.16; mandate of in Syria and Lebanon, 25–27, 126. *See also* DeGaulle, Gen. Charles; Free French; Vichy French

Germany (*and* Germans), 50, 53, 65 n.18, 100–104, 126, 129, 209, 307; foreign policy of, 103–4; interest of in Saudi Arabia and Suez Canal, 53, 195, 206; postwar plans of, 100. *See also* Axis; Hitler; Holocaust; Nazism
Greater Lebanon. *See* Lebanon
Greater Syria, 173, 232
Greece, 328

Hatay-Alexandretta, 27

India, 195, 235, 243 n.30
Iran, 101, 103, 107, 110, 115
Iraq, 28–29, 100–101, 104, 107, 142, 158, 171 passim (chapt. 9), 185, 205, 209, 266, 280, 311 n.20, 322, 323, 324, 325, 326
Israel, 326. *See also* Jews; Palestine; Zionism
Italy, 50, 83, 100, 102, 103, 114, 126, 165, 182, 194, 208, 292

335

Subject Index

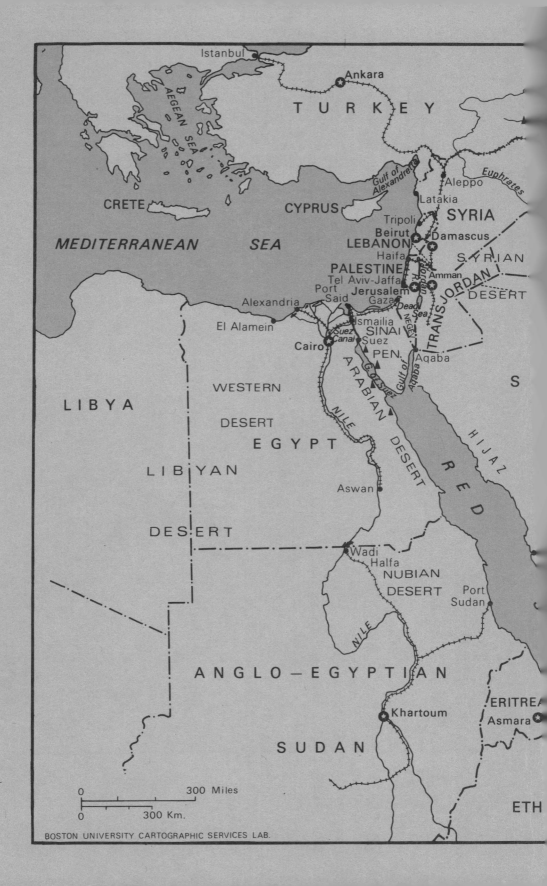

BOSTON UNIVERSITY CARTOGRAPHIC SERVICES LAB.